GENDER IN SOUTH ASIA AND BEYOND

Essays in Honour of Patricia Jeffery

GENDER IN SOUTH ASIA AND BEYOND

Essays in Honour of Patricia Jeffery

Editors
Shruti Chaudhry
Hugo Gorringe
Radhika Govinda

zubaan

Zubaan
128 B Shahpur Jat, 1st Floor
New Delhi 110049
Email: contact@zubaanbooks.com
Website: www.zubaanbooks.com

First published by Zubaan Publishers Pvt. Ltd 2024

10 9 8 7 6 5 4 3 2 1

ISBN 978 93 90514 43 4 (paperback)
ISBN 978 93 90514 48 9 (ebook)

Zubaan is an independent feminist publishing house based in New Delhi with a strong academic and general list. It was set up as an imprint of India's first feminist publishing house, Kali for Women, and carries forward Kali's tradition of publishing world quality books to high editorial and production standards. *Zubaan* means tongue, voice, language, speech in Hindustani. Zubaan publishes in the areas of the humanities, social sciences, as well as in fiction, general non-fiction, and books for children and young adults under its Young Zubaan imprint.

Typeset by in Adobe Garamond Pro/11 pt
Printed and bound at Raj Press, Inderpuri, New Delhi, 110 012

Contents

Preface

"One June evening in rural north India, we mull over the day's happenings: some men complaining about how slowly the Cane Society pays for their sugar-cane deliveries; a woman bringing a head-load of wheat to the village power-mill, pausing to lament her daughter's ill-treatment by her in-laws; a landless labourer transplanting rice seedlings and talking of the lack of employment – and cash – that the imminent monsoon will bring; anxious mothers wanting remedies for the boils plaguing their young children."[1]

So starts Chapter One of *Labour Pains and Labour Power*. The opening words are an exemplar of Patricia (Tricia) Jeffery's lifelong work, work that is honoured and celebrated in this Festschrift.

To me four aspects of Tricia's work stand out as reason for her academic impact. Influence on these points are also what draws together the contributions in the festschrift. The hope is that the individual articles and the collective within this festschrift will, in turn, inspire others.

The first obvious point is the regional focus on the South Asian diaspora in the UK and even more so on the South Asian region itself, with deep delves into different thematic areas including religion, social norms and political structures, livelihoods, education, healthcare and the environment. For over thirty years, the academic literature on the region and its people has been enriched by Tricia's research and ethnography. The contributors to the festschrift all also come with this regional interest.

Secondly, there is the subject matter. The voice and experiences of women are centred in Patricia Jeffery's work, particularly the most invisible and marginalised of them, those engaged in non-monetised or low paid work; the focus on the 'little heard life stories of women' (Rajni Palriwala). The attention is more broadly on gender roles across generations, on kinship and on hierarchies based on social, caste, religious, economic, political and other contexts. By this very lens, looking at individual experiences and the explanatory power of complex contexts, she brings a feminist and social justice perspective to the studies but does so based on the specifics not generalisations or simplest emotion tropes. There is an 'intellectual courage' (Barbara Harriss-White) in this analytical and yet subjective approach to women's lives and their milieu. The contributors to this festschrift are picking up the baton.

Thirdly, there is the methodology that defines Patricia Jeffery's work. This is based on a rich person-centred approach with 'vivid ethnographic accounts' (Jeevan R. Sharma) in defined communities and areas. Case-studies, not just to engage with the theory 'to validate' it and provide some details behind generalisations, but to show ambiguity, paradoxes, complexity. To 'produce surprises' (Barbara Harriss-White). The work is not driven by ideology or a simple narrative but is at pains to show the importance of always a complex reality within which individuals and communities operate.

The consideration given to complexity and the specific individual lived-experiences could result in a difficultly for the reader to follow the main argument or analysis. However, this is never the case, possibly because there is one other characteristic which is the 'accessibility' (Jeevan R Sharma) of the writing, witness the opening to *Labour Pains and Labour Power* quoted at the beginning of this article. Different individual stories are used to paint a wider account with the use of quotes and anecdotes to elucidate and with the title of articles and chapter headings engaging rather than formulaic, often adding humour or including a pun, e.g. *Frogs in a Well: Indian Women in Purdah*[2] and "Plain tales from the Plains: Researching in Rural Bijnor over Three Decades".[3]

Finally, the timeframe, the longitudinal studies, including numerous return visits to the same place, 'the extensive work; and 'vast scholarship' (Ravinder Kaur) also define Patricia Jeffery's work and contribute to the 'rich analysis' (Shalini Grover).

The combination of geographic locality, the focus on women, the real listening and ethnographically rich approach based on deep often longitudinal knowledge combined together is a deep and textured body of knowledge. It provides a layered understanding of the relationship between the individual, their aspirations, their agency and how this relates to social norms, economic and educational changes, formal/legal policies and structures. The analysis shows variety not stereotypes, main patterns but also subsidiary ones, with a particular interest, in fact in the acts of resistance, those that 'upset the gender balance' (Rajni Palriwala).

When academics and even more so development activists – and I count myself amongst them - want to highlight the costs of inequality and marginalisation, there is a tendency for them, for us, to do so with a simplistic narrative, because of a desire to focus on outrage at the oppression and because this is easier. The result is a lack of attention to the shades and the contradictions. Patricia's writings, are much better at avoiding the pitfalls of too simple an account. The lived experience is shown in detail as is how it links to theory or policy in nuanced and complex ways. Marginalisation is spotlighted factually and with empathy and not dogmatically.

Given the focus on the subjective storylines in the bulk of her work, it is not surprising that Tricia was an engaged teacher, Katharine Charsley for example refers to her as an 'enormously inspiring and supportive supervisor'. Tricia also developed long-standing relationships with many of her students and fellow academics, continuing to be interested in their work, drawing in comparisons with her own research findings, these reflections in turn encouraging new lines of thinking or deeper analysis. All of those contributing to this volume are thus honouring, not just her research - seven authored or co-authored books, three co-edited volumes and over 30 articles - which has in different ways moulded their own but also giving thanks to the person behind the research, who in other ways has supported them in their personal and academic journeys. I think this festschrift does Patricia proud and the articles are fascinating. See what you think.

Helen Pankhurst CBE
Advisor CARE International, Prof MMU
Chancellor, University of Suffolk
2022

NOTES

1. 1989: **Patricia Jeffery**, Roger Jeffery and Andrew Lyon: *Labour Pains and Labour Power: Women and Childbearing in India* (Zed Books, London & Manohar, New Delhi), xii + 292 pp.
2. 1979: **Patricia Jeffery**: *Frogs in a Well: Indian Women in Purdah* (Zed Press, London & Vikas, New Delhi), viii + 187 pp. (Seventh impression 1991)
3. 2016: **Patricia Jeffery**: "Plain tales from the Plains: Researching in Rural Bijnor over Three Decades", pp.35-64 in Himanshu, Praveen Jha and Gerry Rodgers (eds): *The Changing Village in India: Insights from Longitudinal Research* (Delhi: Oxford University Press)

INTRODUCTION

Shruti Chaudhry, Hugo Gorringe and Radhika Govinda

It is our privilege and pleasure to collate this set of essays in honour of our colleague, mentor and friend Patricia Jeffery, who is known to us as Tricia. We have all benefitted personally and professionally from Tricia's scholarship, guidance, advice and editorial input, and are delighted to be able to offer this token of our esteem and gratitude. The volume, however, is not just an homage to a wonderful scholar, but also a compelling set of essays casting light on key issues around gender across and beyond South Asia. Most of the essays here were first presented at a symposium to mark Tricia's retirement. This symposium had brought together Tricia's friends, peers, co-authors, colleagues, mentees and students for a day of insightful talks and reflections. The essays in this volume represent original research and analysis that speaks to, draws on, or engages with Tricia's own work. Given this, we wish to use the introduction to offer an overview of her academic life and work and to help situate the essays in relation to that context.

Tricia's academic journey started with an undergraduate degree in Medicine at the University of Cambridge. After a year, she switched to anthropology, completing her degree in 1968. She moved to the University of Nottingham to pursue an MA in Social Sciences (with a specialisation in Race Relations), and then to the University of Bristol where she completed a doctoral thesis on Muslim and Christian Pakistanis in Bristol in 1973 under the supervision of Michael Banton. She was initially denied a studentship for her PhD research on the grounds of being a married woman. Although she eventually received the studentship, this incident fed into her understanding of, and commitment to, addressing gender inequalities that has been at the heart of her work. After completing her PhD, Tricia's PhD examiner, the anthropologist Adrian Mayer, suggested that she could pursue her interest in researching South Asian Muslims among the Pirzada in Delhi's Nizamuddin. It was this advice that took her to India, which has ever since then remained the primary site and focus of her research.

Having completed her doctoral research, Tricia started her career as a temporary lecturer in anthropology at the University of Edinburgh in 1973, subsequently taking up a permanent lectureship in sociology at Edinburgh in 1978 and remaining there for over 30 years before retiring as Professor of Sociology. She also held numerous visiting fellowships including at the Institute of Economic Growth and Jawaharlal Nehru University in Delhi, engaging and fostering relationships with Indian scholars that she has maintained since. Tricia is one of the leading scholars of South Asia in the UK. Her body of work includes seven single or co-authored books and three co-edited volumes and over 80 single and co-authored journal articles and book chapters. What stands out about her work for many is the richness of her data and ethnographic writing that captured so vividly and sensitively the day-to-day lives of those amongst whom she worked. Her work offers a point of departure from the structural-functional ethnographic accounts produced by much British anthropology of the 1940s and '50s where, as Tricia put it, 'the reader got no sense of the people, how they operated within structures or resisted within them' (personal communication 2021).

Over the years, Tricia has held numerous editorial and advisory positions, and among her many achievements is her role in setting up (with others) the Centre for South Asian Studies at the University of Edinburgh – a vibrant interdisciplinary centre. She also served as Chair of the British Association for South Asian Studies from 2014-20. More locally, Tricia supervised 23 doctoral researchers and served as external examiner for 22 (including some of the contributors to this volume). In addition to being a caring doctoral supervisor, she has been a wonderful and generous mentor to numerous younger colleagues at Edinburgh and beyond. Despite this long list of commitments, Tricia has never been an ivory tower academic. When she first moved to Edinburgh she got involved in what was then the Community Relations Council which focused on issues of race and ethnicity. She was also involved with the World Development Movement and subsequently with Scottish Education and Action for Development, for whom she was involved in running workshops and informal conferences for schoolchildren and adults in Edinburgh. Such public engagement and impact have been at the heart of her work, as seen in her later, path-breaking work on oxytocin in home-deliveries in India. It is unsurprising, given this background that a key theme underlying Tricia's research has to do with 'agency'.

Agency, Activism and Social Change

Mindful of critiques challenging the representation of women in the global south, including South Asia, as 'passive and hapless victims', in 'Agency, Activism, and Agendas' (1998), the last chapter of the volume edited by herself and Amrita Basu on women's activism and politicized religion in South Asia, Tricia draws attention to how women in South Asia have been involved in various social and political movements. She notes that whilst many were activists in the independence movements, others were involved in class-based political activities, wherein gender was not the 'primary orientation', and that by the 1970s, a number of them had formed their own feminist organisations. However, agency need not and is not entirely encompassed by political activism. According to her, 'women critique their subordination and resist the controls over them – in personal reminiscences or songs, in sabotage and cheating… Such everyday resistance may seem tame in comparison with the ambitious agendas typical of feminism, but they confirm that South Asian women have a capacity for agency' (Jeffery 1998: 222).

Tanika Sarkar's essay in this volume – on two Bengali women and their relationship with revolutionary and communist politics between the 1930s and the 1950s – is based on exactly such an understanding of 'agency'. Of her own admission, Sarkar had not set out to examine these political women from such a perspective. She had initially treated the life story of Kalpana Dutt 'the activist' and Sabitri Ray 'the housewife' as constituting 'clear mutual contrasts' but the points of identification and overlaps eventually turned out to be much more intriguing to explore. Similar to the biographical approach adopted in *Don't Marry Me To A Plowman!: Women's Everyday Lives in Rural North India* (1996), which centred how women in rural north India were able to influence, often in covert ways, their everyday lives, including their personal and intimate affairs, Sarkar too offers biographical sketches and attempts to retrieve 'the housewife-novelist as a communist in her own right' and to 'reconfigure the activist as a writer, and as a woman, living through tempestuous personal crises'. She argues that these biographical sketches, constructed on the basis of the women's own recollections and fictional writings, shed light on the importance of tracing how political and social change interpenetrate. Interestingly, Sarkar also highlights how even though communist activist women worked shoulder to shoulder with communist activist men in combat, they only covertly evaded familial and gender restrictions in their personal life rather than openly challenging them. This resonates with Tricia's cautionary note about not all women's agency necessarily translating into feminist political activism (Jeffery 1998).

Sarkar is one of the two authors who had contributed to the 1998 volume and who once again reflects on questions of agency and activism in this Festschrift in Tricia's honour. The other is Zoya Hasan. In the 1997 volume, she reflected on the broad theme of gender politics, legal reform and the Muslim community in India. In the Festschrift, she revisits this theme by homing in on the Uniform Civil Code (UCC) debate that has been ongoing in the country for more than seven decades. The debate is over whether such a code would truly be a UCC, a gender-just (and secular) common code or merely the Hindu code. Hasan's essay traces the trajectory of the debate in relation to key developments, in particular, the Shah Bano case and abolition of triple *talaq*, more recently. The Shah Bano controversy began in 1978 when a 62-year-old woman, Shah Bano filed a petition demanding maintenance after her husband divorced her by using triple talaq. In 1985, the Supreme Court granted maintenance allowance for Shah Bano and called for the creation of a UCC which would give all women equal rights irrespective of their faith. This led to a major furore among the orthodox Muslims. To pacify them, the then Congress government overrode the judgement through the Muslim Women's Act, declaring that Muslim women would not have access to civil law in matters of marriage and divorce. This was opposed, among others, by a number of mainstream feminist organisations in the country. These developments taken together stoked the flames of Hindu nationalist forces, giving credence to their claims that Congress and feminist organisations were being pseudo-secular to appease Muslims.

Tricia, in an article titled 'A Uniform Customary Code? Marital Breakdown and Women's Economic Entitlements in Rural Bijnor' (2001), focusing on the implications of the Shah Bano controversy and the accompanying communalisation of politics in the mid-1980s, raised questions about the efficacy of the law in protecting women's rights and its pertinence to the feminist struggle for gender justice. Drawing on her research in rural Bijnor, western Uttar Pradesh, her article sheds light on how the parallels in the domestic lives of Hindu and Muslim women undermined the Hindu nationalist assertions that Muslim women are uniquely oppressed, for instance, in matters related to marital breakdown. It also highlights how the everyday concerns of ordinary Hindu and Muslim women in Bijnor at the time of the Shah Bano controversy were in fact far removed from the controversy itself. Following this thread of argumentation from Tricia's article, Hasan's essay in the Festschrift critically examines the impact of identity politics on gender equality, the approaches and strategies of key political parties, mainstream feminist organisations, and Muslim women's groups toward legal reform, the hotly debated issue of UCC and the challenges of implementing it. It throws light on the crucial role played by Muslim women's autonomous organisations in the Supreme Court's declaration of triple talaq as being unconstitutional and illegal in 2017 and in the introduction of the new Muslim Women (Protection of Rights on Marriage) Act, 2019. It concludes with a warning about how the undue focus on personal laws when it comes to Muslim women's rights has led to glossing over the economic, political and social problems that affect their everyday life. Kaveri Qureshi in her essay in this volume also builds on this argument.

Caroline Dyer and Archana Choksi's essay on pastoralism, education and dignity among Dhebar Rabaris in remote rural areas of the western Indian state of Gujarat engages with a separate but nonetheless related strand of Tricia's work – on education, marginalised communities and social change in contemporary India. Whilst there is a plethora of scholarship that argues that more education results in more agency and empowerment for women (e.g., Dreze and Sen 1996), Tricia's scholarship with Roger Jeffery (1994; 1996; 1998) and also her collaborative writing with Radhika Chopra, in *Educational Regimes in contemporary India* (2005), caution that, in fact, not all education is necessarily empowering, that it need not always translate into an enhancement of the agency of girls and women from marginalised communities. Their work also emphasises the need to go beyond formal schooling and pay attention to education being imparted in non-formal, informal and alternative settings including girls' madrasahs. In Tricia's collaborative writing with Craig Jeffrey and Roger Jeffery, *Degrees Without Freedom? Education, Masculinities and Unemployment* (2008), they interrogate the transformative potential of education. They critically examine the mediating structures of context and agency to explore whether education results in substantive freedoms such as employment and dignity. Specifically, their research focuses on three groups of young men, all of whom see education as holding the key to gaining respect and profitable employment. But for the majority of these men, the educational investment yields neither respect nor employment as the neoliberal economy simply does not have enough employment opportunities commensurate to the level of education they have managed to acquire.

Inspired by such observations, in their own essay in this Festschrift, Dyer and Choksi explore how women and leaders of the

Dhebar Rabari community valued and used formal education as they navigated changes to their livelihoods as mobile pastoralists and the challenges of settlement. They point out how the Dhebar Rabari community associated formal education with the acquisition of respect and occupational diversification (beyond mobile pastoralism). Ensuring that their children had access to schooling was a motivating factor for Rabaris who decided to step out of mobile pastoralism. The authors note that, among other unforeseen consequences, formal schooling has created 'deep lines of intergenerational fracture' in the community. The difference in the values and form of education that the parents experienced (and were at the core of the pastoral way of living) and those that the schooling system is imparting to their children is creating a chasm between the two generations. The education that Rabari children are receiving is – but only very slowly – making a dent in the patriarchal structure of the community. Girls tend to be more studious than boys, but few girls make it to higher secondary education, or beyond. Although boys drop out of school too, girls may be withdrawn because of the gendered division of labour within the household means they are expected to help with domestic chores. But educated girls are getting more say in all-important decisions about marriage, and what they wear. The community has itself begun to question the transformative potential of formal schooling, given that the schools that their children are attending have poor infrastructure and quality of teaching, and that the intergenerational fracture notwithstanding, their investment in their children's education does not seem to be translating into the respect and gainful sedentary employment that they had initially expected.

A striking feature of Tricia's writing – whether produced alone or in collaboration with others, from her second book, *Frogs in a Well: Indian Women in Purdah* (1979) to one of her more recent ones, *Degrees Without Freedom? Education, Masculinities and Unemployment* (2008 – with Jeffrey and Jeffery) – has been the complex life-worlds she is able to portray through rich ethnographic detail and beautifully drawn vignettes. The influence of this signature style is visible in the writing of those whose doctoral/ postdoctoral research she supervised/mentored as well as her close collaborators. It is very much present in Dyer and Choksi's contribution to the volume. After all, Tricia was Caroline Dyer's mentor on Caroline's first postdoctoral research project – the ESRC-funded Literacy for Migrants study – back in the 1990s, on which Archana also worked. Radhika Chopra, one of Tricia's collaborators, herself acknowledges Tricia's influence in her contribution to this Festschrift by noting that her essay 'draws its inspiration from Patricia Jeffery's seminal work *Frogs in a Well* (1979) in which she unpacked a whole universe of gendered hierarchies by concentrating on one neighbourhood in Delhi, and what people did in their everyday lives'. Chopra's essay focuses on a locality called Bootan Mandi, in the city of Jalandhar in the northern Indian state of Punjab, where commerce, colonialism and caste interconnect in relation to leather work and leather workers' everyday lives.

Whilst the essay tackles neither the notion of agency nor that of activism, as such, unlike the other essays discussed so far, it offers a comprehensive insight into how social change has come about in the locality of Bootan Mandi. Various urban legends surround the locality's name, chief among them the identification of the word '*bootan*', with riding boots. Jalandhar was the site of one of the earliest colonial cantonments in north India. Leather workers of the city catered to the demand for boots, saddles, stirrups, reins and sundry other goods for the colonial army and police. More recent twenty-first century websites of shoe manufactures position Bootan Mandi as a place of expertise for police boots, army shoes and sports shoes. The contemporary urban legend of Bootan Mandi lies at the busy intersections of commerce, community, critiques of caste and religious orthodoxy. The Ravidassia movement, oriented toward the veneration of the cobbler Sant Ravidas, is supported by increasingly prosperous non-resident Indian Chamars, empowered by businesses in leather. Migrants from Kanpur (known for its bristle trade), and unskilled labour from Bihar and Uttar Pradesh, move into Bootan Mandi to work in leather, loading hides, curing leather or stitching shoes, all highly visible work on the Bootan Mandi landscape. Based on field work done from late 2018 to early 2020, Chopra's essay analyses the transformative potential of leather as livelihood. This fieldwork was part of a research project on the lives of low-income urban migrant workers in Jalandhar and the city of Guwahati in the north-eastern Indian state of Assam. The funded research involved not only Chopra but also Tricia herself and other scholars, notably, Anuj Kapilashrami and Jeevan Sharma. Sharma also has an essay in this Festschrift.

Kinship, Marriage, Migration/Diaspora

A connecting theme in Tricia's research trajectory has been her work with South Asian Muslims. Sylvia Vatuk, in her essay in this volume, notes Tricia's enormous contribution to the scholarship on South Asian Islam. Tricia's groundbreaking book on the seclusion practices of Pirzada women in Nizamuddin in Delhi, *Frogs in a Well: Indian Women in Purdah* (1979) was published at a time when there was virtually nothing on gender and its intersection with class and religion within sociology. There was a discourse on kinship within anthropology but it lacked, in Tricia's words, 'a gendered political edge' (personal communication 2021). The research in Nizamuddin was initially planned as a study on close-kin marriages that grew out of articles that incidentally Vatuk had previously published on kinship terminology and marriage. The work in Delhi was followed by what is now over four decades of research among Hindus and Muslims in Bijnor in Uttar Pradesh. Vatuk in her essay in this volume, engages with a question that has been a central concern in Tricia's work with Muslims, i.e., the relationship of theology and formal law to the lived realities of informants' lives. Vatuk addresses this relationship through her focus on Islamic inheritance in her longitudinal work in one particular Muslim extended family (*khandan*) in South India. Through an examination of a number of cases of property transmission within and between generations over the course of more than a century, Vatuk shows that in many cases, members of the *khandan* used shari'a succession rules to distribute their assets after their death. Yet, others employed various alternative devices that conformed in most cases with shari'a, while making it possible for owners to pass on property during their lifetime to those whom they most wished to have it. These devices included pre-mortem gifts (*hiba, pl. hibāt*), bequests (*waṣiyya*), and family trusts or endowments (*waqf, pl. auqāf*), or simply taking a prospective immediate heir into confidence concerning their wishes and securing a promise to act accordingly when the time should come. Individuals thus often relied on their own understanding of the approved means of property transmission provided by religious law. Vatuk argues that the assumption that Islamic inheritance law is the key determinant of intergenerational property transmission has led to an over-emphasis in the writing on its details and intricacies and a widespread neglect of actual inheritance practices.

There are striking similarities between Vatuk's work among the wealthy Muslim *khandan* in South India and Tricia's among the high status Syeds in Delhi. When writing *Frogs in a Well,* Tricia was working in an academic vacuum with respect to gender and its intersections with class and religion. This was long before the term 'intersectionality' was coined. In a sense, she was writing about intersectionality without employing the exact term. She drew on the work of Socialist feminists who were working along similar lines and these perspectives informed subsequent research in Bijnor for *Labour Pains and Labour Power: Women and Childbearing in India* (1989) where Tricia's concern centred on what, if any, are the different childbearing experiences of Hindu, Dalit and Muslim women, given their differing marriage practices.

Tricia started her research career with her doctoral research among the Pakistani diaspora in Bristol. Departing from the tradition of community studies of the time, she had convinced her supervisor (Michael Banton at Bristol) to support her to carry out fieldwork in both England and Pakistan thus conducting multi-sited ethnography in the early 70s long-before the terminology existed for what is now a well-established research method. Her PhD research resulted in the publication of her first book *Migrants and Refugees: Muslim and Christian Pakistani families in Bristol* (1976). Several years later Katharine Charsley followed in Tricia's footsteps, literally, going to Bristol combined with a visit to Pakistan to carry out her doctoral research on Pakistani transnational marriages. This research was supervised by Tricia herself at Edinburgh. In her essay in this volume, 'From Ploughmen to Freshies', Charsley reflects on the influence that Tricia's wider work and her role as a PhD supervisor has had on her own writing on gender, kinship and migration. She writes about the inspiration she drew from the 'person-centred' ethnographic style in *Don't Marry Me To A Plowman!: Women's Everyday Lives In Rural North India* (1996). For Tricia, the use of extended biographical narratives in the book was aimed at centering women's own understanding of their lives, but also 'valuing the contexts that women were speaking from' (personal communication 2021). As with her earlier writing, she wanted to counter stereotypes of the passive Third world woman, all the while conscious of her own positionality as a White British woman doing research in India. For Charsley, Tricia's approach provided valuable insights on how the gendered emotional dynamics of British Pakistani transnational cousin marriages could be addressed. These, as she notes, had previously been examined from more 'strategic perspectives'. Whilst Tricia's work in north India focused on women, specifically the vulnerabilities of the incoming young bride in her husband's home (Jeffery et al. 1988), Charsley found a 'gender-reversed echo' in her own exploration of the position of in-marrying migrant husbands from Pakistan. In this sense, Charsley's essay highlights the influence that Tricia's work has had not only on the writing on gender and kinship in South Asia but also its diaspora.

Like Charsley, Kaveri Qureshi engages with Tricia's work in north India by attempting a comparative ethnography of British Sikh and British Muslim women in the UK, akin to Tricia's comparison of Hindu and Muslim women. Like Hasan's essay in this volume, Qureshi draws inspiration from 'A Uniform Customary Code? Marital breakdown and women's economic entitlements in rural Bijnor', published in *Contributions to Indian Sociology* (2001), where one of Tricia's central arguments was that despite the undue focus on Muslims and assertions of Hindu nationalists that Muslim women were uniquely oppressed by their personal laws, in cases of marital breakdown there were parallels in the situation of Hindu and Muslim women. In practice, both faced stigma and their options to leave in situations of marital breakdown were constrained by their economic dependency within marriage and the limits to natal kin support. In her essay, Qureshi builds on these insights in her work on marital breakdown among British South Asians. She notes that as in the Indian context, Muslim family law has been 'exceptionalised' and 'extensively problematized' in political, policy and academic discourse in a way that other minority legal orders have not. Her essay explores how informal mediation is experienced by women of British Pakistani Muslim and Punjabi Sikh heritage. Qureshi notes well-articulated customary differences in the 'kinscripts' associated with natal kin support: while in the Pakistani case, the expectation was that influential family elders would assist in resolving marital conflicts, the *vicholan/vicholi* (intermediary) in Sikh marriages was expected to play this role. In practice, however, Sikh women could not rely much on the assistance of the *vicholan/vicholi*. Further, where mediation was unsuccessful, some participants involved religious practitioners in resolving marital disputes. Qureshi argues that while many studies have criticised the mediation provided by Islamic bodies, such as mosques and sharia councils, on the grounds that they advocate *sula* (reconciliation) even in cases where it is against women's interests, her data suggest that this is not limited to Islamic practitioners and that similar principles are employed by Sikh religious practitioners. In both contexts, her participants actively claimed that they could avail of informal mediation as this was an advantage of having had an arranged marriage. Yet equally, they reported familial pressure to stay in their marriage. To women, what at first felt like a resource for redressing conflict turned out to depend on the 'traditional framework of power'.

Ravinder Kaur's essay on sex ratio imbalances, bride shortages and marriage migration in Uttar Pradesh speaks to another strand in Tricia's work, that is, on gender and demography that has been a running theme since *Labour Pains and Labour Power* (1989). In her essay, Kaur points to long-existing gender imbalances due to persisting son preference and the availability of ultra-sound technologies that have resulted in what she describes as a 'worrying trend of a large number of girls going missing at birth and post-birth' in India's most populous state. She argues that what has also contributed to sex ratios becoming increasingly masculine is contemporary fertility transitions as couples desire smaller but 'son-biased families' resulting in fewer girls and a shortage of marriageable women in future. She explores the implications of the 'marriage squeeze' for marriage patterns in the state. Based on marriage data collected in two districts of the state – one in eastern and the other in western Uttar Pradesh, Kaur proposes the hypothesis that there are 'dual patterns of spatial hypergamy' discernible given the economic and demographic divergence between the eastern and western parts of the state. She suggests that women from eastern Uttar Pradesh, which has comparatively less masculine sex ratios, move internally to marry into more prosperous districts of western Uttar Pradesh which have more severe bride shortages. Men from eastern Uttar Pradesh in turn bring cross-regional brides from states east of Uttar Pradesh such as West Bengal, Bihar, Jharkhand and Assam. Kaur's work speaks to Tricia's long-standing work on issues of fertility and child mortality, son preference, dowry and the devaluation of daughters (more recently Jeffery 2014) yet her observations also differ from the findings in Tricia's forthcoming work focused on Muslims in Bijnor who unlike Kaur's largely Hindu informants are less likely to sex-select and are not experiencing the 'shortage' of potential brides, the resulting 'marriage squeeze' and bride-import reported by Kaur for other parts of Uttar Pradesh.

In her essay, Shalini Grover focuses on low-caste (Balmiki), middle-aged women in an urban low-income neighbourhood in Delhi. Grover acknowledges the influence that Tricia's use of narratives for capturing the everyday reality of marriage has had on her work on lived experiences of marriage among the urban poor. In particular, in her essay, she notes how Tricia's observations on assumptions about low-caste women's economic independence have shaped how she continues to critically interrogate and write about women's intimate lives and labour market experiences. She draws on Tricia's reflections on domestic politics in Bijnor to interrogate female friendships among a group of women belonging to the lowest caste in her study context. The ties of solidarity between women in her research context were expressed through the use of the term '*dharam behen*' (honorary sister or 'sister-friend') and this honorary bond was on par with blood ties. She notes that these ties, that tended to be intra-caste, were formed by women at later life stages when natal kin support was unavailable and they assumed significance within a context of overt caste discrimination. Trust, loyalty, emotional support, empathy and confidence-building based on shared experiences characterised these ties enabling women to cope in situations of crisis, such as male desertion, the threat of reputational damage etc. Yet Grover also points to the limits of female solidarity in relation to domestic violence that was routine and at times extreme for the women in her study. She argues that female friends were unable to offer practical support (e.g. exit options such as shelter) when a friend had suffered violence. This was because wider constraints such as their specific caste-class location as well as patriarchal and community norms limited their intervention. Grover's argument is reminiscent of Tricia's observation in *Don't Marry Me To A Plowman!* 'People have to deal with the social structures within which they live. They cannot ignore them'. Women's resistance is channeled by their understanding that they can act 'within largely unalterable structures' (Jeffery and Jeffery 1996: 16).

Rajni Palriwala's essay, like Grover's, also focuses on non-elite women in Delhi neighbourhoods. She draws on Tricia's work on the relationships of support between women within the domestic sphere and beyond in both Bijnor and Nizamuddin to attend to 'non-sexual intimacy and homosociality' in her study of unmarried women. She presents the stories of three single women (30 years and over of middle and lower middle class and of different ethnic and caste statuses) who were likely to remain never married. She notes that the scholarship on single women that exists in the Indian context has largely focused on widows, divorcees, the deserted or separated, adolescents and the rising age at marriage, and the religious or celibate. The adult never-married woman, she points out, has tended to remain 'invisible' even in rich ethnographic accounts of women. She asks: what could a focus on non-elite single women tell us about trends and questions regarding social relations, socialities, and gender? She complicates current discussions on choice and agency, demonstrating that the three women in her study had remained single due more to circumstance than individual volition, with their lives as single women being embedded within their families. They wanted this last, even as their desire was clearly to marry. In rural contexts such as Bijnor, in contrast to the urban setting of Palriwala's study, remaining single for women, in Tricia's words, is 'virtually impossible'. The only never-married women whom Tricia found through the course of her fieldwork were those considered 'unmarriageable' (e.g. due to a physical impairment such as hemiplegia after polio) (personal communication 2021). As Tricia's research has documented, village women lack marketable skills and remain economically dependent on marriage but also they have little control over arranging their marriages and often have to fall in line with parental commands.

Gender and Development

For those women who do marry, of course, the emphasis shifts to child-bearing and social reproduction. One of the longest running strands in Tricia's work has been her work on gender and healthcare in north India. Jeevan Sharma's essay draws on this body of work to analyse two aspects of maternal and child healthcare in Nepal. The first half of the essay concerns the 'empowerment from above' of Female Community Health Volunteers (FCHV) in Nepal. One of the most ubiquitous development buzzwords since the 1990s has been 'empowerment' and especially 'women's empowerment' a concept embraced by the UN and World Bank amongst others. Sharma notes how the FCHV scheme utilises the language of 'empowerment' and 'community participation' to legitimise the gendered exploitation of female labour and absolves the state from having to provide a wage for increasingly pivotal work.

In the second half, Sharma's analysis speaks to Tricia's consistent call for a gendered political economy of health perspective that would take into account the social, political, and economic context within which childbearing women live. The 2008 paper 'Money Itself Discriminates' details how neoliberal citizens are 'empowered' to exercise consumer choice in health care. Such empowerment, however, is meaningless in a context where 'the state has little capacity to render the health care market accountable and civil society organisations or patients and their families are neither competent nor well-placed to do this themselves' (2008: 63). In an echo of this work, Sharma shows how policies around issues like institutional child delivery in Nepal, are devised in isolation from the daily realities and experiences of the women they are intended to serve. He notes how access to institutions is variable in a context where birthing centres in rural remote villages are poorly equipped and staffed. The emphasis on institutional delivery also offers scope for private health-care providers to expand, with a resulting increase in expensive caesarean deliveries. Analysing health systems in isolation from wider socio-political trends and currents, this reveals, obscures key drivers and impacts of change.

Early feminist critiques emphasised the 'marginal' position of women in development and advocated their 'integration'. Such 'add women and stir' approaches, as seen in the work of the FCHVs above, assume that women's time is elastic and that they are under-employed. One of the key insights of the Gender and Development literature is that women's 'marginality' reflects the systematic gender bias in official statistics and development planning in general, and that women are already affected by and involved in development in locally variable and class specific ways. It was this recognition of the productive and reproductive work in which women were always already engaged that led to the publication of 'Taking dung-work seriously' (1989) – a paper that arose from Tricia's time spent with women in everyday settings. The arduous labour that went into collecting and drying dung for fuel was invisible and gendered work. Similarly, the focus on economic growth and Gross Domestic Product can obscure the by-products of such development. Barbara

Harriss-White's path-breaking work on waste has shone a light on the sheer volume of waste produced in India and its centrality to the informal economy.

In her essay for this volume, Harriss-White revisits the paper on dung-work in analysing waste production and waste related labour in a small south Indian town. The original paper noted that: 'In recent feminist literature, the term "shit-work" has been used in at least two ways. Literally, it refers to dealing with a baby's excreta and its consequences - washing a baby, its soiled nappies and clothes. Metaphorically, it has also been used to describe the general servicing work done by women, either at home or in wage labour - the preparation of food, cleaning, dusting, washing, sweeping. What links these two is that such work rarely allows women direct access to or control over resources, or over the wealth or income such work helps to produce or maintain. Indeed, the term demeans the activities performed and renders them appropriate only for low status menials' (Jeffery, Jeffery and Lyon 1989: WS32). Whilst the marginalisation and invisibilisation of waste workers continues to some degree, the lines between public and private, and productive and unproductive work, are increasingly blurred since much of the work has been commodified. If this reflects the increasingly neo-liberal economy, so too do the conditions of precarity and insecurity that employees face in the sector. Just as the initial paper shifted from the shit-work described above to work on dung for fuel, so Harriss-White shifts the lens to broader patterns of waste including urine, faeces and menstrual waste. The economic marginality of labourers in this field feeds on, and reinforces existing social inequalities and hierarchies. In closing, the essay offers a powerful indictment of the neglect of waste in research and policy work, and echoes calls for inter-sectional analysis of social issues that cut across policy departments and reports.

The final essay in the volume marks a departure from the ethnographic observations of the above in some ways but echoes the themes and issues raised here. Susan Wadley's essay on Mithila art approaches the topics of health, gender, and development through an analysis of paintings produced during, and documenting, the Covid-19 pandemic and the resultant lockdowns in India.

Through fine-grained analysis of the paintings and the context, and through research with the artists, Wadley offers a bottom-up view of how Coronavirus was experienced on the ground. We view the essay as an important contribution on a number of inter-related grounds. Firstly, as Wadley notes, it speaks to Tricia's own love of Mithila paintings. Tricia's appreciation of the art stems partly from the aesthetic value of the images, but primarily from how effectively they capture the issues and themes that have concerned her research. She often used them as teaching aids, and the paintings described in the essay are certainly evocative in capturing issues of gender, class, caste and health-care. Tricia's work has always been centrally concerned with 'putting things across in the way that people themselves put them across' (personal communication, 2021). Concerned, like many feminist researchers, with questions of cultural imposition and whether the subaltern can speak, Tricia sought to foreground the opinions and experiences of her participants. The Mithila paintings reproduced and discussed in Wadley's essay offer an innovative way of capturing local perspectives, values and narratives. Framed in these beautiful images are many of the issues that have animated Tricia's research, highlighting how access to healthcare is mediated by social factors, pointing to state neglect, but also foregrounding the grass-roots efforts of female health-workers in these difficult conditions.

Conclusion

The chapters in this book all reference Tricia's published work, which has informed and inspired generations of scholars. The editors and contributors are all people whose lives and careers she has profoundly affected. Many others share our debt of gratitude and were eager to honour Tricia even though they were not able to offer chapters for the book. In closing we quote from three colleagues, each of whom draws out important ways in which she helped to shape both the field and the scholars working within it. We begin with a quote from long-time co-author, Professor Craig Jeffrey (despite frequent assumptions to the contrary, Craig is no relation – note the different spelling of the name) from Monash University:

Patricia Jeffery undertook pioneering research on the everyday lives of women in India over many decades. Her book, the brilliantly titled Frogs in a Well, became a landmark in studies of women's limited autonomy in highly patriarchal societies establishing Tricia as an ethnographer of the finest calibre. However, it is the work that she has conducted in rural Bijnor district in a small cluster of villages that is her defining contribution. This work, carried out in five different decades, records with incredible compassion, integrity, and attention to detail the changing lives and struggles of women and men grappling with social change.

As I learnt during two years of collaborative work with Tricia between 2000-2002, she combined an extraordinary intellectual capacity with the ability at the daily level to forge connections with an enormous range of people in a wide variety of positions, from leading provincial businessmen to school students, District Magistrates to young women teaching in rural madrasahs. Tricia's capacity to forge connections across boundaries, elicit and recount stories, model ethical fieldwork practice, and suffuse through all her work an ethos of common human feeling will be among her lasting legacies as a scholar, teacher, and friend.

Captured here are two facets that stand out from those familiar with Tricia's work. The first is the emphasis on the detailed and grounded ethnographies which have brought distant places to life for so many readers as noted above. The second, is her ability to connect with and motivate others. Her impact, in other words, extends well beyond the written word.

This point is to the fore in the powerful tribute from Professor Lynn Jamieson, long-standing colleague of Tricia's in Edinburgh sociology:

I got to know Patricia Jeffery as one of the few women lecturing in the department when I was lecturing in Sociology on a series of temporary lectureships in the 1980s. The honours course that Patricia created, Gender and Development, and taught over many years was pioneering in multiple respects. It was both explicitly feminist and outside the Eurocentric focus of most teaching in sociology. Patricia's own training and research on gender and intersecting issues and inequalities in India

> *enabled her to bring the strengths of the discipline of social anthropology as well as sociology to her teaching. This combination was popular with students and added another strand to the possibilities for students of fulfilling the department's explicit commitment to a comparative sociology. Over the years, as Patricia's research and published writing accumulated, ironically this aspect of her work was not always very visible to many of her colleagues. Patricia largely published in area specialist journals which address her primary audience of others studying, working in or seeking to effect social change in India. This did not, however, diminish her impact on teaching in the department or as a colleague providing support to others. She was a mentor and advocate for younger women and played a key role in mainstreaming gender in the curriculum. She was the lead in setting up and defending 'with gender' degrees and an MSc programme in gender studies. They did not endure in this form but the current vigorous genderED network that mainstreams gender in the curriculum, is, at least in part, her legacy.*

The Gender and Development course mentioned here is still going strong. In the course, Tricia articulated a coherent critique of the gender-blind (or at best 'neutral') nature of much development work. Eschewing the tendency to approach issues in a segmented fashion, the course emphasised the need for a more holistic approach that highlighted the interlinked and intersectional nature of social life (although, as mentioned earlier, the terminology around intersectionality did not exist at that point). Tricia encouraged students to think critically about existing assumptions and practices, and to question the implications of development buzzwords and policies. What Lynn's account illustrates is the pioneering nature of much of Tricia's work. She not only helped to diversify the curriculum at Edinburgh long before calls for such change became mainstream, she offered a passionate critique of structures of inequality which she unpacked and explained through research and teaching. In this, as in much of her work, a desire and demand for change shines through. On a smaller scale, Lynn also points to the often unnoticed time and energy that she poured into teaching, mentoring and advising young scholars. All of the authors here can speak to her generosity in terms of time, advice and painstaking editing. Nor was such support restricted to those at Edinburgh. One of Tricia's key concerns as Chair of the British Association of South Asian Studies was to strengthen the Graduate and Early Career section to help emerging scholars. Reflecting on his long association with Tricia, Professor Geert De Neve from the University of Sussex, notes how such encouragement was a hallmark of her interactions with younger scholars:

> *Patricia has been a most wonderful colleague over the years. I met Patricia first as a young scholar at one of the SAAG (South Asia Anthropologists Group) meetings in London more than 20 years ago, where she was immediately tremendously reassuring when my paper had been placed at the very end of the workshop and my discussant had dropped out last minute! But she had read my paper and asked an empathetic question that put me at ease. This was telling of the mentoring role that she fulfilled for so many young scholars over the years, often probably without herself realising how supportive she was to colleagues and how much it meant to them! Patricia is a team player, encouraging collaborators, colleagues, and students to get involved in conferences and networks, and always ready to participate in any workshop or seminar organised by them. Patricia's contributions to the field of gender studies are far too many and wide-ranging to be summarised. I still use even her very early publications on girls' schooling, on traditional birth attendants, and on women's work in rural India in lectures and seminars today. Their ethnographic richness and focused arguments carry a freshness that continues to inspire even the youngest anthropologists-in-the-making today. As always, I look forward to reading her next publications!*

We cannot hope, as Geert notes, to address all of Tricia's research or legacies in this one book. What we have sought to do instead, is to celebrate her work and mark our deep appreciation for her input to our lives and the field more broadly. All of the chapters offered here acknowledge and build on Tricia's contributions to the study of gender in South Asia, but they do so much more than honour a mentor and friend. They offer new data, refreshing insights and original analysis on a range of topics of contemporary importance, and we are confident that they will serve to inspire a new generation of scholars in their turn.

This is not, however, to say that Tricia's research and writing has reached a point of closure. Indeed, those who have followed her work have much more to look forward to. Her forthcoming books focus on a Muslim village where she has worked since the early 1980s, one contextualising the shifts in child mortality and fertility during that period, and the other exploring the implications of demographic transition, economic change, and communal politics for villagers' ability to fulfil the intergenerational contract. The books will present new empirical material alongside her reflections and observations from longitudinal work in Bijnor spanning over four decades. In other words, although this Festschrift emerges from an event to mark Tricia's retirement, her research, analysis and writing continue. From our interactions and conversations with her over the past years, we understand that the best is yet to come.

REFERENCES

Chopra, R. and Jeffery, P. (eds.). 2005. *Educational Regimes in Contemporary India.* New Delhi: Sage.

Dreze, J. and Sen, A., 1996. *India: Development and participation.* Oxford: Oxford University Press.

Jeffery, P. 1976. *Migrants and Refugees: Muslim and Christian Pakistani Families in Bristol.* Cambridge: Cambridge University Press.

Jeffery, P. 1979. *Frogs in a Well: Indian Women in Purdah.* London: Zed Press.

Jeffery, P. and R. Jeffery. 1994. "'Killing my heart's desire': Education and Female Autonomy in Rural North India", in N. Kumar (ed.) *Women as Subjects: South Asian Histories.* Calcutta and Charlottesville: Stree [Bhatkal & Sen] & Virginia University Press, pp. 125-171.

Jeffery, P. and R. Jeffery. 1996. "What's the Benefit of Being Educated? Girls' Schooling, Women's Autonomy and Fertility Outcomes in Bijnor," in Roger Jeffery and Alaka Basu (eds) *Girls' Schooling, Women's Autonomy and Fertility Change in South Asia* (Sage, New Delhi), pp. 150-183.

Jeffery, P. and R. Jeffery. 199. "Silver Bullet or Passing Fancy? Girls' education and population policy" in Cecile Jackson and Ruth Pearson (eds): *Feminist Visions of Development: Gender Analysis and Policy* (Routledge, London), pp. 235-254.

Jeffery, P. 1998. 'Agency, Activism and Agendas' in Patricia Jeffery and Amrita Basu (eds) *Appropriating Gender: Women's Activism, Politicized Religion and the State in South Asia:* New York & London: Routledge: pp.221-243.

Jeffery, P. 2001. 'A Uniform Customary Code? Marital breakdown and women's economic entitlements in western UP', *Contributions to Indian Sociology,* 35(1): pp. 1-32.

Jeffery, P. 2014. "Supply-and-demand demographics: Dowry, daughter aversion and marriage markets in contemporary north India", in *Contemporary South*

Asia 22:2, 171-188 (Special issue 'Innovation: Transforming hierarchies in South Asia', edited by Minna Säävälä and Sirpa Tenhunen)

Jeffery, P. Forthcoming (b). Rural Muslims and the fragile intergenerational contract in north India: Improvised livelihoods intersecting with economic, demographic and political change (Routledge)

Jeffery, P. and Jeffery, R. 1996. *Don't Marry me to a Plowman! Women's Everyday Lives in Rural North India.* Boulder, Colorado: Westview Press.

Jeffery, P. and Jeffery, R. 2008. '"Money itself discriminates": Obstetric emergencies in the time of liberalisation', *Contributions to Indian Sociology* 42(1): pp.61-93.

Jeffery, P., Jeffery, R. and A. Lyon. 1989. *Labour Pains and Labour Power: Women and Childbearing in India.* London: Zed Books.

Jeffery, R., Jeffery, P. and A. Lyon. 1989. 'Taking Dung-Work Seriously: Women's Work and Rural Development in North India', *Economic and Political Weekly,* 24(17): WS 32-7.

Jeffrey, C., Jeffery, P. and R. Jeffery. 2008. *Degrees without Freedom? Education, Masculinities and Unemployment in north India.* Stanford: Stanford University Press.

Patricia Jeffery, Roger Jeffery and Andrew Lyon. 1988. "When did you last see your mother? Aspects of Female Autonomy in Rural North India", in Jack Caldwell, Allan Hill and Valerie Hull (eds), *Micro-Approaches to Demographic Research* (Kegan Paul International, London), pp. 321-333

1

Communist Women – At Home, In the World

Bengal, 1930s to 1950s

Tanika Sarkar

I write about two Bengali women and their relationship with revolutionary and communist politics between the 1930s and the 1950s.[1] One was a novelist, the other an activist. I should begin, though, with a word of caution. I deeply respect their work, but I do not assume that women's words and memories are necessarily or especially accurate or transparent: or that they are windows into an unmediated reality.[2] Like all other recollections, these contain layers of mediations, displacements, subterfuges. But even if memories are knowingly or unwittingly manipulative, still 'they allow us to recognize the interests of the tellers and the dreams and desires beneath them'.[3] Their value lies precisely in this.

Kalpana Dutt, later Joshi, was an iconic revolutionary in the 1930s before she joined the Communist Party of India.[4] Sabitri Ray, wife of a Party member, fictionalised political lives between the 1930s and the 1970s. Feminist literary historians have recently pulled her out of obscurity, primarily as a partition novelist.[5]

I had first presumed that the activist and the housewife constituted clear mutual contrasts. Their points of difference, or of identification, eventually turned out to be rather more intriguing. By retrieving the housewife-novelist as a communist in her own right, and not simply as the wife of one, I add a new layer to the category of political women. I also reconfigure the activist as a writer, and as a woman, living through tempestuous personal crises. The purpose is to see if women had a distinctive relationship with politics – and a language of their own to express it. The effort may complicate a widely held assumption that women's writings and politics invariably shared generic features, standing in clear contrast to male literary and political tropes.

Several feminist scholars have revealed how communist movements marginalised women cadres and troubled the promise of egalitarianism.[6] There are a few similar studies of women in the politics of revolutionary terror.[7] My work bears out their findings to a large extent, although it adds personal and intimate domains to their experiences. Apart from emphasising a generalised subordination, I also probe the different ways in which they navigated and displayed the problems of their location.

Priyamvada Gopal describes how men and women understood and represented gender in the Progressive Writer's Association. Her approach is finely tuned and complex, revealing powerful forms of autonomous political understanding and literary expression. Ania Loomba establishes a complicated dialectic among the personal, the political and the representational, showing how they reconfigured one another.[8] Together, they have cast communist women as exciting and complex historical actors. By narrowing down the ambit to two figures, I hope to retrieve some more interesting aspects.

I begin with the broad political context over the two decades, which I then follow up with a broad but brief account of sociocultural changes that affected political women. I focus on Dutt and Ray in the last two sections.

I

Several parallel political streams opened up in Bengal in the 1930s. Congress politics certainly dominated the scene, but were occasionally overshadowed by spectacular upsurges of revolutionary violence. Communist ideology spread fast at the same time, despite a temporary setback in 1929 when some leaders were arrested for organising what the government termed as a 'conspiracy against the King and Empire' and launched the Meerut Conspiracy Case against communist labour activists. The simultaneous existence of three possible courses of action created a problem of choice. It also marked important shifts from one strand to another.

The Congress had resolved to struggle for full independence at its Lahore session of 1929. In 1930–31, a highly organised Gandhian leadership confronted the state with an immensely powerful and widespread civil disobedience movement against specific laws. Villagers refused to pay the police or the *chowkidari* tax, and Congress volunteers fanned out into coastal areas to prepare contraband salt in public view, despite enormous police repression. Salt was sold in cities where foreign products were boycotted and burned, and shops were picketed. Streets filled up with protest demonstrations and slogans. Although suspended temporarily in 1931 by the Gandhi-Irwin Pact, the movement was resumed when the First Round Table Conference in London failed to meet Congress demands. The initial energies were spent by this time and the movement contracted into individual *satyagraha* between 1932 and 1934.[9] There was yet another huge Congress uprising in 1942, after the British dragged India into the Second World War without consulting its leaders. The Quit India movement developed an underground apparatus and there were occasional flare-ups of popular violence. Parallel governments were briefly set up in parts of southwest Bengal.

There was a resurgence of revolutionary terrorism from 1928, involving assassinations of British officials, and an armed uprising at Chittagong in April 1930, which we shall discuss later in some detail.

The Communist Party of India (CPI) was founded in 1925, although, according to a different reckoning, this happened in 1920. Its strategies were formulated within an overarching frame of Communist International guidelines, as dictated by the Soviet Union – which, in turn, were dictated by Stalin. This resulted in some startling policy turnabouts.[10] The CPI denounced the 'imperialist war' in 1939. But an imperialist war soon became the 'People's War' when Nazi Germany attacked the Soviet Union in 1941, and the CPI turned around to support British war efforts. In 1947, as the Cold War accelerated, the Soviet Union tried to hasten communist seizures of state power wherever possible. Simmering sharecropper struggles in North Bengal developed into full-blown resistance to tenure-holding *jotedars*. Indian communists condemned independence as 'fake', and a militant B.T. Ranadive replaced P.C. Joshi – Kalpana Dutt's husband – as General Secretary in 1948. The Party was briefly banned.

But the Soviet Union did a *volte face* when it identified Nehru as a reliable ally. It asked the CPI to reinvent itself as a responsible parliamentary opposition. Ranadive's line was thoroughly discredited, and Joshi, suspended in 1949, was readmitted to the Central Committee in 1956.

If the broad policy framework was dictated by the Soviets, Indian communists creatively filled in the details with impressive movements of their own fashioning. Joshi organised a brilliant cultural upsurge to raise funds for famine relief in Bengal.[11] P. Sundarayya and Rajeshwar Rao presided over the huge Telengana uprising – opposing the Nizam's rule in Hyderabad, and demanding radical land reforms as well as the abolition of untouchability (caste had eluded the attention of Bengal communists). Ranadive tried to organise an urban insurrection.

While at the Party's helm, Ranadive ruthlessly persecuted communists who were close to Joshi. Ray's husband was one of them.

II

These decades also saw momentous social changes in India, which historians are yet to address. In many ways, they offer a parallel with the May 4th movement in contemporary China, which similarly braided the social and the political. They threw up a fresh generation of 'new' women from the upper and middle classes. Many studied at colleges and universities, and moved to hostels, away from family control. Several went abroad for higher studies, others joined political organisations, and quite a few cultivated a new female athleticism – an important, though neglected, sign of changing times.[12]

A few young people from elite families also experimented with a somewhat libertarian lifestyle: pre-marital, even extra-marital relationships, love marriages (which could be inter-caste or intercommunity) and runaway marriages. Many inhabited more than one of these new spaces. Ray and Dutt, for instance, went to college, lived in hostels, married men of their choice, held and acted on dangerous political views. Trade unionist Prabhabati Dasgupta and nationalist leader Aruna Asaf Ali – both upper-caste Hindus – married Muslims.

We need to read political and social change together, to track how they interpenetrate. During civil disobedience, women led demonstrations, picketed, courted arrests – even death in police firing – made contraband salt. Peasant women became 'dictators' of local committees, and middle-class women worked with them.[13] During the Quit India movement of 1942, Aruna Asaf Ali organised the underground apparatus for nationalist resistance. Nationalism did not erode social barriers, but it did make them somewhat porous at peak points.

Gandhi hoped this was a temporary break from class, caste and gender boundaries; women might have thought otherwise.[14] Bengali revolutionary 'terrorists' admitted women to their front ranks in the 1930s – the only Indian revolutionaries to do so. Women trade unionists began to work in slums from the early twenties.[15] The first generation consisted of politically unattached women, who organised various categories of factory and sanitation workers on their own, with ingenious mobilising tactics.

Congress, as well as revolutionary terrorists, had created special fronts for women students and volunteers from the late 1920s. *Samitis* were ostensibly founded to train nationalist volunteers. But a small secret core of hand-picked recruits to terrorism emerged. Postgraduate student, Ila Sen, ran the Kasba Chhatri Sangha at 24 Parganas to teach lathi and dagger play to schoolgirls, some of them mere children.[16] Parents and schools happily imagined that their wards were becoming strong-bodied patriotic mothers and wives, little knowing that an inner band had formed to shoot down Europeans.[17]

Clearly, physical training was no longer a rare or completely forbidden activity for young women. Two teenage school students, Shanti and Suniti, assassinated District Magistrate Stevens at Comilla in 1931. They visited him on the pretext of being acclaimed swimmers who wanted his permission to demonstrate their skills at a public event.[18] Obviously, theirs was a fairly credible story. Bina Das, a college student, fired on the Bengal Governor in 1930 at a Calcutta University convocation ceremony. Her brother testified that both his sisters, Kalyani and Bina, were ardent cyclists. So were Kalpana Dutt and her friends. Wikipedia shows a childhood photograph of Ila Mitra, communist leader of the Nachole *adivasi* peasant movement at Rajshahi in 1950, who was brutally tortured in an East Pakistan prison for four years. She stands in shorts and shirt, in front of a shelf full of cups and medals, won for athletic feats in the early 1930s.[19] Sports would have eroded typically feminine inhibitions about physical deportment and conduct, and created a more robust and confident relationship between women and their bodies.

Once brought into the inner circles of revolutionaries, these young people lived double lives, parts of which were jealously hidden from families and could only be shared with one another. Intense political closeness among comrades was, therefore, bound to slide into emotional intimacy, even though terrorists took a vow of celibacy. Surya Sen, leader of the Indian Republican Army, tried to keep men and women apart within the organisation and minimise mutual contact.[20] But social distance crumbled at times of terrorist action.

Suhashini Ganguly, member of the Calcutta Jugantar Group of revolutionaries, set up a safe house for Chittagong terrorists at Chandernagore, along with a male revolutionary. They posed as a married couple.[21] Her 'husband' developed an unrequited love for her which complicated life in the hideout. She herself loved Ganesh Ghosh, a leader of the Chittagong Armoury Raid.[22]

By admitting young women into their ranks, Bengal revolutionaries took grave risks with entrenched gender norms they had no desire to challenge. This put them in a bind, which they resolved with the pervasive motif of sacrifice. Women could forsake their feminine identity – but only in exceptional times, and only for an exceptional cause. A non-gendered political mission was not seen as a desirable freedom, but as a necessary loss of their authentic identity.

Revolutionary men also took enormous risks when they plotted violent action. Male violence does not overturn codes of masculinity – rather, it conforms to the traditional warrior-caste ethos. Women in violence, on the other hand, overthrew deeply entrenched norms. Even their vow of lifelong celibacy was transgressive, since marriage, domesticity and procreation are their prescribed vocation, whereas male celibacy is compatible with the ascetic ideal. Women revolutionaries, therefore, had to account laboriously for their violent act, and their testimonies oscillated between great pride and deep discomfort.

Bina Das subtly crafted her confession to straddle both womanliness and violent patriotism. The assassination attempt was 'an outrage against my nature', which was otherwise gentle and pious – in other words, perfectly feminine. But she had to

> die fighting against the despotic system of government which has kept my country in perpetual subjection … a slave cannot realize God. My sense of religion and morality is not inconsistent with my sense of political freedom … freedom is originally connected with religion.

She thus assimilates violence within worship, which is an acceptable female prerogative. Above all, her own expected death after capture redeems her violence. She asked, 'would not the immolation of a daughter of India and a son of England awaken India?'[23] Her reference to immolations (associated with widows) or *sati* in a modern political context is interesting. It blends ritual suicide with patriotic politics without any sense of discrepancy between what is indubitably, even aggressively, modern, and what is a traditional prescription for virtuous Hindu widows.

Their unprecedented closeness to male comrades posed another momentous problem. Kalpana and Pritilata Waddedar went underground with young men, and Kalpana spent several years in hiding with them. Both fell in love with comrades who were killed in action. Even had they lived, their love was doomed. Their vow of celibacy was meant to safeguard conventional norms of gendered social distance. It also offered up a flawless, perfect sacrificial object to the Motherland. For all their mutually opposed politics, Gandhians and terrorists shared the motif of self-sacrifice and the destruction of personal loyalties and emotions. Religious faith provided an additional bulwark against unruly desires.

What was actually a spectacular break with gender norms did not, therefore, display itself as such. Equality in combat was restricted to violent moments and, sadly, heroic women spared little thought for ordinary ones.[24] Although they abandoned familial and gender restrictions, they refused to question them. Patriotism was, therefore, both enabler and roadblock. Their politics certainly pushed back the limits of feminine existence. But the limits were evaded covertly.

Communists, on the other hand, did not prohibit sexual desire. They endorsed divorce and accepted love marriages as the preferred norm. Nor were they unduly troubled by the occasional eruption of extra-marital relationships in their ranks. Bani Dasgupta, a 'wholetimer', who devoted all her time to Party work, told me in 1998 that local people mocked their Barisal Party office as a '*prajapati* (butterfly) office' – a place of romance, sometimes illicit. Obviously, romances were more disturbing to their neighbours than their political or ideological work. For a while in the 1940s, people lived in communes, abjuring a family life for a collective and shared one.[25]

Communists were indeed making social revolution in practice. Yet, they did not reflect seriously on what gender equality involved, nor did they develop a critique of patriarchy. Gender – like caste – was relegated to an epiphenomenal sphere: acknowledged, but so subordinated to class that it did not merit special elaboration. There was a strong imperative for self-sacrifice and for subordinating family needs to Party commands, especially for the ordinary cadre.

Women turned to communism from the late 1930s, receiving – as did communist men – a rather crude Stalinist creed for political education. Stalin's *History of the Communist Party of the Soviet Union* was their staple political-intellectual diet. Given that Marxism is an intensely theorised political philosophy – and given that Indian middle-class Marxists were highly erudite and cosmopolitan – such theoretical poverty is surprising. Moreover, no communist woman reflected on communist doctrines. Ideological production was left to the men and the women's activism was practical, not intellectual.

Going by the books that Kalpana Dutt read when she came out of prison in 1939,[26] they learnt primarily about international workers' struggles. More inspirational was a utopian mythology about the Soviet Union. Soviet women's journals were translated into Indian languages and Indian communist women sought in them the image of their own future.

Communist women started their political career in student unions. They raised relief funds during the devastating Bengal famine of 1943 through theatre and song squads.[27] It was quite rebellious for young middle-class women to travel to distant famine-stricken villages with their plays, to live rough and in unprecedented intimacy with men. At least one divorce and a second marriage came out of it, creating something of a sensation when Shobha Sen left her husband and son to join co-actor Utpal Dutt.

Mahila Atmaraksha Samiti – MARS, a broad women's front, coordinated by communists – expanded the scope of their work. Middle-class activists trekked to villages to mobilise women for relief kitchens. They taught embroidery to urban famine victims and marketed their products. As a women-only space, MARS performed typically domestic and nurturing functions.[28] But domesticity, thus repurposed, provided a useful launching pad for full-time political work on other fronts. It also brought together women of different classes in daily contact, and transformed a few conservative ones in the process – Bimala Maji, a rural child-widow, was encouraged to remarry, for instance. It also expanded the social world of middle-class communists.

Relief work segued into vigorous street protests in the mid-forties, when MARS organised marches of refugee women for better rations, and when a few women joined militant sharecropper movements in north and southwest Bengal.[29] Peter Custers argues that they only came into their own when state repression forced male leaders into prisons or underground.[30] A situation that was reversed when the men returned.

Leadership remained firmly in male hands and leaders could casually and hurtfully reprimand women activists in public.[31] Theory and practice therefore chased each other in both preserving and challenging social values. The result was a complicated circularity between desire, articulation and practice.

III

Kalpana Dutt, granddaughter of Rai Bahadur Benode Dutt of Boalkhali in Chittagong, has been widely revered as an *agnikanya* – a daughter of fire. Even Rabindranath Tagore, otherwise a harsh critic of terrorist politics, interceded with the colonial authorities for her release from prison. She contested as a communist candidate against veteran Congress leader, Nellie Sengupta, in the 1946 elections. Nervous of her great popularity, Nehru himself came to campaign against her. But he began his speech with a tribute to the *bahadur ladki* (the heroic girl) of Chittagong.[32]

Her name first enters police files in February 1931 as a dangerous Bethune College student, close to Surya Sen. Sen and his Hindustan Republican Army, inspired by the Irish Easter Uprising of April 1916, had organised a remarkable conspiracy in April 1930 in the East Bengal town of Chittagong. A small group seized the armoury, cut off the town's communication lines, shot dead many Europeans and held the town captive for several days before the British could overcome them. Along with a few comrades, including Kalpana, Sen remained underground for three years, to be executed in 1934.[33]

Kalpana excelled in lathi and dagger play and was an excellent shot. She travelled frequently between her Calcutta hostel and her

Chittagong home to bring gun cotton for Sen, adroitly evading police searches. She was first arrested in September 1931 and her influential father signed bonds to defer her conviction. Almost immediately she went underground. She was arrested again in September 1932, but was released on bail once more – another instance of her family's high standing. She absconded yet again in December and was re-arrested in August 1933. She spent the years in male attire. Once, when she was captured with the men and asked by the police to strip, she burst into tears. The police gleefully realised that their trophy was the ever-elusive woman terrorist. She was sentenced to life transportation at the dreaded Andaman Cellular goal. A spirited public campaign stopped that and procured her release in 1939.[34]

Kalpana's defiance – of family and state – was boundless, as was her courage.[35] Yet, she let Surya Sen monitor her every movement and demand that she repeat to him every word that passed between her and the man she loved. She accepted the humiliating surveillance, complaining about it only at the end of her life. In a newspaper interview, she sharply criticised Sen's moral policing. She recalled that she had told him she had not endangered her loving family to submit to his relentless suspicion. But she subsided immediately after her brief flare-up.[36] We find a similar reticence in Manikuntala Sen who was furious when P.C. Joshi berated women comrades for their presumed lapses at a public conference.[37] Other women prodded her to speak up, but she would not defy the General Secretary. She revealed it much later, after she had resigned from the Party.

After her release in 1939, Kalpana slowly turned towards communism. She worked hard for famine relief at Chittagong in 1943 and joined the MARS.[38] She wrote a book in 1945 to eulogise her Chittagong associates and to narrate her thrilling experiences in the terrorist movement. The Party had commissioned it, even though it opposed terrorist politics. It had to live down its support to the British war effort during Quit India, and regain its patriotic credentials. Kalpana's recollections reminded readers of her role as a nationalist heroine. It also reminded them that she now belonged to the communists.

She closed the gap between patriotism and communism to stress continuity between her two political identities. As both terrorist and communist she was 'serving her country'.[39] She never quite explained why, in that case, she chose to shift to communism.

The shift was not easy. Her male revolutionary associates had already converted to communism by early 1939 but she continued to vacillate until November. She remained at her parental home, and the police – now keeping only 'a periodical watch' – were relieved to find her 'inactive' and 'seldom coming out of her house'. Soon, they withdrew their surveillance. She would not meet her terrorist friends who had, by then, turned to communism. In an intercepted letter of July 1939, Manoranjan Roy reproached her for avoiding them, for suspecting them of 'insincerity', for not joining them to work in the slums.

As she struggled with melancholy introspection, Kalpana Dutt confided in terrorist women instead. She wrote to Bina Das (Manudi) in July:

> Nothing interests me. I am in a state of indecision from which I cannot emerge, the instructions coming from everybody are creating more obstacles in my attempt at self determination. Manudi, to be frank, I cannot believe anybody. I do not get satisfaction from conversing with anybody. I do not go out of home now at all … Manudi, will you write clearly what I should do now? Won't you come here once?

She wrote to Suhashini Ganguly (Putudi) at the same time: 'I shall not leave you alone. I shall trouble you often … Please do come here soon.'[40]

Male comrades did not offer her a space where she could express her doubts. Manikuntala articulated a similar problem, of failing to find common ground between her religious beliefs and her communism, she could not bring her distress to Party circles.[41] The Party was instrumental in what it harvested from its whole-time cadres. It put part-selves to political use, ignoring the whole person.

By November Dutt had made the shift, although she never explained why she did so. As she had earlier accepted Sen's policing, now she obeyed Party instructions. General Secretary P.C. Joshi fell in love with her. She spurned him because her beloved terrorist comrade had asked her to wait for him. Joshi pointed out that he had been killed, but she remained adamant. The Party stepped in and insisted that she marry Joshi. She complied, and they were married in 1943.[42] When Joshi was suspended from the Party in 1948, she was put under great pressure to leave him. She stood by him, but did not face suspension herself; so great was her public standing outside the Party that it could not afford to punish her. The marriage was fairly stormy, and in one of his last letters to a friend, Joshi wrote: 'My family is alright but each lives his own life. I am a misfit.'[43]

Clearly, her turn to communism and to Joshi had been inspired by a new political commitment and a new love. But she chose to be silent about the first, and represented the second as obedience to Party commands.

After independence, the Indian government renewed surveillance far more implacably than the colonial police ever did. She was arrested in October 1949, and had to plead piteously with the prison authorities for a visit from her two sons – three and two years old – who had been left alone at home as their father was then away. It took quite a while for the police to ascertain that she had been arrested under a wrong charge. The authorities ignored the fact that her husband had always urged unity with the Congress. Indeed, so powerful was Joshi's dislike of B.T. Ranadive's insurrectionary line that he secretly tried to persuade some comrades to break away from the CPI and form a new 'White Flag Party'[44] – no doubt influenced by a Burmese revolutionary organisation with the same name. His 'soft' communism, nonetheless, failed to temper state suspicion. Only when the Party split in 1964, and the Joshis embraced the moderate wing of the CPI, was the police posse withdrawn and the file on Dutt closed.

Her last interview strikes a baffling note. Joshi was very shabbily treated by B.T. Ranadive, who succeeded him as General Secretary. However, Dutt never mentioned that. Instead, she abruptly interrupted her life story to say: 'I liked Ranadive. He was a true gentleman and always very nice to me'.[45] A strange tribute to a man who had destroyed their political credibility and who, later as a CPI(Marxist) leader, split away from her own Party. What can one make of this unexpected eruption? An assertion of autonomy? And why was it tucked obliquely into her life story?[46] Why was this dazzling public figure so remarkably reticent about her political and personal thinking?

I resuscitate her brief and faltering anguish, to emphasise a hidden history of unexpected anomalies that coexisted with great courage. Her vulnerabilities did not define the 'real' Dutt. But, by acknowledging their existence, we complicate the conventional vision of heroism as a seamless, self-identical whole: never interrupted nor haunted by its Other.

Dutt later worked for famine relief at Chittagong and, later still, for the CPI women's front – the National Federation of Indian Women. We know little about her role in the organisation. She wrote a few pieces for the communist newspaper, *People's War,* where she discussed the prevalence of communal harmony at Chittagong at a time of great strife elsewhere. She recalled how Muslim peasants sheltered revolutionaries;[47] how a Muslim prison cook prepared special dishes for her – better even than those she received as a Division 1 inmate; and how, after her release, many town Muslims came to congratulate her. She told stories of Muslim peasant women who, deserted by husbands during the famine, formed self-help committees on their own; and how Muslim youths rescued women from the clutches of drunken soldiers.[48]

She wrote in vivid and unusual words about child patients:

> Children were the worst sufferers … they were wild and strange. Their hands and legs were thin and straight like wooden sticks. They had enlarged spleen and swollen stomach. Their faces were puffed up through undernourishment, sickness and tears of hunger and misery. Their eyes alone sparkled – like those of some hungry wild animal appearing in the night.[49]

She recounted tales of ordinary Samiti women who distributed food and worked with the Friends' Ambulance Unit; of how they snatched time to soothe child patients with night-time stories despite their heavy workload. She described how the Party set up milk canteens, apart from working in Government-funded relief units, which they took over. Sometimes teashops enticed children to sell their share of milk to them; communists stopped that.[50] As a talented journalist, she reported stories that most others forgot.

Few, however, commemorated Kalpana as a communist; neither public memory, which had been exuberant about her terrorist achievements, nor communist histories.[51] The aura of her name belongs to a past she chose to leave behind. It is not associated with Kalpana Joshi, wife of a charismatic General Secretary and active and ardent communist herself.

While her newspaper reports show a rare eye for detail about ordinary people, she wrote practically nothing about her long and crowded political life as a communist. Nor did she mention momentous events in the life of the Party: her husband's leadership; his overthrow; the insurrectionary turn in Party strategy; the post-colonial Congress repression she'd suffered from; the effects of de-Stalinisation; the Party split in 1964. The political figure fell silent when it came to the political life that she had lived for the longest time.

IV

> I sometimes feel that when future generations remember all of you, will they ever think of Alys (Faiz Ahmad Faiz's wife) or me. We have always walked with you, though you were a step ahead of us. Sometimes you would look back to perhaps make sure that we were still there, following behind you. And we would reassuringly smile back although our hearts would cry out in pain.[52]

Referring to the early Communist Party of Pakistan, this fragment from a wife's letter sums up the self-perception of Party wives: always a step behind husbands, hiding their pain behind a smile. Yet, the writer does manage to articulate their marginalisation by the Party they believed in, and in the lives of husbands they loved: not in anger, but as a gentle, subdued question, half-spoken, half left in the air. Sabitri Ray also spoke in such a soft, sad voice.

Ray's life and writings thrust up a new political figure: communist wives. Although they were not cardholding activists, they were nonetheless communists in their conviction. Ray married a middle-ranking cadre who had earlier been a terrorist. He was too busy with Party work to help with domestic responsibilities.[53] Although communists did not demand celibacy, in practice, they imposed an equally strong self-abnegation on their adherents, making it clear that Party responsibilities must supersede personal and familial ones, however urgent.

A frail Ray carried childcare and domestic chores single-handed. She also looked after her oppressively orthodox matrimonial family. In the early 1940s, Joshi had advised married cadres to integrate themselves with larger family units, however conservative, to retain a support structure for themselves and for their children in times of repression.[54] For young modern wives, hoping to become companion comrades to their husbands, the pragmatism could prove stifling. Ray had married in spite of parental disapproval, without any religious ceremony. But her husband asked her to put the vermillion line on her hair-parting – the mark of a Hindu married women – as they entered his village. That startled and dismayed her.[55] She never forgot it.

Ray frequently counterposed communist wives to the growing number of women activists, often cushioned by well-off and illustrious families. She describes them – perhaps with more passion than accuracy – as complacent and insensitive, swollen with self-importance about their rarity value, and with the admiration of male comrades. They dismissed wives with contempt, as useless appendages. Wives resented the political intimacy their husbands shared with these women.[56] They were isolated precisely because they chose to marry communists, accepting the attendant risks and privations that thrust them into domestic drudgery.

Ray, suffering from bouts of depression and low self esteem, stayed away from Party activities. She did not even join MARS, which enabled home-bound wives to come to the aid of subaltern slum women.[57] Caught up in family responsibilities and illness, and cooking endlessly to feed comrades who hardly noticed her, she lived in a narrow world. Her fictional plots, characters and emotional situations, therefore, replicated the limited repertoire of personal experience. Because she wrote intermittently, hard-pressed to write between spokes of the domestic wheel, narrative construction was sometimes awkward and shapeless, bulging with excessive details and meandering, sentimental monologues.

Not all communist women wrote in a similar vein. In sharp contrast to Ray's tremulous prose, Sulekha Sanyal – a remarkable and sadly forgotten novelist – used a dry, harsh staccato and minimalist language, which was closer to male communist writers. Her protagonist Chhabi is a perpetual question mark: full of anger at injustice and cruelty; lashing out against norms, emotions and obligations that seek to tie her down. Unlike in Ray's writing, which is lyrical about the beauties of nature, of men and women, in Chhabi's world human beauty decays under hunger and cruelty before it can bloom, and nature offers no solace. Their divergences appear greater than their commonalities, and no single voice, language or sensibility offers a distinctively female communist tonality.[58]

In most of Ray's novels, the woman protagonist first loves a terrorist: romance of the pistol and pre-marital love enhancing each other's contraband allure.[59] She changes abruptly when the man turns to communism. Ray navigates the shift by partly denying it, as Dutt had done. She struggles to make communism as full of romance, danger and heroic patriotism – and, therefore, as deserving of self-sacrifice – as terrorism had been.[60]

The wife soon realises that she can never achieve the promised romance of a fulfilled communist life, as she'd envisioned when she fell in love. She accepts her fate. The fictionalised husband's personality is inextricably shaped by his ideology and movement, he is nothing without them. She cannot love one without loving the other. But she muses interminably on her pain in an everlasting conflict, where triumphalism and tragedy jostle, neither ceding ground.[61]

If the emotional world of Ray's fiction is circumscribed by this invariant narrative trajectory, it nonetheless analyses a complex political world with surprising incisiveness. Surprising because

Ray was a solitary housewife, stranded in punishing domesticity, eavesdropping on Party meetings from the kitchen, and reading Party journals left at home in brief, hurried snatches. Neither husband nor visiting comrades had the time or the inclination to enlighten her. She wrote in a letter: 'I listen to what people say, at home, outside, on buses and trams, I listen with all my heart, all my mind, I write on that basis.'[62]

Swaralipi was her third novel, and her first mature piece of fiction. Driven by uncharacteristic anger about the Ranadive period, it is sharper and less ambivalent than her usual tentative prose. Its tragic protagonist – Sheeta – is rejected by terrorist Prithvi because he must renounce earthly pleasures. Heartbroken, she marries a Congressman she does not love. She spends just one night with him as he is imprisoned the next day. But it leads to pregnancy and a daughter. He dies later.

Most of Ray's wives embrace their loss and pain rather than try and overcome them. Resignation – bitter but concealed – constitutes an integral part of their personality. They brood on their grudges, even as they outwardly compromise with unjust orthodoxy. Sheeta grumbles about domestic tyranny and chafes against her mother-in-law's impositions, but she also accepts them. Although she loves Prithvi, she clings to the discipline of widowhood. As the novel ends, she gives up her freedom and her child when she returns to her husband's village in East Pakistan to bring her ailing mother-in-law back to Calcutta. She is arrested on the way and taken to prison – a clear parallel to the arrest of Ila Mitra by the Pakistani police. An ambiguous fidelity to the chains that bind shapes her idealism, and sacrifice constitutes the stuff of female heroism.

The husband dies early, leaving Sheeta with a terrible burden of guilt. Even though Prithvi – now a communist, no longer committed to celibacy – is keen to renew the relationship, she does not agree. In many ways, she remains a widow at heart. Nor does he insist too strongly. Ray's male protagonists are gentle, introspective men, possessed of an infinitely romantic – rather than masterful – masculinity.

As Sheeta cannot decide, and as Prithvi is distanced again and again by political vicissitudes, love's consummation is perpetually desired yet deferred – a standard hazard of communist lives at this time. There is yet another constraint on desire. Since the Party was banned in 1949, the activist couple, Sagari and Rathi, avoids sex for fear of an unwanted pregnancy. Aching for each other, they sleep apart.

If these tragedies are, in some ways, the unavoidable collateral damage of a great cause, politics also separates loving couples in more vicious ways. Sagari is compelled by Party orders to leave Rathi, who does not toe the Ranadive line. Ray depicts the new leadership as sexually and morally corrupt. Leader Nandalal lives in inappropriate luxury, while cadres suffer great privation. He forces comrade to betray comrade, wife to leave husband. When Sagari leaves Rathi, Nandalal tries to seduce her. Belatedly realising the costs of her blind loyalty, Sagari leaves for North Bengal to work for the Tebhaga movement, where she is shocked again by the Party's reckless adventurism and the accelerating violent action against even minor and friendly tenure-holders. While opposing it, she dies under police fire, leaving a loving letter for Rathi.

As an apocalypse threatens, the new Soviet line appears, denouncing sectarian divisions and insurrectionism. The Party is redeemed. Erstwhile supporters of the Joshi line, who had betrayed him under pressure, now repent and return to his fold, and wounds are healed. Ray's narrative thus returns to a familiar socialist optimism, but only after relentlessly revealing its faultlines. No other Bengali communist novelist ever went that far in exposing and criticising Party decisions.

The personal and the political in Ray's narration of the Ranadive period may be debated. We cannot ascertain her allegations of corruption. Since sexual predatoriness is the unfailing sign of villainy in Bengali fiction, she could have mobilised it to put the final stamp of denunciation on Ranadive's leadership. Although communist women arranged logistic support and worked to keep lines of communication open between Party and ground level activists, Ray had imagined them as fully fledged comrades-in-arms.[63]

More impressive is the implicit – maybe even unselfconscious – questioning of the communist distrust of individual conscience, emotional intelligence, independent judgement and a blind reliance on Party diktat. Even comrades who cannot bring themselves to trust Ranadive, do not believe that they might be right and the Party wrong. Do we detect gentle irony when 'old-liners' are reprieved by the new Soviet perspective which restores their faith in their own political understanding? Even if it is an unintended irony, as it probably was, Ray intuitively observed a deep deficit in the communist personality without, perhaps, fully realising its implications. But she was the only person who did register it.

Surprisingly, although she was very close to the Joshis, Ray does not defend Joshi's strategy of a broad unity with bourgeois nationalists, nor does she mention the imaginative cultural upsurge that Joshi had organised in the People's War phase. Although the new Soviet line of moderation validates Joshi's stance, Ray does not invest him with the vibrant excitement that Ranadive's 'wrong' line had stimulated; the romance of the revolutionary moment at the barricades seems to depart with the exit of Ranadive, the problematic and intolerant leader. Prithvi admits that the Party under Joshi was much too inclined towards courting the middle-class intelligentsia, while the Ranadive period, in its initial phase, had resonated with true communist passion.

Even though Joshi was quite pro-Congress, Ray depicts it as the ruthless enemy of working-class and peasant struggles; as the new nation state following in the footsteps of the colonial masters. The first intimation of an insurrectionary line – thundering speeches made at an open mass meeting by a working-class leader, proclaiming that 'the path of Telengana is our path'[64] – thrills communist hearts, fatigued by the hitherto-banked fires of political passion, even though one comrade quizzically asks, 'must he say all this in a public meeting?'[65]

However, Ray problematises Ranadive's 'left adventurism', not so much to defend the new Indian state or the potential of Congress for self-reform, nor with a total rejection of the insurrectionary ideal. Rather, she closely questions the Party strategy of alienating intermediary and small tenure-holders by advising peasant rebels to loot their crops along with those of larger landlords. She also questions the wisdom of provoking a well-armed state when peasants are unarmed, and when the banned Party is teetering on the edge of extinction.

It is interesting that the retiring housewife described and analysed Party experiences more presciently and independently than did Kalpana Joshi, the daring activist. Her analysis of the Ranadive line comes very close to Manikuntala Sen's later description. Unlike Ray, Sen did refer to Stalin's purges and to the Indian Party's imitation of the Great Leader with the dictatorship of its own General Secretary. But she did so through a series of troubled questions, not with a critical analysis.

Swaralipi probes tensions in the political-emotional sensibility of communists: when the political absorbs profound emotional turbulence, and the emotional and the relational are tangled in the formally political. Each partakes of the other's essence in a dialectical spiral.

When he was at the Party's helm, Ranadive had ruthlessly persecuted communists who were close to Joshi. Ray's husband was one of them and she wrote *Swaralipi* in 1952 to denounce the Ranadive line. Aghast at her insubordination, the CPI notified its members: 'The Central Committee of the Communist Party of India directs that no book written by the authoress of *SWARALIPI* should be advertised by our Party journals until she unconditionally express regret for writing the book'.[66] Even though Joshi was later rehabilitated, Ray's writings were not.

After the Central Committee proscribed *Swaralipi*, Ray wrote in a letter:

> Now I think, why did I even try to write this? Maybe someone else could have written this far better. But no one else did, I alone made the effort, and I did so in all sincerity. I am deficient in political wisdom, I could have made mistakes. But was this the only way of correcting them?[67]

NOTES

1. Patricia Jeffery's lively interest in women's lives and agency, and in socialism, makes me hope this chapter is not a misfit in this felicitation volume.
2. Here I differ from the total reliance that Kavita Panjabi places on women's recollections as a superior mode of understanding the past. Panjabi, K. 2016. *Unclaimed Harvest: An Oral History of Tebhaga Women's Movement.* Delhi: Zubaan.
3. Alessandro Portelli, A. 1991. *The Death of Luigi Trastulli and Other stories*, p. 2. New York: SUNY.
4. For an excellent account of Dutt's work in the Chittagong uprising, and also for a history of the uprising itself, see Chatterjee, M. 2010. *Do or Die: The Chittagong Uprising 1930–34*, Delhi: Picador.
5. See Sudakshina Ghosh's biographical introduction in Samanta, S. (ed.) 2005. *Sabitri Ray Rachanasamagra, (Collected Works of Sabitri Ray)*, Vol. 1. Calcutta: Granthalay Private Ltd. (henceforth, *Collected Works*, using *Swaralipi (Notation)*).
6. Above all, Sangathana, S.S. 1989. *We Were Making History: Women and the Telengana Uprising*. London: Zed Books. Also Panjabi, *Unclaimed Harvest.* The tradition continues in feminist studies of women in Maoist movements. Ania Loomba has recently made an invaluable addition to the corpus (see, 2018. *Revolutionary Desires: Women, Communism and Feminism in India.* Delhi: Routledge). Loomba's work is the template for my piece, although it is an impossibly hard act to follow. Maclean, K. 2016. *A Revolutionary History of Interwar India*. Penguin.
7. Maclean, *A Revolutionary History.*
8. Gopal, P. 2005. *Literary Radicalism in India: Gender, Nation and the Transition to Independence*. London and New York: Routledge.
9. Sarkar, T. 1987. *Bengal 1928–1934: The Politics of Protest.* Delhi: Oxford University Press.
10. On this, see the excellent history of Communists by Praful Bidwai (2015. *The Phoenix Moment: Challenges Confronting the Indian Left*. Delhi: HarperCollins India).
11. Requisitioning of essential materials for British war efforts and a scorched-earth policy to block Japan's possible entry into India led to a catastrophic famine in Bengal in 1943.
12. See Elena Valdemari, 'Physical Education and femininity in India: Global Trends and Local Politics towards Crafting Women Citizens', I am grateful to her for allowing me access to her unpublished article.
13. Sarkar, T. 1989. 'Politics and Women in Bengal: the Conditions and Meanings of Participation', in J. Krishnamurty (ed.), *Women in Colonial Bengal: Essays on Survival, Work, and the State*. New Delhi: Oxford University Press.
14. While many important Congress leaders were socially conservative, some, like Jawaharlal Nehru and Subhas Chandra Bose, were far more liberal and

gender-aware. Sarkar, T. 2010. 'Gandhi and the Problem of Social Power', in Judith Brown and Anthony Parel (eds), *The Cambridge Companion to Gandhi*. Cambridge, London and New York: Cambridge University Press.

15. Santoshkumari Gupta, who worked with jute labour in early 1920s, and Prabhabati Dasgupta, who organized jute workers and Corporation sweepers in the late 1920s. Begum Sakina, another trade unionist who worked among municipal sweepers, was the first woman to be elected as a municipal councillor in Bengal in the mid-1930s. Also, Sarkar, T. 1987. *Bengal 1928–1934: The Politics of Protest*. New Delhi: Oxford University Press.
16. Intelligence Bureau Files (henceforth IB Files), 172/32 of 1932 Part III.
17. IB Files, File 850/31, ibid.
18. IB Files, File 850 – 31 of 1931, Confidential. Assassination of S.B. Stevens, District Magistrate Tipperah, on 14/12/1931.
19. En.wikipedia.org/wiki/Ila_Mitra
20. Singh, A. 1968. *Agnigarbha Chattogram (Chattogram on Fire)*, p. 317. Calcutta: Bidyodaya Library.
21. Letter from Police Superintendent, Chittagong, to Special Police Superintendent, Calcutta, 10/7/ 1939, IB Files, 172/32 of 1932, Part II.
22. Personal communication from Sumit Sarkar, whose family was very close to Suhashini or 'Putudi', as she was called.
23. Letter from Police Superintendent, Chittagong, to Special Police Superintendent, Calcutta, 10/7/ 1939: IB Files, 172/32 of 1932, Part II.
24. Once the Chittagong group went into hiding, it had to survive entirely on the mercy of peasants, mostly Muslims, whom they had so far completely ignored. When in jail, they depended on untouchable sweepers to carry secret messages among cells. It is no surprise, therefore, that most turned to communism after their release. Singh, *Chattogram,* p. 208.
25. Ania Loomba discusses this little-known aspect of communist experiments. She also has an excellent discussion of communist romances in Loomba, *Revolutionary Desires*.
26. IB Files, File 493/31 of 1931, Part 11, West Bengal Intelligence Bureau Archives.
27. Renu Chakravartty narrates the first two decades in *Communists in Indian Women's Movements* (1980. Delhi: Peoples Publishing House).
28. For an excellent account, see Sen, M. 2001. *In Search of Freedom: An Unfinished Journey*. Calcutta: Stree.
29. Chakravartty, G. 2015. 'Emergence of Mahila Atmaraksha Samiti in the Forties: The Calcutta Chapter', in S. Bandyopadhyay and T. Sarkar (eds), *Calcutta: The Stormy Decades*. Delhi: Social Science Press.
30. Peter Custers, P. 1987. *Women in the Tebhaga Uprising: Rural Poor Women and Revolutionary Leadership, 1946–47*. Delhi: Naya Prakash. See also Panjabi, *Unclaimed Harvest*.
31. Sen, *In Search of Freedom*, p. 145.

32. Personal communication to Sumit Sarkar from the late Professor Parthasarathi Gupta, who attended the meeting as a child and vividly remembered the episode.
33. An excellent account in Chatterjee, M. 2010. *Do Or Die: The Chittagong Uprising, 1930–34*. Picador. For a chapter on Kalpana, although her focus is quite different to mine, see also Bose, B. 2020. *Intervention Narratives: Afghanistan, the United States and the Global War on Terror*. New Jersey: Rutgers University Press.
34. IB Files, 172/32 of 1932, Part II. Also my interview with Dutt, Delhi, October 1974.
35. As an interesting aside, I had a conversation with her in October 1974. She told me she used to slink out of her home with a bomb or a pistol at the dead of night to meet a contact in a deserted place. She never feared the police, informers or capture. But she would tremble at the thought of ghosts lurking around.
36. Dutt, K. 2013. *Chattogram Astragar Akramankarider Smritikatha*: *Agniyug Smritimala*, Vol. 1. Calcutta: Radical Press.
37. Sen, *In Search of Freedom* pp. 145-6.
38. Chakravartty, G. 2007. *P.C. Joshi: A Biography*. Delhi: National Book Trust. pp. 114–15.
39. Dutt, K. (trans. A. Bose and N. Chakravartty). 1945. *Chittagong Armoury Raiders: Reminiscences*. Delhi: Peoples Publishing House.
40. IB Files, File 493/31 of 1931, Part 11.
41. Sen, *In Search of Revolution: An Unfinished Journey*, Bhatkal and Son, Calcutta, 2003.
42. Interview with Ashok Kumar Mukhopadhyay in *Desh*, 18 December 1991. Reprinted in Dutt, *Chattogram Astragar Lunthaner*, pp. 113–23.
43. Chakravartty, *P.C. Joshi*, pp. 115–18.
44. IB Files, File 493/31 of 1931, Part II.
45. Interview with Ashok Kumar Mukhopadhyay, in *Desh*, 18 December 1991. Reprinted in Dutt, *Chattogram Astragar Lunthaner*, pp. 113–23.
46. Ibid.
47. She wrote an article on this later, 'Chittagong Uprising and the Role of Muslims', for the Chittagong Uprising Golden Jubilee Committee in Ray, N.N. 1984. *Challenge: A Saga of India's Struggle for Freedom*. Delhi: Peoples Publishing House.
48. Dutt, K. 1945. 'Hindu Muslim Unity', *People's War,* 30 August.
49. Dutt, K. 1945. 'Only Children's Hospital in East Bengal', *People's War*, 26 August.
50. Dutt, K. 1945. 'Post Famine Self Help Movement in Chittagong', *People's War*, 23 December.
51. She is not mentioned by Renu Chakravartty in *Communists in Indian Women's Movements* (1980. Delhi: Peoples Publishing House). Gargi Chakravartty's

biography of Joshi has just a few scattered sentences that refer to her, even though the author was very close to the entire family.

52. Excerpt from letter by Razia Sajjad Zaheer to Faiz Ahmad Faiz, in 1951, cited by Ali, K.A. 2015. *Communism in Pakistan: Politics and Class Activism, 1947–72*. London: Bloomsbury Academic, p. 50.
53. Ray's daughter, Gargi Chakravartty, shared these experiences with me.
54. Sarkar, S. 2018. 'Thinking about P.C. Joshi', in *Essays of a Lifetime: Reformers, Nationalists, Subalterns*. Ranikhet: Permanent Black.
55. Ghosh, 'Introduction', in *Collected Works*, p. 6. Several of her early novels, written shortly after her marriage, expressed the wife's bafflement.
56. See *Srijan (Good People)*, first published in 1946, reprinted in *Collected Works*.
57. Reba (Babli) Sarkar told MARS that she could only work from home. They sent slum women to her to learn Kashmiri embroidery. Interview on 11 June 1974.
58. Sanyal, S. 1958. *Nabankur (New Seedling)*. Calcutta: Nabayan.
59. See, for instance, *Paakaa Dhaaner Gaan (Song of the Ripe Paddy)*, Ray's later trilogy on the Tebhaga movement.
60. For the women's role, see Panjabi, *Unclaimed Harvest*.
61. Note Lata's predicament in *Paakaa Dhaner Gaan (The Song of Ripe Paddy)*, or Khana's in *Badwip (Delta)*.
62. Cited by Ghosh in *Collected Works*, p. 9.
63. Sen, I. 2012. 'Women's Politics in India', in R. Ray (ed.), *Handbook of Gender*, Delhi: Oxford University Press.
64. *Swaralipi (Notation)*, in *Collected Works*, p. 311.
65. Ibid, p. 313.
66. See Samanta, *Sabitri Ray Rachanasamagra*, p. 8.
67. Cited by Ghosh in *Collected Works*, p. 9.

2

The Uniform Civil Code Debate and Gender Justice

Zoya Hasan

The re-election of the BJP government in 2019 brought to the forefront the question of a uniform civil code (UCC), an issue that had been at the centre of political and legislative debates since independence. One point was whether religion-based personal law should be continued or a UCC instituted. Seven decades after independence public opinion remains sharply divided. There is agreement that religious personal laws are discriminatory toward women and must therefore change. However, there are disagreements over the means to achieve this objective. There is also disagreement about whether such a code would be a UCC, a gender-just common civil code or simply the Hindu code.[1]

This chapter traces the trajectory of the UCC debate in the context of key developments, notably, the Shah Bano case and abolition of triple talaq. It touches on two of the issues that arise: the role of legal reform and how feminists can engage with the state. It examines: the impact of identity politics on gender equality; the approach and strategies of influential political parties, women's organisations, and Muslim women's groups toward legal reform; the contested issue of a UCC; and, finally, the challenges of introducing a UCC. The UCC would provide one law for the entire country, which entails the legal unification of the civil codes of different religious communities and enforcing a uniform code in matters of marriage, property inheritance and adoption.

The UCC debate centres on the argument about replacing individual personal customs and practices of marriage, divorce, adoption and succession with a common code. Those in favour of one code argue that it will end religious discrimination. Detractors contend that it will rob the nation of its religious diversity and violate the fundamental right to practise religion enshrined in Article 25 of the Constitution. In fact, they hold that a state action to introduce the UCC is against the quintessence of democracy. The critics have directed their energies to what they perceive as an unequal exercise of power of the state, reforming the institutions and practices of Hinduism, while not deploying this power in relation to Indian Islam. Clearly, the system of personal laws has created a legal and social quagmire.[2]

Patricia Jeffery, while exploring the implications of the Shah Bano controversy in the mid-1980s and the associated communalisation of politics, pointed out in her article 'A Uniform Customary Code? Marital breakdown and women's economic entitlements in rural Bijnor' that the problems of marital breakdown and its impact on women's lives are not unique to Muslims.[3] Apart from raising questions about the relationship between formal law and theology on the one hand and the lived realities of Muslim and Hindu women on the other, Jeffery questioned the efficacy of the law in protecting women's rights and its strategic priorities in the struggle for gender equity – issues that remain central to the quest for gender justice in India. She noted the crucial parallels in the everyday domestic lives of Hindu and Muslim women, which challenged the Hindu right's assertions that Muslim women are uniquely oppressed by their men and victimised by Islam.[4] Despite a commonality of experience, a central element of the Hindu right's anti-Muslim rhetoric is that Muslim wives are routinely being repudiated in contrast to Hindu women, which is not borne out by empirical data. 'The triple talaq is simply not part of Muslim men's everyday repertoire, any more than secular law courts are a part of Hindu men's,' she remarked.

Nonetheless, these 'communal contrasts' form the basis of the BJP's campaign for a UCC, which is the focus of this chapter.

The UCC was mentioned in the BJP's election manifestoes in 2014 and 2019.[5] This issue is not new for the BJP or for Indian politics. For the BJP, after the abrogation of Article 370 revoking the special status of Jammu and Kashmir, the passing of the Citizenship Amendment Act, criminalisation of 'triple talaq' among Muslims and the construction of a Ram Temple at Ayodhya, the UCC has been on their agenda for a long time but remains unaddressed. The BJP was the first party to promise the implementation of the UCC if it were elected, whereas most other political parties are either opposed to or ambivalent about it.[6]

Equality Before Law

Equality before the law is a principle that seeks to promote gender inclusiveness and Articles 14 and 15 of the Indian Constitution explicitly state this. However, one of the greatest challenges relating to gender equality pertained to the domain of personal laws.[7] After Independence, reform of personal laws became necessary to meet the needs of secularism and modernisation, and to render personal laws fair, just, and non-discriminatory. India's post-colonial modernist leadership demonstrated a willingness to intervene in matters of personal law which are widely seen as the domain of religious and traditional authorities, and where religious and customary precepts (the latter often giving women even fewer rights than the former) continue to hold sway. However, only Hindu laws were singled out for reform which gave more rights to women in marriage and divorce, whereas Muslim women are still governed by the Muslim Personal Law (Shariat) Application Act, which the British government enacted in 1937.

Article 44 of the Directive Principles in the Constitution says the 'State shall endeavour to provide for its citizens a UCC throughout the territory of India.' The objective of this endeavour should be to address the discrimination against vulnerable groups and harmonise diverse cultural practices. The Constituent Assembly debates reveal a lack of consensus on what a potential UCC would entail. While many thought the UCC would coexist alongside the personal law systems, others thought that it was to replace personal laws.

The codification of personal laws has historically generated protests. The Hindu Code Bill, one of the foremost pieces of social legislation, had triggered enormous opposition. But the Congress government under the leadership of Prime Minister Jawaharlal Nehru went ahead within a few years of independence to enact a number of progressive laws in relation to marriage and divorce (1955), adoption and maintenance (1956), minority and guardianship (1956), and succession and inheritance (1956) among others. These broke away from the scriptural tradition and represented important steps in the direction of, first, the liberalisation and secularisation of Hindu personal law and, second, the eventual formulation of a UCC.[8] Nehru hailed this reform as revolutionary and 'the most outstanding achievement of his time'.[9] These changes went quite far in the direction of gender equity but not complete equality. In later years, women's organisations were to argue that they did not go far enough, not in practice giving equal rights to women, and most of these laws are flouted with impunity. For example, the Hindu Marriage Act 1955 permits the marriage of a girl at 18, but not of a boy until the age of 21. Similarly, the Hindu Succession Act provides for different schemes of succession for male and female intestates.

More contentious than the shortfalls of Hindu law reform was the state's reluctance to adopt a similar approach toward reform of the religious personal laws of minority communities (i.e. Muslims, Christians, Sikhs, and Parsis) to bring them in line with modern notions of gender justice. Muslim personal law relegates Muslim women to the private sphere and increases their financial dependence on their families and communities. This asymmetric treatment created an aberration in the very notion of equal citizenship: if it was accepted that the state could intervene to provide equal rights to members of one community, then what ground was there for not doing the same for others?

Although Nehru considered legal reform of all personal laws necessary and a UCC (codification and the legal unification of the civil codes of different religious communities in India) for the country as a whole essential and a vital element for national development, he was apprehensive that any imposition on minorities, without their consent, would be imprudent. Hence, the policy of merging personal laws of different religious communities into a set of uniform and equal laws was indefinitely postponed until such time as the minority communities were ready for it and/or willing to initiate it. The aspiration for a UCC was placed in the non-justiciable Directive Principles of State Policy (Article 35 in the draft Constitution and Article 44 in the present Constitution), leaving personal codes in place.

Narendra Subramanian points out that some prominent Muslim public figures and community leaders did support a full or partial codification of personal laws in the decades following Indian independence. These included Abul Kalam Azad, Naziruddin Ahmad and Hussain Imam who argued for constructive amendments or the full or partial codification of Muslim personal laws according to constitutional values.[10] In the early 1970s, jurist Tahir Mahmood compiled two companion volumes advocating the codification of Muslim personal laws, to bring them into line with common civil laws and abolish some of its practices.[11]

However, Muslim personal laws have remained uncodified and unchanged. There was reluctance to impose the will of the majority on a minority that was disadvantaged and under-represented in legislatures and government. Muslim opposition to government interference, a lack of political will, and the conflation of the principle of personal law reform with a UCC deterred governments from any serious legislative moves toward the codification of Muslim personal laws.[12] Even women's rights activists, who had in earlier decades pushed for legislative reform of Muslim personal laws or moves toward a common civil code, have favoured internal reform as a mechanism to improve women's rights rather than the necessity of extensive legislative involvement. The internal reform of personal laws to bring them within the ambit of equal protection and other fundamental rights has proved to be just as complicated. It is difficult to accomplish this goal even with the best intentions and will, and even with the considerable involvement of Muslim women. [13]

The Long Fight

It all started in April 1978 when a 62-year-old woman, Shah Bano a Muslim divorcee, filed a petition demanding maintenance of her marriage after her husband divorced her by using triple talaq. In a defining verdict delivered in 1985, the Supreme Court called for the enactment of a UCC which would give all women, regardless of faith, equal rights – for example the right to alimony or maintenance once divorced. This landmark judgement granted a maintenance allowance to Shah Bano, a 73-year-old Muslim divorcee, to be paid by her husband under the Criminal Procedure Code (CrPc). The court ruled that Section 125, as part of the criminal rather than civil law, overrides all personal law and is uniformly applicable to all women, including Muslim women.

At stake in this case was the right of a divorced Muslim woman to claim maintenance from her former husband under the CrPc. Avoiding the constitutional question of equality, the court dilated at length on the compatibility of the CrPc and the *Quran*. Although she won her case, the Rajiv Gandhi government panicked and overturned the judgement in 1985 to avoid alienation from Muslim orthodox elements.

This sparked off a major political uproar which the Rajiv Gandhi government pacified by means of the Muslim Women's (Protection of Rights on Divorce) Act (MWA), to override the judgement and thus exclude Muslim women from the purview of the CrPc, to which otherwise all citizens have recourse. Acting on the advice of the clergy, the government took the decision to nullify the court's verdict and enact the MWA in 1986, declaring that Muslim women would not have access to civil law in matters of marriage and divorce.

The new law created problems not only for sex equality but also for non-discrimination on grounds of religion: Muslim women were the only ones denied this remedy under the criminal code.[14]

The events soon became national news, and were followed by a campaign against this reversal. In 1986, the government implemented the Muslim Women's (Protection of Rights on Divorce) Act to nullify the Shah Bano judgement, granting paltry alimony to Muslim women.[15] But it was strongly opposed by progressive women's groups and by many Muslim men too. They rejected the priority accorded to the interests of a religious community over gender and the construction of identity predicated on narrow doctrinal principles that distinguished Muslims from others. The Muslim Women's Act, stipulates that divorced Muslim women must be supported by relatives or *waqf* (charity) boards which reinforced the dependence of women on male relatives of the the natal family or the Waqf Board.

The reversal of the Shah Bano verdict breathed life into the ideology of the Hindu nationalists who condemned the Congress party and its governments for its appeasement of Muslims through this legislation. While it is doubtful how much Muslim support Rajiv Gandhi garnered in terms of Muslim votes in the 1989 parliamentary election, his move certainly alienated a large section of the Hindu community, especially the middle classes which saw him as 'appeasing' Muslims. This decision was cited again and again by Hindu political activists to claim that Hindus as a majority community are discriminated against. This is an absurd charge, since the discrimination is against Muslim women, rather than Hindu men.

The Congress abdication in the Shah Bano case gave the BJP the political opening. After the Shah Bano controversy resulted in the Muslim Women's (Protection of Rights on Divorce) Act, 1986, which denied divorced Muslim women the same rights to maintenance as other Indian women under the Criminal Procedure Code, Hindu organisations stepped up their advocacy of uniform laws, primarily as a means of eradicating the 'privileges' of minority men.

BJP's Advocacy of UCC

The BJP is the biggest advocate of a UCC while Muslim conservatives are among its strongest opponents. The Muslim leadership fears that such laws would inevitably lead to uniform cultural practices and alien customs being foisted upon them. They claim protection of their personal laws under Articles 25 and 26 of the Constitution which guarantees the right to religious freedom. Many Hindu leaders had taken the same oppositional position against reform of Hindu personal laws during the parliamentary debates in 1955–56 but were overruled;[16] this was possible because the majority in parliament comprised Hindus who were agreeable to changing these laws.[17]

Muslim leaders have vocally opposed a UCC, insisting that personal laws are an intrinsic part of their religion, and therefore, the state should not legislate on it. The All India Muslim Personal Law Board (AIMPLB) has opposed any attempts to adopt a UCC. It is the AIMPLB that had organised pressure on the Rajiv Gandhi government in 1986, in the aftermath of the favourable decision in Shah Bano, to adopt the Muslim Women's (Protection of Rights on Divorce) Act. It was a major step backward for the country, though an activist judiciary had upheld significant principles of law that should have been accepted. Clarifying its stand on the issue of the UCC, the board said India is inhabited by multicultural and multireligious people and each group has the constitutional rights to maintain its identity. It further said that the very concept of UCC is a threat to the diversity of India and it is the duty of the board to oppose it by democratic and peaceful means. The AIMPLB has been dragging its feet on even drafting a model nikah namah or written marriage contract which would clearly specify the rights of both spouses.

In between are many who believe uniform laws are desirable but that as a country we are not quite ready for it and, therefore, it is best not to raise the issue especially at this juncture when a majoritarian government is in power. The overlaps between the conservative Hindu and Muslim positions are striking; both are overtly communitarian and covertly patriarchal, impelled by the need to preserve gender hierarchies as well as retain their own religious authority and autonomy.

Typically, politicians associated with the BJP who have been the most vocal in expressing sympathy for the plight of the Muslim woman in their battle against the Muslim clergy are the ones who 60 years ago were at the forefront of opposing reform of Hindu marriage and inheritance practices that deprived Hindu women from equal rights with men. Nonetheless, the BJP was the first party in the country to promise the implementation of UCC. In 1998, the party promised to institute a UCC if it came to power. Until then, it had raised the UCC issue principally to embarrass the Congress party which was reluctant to change the status quo in the face of Muslim opposition to it. It was keen to draw a parallel between the Congress's capitulation to Muslim conservatives in the 1950s and again in the 1980s in the Shah Bano case to underscore this tendency. To its way of thinking, leaving Muslim law untouched implies unequal and asymmetrical treatment. This asymmetry has formed the basis for the charge that secularism, especially secular practice, implies pandering to Muslims for electoral gains. BJP criticised the unequal exercise of state power which intervened to reform the Hindu personal laws whereas the same was not done in relation to Muslim personal law. Hindu nationalists underpinned their calls for a UCC with criticisms of gender-unequal features of Muslim personal law, but not similar infirmities in Hindu law. This has given the dominant Hindu community a sense of 'liberal superiority' over other 'unreformed' communities, in particular Muslims.

The call for a UCC found mention in the party's 2019 manifesto. Rashtriya Swayamsevak Sangh (RSS), ideologue Seshadri Chari asked the BJP government to bring in a UCC on the heels of the revocation of Article 370 in Jammu and Kashmir which also reduced the state to a Union Territory in August 2019.[18] Speaking to the media in Dehradun, the Union Defence Minister suggested that following the Supreme Court's landmark verdict on the Ayodhya case (9 November 2019) this is the time to implement a UCC. The BJP derides and decries minority rights as an unwarranted privilege, but it supports Muslim women's rights to expose the unreformed character of Muslim personal law and therefore seek its abolition.

Strategic Shift

The problem with the UCC debate has been its gratuitous emphasis on uniformity which found its reflection in terming it a uniform civil code. Both in judicial pronouncements and public debate, the need for a UCC was justified as essential for national integrity, and plural systems of law undermine it. For a long time it was rarely articulated in the public consciousness as a feminist issue.[19] It became a debate about uniformity versus minority rights, secularism versus religious laws, and modernisation versus tradition.[20] The critique of the state in this context is either that it intervenes too much, as when the government passed the Muslim Women's Bill, or too little, as in its reluctance to enact a UCC. As for feminists, Patricia Jeffery had summed up the problem in the earlier mentioned article thus: If feminists supported the UCC and opposed the Muslim Women Bill, they would risk being co-opted to the agendas of the Hindu right and antagonising many Muslims by intervening in community affairs. Not to press for gender-equitable legislation pertaining to family matters, however, could leave unchallenged personal laws that are all premised on gender inequity. Not surprisingly, feminist activists in India remain divided over how to define the key issues and how to campaign for gender equity.[21]

Over the years the debate on legal reform in the women's movement has shifted from a position that virtually ignored religion to an attempt to work for reform from within. This shift occurred at a time when the communalisation and politicisation of religion was apparent in the series of events discussed in the preceding section that led to the waning of secularism and attacks on minority rights. As the issue of minorities catapulted to centre stage, Muslim women's rights became a subject of considerable debate, typically with reference to the status of Muslim personal law and the conflicting claims of personal law, identity, and gender. This was most clearly underlined during the Shah Bano controversy already alluded to.

The decisive shift occurred after the dramatic growth of Hindu nationalism which increased apprehensions of the imposition of a 'Hindu' code. This led to the move away from the long term goal of homogenisation of family law to the reform of group specific personal laws. It signalled an acknowledgement that gender equality needs to be delinked from uniform laws. Earlier it was believed that UCC was the optimal path to women's empowerment in family law, from the 1990s a more nuanced position emerged, which combined the options of reform from within personal laws with the formulation of gender-just laws deriving from the concept of a common civil code. The term uniform was practically dropped within the women's movement, even by those groups who endorsed state legislation.[22] The women's movement remained committed to equality, but it had to reckon with a political climate vitiated by communal politics and religious identities. Aware that legal change cannot be isolated from the wider political contradictions in the context of communal politics, women's groups began to seriously rethink the demand for a UCC.

Muslim Women's Activism and Gender Justice

The most important development over the past few years has been the wider growth of women's rights activism in India and the emergence of Muslim women's activism seeking to promote women's rights rather than focusing all energies on changing personal laws.[23] This has added a new dimension to the public debate on this issue. Muslim women's activism was propelled by the growth of non-party, autonomous women's groups. The most significant factor, though, is the wider growth of women's rights activism in India. Non-party, autonomous women's groups have taken the lead in pushing for change.[24] The alliance of Muslim women's groups with the women's movement, together with movements for secularism, democracy, and human rights, has also been crucial in broad-basing the struggle for women's rights. Consequently, Muslim women are willing to speak out against gender injustice, and find ways to challenge structures of power and authority within the community and the state at multiple levels. These groups seek to promote equal citizenship rights pertaining to all fundamental rights mandated by the Constitution rather than focusing on changing personal laws to enhance their rights; this partly accounts for their success in mobilising women from all religious background to fight for gender equality.

Two networks are at the forefront of this process: the Bharatiya Muslim Mahila Andolan (BMMA) and the Bebaak Collective. Both have questioned the authority of the Muslim Personal Law Board to speak for the Muslim community and women in particular. Both these networks, in different ways, place the exclusion of Muslim women in the wider context of the discrimination faced by Muslims in India in general, such as the recent issues regarding beef bans for example. These multifaceted efforts have seen the beginnings of serious debate on social reform and gender justice within the community.

BMMA has taken the lead with regard to the campaign for the reform of Muslim personal laws, particularly triple talaq. Muslim women's activists have been emboldened by the support of BJP which has used them to push for triple talaq abolition. For the same reasons the political influence of Muslim clerics and religious organisations, who have acted in the past as a force blocking state intervention in Muslim personal laws, has been eroded. Compared to other Muslim women's organisations, the BMMA has shown willingness to formulate its own conception of laws and more willing to engage with the BJP government which was the prime mover behind triple talaq abolition. It prepared the blueprint for a progressive Muslim family law as a public need. This draft Act was the result of some six years of consultations among Muslim community leaders and women's organisations and was intended to prompt community and political debate about the codification of Muslim family laws in India.[25]

The abolition of triple talaq is a case in point. The practice of triple talaq had been under the judicial scanner for quite some time. This practice that many Muslim men employ to divorce their wives instantaneously and without their consent, merely by uttering the word talaq (divorce) thrice is oppressive and anti-women by any standards and is considered unacceptable not only by people belonging to other religions but also by Muslims. Most Muslim countries do not have this practice. Pakistan, Morocco, Algeria, Indonesia, Iran and Tunisia are some other countries which had de-recognised instant triple talaq. Triple talaq gives a Muslim man the right to divorce his wife unilaterally, with the wife not having any say in the matter. Women's vulnerability to arbitrary, unilateral divorce underlines the main problem of triple talaq.[26]

Women can obtain divorce only by approaching the court on the specific grounds provided under the Dissolution of Muslim Marriage Act, 1939. It discriminates between Muslim men and women and it discriminates between Muslim women and women of other religions who possess more legal rights.[27] This egregious practice was declared unconstitutional and illegal by the Supreme Court in 2017.[28] The operative part of the split judgement had declared that, 'In view of the different opinions recorded, by a majority of 3:2 the practice of *talaq-e-bidat*, triple talaq, is set aside.' Public opinion against this practice gathered momentum when Muslim women's organisations stood up to the community's conservative elements and challenged their patriarchal mindsets.

The New Law

The Muslim Women (Protection of Rights on Marriage) Bill was passed by parliament on July 30, 2019. The new law was the outcome of a court case filed in 2016 by Shayara Bano, a Muslim woman who had fallen victim to triple talaq.[29] She challenged the constitutionality of the practice of triple talaq along with other practices like nikah-halala and polygamy. BMMA conveners co-filed a PIL (Public Interest Litigation) application to the Supreme Court, seeking the abolition of *talaq-i-bid`ah*, a form of instant Islamic divorce by which a husband can unilaterally repudiate a wife. The petitioner contended that triple talaq is invalid as it is fundamentally un-Islamic and hence should not be part of Muslim personal law.[30] Five women – Shayara Bano, Gulshan Parveen, Afreen Rehman, Atiya Sabri and Ishrat Jahan – who spearheaded the fight refused to heed requests from the conservative clerics of the AIMPLB to withdraw their petitions.[31] While the AIMPLB has argued that triple talaq is an essential practice within Islam, the petitioners, the central government and organisations like BMMA and Bebaak Collective had all argued that it is not.[32] A five-judge constitutional bench headed by Chief Justice J.S. Khehar in Shayara Bano vs Union of India declared the practice to be unsupported by the sources of Muslim personal law and therefore, illegal in the eyes of the secular state.

The Muslim Women Act, 2019 made the practice of instant divorce through triple talaq a punishable offence.[33] Ending the discriminatory practice of triple talaq was a much needed reform. The prime minister's celebratory tweet claimed that: 'An archaic and medieval practice has finally been confined to the dustbin of history! Parliament abolishes Triple Talaq and corrects a historical wrong done to Muslim women. This is a victory of gender justice and will further equality in society. India rejoices today!'[34] But beyond this political claim, the verdict highlights the changing social and political landscape in India, which enabled a group of Muslim women to successfully take on orthodox elements in their community.

However, the law is controversial because it criminalises the practice of *talaq-i-biddat*, rather than simply confirming that a divorce pronounced in this way is invalid. Supporters say the new measure protects Muslim women. Opponents say the punishment is harsh and open to misuse. Many activists condemned the criminalisation of triple talaq as it would make it easier to incriminate Muslim men. Rather than protecting women, the government's main intention has been to make Muslim men vulnerable to arrest. The law criminalises the pronouncement of talaq itself, irrespective of whether it is accompanied by violence or any form of abuse.[35]

The new law decrees that any husband pronouncing triple talaq, whether spoken, written or electronic, can be punished with a fine and three-year jail term. Arrests can be made without a warrant, and bail is given only at the discretion of a magistrate. And the law applies retrospectively meaning that earlier transgressions can now be filed with the police. The new law conflates civil law and criminal law. The Act has introduced penal legislation, specific to a class of persons based on religious identity. It does not have any procedural safeguards and can be easily misused.[36] The new law has consciously set punishments for merely uttering words that, ever since the Supreme Court's judgement, have no legal meaning. Rather than protecting women, they argue, the government's main intention has been to make Muslim men vulnerable to arrest. Criminalising triple talaq in the name of deterrence is excessive and more so given the anti-Muslim bias afflicting the Indian criminal legal system.[37]

The 2019 Act has already been the subject of several legal challenges from Muslim religious organisations, which see the law as disproportionate and a political move against minorities.[38] However, the significance of the abolition of triple talaq shouldn't be underestimated. At the same time, it is clear that its abolition is not a panacea for the deep and serious problems these women face. It does nothing to improve the status of Muslim women who suffer from numerous other difficulties. There's abundant evidence that Muslim women rank below the national average when it comes to literacy, schooling and workforce participation.

This marginalisation is compounded by the fact that Muslim women's issues are often only discussed as religious ones. This doesn't just reinforce the centrality of personal laws, but glosses over the economic, political, and social problems that define the everyday experiences of Muslim women. It is clear that their deprivation stems from a shortage of three essentials: knowledge (measured by literacy and average years of schooling), economic power (work and income), and autonomy (measured by decision making and physical mobility). Gender discrimination coalesces with class inequalities and pervasive social hierarchies to compound the marginalisation of Muslim women. These issues are conspicuous by their absence from the world of politics, bureaucracy, universities, and the public and private sectors.

A Way Forward?

Despite considerable disparagement of secular parties and reviling Muslims for their refusal to embrace a UCC, the BJP did not devise proposals to advance this project when it was in power in a coalition from 1998 to 2004 and from 2014 to 2019. The Law Commission was mandated to deliberate on this issue in 2018.[39] The Law Commission's public consultation on the feasibility and potential content of a UCC was a welcome step. The Commission issued a 'questionnaire' to test the waters on the UCC. The questions included 'what measures should be taken to sensitise society to a common code or codification of personal law,' and would the UCC ensure 'gender equality'.

The Law Commission has recommended codification of personal laws over the UCC as a way to end discrimination within religions. In its 2018 report, it said:

> While diversity of Indian culture can and should be celebrated, specific groups or weaker sections of the society must not be dis-privileged in the process. Resolution of this conflict does not mean abolition of difference. This Commission has, therefore, dealt with laws that are discriminatory rather than providing a UCC which is neither necessary nor desirable at this stage. Most countries are now moving towards recognition of difference, and the mere existence of difference does not imply discrimination, but is indicative of a robust democracy.[38]

Codification of various practices and customs would make them 'law' under Article 13 of the Constitution. Any 'law' that comes under Article 13 should be consistent with the fundamental rights, the Law Commission reasoned. This would protect the plurality of religions, too, and may be the way forward for the near future. In fact, the Law Commission stated that the UCC is 'neither necessary nor desirable at this stage in the country.'[40] It said a unified nation does not necessarily need to have 'uniformity'.[41] The former Chairman of the Law Commission suggested that the government should start working on reforms of family laws across communities. Whatever best practices are available should be extended to other communities.

The current debate over the UCC is marked by uncertainty and division about whether a UCC will enhance gender justice or will it simply enhance the Hindu right's agenda of uniformity. A gender-equitable UCC was a central demand of feminists in India, however, once the Hindu right appropriated the idea of the UCC during the Shah Bano and triple talaq controversies, feminists found themselves on the horns of a dilemma with regard to legal reform, especially the question of the UCC. Women's groups have drawn back from supporting a UCC after the communalisation of the issue and favour an intermediate approach instead. The way forward, as argued in this article, is the middle path of combining reform of family laws of all communities and voluntary adoption of a progressive UCC. This is the position generally favoured by feminists and is in line with Dr B.R. Ambedkar's (Chairman of the Drafting Committee of the Constitution of India and the country's first Law Minister), initial vision:

> It is perfectly possible that the future parliament may make a provision by way of making a beginning that the Code shall apply only to those who make a declaration that they are prepared to be bound by it, so that in the initial stage the application of the Code may be purely voluntary.[42]

NOTES

1. Subramanian, N. 2014. *Nation and Family: Personal Law, Cultural Pluralism and Gendered Citizenship in India*. Stanford: Stanford University Press.
2. For a review on the subject see Herkolotz, T. 2017. 'Law, religion and gender equality: literature on the Indian personal law system from a women's rights perspective', *Indian Law Review* 1(3).
3. Jeffery, P. 2001. 'A Uniform Customary Code? Marital breakdown and women's economic entitlements in rural Bijnor', *Contributions to Indian Sociology*, 35(1): 1–32.
4. Ibid.
5. Bharatiya Janata Party. 2019. *Sankalp Patra Lok Sabha*, Manifesto of the Bharatiya Janata Party. https://www.thehinducentre.com/resources/article26769375.ece/binary/BJP-Election-2019-english.pdf.
6. Mathew, C.K. 2019. 'Uniform Civil Code: The Importance of an Inclusive and Voluntary Approach', *Issue Brief No. 10*, https://www.thehinducentre.

com/publications/issue-brief/article29784007.ece (accessed 19 October 2020).

7. The term Muslim personal law refers to family law that governs the domestic relations of Muslims in India. It operates in matters relating to inheritance, marriage, divorce, maintenance and adoption, which are regarded as personal issues because they relate to the family or personal sphere.
8. Parasher, A. 1992. Women and Family Law Reform in India: Uniform Civil Code and Gender Equality. Delhi: Sage Publications.
9. Som, R. 1994. 'Jawaharlal Nehru and the Hindu Code: A Victory of Symbol over Substance', *Modern Asian Studies*, 28(61).
10. Subramanian, N. 2014. Nation and Family: Personal Law, Cultural Pluralism and Gendered Citizenship in India. Redwood City, CA: Stanford University Press.
11. Mahmood, T. 1972. 'Progressive Codification of Muslim Personal Law', in T. Mahmood (ed.) *Islamic Law in Modern India*, pp. 80–98. Bombay: N.M. Tripathi Ltd.
12. Jones, J. 2020. 'Towards a Muslim Family Law Act? Debating Muslim women's rights and the codification of personal laws in India', *Contemporary South Asia*, 28(1): 1–14 https://www.tandfonline.com/doi/abs/10.1080/09584935.2019.1684444. (accessed 19 October 2020).
13. Nussbaum, M.C. 2008. *The Clash Within: Democracy, Religious Violence and India's Future*. Cambridge, MA: Harvard University Press. p. 175.
14. Hasan, Z. 1998. 'Minority Identity, State Policy and the Political Process', in Z. Hasan (ed.), *Forging Identities: Gender, Communities and the State in India.* New Delhi: Kali for Women.
15. The Muslim Women (Protection of Rights on Divorce) Act, 1986, May 19. http://legislative.gov.in/sites/default/files/A1986-25_1.pdf
16. The government succeeded in passing four Hindu Code Bills, including the Hindu Marriage Act (1955), the Hindu Succession Act (1956), the Hindu Minority and Guardianship Act (1956) and the Hindu Adoption and Maintenance Act (1956).
17. Mehta, P.B. 2008. 'Reason, Tradition and Authority: Religion and the Indian State', in I. Creppel, R. Hardin and S. Macedo (eds) *Toleration on Trial.* Lanham, MD: Lexington Books.
18. Nair, P. 2019. 'It's Time For Uniform Civil Code. This Will Help Muslims Break Taboos: Seshadri Chari', *Outlook*, 29 August. https://www.outlookindia.com/magazine/story/india-news-its-time-for-uniform-civil-code-this-will-help-muslims-break-taboos-seshadri-chari/302081 (accessed 11 January 2022).
19. Menon, N. 2001. 'Introduction', in N. Menon (ed.), *Gender and Politics in India*. New Delhi: Oxford University Press.
20. Rajan, R.S. 2003. *The Scandal of the State: Women, Law, and Citizenship in Post-colonial India*, New Delhi: Permanent Black.
21. Jeffery, P. 'A Uniform Customary Code?'.

22. Ibid. 1997: 253–63
23. See Tschalaer, M.H. 2018. *Muslim Women's Quest for Justice: Gender, Law and Activism in India*, Cambridge: Cambridge University Press.
24. This interpretation was also common to much newspaper coverage, e.g. *Hindustan Times*, 23 August 2017; *The Indian Express*, 23 August 2017.
25. 'Triple talaq debate: Islam gives equal rights to women, says Muslim personal law board', Scroll 28 March 2017. https://scroll.in/latest/833014/triple-talaq-debate-islam-gives-equal-rights-to-women-says-muslim-personal-law-board (accessed 12 October 2020).
26. Hasan, Z. 2017. '"Triple talaq" abolition is only the start of a larger campaign for gender justice in India', *Conversations*, September 7. https://theconversation.com/triple-talaq-abolition-is-only-the-start-of-a-larger-campaign-for-gender-justice-in-india-83089 (accessed 12 January 2022).
27. Idiculla. M. and S. Prasoon. 2010. 'Untangling the Debate on Triple Talaq', *The Wire*, 16 June. https://thewire.in/law/untangling-debate-triple-talaq (accessed 12 October 2010).
28. Mandal, S. 2018. 'Out of Shah Bano's shadow: Muslim women's rights and the Supreme Court's triple talaq verdict', *Indian Law Review*, 2(1): 89–107. https://doi.org/10.1080/24730580.2018.1510162 (accessed 19 October 2020).
29. Das, K. 2020. 'Triple Talaq crusader Shayara Bano joins BJP in Dehradun', *Hindustan Times*, 11 October.
30. Shayara Bano v Union of India and Others AIR 2017 SC 4609.
31. Shayara Bano joined BJP in 2020 stating, 'Not only was I highly influenced with BJP's principles, I also looked upon PM Modi as my ideal. These are the reasons that I decided to join BJP.' Das, 'Triple Talaq crusader'.
32. Jones, J. 2020. 'Towards a Muslim Family Law Act? Debating Muslim women's rights and the codification of personal laws in India', *Contemporary South Asia*, 28(1): 1–14. https://doi.org/10.1080/09584935.2019.1684444 (accessed 10 October 2020).
33. PRS Legislative Research. 2019. The Muslim Women (Protection of Rights in Marriage) Bill, 2019. Ministry of Law and Justice. https://www.prsindia.org/billtrack/muslim-women-protection-rights-marriage-bill-2019 (accessed 11 January 2022).
34. India Today Web Desk. 2019. 'Archaic practice confined to dustbin of history: PM Modi after triple talaq bill passed by Parliament', *India Today,* 30 July.
35. Ibid.
36. Since the 1960s, Indian courts have restricted freedom of religion further through a unique doctrine known as the 'essential religious practices' test. As per this doctrine, Article 25 protects only those practices that are essential and integral to the religion, as determined by the courts. Courts examine the validity of a specific religious practice by testing it against religious canons instead of constitutional norms.
37. Mandal, 'Out of Shah Bano's shadow', p. 18.

38. Agnes, F. 2018. 'The Politics behind Criminalising Triple Talaq', *Economic and Political Weekly*, 53(1). Also see Punwani, J. 2018. 'Triple Talaq Judgment and After', *Economic and Political Weekly*, 53(17).
39. Law Commission of India. 2018. *Consultation Paper on Reform of Family Law*, Government of India, 31 August. https://www.lawcommissionofindia.nic.in/reports/CPonReformFamilyLaw.pdf (accessed 11 January 2022).
40. Ibid.
41. Rajagopal, K. 2018. 'What is the debate on uniform civil code all about?', *The Hindu*, 8 September. https://www.thehindu.com/news/national/what-is-debate-on-uniform-civil-code-all-about/article24903560.ece (accessed 11 January 2022).
42. B.R. Ambedkar quoted in Mathew, 'Uniform Civil Code'.

3

Reaching for the Mango Tree?

Pastoralism, Education and Dignity Among Dhebar Rabaris in Gujarat

Caroline Dyer and Archana Choksi

Introduction

> Now imagine it is very hot and they know there is a mango tree ahead but there is an acacia tree here so they will sit under acacia because for now it gives that security. Otherwise we would try and find mango tree and not sit under an acacia tree.

We begin with Hasuben's evocative words to Archana while discussing dignity, education and change in her life as a mobile pastoralist woman. Hasuben invokes a sense of movement, in moving from one tree to another, that reflects the macro and micro contexts of both geo-spatial and social mobility in pastoralists' lives. Her words articulate, too, the act of balancing what you have in hand at present – the slightly inadequate but secure shade of an acacia tree – against risking its loss in the search for something better – the larger, leafier space under a mango tree and its promise of delicious fruit. This metaphorical journey, from one tree to another that is presumed to be better, is shaped by pastoralists' individual and collective experiences of the absence, promise, and contact with formal education. It is on this journey, on how education is situated in pastoralists' lives and on how it shapes their notions of dignity ... that we focus in this chapter.

In the opening chapter of her co-edited collection of papers on educational regimes in contemporary India, Jeffery (2008, 13) pointed out that: 'education and schooling are not necessarily or unambiguously life enhancing or passports to success. Education *as it is practiced* is profoundly ambiguous in its effects, and a focus on values in isolation would be insufficient'. Her observation prompts us to ask how Hasuben, and other women and leaders in their community, value and use formal education as they navigate changes to their livelihoods as pastoralists; and what now prompts, for some of them, a re-evaluation of pastoralism as a dignified occupation for 'educated' young people?

Mobile pastoralism is the practice of moving domesticated animals to pasture in response to seasonal resource variation in the highly uncertain environments that characterise global drylands (Krätli 2015). It has been practised in the semi-arid zone of what is now western India and south Pakistan for about 6,000 years (Choksi 1995). Kachchh, a region in these once contiguous grasslands and now a District of Gujarat, is home to 13 sub-groups of pastoralists, who are known locally as *maldhāri* (keeper – *dhāri* – of animal stock – *māl*). The Rabaris of Kachchh are one of these 13 groups. Dhebars are a major Rabari sub-grouping (along with Katchis and Vagads) and traditionally have had some of the largest animal holdings among all Rabaris in the region. From the vantage point of the state, Rabaris in Gujarat are almost all categorised as Other Backward Classes (OBC), and as a Socially and Educationally Backward Caste (SEBC).

Our first encounters with Rabaris were in the early 1990s, when we spent three years working ethnographically on adult literacy and contributing to conceptualisations of socially situated literacies within the, then emerging, New Literacy Studies (Street 1984; Dyer and Choksi 2001). This research also identified multiple structural and other barriers to creating any kind of fit between a mobile pastoralist livelihood and the formal schooling system (Dyer and Choksi 2001; Dyer 2014). Following brief visits to Kachchh in the aftermath of the 2001 earthquake, and an in-depth study of the Rabari residential school in 2008, we began another study in 2018 that included Rabaris: a qualitative investigation of dignity and heritage among mobile pastoralist women in Gujarat, Maharashtra and Himachal Pradesh. This chapter is informed by all three research episodes, but draws primarily on the 2018 study, which revealed significant intergenerational, and gendered, tensions around changing values of dignity.[1] These are captured here mostly through the eyes of Rabari women who have grown up, or are still actively involved, in mobile pastoralism and are now themselves mothers (some are grandmothers), supplemented by insights from casual encounters with unmarried adolescent Rabari girls and interviews with male community leaders. All participant names are pseudonyms.

The chapter looks first at education and dignity in pastoralism in the late 1990s; then at the effects of the 2001 earthquake in Kachchh on regional development and pastoralist futures; then at the diversification, schooling and employment that Rabaris now associate with respectable identities. The conclusion reflects on another turn in the contested dignity of pastoralism: a re-evaluation by some, in the light of failings of schooling, of its potential as a viable livelihood for 'educated' young people.

Education(s) and dignity in pastoralism

Rabaris are traditionally camel breeders. According to their myth of origin they were fashioned by Lord Shiva, at the behest of his consort Parvati, to look after the camels that Parvati had fashioned from dust and into which Lord Shiva had breathed life (Dyer 2014). Few Rabaris now keep camels, owing to a decline in demand, and have diversified into keeping cattle, sheep and goats. Spirituality, reflecting its divine origin, and the moral stewardship of animals, are fundamental tenets of pastoralism in the Rabari tradition. This places keeping animals 'happy' (*sukhi*) at the heart of human wellbeing, and is a lens through which Rabari views on education(s) are always filtered:

> If they [animals] are happy that will make us happy too (Women's focus group, December 2018).

PASTORALISM AND EDUCATION WITHIN IT: A VIEW IN THE 1990S

Mobile pastoralism carefully balances animal holdings with labour requirements, and mobility is used to access resources in the 'uncertain' environments of drylands. The annual cycle of transhumance is a negotiated, highly planned and managed process of securing water and fodder, during which pastoralists encounter an array of land regimes (Bhardwaj and Mahajan 2006; Sud 2012). In Gujarat, this array includes various categories of: state-owned land, such as forestry, wasteland and road margins; village lands (notably *gauchars*, designated fodder areas); and privately owned agricultural land, where farmers rent space to pastoralists so that migrating animals consume crop residues and deposit dung and urine as fertiliser in exchange for safe passage. Dhebar Rabaris often keep animals outside Gujarat, where better access to resources enables them to keep very large flocks, returning to Kachchh only for the monsoon and to celebrate the festival and wedding season that falls around Lord Krishna's birthday. Hasuben recalled:

> We used to live with sheep and goat and only come for weddings, when we will stay for 15 days here. We used to come, attend weddings, stay for 15 days, lock the house and go back to the animals. I had lot of animals, around 1,000–1,500. I have roamed everywhere – Nagpur, Chattisgadh. We used to go wherever our animals enjoyed (*māl ne māza*) ... [laughs] wherever our *māl* is happy (Hasuben, January 2019).

In traditional 'extensive' Rabari pastoralism, each family member contributes labour in roles, learnt from childhood, that are clearly gendered and mutually indispensable. Women take care of the hearth, young children, small animals and the purse. Men take care of the flock and daily routines of grazing, watering and moving animals. In the 1990s, several families would come together to form a joint migrating unit (*dang*) for safety and companionship, and to share the work of pastoralism, while each maintaining a family hearth. Women such as Hasuben would load up the pack camel and move to meet the menfolk and animals at the next camp. Rabari women were responsible for shopping and keeping cash, which brought them into contact with other communities in villages. They would move relatively freely in the public domain, their social interactions guided by a strict code of behaviour around men (including maintaining a physical distance, keeping their head covered and covering their face from older men [*lāj*]).

During our first period of fieldwork, women of the *dang* would sit together in the shade of a tree in the early afternoon. With domestic and animal-rearing chores completed until the men and animals returned, they would chat and do embroidery. Daughters would join mothers, stitching in their company, and adding this skill to the many others – how to milk, churn buttermilk, fetch water and wood, manage the camel and run the household – that their mothers passed on. Gradually, each girl expanded the dowry of embroidered items she would take to her marital household: door hangings, camel bags, large sitting mats, bodices, shawls and spice bags – all in the specific repertoire that marked her out not just as a Rabari, but also as a Rabari from a specific sub-group (Frater 2002). Her daily routine of situated learning (Lave and Wenger 1991) endowed her with practical skills as a pastoralist woman in the gendered, yet mutually constitutive and respected, labour roles in the migrating unit; and passed on the values of dressing, manners, dignity, religiosity and propriety of conduct (*mariyāda),* that she would be expected to live by and uphold as a Rabari woman.

Reflecting on lives 'under the acacia tree' in those days, older women talked about migration with animals as a livelihood that, despite its difficulties, has an intrinsic dignity because it enables a form of freedom that, having now settled, they see much reason to value:

> There are problems as there is rain, the land is not good for grazing, people will not let you stay. It is not that a *maldhāri* is happiest, there are many problems also. But it is ***your own business*** (Mighuben, January 2019 – emphasis added).

We did not come across any parents who could read or write, but among migrating families we did find the occasional child who had fleetingly attended school. This brief skirmish with schooling was testament to an educational intent that had been thwarted by schooling's 'terms of inclusion' (Dyer 2013), one of which is that a child is available to attend, daily, in the same place, for the same amount of time. In the 1990s, since children mostly migrated with their parents, actual numbers attending school were very small. Reports of schools' failings, however, circulated widely: of teachers who were often absent and, when present, would indulge in small acts of everyday violence; and of taunts from other children (Dyer 2014). These reports chime with research findings of the poor quality institutional arrangements for formal schooling that continue to leave many children in India in 'learning poverty' (Beteille et al. 2020). Such conditions, coupled with the logistics and emotional distress of having to leave a child with relatives in a village to access school, and a reluctance to mix with children of lower castes who also use village schools, were further 'terms of inclusion' that were implicated in Rabari families not using formal schools.

Yet, at the same time, leading a life with dignity as an 'uneducated' pastoralist was becoming difficult. Adults saw being able to read and write as an advantage that meant not having to ask someone else which is the right bus. For women particularly, having to ask a stranger for help was undignified. They disliked this form of dependence, and their sense of *mariyāda* was reflected in the concern that such a person might not be 'good' and would be rude to them. At the same time, Rabaris were forming a view that 'education in India is the new caste' (Chantia 2006, 267) (which Jeffery [2008] rightly contests). They found that the dignity of their ascribed status as caste Hindus was undermined, for example, when educated but lower-caste officials exerted the authority of their position to bar them from accessing state-owned land, and demonstrated that schooling helps one to acquire the voice of power – or, as Gee (2012) puts it, the 'Discourse' of the educated. Since a livelihood in pastoralism is necessarily lived in what education policy discourses describe as 'remote rural' areas and Rabaris themselves call, without pejorative intent, 'the jungle', from where schooling is inaccessible, transhumant Rabaris we met in the 1990s saw formal education as an idealised good that conferred recognisable positional advantage but was out of reach for them. Thus, they heard from others, and repeated, that the jungle is place of, and for, the uneducated, and applied to themselves the derogatory label of being 'jungli' people. All of this led them to describe themselves as 'left behind' (*ame pāchal rahe gaya*) – long before the international development industry mobilised the very same term.

'PROGRESS' THROUGH EDUCATION AND GETTING OUT OF ANIMALS: LEADERS' ADVOCACY

Among Dhebar Rabaris, the community council (*nāt*), led by male figures of traditional authority, regulates what constitutes a respectable identity. In the 1990s, their authority was effectively brought to bear on customs relating to marriage, conduct of weddings and divorce by invoking peer pressure, fines and the ultimate possibility of outcasting and total social ostracisation – a devastating status in such a tightly knit and co-dependent community. Leaders were advocating vigorously for 'improvement' (*sudhāre*) and 'progress' (*āgal vadhvun*) in response to Rabaris' 'left behind' positioning. In their view, this would be accomplished through schooling and a mass exit from pastoralism, a vision captured in their mantra, 'Get out of sheep and goats, and get into education'. They also established a residential school for Rabari children in Anjar, staffed and governed by community members, hoping to enable a generation of educated children to get into a successful life outside pastoralism (Dyer 2014).

Underpinning leaders' advocacy, however, was a concern with an undignified transition of the moral tradition of Rabari pastoralism into an occupation based on what they called 'blood money'. As pastoralism had become increasingly enmeshed in the market economy, Rabaris had gone from only drinking milk, to selling wool, to selling animals for meat markets to raise cash (Choksi and Dyer 1996). Leaders sought to end this through schooling, which they saw as the means to occupational diversification and a respectability that pastoralism could no longer ensure. In our many conversations with them, they had no clear answers as to how this added up when schools were not accessible to pastoralists; or what people would do instead of pastoralism, if they did leave sheep and goats; or what could be done about the poor environments for learning that local schools offered.

In the larger context of a BJP-governed Gujarat (Simpson 2006; Mehta and Mehta 2010), aspirational positioning for the Rabari community would probably benefit from adherence to the norms of Hindutva (see Chako 2019), but this aspect of 'progress' and problematic 'blood money' was then a distant concern. A more pressing community governance issue was the knotty issue of bride price, which, alongside other expensive social customs around marriages (Dyer 2014), was fuelling the need for 'blood money'. Rabaris marry endogenously; and in the 1990s child engagement was common, sometimes involving intergenerational obligations, and a bride price was usual.[2] Cash constraints and escalating costs were leading to delay in sending the girl to the husband's home, sometimes to such an extent that child-bearing was compromised. In public, parents would give the still unfinished dowry of embroidery as the reason for not sending the girl; in private, the bride price was the main hindrance. Since bride price practices were what much of the 'blood money' was used for, an uncomfortable fact that could not be openly confronted, leaders banned embroidery instead; and they legitimised their action by claiming that this freed a girl to attend school, as she would not have the competing demand on her time of stitching her dowry.

Despite their vigorous advocacy of formal education for both boys and girls, when it came to livelihoods, leaders focused only on diversification for men. There was no acknowledgement of women having important income-generating roles then or in the future. In that respect, their promotion of schooling for girls was not rooted in any notion of gender equality, or a reflection on productive female livelihoods. Rather, it stemmed from a patriarchal insistence that female orthodoxy and adherence to old-fashioned customs – of which embroidery was symbolic – were the barriers to 'improvement' and 'progress' of the whole Rabari community; and schooling was the obvious instrument by which those barriers would be removed.

This – deeply gendered – stance was also embedded in a notion of Rabari social structure as egalitarian in principle. Since the social capital of education was understood to be imbricated in dignity for the Rabari community as a whole, and the meta-narrative of education as 'progress' was situated alongside the principle of egalitarianism (even though practices and principles may diverge), leaders largely just assumed that both boys and girls in their community should acquire that capital, but did not foresee the contradictory and gendered outcomes of schooling that ensued.

The Earthquake and Transformation of Kachchh

The earthquake that shook Kachchh in January 2001 catalysed changes that would have far-reaching effects on pastoralists. During reconstruction, in this localised version of India's ongoing 'great land grab' (Shiva et al. 2011), thousands of hectares of land changed hands, and often went into private ownership. Ramani (2010, 18) comments on the absence of nuance, sensitivity or involvement of the people of Kachchh as stakeholders; and Simpson (2014) reveals the disparate motivations of the reconstruction's architects, and how these shaped its long-term effects. The approach to post-earthquake reconstruction was entirely cast in the neo-liberal industrial model of development on which the government of Gujarat prides itself (Simpson 2006), in a state where, in as much as mobile pastoralism is seen at all, it is seen as antithetic to 'progress' within this model (Dyer 2014).

Although pastoralism was a dominant local livelihood, attention was not paid to its reliance on access to land that provided fodder and water for large numbers of animals. Tracts of state-owned 'waste land', understood by state authorities to be barren and unused (Bharwada and Mahajan 2006), village *gauchars* and unirrigated land owned by agriculturalists but often used by pastoralists, were quickly fenced off. Between 2001 and 2009, according to a list we obtained in 2009 from the District Collector's office, 318 factories were established (Dyer 2014); and by 2011, the reported number had risen to 441 (GSIDS 2016, 131). The region's rich and largely unexploited mineral reserves were a magnet for new industrial development, nearly two-thirds of which comprised oil and refinery, petrochemical and mineral-based industries (GSIDS 2016). Kachchh became what Ramani (2010, 18) describes as an 'industrial mine' for investors and developers. Blind to the presence of pastoralism, the district's 2014 *Human Development Report* stated that, 'Infrastructure, construction material, manufacturing of engineering goods, mineral processing & fabrication are major employment generating segments within the district' (GSIDS 2016, 130). Many wind farms popped up and, in 2018, public interest litigation challenged the allotment of *gauchar* land in the district to private companies for windmills.[3] Roads were widened to enable the transportation of massive turbines, at the cost of the planted margins that provided fodder, shade and safe passage for pastoralists' animals. Stopping encroachment on *gauchar*s, and obtaining recognition and political representation for the rights of pastoralists, are ongoing battles for Kachchh-based civil society organisations in the wider war over the impact of the 'Gujarat model' on fragile natural resources and sensitive ecosystems (Mehta et al. 2019; Shah 2005).

The earthquake and its aftermath brought many – but not all – pastoralists back to Kachchh. While the trend of sedentarisation has intensified since then, this is when it began. Remembering the immediate post-earthquake years, Rajiben said:

> [Before], they had to look after *māl.* There were many sheep and goats. Very few people lived at home. They started staying at home only after the earthquake. Previously if there were four brothers between them they only had one house and there was no space for everyone. Very few people lived in the house. Their main subject was *māl.* After the earthquake many organisations came and started helping. They built houses for them – for example in Bhimasur village if your son separates from you he will be given a plot. So people have got a facility to stay, so they started living in the house.

> Once people started living in the house they reduced the number of animals (Rajiben December 2019).

If the allocation of individual plots incentivised settlement, it was not the only reason pastoralists began to reduce animal holdings. Land privatisation and redeployment meant that in the annual return to Kachchh for the monsoon, sources of fodder and water dwindled, and the pressure on resources that were left escalated accordingly. A collective attempt to manage the land-to-animal ratio meant that the number of animals had to be reduced, or an alternative to pastoralism sought.

The kind of exit from pastoralism that leaders had advocated, and was now becoming a distinct, rather than distant, possibility, rests on two important premises. One is that alternative means of generating an income can be secured. In post-earthquake Kachchh, the new factories – known locally as companies – introduced alternative livelihood possibilities that had not previously existed. Although they attracted an influx of labourers from other parts of India, as well as from Gujarat, companies generated new jobs for men and women, both directly in production and ancillary positions; and indirectly through their catalytic effect on the local economy, which generated a need for drivers, shopkeepers and guards – jobs for men; and, for women, sewing, and domestic labour in the households of the growing numbers of middle-class families. The second premise is that children would be able to attend school and establish themselves on the trajectory of qualification leading to employment. Sedentary living foregrounded this as a real and relevant possibility by removing the 'terms of inclusion' around school access.

In reconstructed Kachchh, some families have settled entirely and sold off their animal holdings; some have engaged in pastoralism at arm's length by diversifying occupationally but keeping animals in the care of others (often, a male *gowal* [helping hand]); and some have future-proofed by splitting their household, a common adaptation strategy among pastoralists. Splitting leaves men in pastoralism, while women and child(ren) return to the village. The deep gendering of mutually dependent roles in Rabari pastoralism may mean, however, that deploying female labour away from the migratory unit and into the sedentary household makes the family worse off. Rajiben explained:

> Without a woman it's not possible to keep animals as you require someone to make food and things. If a woman stays back home he will still need food and other things. If one brother has up to 100 sheep he can stay with someone else, but if another brother has 400–500 sheep how can he stay with someone? You can't just depend on a *gowal*. Because of that, slowly the number of animals got reduced (*māl ocho tha-to gyo*) (Rajiben, December 2019).

This (commonly heard) perspective takes for granted both that the domestic role is indispensable within the migrating unit's overall organisation of labour, and that it is designated to women, even as this apparently immutable norm of labour division is implicated in an increasingly common trend of declining family fortunes.

'Now is the Time for Education': Diversification, Schooling and Employment

The undermining of pastoralism's viability, alongside schooling's instrumental importance in fulfilling ideas of 'progress' and 'improvement', has, as Sitaben put it, 'seduced' many women into major life changes to fulfil their aspirations for the next generation:

> Like me most of them are seduced by the idea 'I want to send my children to school so I will work hard, do labour work and not go to graze animals'. That is the reason people with animals have to get back here. They just want to settle and make their children study (Sitaben, December 2019).

Community leaders speak of this as 'the time for education', a view that women such as Sitaben and Rajiben share, even as they themselves miss pastoralism:

> It was a good activity and I miss it a lot. But now, we can only miss it. We had to stop roaming around places to herd our animals so that we can provide education and stable lives to our children. Now, the time is not right to be in the herding business (Rajiben, December 2019).

ADVERSE INCORPORATION, AND THE DIGNITY OF WORK AND HOSPITALITY

Against the 'seduction' of settling in order to access schooling and work outside pastoralism, realities of this transition suggest that it is often a process of 'adverse incorporation' (Dyer 2012). Sustaining dignity is a struggle in the face of sharp challenges to social values that, while essential in pastoralism, lack a similar coherence in the new setting. Most immediately, and with many ramifications, there is a new experience of poverty, and a focus on economic status. In many of the villages of Kachchh where Rabaris have come to live, the land is dry, labouring work is difficult to come by, and there are no factories to provide local jobs – and newly settled adults are unable to read and write, and have no educational qualifications. Then:

> Once you leave *māl* it's poverty. They are all new, they have just settled recently a year or two ago. Even people who have come 10–12 years ago, they also haven't got settled in any other business. They are all doing labour work (Rajiben, August 2019).

In Gujarat, the state of the business-minded (Simpson 2006; Simpson and Kapadia 2010; Desai 2011), 'business' (in English) – and the ability to succeed in it – is a perennial topic. Business is an unlikely avenue to economic security for Rabaris who have grown up in their hereditary occupation of pastoralism: start-ups often fail, and they are not 'business' people, as Mayaben explained:

> People like us who have been *maldhāri* are not able to do business because business is not their subject. They have come from *māl* and this is not their subject at all (Mayaben, January 2019).

Even if it was, a new business needs start-up capital, which tends to put this possibility out of reach unless the exit from pastoralism has been profitable:

> None of them could start their own business. Who can start the new business? Only the one who has Rs. 5–7 lakhs cash in his hand can start their own business. But you can't start your own business with Rs. 50,000, even if you want, what can you do with Rs. 50,000? With that money do you feed your family or start a business? It just can't work. So every morning he has to think that I will go and work as a

> labourer and earn Rs. 200. That's what they think about (Mayaben January 2019).

Poverty is a pressing aspect of adverse incorporation for many who leave pastoralism. However, what we want to foreground here is not so much how women deal with its material dimensions, but how they negotiate dignity in the transition from owning the means of production (animals), with its associated freedoms, to being drawn into relations of power and subjugation associated with working for others. Rajiben said:

> If I talk about the previous time only, that was good. At that time people didn't like to be anyone's slave (*gulāmi pasand nohti*). They had *māl* so they didn't want to do anyone else's business (*parko dhandho*). Even today we think if we had *māl* we wouldn't need to do someone else's business. Girls who are going to the company will not go there if they had their own property. Even if they had some farming land they wouldn't go somewhere else, leaving their farming land. But for many they don't have either land or animals, that's why they have to go somewhere else (Rajiben, August 2019).

Even as the need to work for income is now foregrounded for sedentary women, they associate productive work with dignity. Although the work they can now get is very different from working in pastoralism, it provides income and self-respect. Older women have an unnegotiable criterion of dignified work that they do not ask of their daughters: beyond generating an income and not requiring literacy skills or educational qualifications, it must not require them to change their clothing. For this generation, wearing community-specific clothing is an essential marker of individual and collective Dhebar Rabari identity (Frater 2002), although they do accept that their daughters may prefer generic local clothing – providing modesty is preserved. In rural areas, work that conforms to older women's norms of attire is most likely to be manual labour, or sewing piece work. In urbanised settings, older Rabari women can find employment as domestic helpers. Working in others' homes is hard – 'a woman may work in four different houses', using 'methods of cleaning that are different', and lacks the relative autonomy that pastoralism offered. Despite such changed circumstances, they see dignity not only in working, but also in doing this, different, work well:

> People started staying at home but the question was what to do sitting at home too? If we go and work in someone's house at least we will earn Rs. 500 a month. … Woman like me can't work in the company as company has a rule that you can only work there if you wear dress [company uniform]. You cannot enter in a company without the dress. You can enter but can only work in the garden, or sweep and we won't enjoy those kind of things. Instead, if we go and clear some utensil in 3–4 houses one can earn Rs. 1,000–1,500 a month. What does one do sitting for a whole day in the house, now your own housework gets over quickly? … We do the work, practically, with respect [*ijjat*] … this woman came, did her job properly, talked properly and left (Rajiben, December 2019).

Paid employment does not have the intrinsic security blanket that pastoralism offers, nevertheless. Precarity is emerging among families who have divested from animals, since animals are flexible assets that can be sold to generate cash, or loaned to help another family in need. Families in fragile economic health find that emergencies, particularly when medical, outstrip their financial capacity to cope (see also Jeffery and Jeffery 2008); and, if they need to borrow, those who would help are themselves often in similarly straitened circumstances.

While incidents such as a medical emergency are a shock, precarity also causes stress, which can lay bare a fracture in notions of female propriety and norms around the collective. For example, *mehmangati* – looking after guests – is an integral part of female Dhebar *mariyāda*; but settled Dhebar women are now found to be refusing their obligations of hospitality, for reasons of constrained time and expense. They are judged by older women used to the ways of the *dang* to be lacking the respect for guests that 'should be within you' [*man mā hovu joiye*]. Older women's reminiscences on this theme – and, particularly, their emphasis on co-dependency – underline the sense of fracture that they are experiencing:

> was a beautiful co-dependency among people in herding. If one family was expecting guests, then another family would offer a jar full

> of ghee to them. People had abundance without the need of money. ... We could share milk and ghee with others. Sometimes, people shared flour, too. This kind of kindness and co-dependency still exists in the herding business and within a *dang* (Sitaben, December 2019).

Even if somewhat redolent of a reconstructed golden past, women who have lived in pastoralism and experienced the sharing, kindness and co-dependency on which it depends, find these norms of collective flourishing are challenged by the adversities of sedentary living.

GETTING INTO EDUCATION: THE IDEAL OF EDUCATION AND THE REALITIES OF VILLAGE SCHOOLS

Since accessing schools was such an important aspect of deciding to return to villages, Rabaris who now live in Kachchh are conscientious about enrolling children in the local school. In most of these families, this is the first generation to attend school. But schooling is often not fulfilling the instrumental purpose that had been expected of it, it is unleashing unanticipated social consequences (see also Jeffery 2008). Idealised expectations of the benefits of getting an education collide – sometimes brutally – with the realities of using 'government' schools.

Although there is no disaggregated information about Rabaris specifically, the village schools that they mostly use reflect the Gujarat-wide trend of high rates of initial enrolment but poor learning outcomes. The 2018 rural ASER round reported for Kachchh that just 40.1 per cent of children in Grade 5 could read Grade 2 level text, while a mere 29.8 per cent could do 'at least subtraction'; among students in Grades 6–8, the proportion of those who could complete a Grade 2 level text was 65.6 per cent, while just 35.2 could 'do division' (ASER 2019). Gujarat's rate of transition to upper primary levels (Grades 6–8) was India's lowest through the 1990s: according to Govinda and Bandyopadhyay (2008) it stood at 73.9 per cent, against the national average of 85.9, in 1999; but by 2014 it had risen to 97.9 per cent (against the national average of 89.7 per cent) (GCRSA 2016).

Progression without learning is common all over the country (ASER 2019; Beteille et al. 2020). In part this reflects a policy of automatic promotion, rescinded in 2019, that intended to reduce the stress of examinations and grade repetition. Rabari children are not the only ones to have learnt that progression at school is not related to work, attendance or, indeed, any effort beyond merely enrolling in the school. The corrective of the Grade 8 Board examination (end of upper primary stage) comes as a shock and marks a critical point where engagement with schooling is likely to end. Rajiben remarked:

> Government sent a circular that till Standard 8 no child should be failed. So the value of studying disappears. They know, no matter whether they go or don't go to school, they will be passed till Standard 8. … Children think they will be promoted sitting at home till Standard 8 so what is the need to go to school? So they don't go. Kids think, 'I will get the certificate whether I go or not'. But by the time they come to Standard 9, what can they do? Can't even read and write. So they leave (Rajiben, December 2018).

Despite this fault-line in the system, community leaders and teachers blame parents' apparent carelessness for not making sure their children attend school, which they attribute to parents' lack of education. Blame shifting is common, but does not acknowledge that formal schooling has 'rules' that are hard to know, inconsistent and often difficult to follow for those who have never experienced it themselves. Unschooled Rabari parents talk of schooling as 'the subject' of teachers, and do not expect themselves to know a subject that is not their own. At the same time, as Rajiben put it, 'A teacher is a second foundation like mother (*māno bijo payo*)'. It is to these teachers that parents assign the responsibility of educating children into the ways of abstract knowledge and reasoning that constitutes formal education and is associated with 'progress' and 'improvement'; and which, in the contemporary era, trumps the experiential knowledge that comprises the education within, and for, pastoralism, that parents themselves have experienced. Yet, in a government school, the teacher is constantly negotiating the competing norms of a role that embodies being simultaneously an educator and a low-level representative of the Indian state, encumbered by its administrative demands (Ramachandran 2016). The resulting tension is often reflected in a teacher's unreliable presence (Kumar 2018) and limited engagement with children. Rajiben noted, in passing, 'Now they get so much work from above – what can a teacher do? Teach or do that work?'.

Formal schooling is creating deep lines of intergenerational fracture, as the values and form of education that parents experienced, and are foundational to pastoralism, are challenged in the context of sedentary modernity. Schooling constructs childhood itself and autonomy, in ways that are different from the situated livelihood learning that parents experienced. In pastoralism, children have, from an early age, significant responsibilities within and to the collective. Individual autonomy and self-regulation are learnt within the clearly scaffolded and close-knit collective setting that we described earlier, in which respect for elders, obedience towards parents, gendered propriety, 'working' and following community customs, all help to ensure social cohesion and collective capacity to keep animals happy – the fundament of successful pastoralism. Government schools are often not a purposive setting, nor do teachers provide an appropriate scaffolding. Parents enrol their children, but are not accustomed to exercising control over them in the way that schooling envisages (such as monitoring attendance and overseeing homework), and even less so when the 'rules' of schooling are unclear. Parents are not necessarily there to do this anyway, since many families are still exercising the option of household splitting and are away with animals while children stay with relatives to enable them to attend the village school. Rabari boys reportedly often absent themselves from school, making the most of their autonomy of movement in the public domain and the low likelihood of teachers noting their absence or being concerned for their safety. Girls are reportedly more studious than boys, and do better in tests at school; but even if a girl is studious, splitting can mean that she is expected to adopt gendered responsibilities in the household, and has to drop out of school to do so:

> In villages they drop out after Standard 7 or 8 because their parents are in herding. The children may be studying here. They ask the girl

> to leave after Standard 7 or 8 so she could look after the younger ones and their education (School Principal, December 2019).

Even if girls succeed in getting through the Standard 8 Board exam, secondary Board examinations almost always mark the end of the line:

> Most of the girls leave education after Standard 10, 11 or 12. So till today, not a single one of them has got a government job. Usually, they don't pass (School Principal, December 2019).

Engagements with schooling are often unsatisfactory for both girls and boys, and do not fulfil expectations of enabling access to a good job. Many young Rabaris are joining the ranks of the 'half-educated', uncompetitive in the formal job market, and lacking the skills or capital to be self-employed. Often, they are unwilling or unable to be reabsorbed into a life in pastoralism that the family has left behind. Sitaben, for whom educating her two boys was a major reason for settling in the village, is disappointed that although they had reached Grade 12, both were now at home, working 'if they find some work to do'. Community leaders recognise that 'How to give livelihood (*rojgari*) to the educated ones – how to make them move forward is the main issue we have' (School Principal and Community Leader in conversation, December 2019); and while this is seen as more pressing for boys, it is also recognised as an issue for girls. For some boys, when schooling fails to deliver the expected 'progress', poor schooling outcomes can be mitigated by returning to pastoralism, which is a livelihood that flexes to suit labour availability. Pragmatically, the current shortage of male labour in pastoralism facilitates re-absorption of boys (as a *gowal* for others, if not directly in the family's own herd):

> Their fathers think that it's better to pay their own sons than paying Rs. 10,000 to helpers. Parents take their children back [into pastoralism] as they are not doing well in their studies. They studied till Standard 8 and went back to herding animals (Sitaben, December 2019).

A sub-text of these concerns about finding work for boys is that nowadays some Rabari boys, out of school when they should not be, or with nothing to do, are hanging around in public spaces and behaving with an absence of propriety towards young women that contravenes the older generation's view of dignified behaviour. In some cases, young males' behaviour is putting pressures on girls to collude or resist that they find very hard to manage.

BRIDE PRICES AND SUITABLE BOYS

The intersections of schooling, employment and income-generating capacity have important influences on marriage matches and put particular pressures on boys. Within the social institution of marriage, the heteronormative and patriarchal norms of Rabari society expect a male to provide security for his wife and family. In the eyes of the community and traditional leaders, an inability to do so is a valid reason for a marriage to be dissolved. Bride prices persist and by 2018 were unlikely to be less than Rs. 700,000. These realities require a cash flow that neither the individual nor his family can sustain in the absence of a secure source of income. In sedentary settings, a boy who has been to school and achieved a low level of education, but failed to obtain (good quality) employment is a poor prospect: 'If he doesn't have any work or career, who will give him their daughter?' (Sitaben, December 2019). Coupled with this is a new value of conspicuous consumption and, for boys in sedentary settings, owning a motor bike and smart-phone are a marker of status (Jeffrey et al. 2004) and evidence of capacity to generate the cash needed to acquire material assets.

Whether on wages for daily labour, or in the low-level jobs in companies that elementary education may enable, it can take a long time to save up for a marriage. Since a young man may make his way without higher education, but not without a wife, the immediate reality of ensuring marriage is likely to be more pressing than attempting to pursue schooling. Alongside its value in ensuring boys are occupied rather than hanging about, this is another factor that puts pastoralism, re-recognised as a profitable and steady business with liquid assets, back in the frame:

> The boys dropped out of schools as they wanted to earn and save money to buy ornaments for their future wives. They started herding

> animals as they thought they can save some money by selling animals. Usually, people sell animals worth five to six lakh in a year and they have a chance to save some money in a year or two. They can't save Rs. 500,000-600,000 if they earn Rs. 10,000 per month. So, they again started herding animals (Sitaben, December 2019).

Older women report that while they themselves did not have the agency to choose their husband, the next generation of educated girls is likely to claim at least a role, if not the final say, in this decision making. This appears to be a dimension of autonomy in the next generation that unschooled mothers are reluctantly seeing as acceptable, providing that the rules of endogamous marriage are followed:

> Mothers feel bad but now the girls are studying so they can decide about their future. If they can find well educated boys for marriage from our Rabari community, then they do not feel bad (Sitaben, December 2019).

In general, Rabari asserts that a boy would not prefer a girl who is more educated than himself points to a discriminatory gendered norm taking root in the 'time of education' (see also Tilche and Simpson 2018). Schooled young Dhebar women reported that they prefer educated boys, but the still shaky and uneven progress of both boys and girls through schooling means that the conditions for hypergamy through formal education are largely still absent. Educated girls who had never practised pastoralism generally showed no inclination to migrate themselves, but somewhat to our surprise, some said they would take seriously an offer of marriage from a boy who has been to school but is working in pastoralism. With marrying out of the community still proscribed, being 'educated' and earning a good income from pastoralism was, for them, a potentially attractive combination of attributes in a future husband.

Dignity in Pastoralism Re-evaluated

The possibility of marrying into pastoralism that these Dhebar girls admit reflects a new contemporary narrative of pastoralism, which is now often being termed and presented as a 'business' that is both self-sustaining and has good potential to make money.

> In jobs, one gets a salary of Rs. 10,000 per month but if you have 100 animals, you will have income of Rs. 250,000–300,000 per year through the sale of wool, sheep and goats (Women's focus group, January 2019).

The business potential of pastoralism, however, is set in the context of significant externally generated pressures on pastoralism itself, as well as continuing contestations over whether it is a dignified contemporary occupation.

There are increasingly sharp concerns, for example, about insecurity on migration. In the 1990s, occasional animal theft was an occupational hazard, but was countered by remarkable feats of tracking, using knowledge of individual animals, to find a stolen animal, sometimes years after the event. Now, there is a new nuisance of looting by organised gangs, who come at night, armed, and load animals onto a truck. Women interviewed in 2019 talked about such incidents, and the challenges of keeping girls safe, often juxtaposed with reference to the dignity and sanctity of pastoralism, and the moral depravity of the thieves:

> Those who do such work (steal) can't be happy. Our money is called *jogi* (holy income). It comes from real hardships. Those who steal our animals can't enjoy that money (Maiaben, January 2019).

Out-of-state Dhebar pastoralists are finding themselves unwelcome, as land pressures everywhere create growing competition for dwindling resources. Women still in pastoralism in 2019 talked of being positioned by others as 'outsiders', and of the joy in pastoralism that they find is now largely gone:

> When can you enjoy *māl*? When the land is open and animals have food to eat (*charva*). Then *māl* is good. But that is not the situation now ... animals are in real difficulty now. People with animals are now facing nothing but problems (Miraben, January 2019).

While the income that pastoralism as a 'business' can generate is recognised, to see pastoralism as a business is, for many, to misrecognise it. From this perspective, marketising pastoralism has undermined its dignity, and there is discomfort about making a profit from animal death. A future in pastoralism may then be rejected with reference to the 'blood money' discourse, from a stance of spirituality and moral propriety that associates Rabari pastoralism with an ideal form of animal custodianship:

> There is money in this business but it is blood money. For example, if you have 200 animals, from that 150 gave birth, so those 150 sheep will be sold off. The animals will be sent to the butcher. There is lots of money with people but the money one earns from killing these animals is not good money (Sitaben, December 2019).

For those who have been to school and return to pastoralism, although the presumptive capacity of schooling to free them from pastoralism has not succeeded, they have at least gained an element of 'educated' social capital that elevates them from the status of the disrespected non-literate adult. Perhaps this will elevate pastoralism from the current framing of being a low-status occupation for illiterate people, an indignity that, in the light of 'progress' since the earthquake, is very sharply felt:

> How can we sustain without *māl*? We are illiterate. His father doesn't know so much as [counting to] one (*ekdo*). Who will let him enter in a company? If he had some education, he could have worked in security or could do any business. Nowadays an illiterate person has no respect (Maiaben, January 2019).

At the end of their paper, 'Degrees without Freedom' (Jeffrey et al. 2004, 983), the authors conclude that 'the educational strategies of formerly disadvantaged social groups in South Asia may not follow a simple line of increasing investment over time, but be subject instead to reassessment and reversal as the expected gains from formal education fail to materialize'. Our discussion here of 'investment' in education among Rabaris in Kachchh shows that, since the earthquake in 2001, there has been an accelerating trend of change, in which many parents have often gone to the extraordinary lengths of sedentarising and accepting considerable hardship for themselves in order to access schooling for their children. The expected fruits of this investment are occupational diversification, secure and good quality work, and a social standing that, by embodying formal education as a constitutive element of individual, family and community identity, is recognisably dignified.

Yet the schools that most Rabaris can access in rural Kachchh rarely provide a smooth – if indeed, any – transition into what is envisaged by stepping away from pastoralism. The pathway to the mango tree, and its fruits, it seems, is elusive. Schooling and sedentarisation are creating intergenerational fractures and diverging social norms around dignity (see also Tilche and Simpson 2018). The moral codes on which successful pastoralism depended, and which guide older Rabaris' notions of propriety, particularly for women, and of collective wellbeing, do not necessarily map easily onto the circumstances and aspirations of boys and girls now attending school and living lives outside pastoralism, in sedentary settings. Ironically, amid these tensions, pastoralism is, for some, a route to the prosperity and status that low-level schooling and poor quality, or no work are not able to supply. Perhaps the new generation of schooled pastoralists will have gained skills and a voice that enable them to engage with the causes of the deteriorating context for mobile pastoralism – but how this might unfold remains to be seen.

NOTES

1. We acknowledge with gratitude the financial support provided by the UK's Economic and Social Research Council, the Nuffield Foundation and the British Academy.
2. Tilche and Simpson (2018) cite literature suggesting that bride price is a sign of a relatively 'equalitarian' society, unlike the practice of dowry, an observation with which we broadly agree.
3. The Suzlon wind farm, aiming to be a 2,000 MW farm at full capacity, had already completed installation of 1,100 MW of hybrid windmills by 2014, *en route* to being the world's largest wind farm at a single location (https://ejatlas.org/conflict/suzlon-energy-in-kutch-district). Also see: https://mercomindia.com/gujarat-high-court-notice-wind-projects/.

REFERENCES

ASER Centre. 2019. *Annual Status of Education Report (Rural) 2018*. New Delhi: ASER Centre. http://img.asercentre.org/docs/ASER%202018/Release%20 Material/aserreport2018.pdf (accessed January 2022).

Beteille, T., N. Tognatta, M. Riboud, S. Nomura and Y. Ghorpade. 2020. *Ready to Learn: Before School, In School, and Beyond School in South Asia.* South Asia Development Forum, World Bank. https://openknowledge.worldbank.org/handle/10986/33308 (accessed January 2022).

Bharwada, C. and V. Mahajan. 2006. 'Quiet Transfer of Commons'. *Economic and Political Weekly,* 41(4), 313–15. DOI: 10.2307/4417728.

Chako, P. 2019. 'Marketising Hindutva: The state, society and markets in Hindu Nationalism'. *Modern Asian Studies,* 53(2), 377–410. DOI: 10.1017/S0026749X17000051.

Chantia, A. 2006. 'Education as a Means of Social Change: study with regard to dhankut, a group living in District Bahraich, Uttar Pradesh'. *The Anthropologist,* 8(4), 267–74. DOI: 0.1080/09720073.2006.11890975.

Choksi, A. 1995. 'Ceramic Vessels: their role in illuminating past and present social and economic relationships'. *Man and Environment,* 20(1), 87–108.

Desai, K. 2011. 'Review: On Constructing the Idea of Gujarat'. *Economic and Political Weekly,* 46(48), 32–5.

Dyer, C. 2012. 'Formal Education and Pastoralism in Western India: Inclusion, or adverse incorporation?' *Compare,* 42(2), 259–81.

Dyer, C. 2013. 'Does mobility have to mean being hard to reach? Mobile pastoralists and education's 'terms of inclusion'. *Compare,* 43(5), 601–21. https://www.tandfonline.com/doi/abs/10.1080/03057925.2013.821322.

Dyer, C. 2014. *Livelihoods and Learning: Education for all and the marginalisation of mobile pastoralists.* Oxford: Routledge.

Dyer, C. and A. Choksi. 2001. 'Literacy, Schooling and Development: Views of Rabari nomads, India'. In B. Street (ed.) *Literacy and Development: Ethnographic Perspectives.* London: Routledge. DOI: https://doi.org/10.4324/9780203468418.

Frater, J. 2002. ' "This is ours": Rabari tradition and identity in a changing world'. *Nomadic Peoples,* 6(2), 156–69.

Gee, J. 2012. *Social Linguistics and Literacies: Ideology in discourses.* 4th edition. London: Routledge.

Jeffrey, C., R. Jeffery and P. Jeffery. 2004. 'Degrees without Freedom: The impact of formal education on Dalit young men in North India'. *Development and Change,* 35(5), 963–86. https://doi.org/10.1111/j.1467-7660.2004.00388.x.

Jeffery, P. 2008. 'Introduction: Hearts, Minds and Pockets', in R. Chopra and P. Jeffery (eds.) *Educational Regimes in Contemporary India,* pp. 13–38. New Delhi: Sage.

Jeffery P. and R. Jeffery. 2008. 'Money Itself Discriminates: Obstetric emergencies in the time of liberalisation'. *Contributions to Indian Sociology,* 42(1), 59–91. doi:10.1177/006996670704200104.

GSIDS. 2016. *District Human Development Report, Kachchh.* Gujarat Social Infrastructure Development Society/Government of Gujarat. https://www.undp.org/content/dam/india/docs/human-development/District%20

HDRs/13.%20Kachchh_DHDR_2016.compressed.pdf (accessed January 2022).

Govinda, R and M. Bandyopadhyay. 2008. *Access to Elementary Education in India. Country Analytical Review.* CREATE consortium. New Delhi: NUEPA. https://assets.publishing.service.gov.uk/media/57a08bb7ed915d3cfd000ec0/India_CAR.pdf (accessed January 2022).

Krätli, S. 2015. *Valuing Variability: New perspectives on climate resilient drylands development.* London: IIED. Available: https://pubs.iied.org/pdfs/10128IIED.pdf (accessed January 2022).

Kumar, K. 2018. Diagnostic Trouble. In 'Are our children learning: a symposium on the crisis in learning afflicting our schools'. *Seminar* # 706. Available: http://www.india-seminar.com/2018/706.htm (accessed January 2022).

Lave, J. and E. Wenger. 1991. *Situated Learning: Legitimate Peripheral Participation.* Cambridge: Cambridge University Press.

Mehta, N. and M. Mehta. 2010. 'Gujarat beyond Gandhi: notes on identity, conflict and society'. *South Asian History and Culture*, 1(4), 467–79. DOI:10.1080/19472498.2010.50701.

Mehta, L., S. Srivastava, H. Adam, Alankar, S. Bose, U. Ghosh and V. Vijay Kumar. 2019. 'Climate change and uncertainty from "above" and "below": perspectives from India'. *Regional Environmental Change*, 19, 1,533–47.

Ramachandran, V. 2016. *Teachers in the Indian Education System: Synthesis of a 9-state study.* New Delhi: NUEPA. DOI: 10.13140/RG.2.2.32276.30085.

Ramani, S. 2010. 'Development and Displacement: Resentment in the Kachchh. Commentary'. *Economic & Political Weekly*, 45(8), 15–18.

Shah, A. 2005. *Poverty and Natural Resources: Understanding the Dynamics in the Content of Dryland Regions in Western India.* Chronic Poverty Research Centre Working Paper. http://dx.doi.org/10.2139/ssrn.1756848 (accessed January 2022).

Simpson, E. 2006. 'The State of Gujarat and the Men without Souls'. *Critique of Anthropology*, 26(3), DOI: 10.1177/0308275X06066581.

Simpson, E. 2014. *The political biography of an earthquake: Aftermath and amnesia in Gujarat, India.* Oxford: Oxford University Press.

Simpson., E. and A. Kapadia. 2010. *The idea of Gujarat. History, ethnography and text.* Hyderabad: Orient Black Swan.

Shiva, V., S. Jani and S. Fontana. 2011. The Great Indian Land Grab. New Delhi: Navdanya. https://www.navdanya.org/attachments/RFSTE_The%20Great%20Indian%20Land%20Grab_28-9-2011%20(1).pdf (accessed January 2022).

Street, B. 1984. *Literacy in theory and practice.* Cambridge: Cambridge University Press.

Sud, N. 2012. *Liberalisation, Hindu Nationalism and the State: A Biography of Gujarat.* New Delhi: Oxford University Press.

Tilche, A. and E. Simpson. 2018. 'Marriage and the crisis of peasant society in Gujarat, India'. *Journal of Peasant Studies*, 45(7), 1,518–38.

4

Converting Life to Leather

The Making of an Urban Neighbourhood

Radhika Chopra

This chapter draws its inspiration from Patricia Jeffery's seminal work *Frogs in a Well* (1979) in which she unpacked a whole universe of gendered hierarchies by concentrating on one neighbourhood in Delhi, and what people did in their everyday lives. Discerning hierarchies embedded in the nuanced veiling practices among the women of Pirzade families, the custodians of the Auliya shrine of Nizam-ud-din, Jeffery analysed the significance of uses of space to discern the structure of practice. What is striking in the analysis is the manner in which a neighbourhood as a social, cultural and ethical universe came to the surface in the descriptions.

In this chapter I present a single neighbourhood called Bootan Mandi, in the city of Jalandhar in Punjab, as a place where commerce, colonialism and caste interlock. As material and commodity, leather has played an elemental role in transforming the life of the residents of Bootan Mandi, including migrant workers. Rather like *parda*, as material and process, *chamra* (hide/leather) animates life around itself, evident in the labour-intensive processes of converting skin to leather that I describe in some detail. This potential of leather is not unique to Bootan Mandi and its Chamar leather workers. Owen Lynch's study of the Jatavs of Agra and Maren Bellwinkel-Schempp's of the Khatiks of Kanpur, demonstrate how trading in leather and bristle altered the lives and worlds of the urban lower castes in Agra and Kanpur, respectively. Karen Coleho and M. Vijayabhaskar's work on leather production in Ambur in Tamil Nadu and Marie-Caroline Saglio-Yatzimirsky's work on contemporary Dharavi's leather workers demonstrate the strong sense of identification with leather. Important in Coleho and Vijayabhaskar's and Saglio-Yatzimirsky's work are the migrants who have made Ambur and Dharavi their home, and their sense of place making rooted in leather. Taking a cue from these writings, I outline some aspects of Bootan Mandi's history, in particular its identification as a space for tanning and curing leather. Leather tanning has relegated the neighbourhood to the position of an undesirable quarter of the city of Jalandhar. At the same time, leather provided significant economic and business opportunities for Chamars, the leather workers who laboured almost exclusively on tanning and curing leather and making shoes. I focus on the low-income migrants of Bootan Mandi. Fieldwork makes clear that the conversion of skin to leather provides security and entwines with personhood. The labour of conversion is central to identification and forms an important part of my discussion.

Since 2018, Patricia and I have been part of a funded project, housed simultaneously at the University of Edinburgh, the University of Delhi and the North-East Network, studying the lives of low-income urban migrant workers in two cities – Jalandhar and Guwahati. This chapter draws on research from that collaborative project.[1] I draw on discussions between all the members of the project from when the project began in 2018 through to the summer of 2020, a time riven with dissent, disease and dislocation. I hope I have learnt sufficiently well from Patricia Jeffery's exemplar ethnography to be able to say something sensible and, hopefully, interesting about Bootan Mandi and what it takes to make leather.

Bootan Mandi, a Life Told in Leather

In the history of leather processing in Punjab, the urban quarter of Bootan Mandi was closely identified with leather work.

A leather worker stitching hide with bamboo fibre, Bootan Mandi, Jalandhar, Punjab. Photograph, Dr. Jeevan Sharma, October 2018.

The commercial hub of Jalandhar, where Bootan is located,[2] had one of the oldest military cantonments, established in the mid-19th century, making it an important centre of trade and commerce. Urban legend has it that the demand for riding boots, saddles, harnesses and other accoutrements required by the British military gave Bootan its name.[3] Colonial institutions gave a push to the demand for leather, and modernised the processes of converting hide to leather. 'Early British intervention in the leather industry led to its urbanisation, involving social mobility for the communities involved in the profession' (Sujatha 2002, p. 4,673). The presence of cantonments in cities such as Jalandhar, Agra and Kanpur created a demand for leather and encouraged internal migration. Chamars from villages within Punjab and migrants from beyond Punjab moved to Bootan. The incoming migrants were primarily Chamar, a caste widely known for their expertise in shoe making and leather processing (Saberwal 1976). Bootan's leather workers, like the leather processing and bristle harvesting Khatiks of Kanpur (Bellwinkel-Schempp 1998) or the Jatavs of Agra (Lynch 1969), benefited from a burgeoning leather industry during and after the colonial period. Karen Coleho and M. Vijayabhaskar's work on the town of Ambur in Tamil Nadu (2014), brings the issue of leather processing into the 21st century and has a particular resonance for analysing the contemporary leather business in Bootan Mandi, as does Saglio-Yatzimirsky's work on Dharavi (2013), particularly in relation to how leather enabled critiques of caste hierarchies.

Although leather as a material was in great demand, leather workers themselves remained at the lower end of the value chain, and their work was confined to tanning leather rather than earning and prospering from selling high-value leather products. Unfortunately, the kinds of shoes that suited colonial or urban tastes were not made by local leather artisans, but by specialised tanneries and shoe makers who had networks with 'leading manufacturers in England' (Sharma 1983, p. 542), such as Cooper Allen and Co. Ltd. 'Raw hides and semi-tanned leather soon became important items in Indian exports to England in the early 20th century' (Sujatha 2002, p. 4673). Such lucrative markets were basically inaccessible to local leather workers. Nevertheless, the highly segmented nature of urban markets fuelled demand for a variety of locally produced shoes at the lower end of the market, simultaneously with the more expensive boots and laced shoes (Coleho and Vijayabhaskar, 2014). Local leather workers and shoe makers who were settled within identified urban quarters, benefited from the possibilities offered by market segmentation.

Two additional and definitive social processes were critical to the transformation of life in Bootan. The first was the emergence of a political religious community, inspired by the Bhakti movement, aspects of which have been discussed by Mark Jugensmeyer in his work on religious rebels, the Ad Dharmi, (1988) and by Ronki Ram's in-depth discussion (2004) of dalit consciousness and caste-based religious movements in Punjab. In Jalandhar, the concentration of leather curing and production within Bootan, during and after the colonial period, enabled some Chamars to move from the task of curing and tanning leather to actually trading in leather. The ability to read bills of sale in English and the functional literacy required for trading spurred the desire for literacy. Despite such discriminatory practices as being made to sit outside classrooms or being prohibited to socialise with upper-caste classmates (Ram 2004), the few who managed to finish school, prospered. The combination of money and functional literacy enabled individuals and families from Bootan Mandi to migrate transnationally, to Africa, the UK and the USA. Some key figures in the anti-colonial movements were Chamar migrants to the USA. Transnational migration enabled by the lucrative business of making leather fostered religious rebellion rooted in critiques of caste. The anti-caste Adi Dharm movement waned soon after independence, but the sentiments and memories it engendered influenced the emergence in the late 20th century of the Ravidassia movement, coalesced around the cobbler saint, Ravidas. I haven't the space to discuss the unfolding contours of the Ravidassia movement, but the rich literature draws attention to leather as the terrain on which radical critiques, community formation and international migration unfolded (Ashutosh 2014; Jodhka 2009; Ram 2004, 2009; Singh 2012; among others).

The second important phenomenon in the latter half of the 20th and the early 21st centuries is the in-migration to Bootan of labour from beyond Punjab. Leather empowered the more affluent Chamars of Punjab to migrate transnationally, and leather was the 'pull' factor that encouraged migrants from different parts of India to migrate into Punjab (and Bootan) to undertake the labour-intensive work of curing leather. Tied into both movements is leather as a commodity and a process. Based on fieldwork done from late 2018 to early 2020, I first analyse leather as livelihood. Any essay on leather cannot ignore the material itself, nor what is entailed in labouring on leather. I draw on narratives of workers and the graphic nature of the work entailed in converting a living body to an inanimate object.

Statistics tell us that, from a commercial perspective, leather is an extremely important commodity in India. Home to 20% of the world's cattle and buffalo, and 11% of the world's sheep and goat populations, India has an abundance of four-legged animals whose skins are particularly amenable for conversion to leather. The hide is most commonly used for footwear, but it is also used for saddlery, clothing, weaponry, water storage containers and other goods. In the 1990s, the Council for Leather Exports put plans in place to step up leather exports from Rs. 5,000 crore in 1995 to Rs. 10,000 crore by the turn of the century (or about 4% of the country's export earnings, Damodaran and Mansingh 2008). The expansionist plans envisioned a move away from the small-scale manufacture of leather goods toward encouraging large corporations and international joint ventures to produce high-value leather products – industrial machine belts, for example (EPW 1989, p. 2,099). Given the wealth of 'raw' material available, the leather industry is positioned as a key sector in India's industrial landscape, employing over four million people (Khan 2020). By the time of our fieldwork in 2018, the Leather Council's expansion plans were in place in cities such as Jalandhar, where special industrial zones were established for the large-scale production of leather and leather goods. Smaller, artisanal workshops were confined largely to Bootan Mandi.

As urban infrastructure developed and the city expanded, Bootan Mandi's inclusion within municipal limits became a point of aggravation. Leather processing, curing and tanning are classified as noxious and polluting industries. Under new zoning regulations leather manufacturing was moved out of Bootan to larger leather factories along the city outskirts.[4] State investment in leather as a major foreign exchange earner and the creation of a new industrial zone, resulted in the flight of leather manufacture a fair distance from Bootan, to the Wariana Industrial Area and the Leather Complex on the north-west outskirts of the city along the Jalandhar-Kapurthala Road. Some of the Ravidassia owners of tanneries moved to the Leather Complex.

The move did not entirely dispossess Bootan of leather. Businesses classified under state industrial policies as micro, small and medium enterprises (MSMEs) created an export-oriented market within Bootan. Although their commercial networks (and presumably their net worth) are not expansive, they spearheaded the modernisation of leather production. For example, the Modern Skin Company, a private limited company with its headquarters in Chandigarh and listed as a small enterprise (authorised capital Rs. 5 lakhs), located in Bootan. Ravi Leather Craft of Bootan is a medium enterprise that specialises in the export of finished leather. Nevertheless, it is not finished products that form the identity of Bootan, which, even today, is better known as a hide market than as a place for high-value leather commodities.

What did the shifting contours of leather production do to migration patterns? Since the start of the green revolution in the mid-1960s, migrants have been drawn to the city of Jalandhar. The increase in rice cultivation in the 1970s drew migrants to Punjab. Through the 1970s and 1980s, migrants arriving at railheads (including Jalandhar) were taken directly to villages in tractor-trolleys by labour-hungry Punjabi landholders. However, in the period of approximately three months between rice transplanting and rice harvesting, there was little employment in village economies; many migrants moved into the city to ply cycle *rikshas*, to work in *bazaars* and roadside eateries or in brick kilns. Numerous niches of the city's economy depended on such seasonal movements of migrant labour. The usual pattern was to move from the agrarian economy to the urban economy, and back again. Movements were tied to the rhythms of the agrarian calendar, rather than to the demands for labour in the city. Labour mobility created a distinctive form of circular migration between agrarian and urban economies, that of migrant labour circulating between sectors *within* Punjab. Their movements redefined what circular migrations meant, for they moved between their places of emigration, and spaces/economies within the space of immigration, in the process redefining the notion of home. In Bootan, migrants worked as loaders or in the numerous processes of curing and tanning. Over time, the more skilled migrants were greatly sought after and were offered regular employment as valuable members of Bootan's leather economy. Some were already conversant with flaying, curing and tanning, especially migrants from around Kanpur and Rai Bareilly. The combination of artisanal workshops, export-oriented business enterprises and commerce in leather continued to encourage the in-migration of labour to Jalandhar and Bootan.

The migrants of Bootan Mandi buck the primary all-India trend of short-term migration. Studies estimate that 80% of migrants in India who leave rural areas for work each year spend less than six months away from their village (Coffey et al, 2015). Our project survey pointed out that most migrants into Jalandhar have been coming to the city or have lived in the city for over 10 years. Out of 100 surveyed migrant workers in Jalandhar in 2018–19, only 13 had come to Jalandhar in the previous year. Of the 100 migrants surveyed in detail, 80 had been in the city for more than 10 years. Of these, 59 had come with families, or had family members living together. While migrants still viewed their villages of origin as home, the presence of children meant irregular and carefully planned visits back there. The reasons were various and included: children's school calendars; rents paid in advance; the loss of wages or even of jobs; and the increasing intensity of social and economic support systems in Jalandhar.

Quite apart from bifurcating the sense of home experienced by longer-term migrants, and what this has meant to their social and familial biographies, the presence of migrants significantly transformed Bootan's cultural landscape. In the following excerpt from the fieldnotes, Chandu,[5] a migrant worker, exemplifies the intricacies of ties between livelihoods, leather and migration:

> Chandu, a migrant from Vaishali Gadh, Bihar, has been in Punjab since 1972. He said that earlier he was a helper in a truck, but ran away after a person was killed in a road accident. He settled in Jalandhar after his marriage in 1973. He has six children, four sons and two daughters. Two of his sons have been brought up and educated in Punjab. His grandchildren also live in Jalandhar. When I first met him, he was working on flayed skins, heaving them out of the solution of lime and water, first rubbing them with a brick, then with a *rambhi* (a slim sickle). He was paid Rs. 15 per skin. A little later, he and Shekhu, another migrant, soaked some skins in the solution of *babul* husk,[6] the *saak*, which he called *manni*, and then hung skins after overturning. Chandu also looked after skins drying in the sun, shaping them, and scraping off the *saak* stuck to each. He received a separate payment of Rs. 10 per skin for scraping. Chandu was quite

> experienced and was paid per piece, earning around Rs. 500–600 per day.
>
> Chandu's elder son works in a raw leather unit of the Wariana Leather Complex. He was well versed in intricacies of the leather trade. At the Leather Complex, Chandu's son is paid a daily wage. When there is work, he can earn up to Rs. 400–500 per day but sometimes he remains unemployed for months. In his assessment, the leather trade is on the decline. Even shop owners in Bootan Mandi are having a hard time. Leather factories located in the modern industrial Leather Complex, corner most of the orders and the resultant profits. Chandu told me that for last 10 years, work has been declining rapidly. Earlier, owners of almost every establishment in Bootan used to employ him, and get their work done faultlessly and efficiently. But that has stopped; he now works exclusively for Chhotelal, who is also a migrant from Uttar Pradesh [UP]. Part of the reason for the decline is the machinery in the leather factories which manages to 'peel' at least three layers from each hide which is not possible with manually cured hide.

When asked if they faced discrimination in the city, Chandu's elder son assured me that they are treated as family by neighbours. But people do draw distinctions. Though Chandu's grandchildren have grown up in Punjab, they are still identified as *Chawl khani jaat* (rice-eating caste/community) and *bhaiyye*.[7]

Two aspects emerge from Chandu's account. The first is the segmentation of the business of leather into the factory production system located in the Leather Complex, where Chandu's son works, from the older, manual styles of curing and tanning in the small tanneries of Bootan Mandi. Leather, historically so significant and so well entrenched in Bootan, was not easily displaced to the Leather Complex, although it certainly suffered a decline. Smaller tanneries, of the kind where Chandu worked, started to dwindle. Instead of tanning, Bootan has become known as a *Chamra Mandi*, a collection centre for hides. However, transactions in hides have suffered strains of various kinds. The President of the Hide Market Association, Joydeep, said that over the last few years business had declined dramatically for various reasons.[8]

> Our people, people of our caste (*saade loki*) are being hounded by police and members of Hindutva groups, like the BJP-RSS. Some days ago, Chamars who pick up dead animals from *gaushalas* (cow-shelters) were beaten up by upper-caste Rajputs in the name of cow-protection (*gau-raksha*). The *gaushala* manager refused to accept any responsibility for the assault, insisting that his sole responsibility was to allow people to carry the skins, and neither he nor the *gaushala* are associated with those who collect the skins or those who object. After some insistence, and as a way to avoid violent assaults in future, the Chamars got a letter from the *gaushala* manager, stating that they are permitted to carry skins away from the *gaushala*. The letter was crucial to try and ensure that in future the manager did not deny the need for carcasses and skins being taken away. Following this instance, Joydeep asked the person who collects skins from the Doaba Chowk Gaushala in Jalandhar to get a similar letter from its manager as a protective measure.
>
> Joydeep insisted that such violent assaults resulted in fewer skins arriving at the *Chamra Mandi*, and the consequent decline in trade. Many workers shifted to find alternative work, like furniture making, welding, construction, real estate and so on. 'There is no income in this occupation,' he said. Another member of the market association from Cheeka, Kaithal district of Haryana, who was also present during the course of the interview, agreed. He was very vocal in pointing out the injustice of the event and its aftermath. *Gaushalas* are managed by upper-caste Brahmins and Baniyas and they are the only beneficiaries of the *gaushala* economy. 'You [referring to the upper castes] drink the milk, eat the cheese, consume the *ghee*, get all the donation money … what do we Chamars get? We Chamars clean the shit of the animals, we Chamars clear the carcasses. And we Chamars get beaten by goons' (*gai ka doodh tum piyo, paneer tum khao, ghee tum khao, daan ka paisa tumhe mile … aur haemin kya milta hai, ye janwaron ka gobar saaf karein hamare log, mare janwar ko uthayein hamare log, aur gundon ke haathon pitaya bhi khayein hamare log*). 'We are not allowed to beat up an upper-caste person, or ask them to chant "*Jai Bhim*!" We shouldn't be beaten up either.'

The decline in the availability of skins is spoken of quite widely; nevertheless, the hide market continues to be a busy commercial space, imparting a quickness to the rhythms of life in the neighbourhood.

Open all days of the week except Sundays, the market receives the hides and skins of a number of different animals, although the hides of buffalo and cow, and the skin of goat and sheep, predominate. Ringed around the hide market are small warehouses, where hides are stored for subsequent sale. The market is regulated by an association, and only its members can sell and purchase hides in the *Chamra Mandi* of Bootan. These warehouses (referred to as godowns) usually employ migrant labourers for transporting, loading and offloading the hides. Buyers from the Leather Complex, including owners of leather factories, come to Bootan to purchase raw hide.

There is an additional shift in the urban landscape. Small enterprises making synthetic-fibre sports and walking shoes have mushroomed, and are overtaking those that make leather boots and shoes. This is perhaps the clearest indication of the commercial imperatives that confront leather. An entire lane is dedicated to stitching synthetic shoes, largely by migrant labour.

> Mahinder is from Unnao, UP, and lives with his wife and son in a rented room in a rooming house near Bootan.[9] He has been living in the city for more than twenty years. He said that he has been working in this shoe stitching shop [where the interview was conducted] since he had come to Jalandhar. In a single day he is able to stitch one lot of shoes [one lot is 32–40 pair of shoes] and earns around Rs. 500–600 per day.
>
> Another migrant, Amrit, said that most migrants working in small shops stitching and making shoes for the wholesale markets, are from UP, from the Kanpur-Unnao-Rai Bareilly area. Some migrants who have lived in Punjab for many years own MSMEs in the by-lanes of Bootan. They usually get orders from people who come by their shops, though this system has been replaced by mobile sales people who travel to shoe shops and market the products. Many orders are placed over mobile phones, especially from those who are frequent buyers.

The transfer of production from Bootan to the Leather Complex has poised the neighbourhood between its past and its future. Work and production have shifted perceptibly away from natural raw hide and leather toward newer, man-made fibres that are light, cheap and have muscled in on leather. Within Bootan, the shift toward synthetic fabric is understood as a 'preference', expressed by younger migrant men, to work in the leather factories where machines 'handle' the leather processing, including flaying, cutting and so on. The fact is that this is where work is usually found, and migrants follow the work. Khairchand, an older and more experienced worker, lamented that the business of selling finished leather in Bootan Mandi has almost ceased. Despite the existence of MSMEs engaged in leather transactions, the general perception among residents is that the leather business of Bootan has diminished overall. Whatever remains is handled by migrants from UP and Bihar, from Kanpur, Unnao and Rai Bareilly. In-migration into Bootan is certainly evident in the interviews of workers engaged in the multiple tasks of making leather. The challenge to Bootan Mandi's leather business is not from synthetics but from the transference of production to a state-supported factory system in the special economic zones of the Leather Complex.

Leather Tanner, Bootan Mandi. Photograph, Jeevan Sharma, October, 2018.

So, has leather vanished in 21st century Bootan? If not, where is it in the neighbourhood landscape? The intersectional mobilities and trifurcation described by Mahinder and Amrit between the tanning/curing of raw hide, the sale of hides and the stitching of non-leather shoes should not be read as an indication of the receding significance of leather. Hide processing and tanning have moved to the Leather Complex, to the detriment of tanneries in Bootan, but small leather workshops and tanneries still exist. Most are situated behind the *Chamra Mandi,* the hide market. These tanneries use the manual methods of tanning and curing and are a key reason for the continued presence of Punjabi and migrant labour in Bootan. As you walk through the area, the strong smell of curing leather pervades the air and makes it clear that tanning remains a neighbourhood occupation, although it has receded into by-lanes and back lanes. Visually, olfactorily, conversationally, as well as in the patterns of neighbourhood life, leather as product, as labour process and as business enterprise is everywhere (see Figures 0.1 and 0.2).

What is less obvious is the idea of leather as an encounter between human and animal. The carcass and the hide are material evidence of mortality, with which the living engage for their livelihood. The sensorium of making leather emerged from interviews conducted in the neighbourhood. Not everyone had the time for an extensive interview. But the few workers and owners of small tanneries who did speak at length, provided vivid accounts, and fleshed out the milieu of Bootan's leather business. One of the Chamar leather workers of Bootan Mandi described the process of transforming skin to leather : *khal se chamra.*[10] The account lays out the details of the work and gives us a sense of the labour entailed in making leather.

> When a cow or buffalo dies in a village, *apne loki* [literally, our folk; a reference to members of the caste group] take it to a place called *Hada Rehri* [*hada*: boundary; a reference to a place on the boundaries of a village, usually adjacent to a road or a water source] to decay after death. The carcass is wrapped in salt and sacking, to preserve it for storing before it is transported. The salted carcass is brought to Bootan Mandi for sale.[11] Owners of small tanneries usually buy the carcass or hides. Like this buffalo hide [indicating the hide he was working on] was bought for a thousand rupees. The hide is taken

to the tannery yard, and immersed in normal water overnight, then washed the next day to remove the salt. Afterwards it is immersed in water and lime (*chunna*), in pits (*kund*). One *kund* is large enough to contain about 16 hides at a time. The hides are immersed for about 10–12 days, till the time the hair loosens and starts falling off the hide. It might take longer, up to 20 days in winter. Every day the hides are taken out of the pit, checked and put back. The lime solution is stirred thoroughly before the hide is soaked again. As the hair loosens, it is rubbed off with a *ramba* [a semi-circular tool]. The hide is resoaked in a fresh solution of lime and water for another 2–3 days or up to 5 days, till hide swells and the skin tightens. Next it is flayed to remove the fat and meat with a *rambhi* [a slimmer sickle]. This fatty meat can be collected for use for lipsticks, *bindis* and so on. But since there are no cosmetic processing units near Bootan, the fat and particles just decompose and are thrown away. It is decomposed in a water pit, the *garki*.[12] Meat decomposes and lime deposited in it gets separated. The lime can be used again for soaking. Decomposed meat and fat needs to be cleaned from the *garki* twice a year. After this, the hide is immersed in water overnight, till it becomes white and soft. It is rubbed with brick first and *rambha* later, to give it a smooth finish.

Then it is immersed in a solution (*manni*) of water and *kikar da saak* (*babul* husk). It's rotated in this solution for about 2–3 hours. Then the hides are taken out, more husk is added and hides are immersed in the same solution for another 3 days. After that, the pieces of hide are stitched or bound together with long bamboo or plant fibre (*khane*). After stitching, the hides are hung and the *babul* husk solution is poured over them. The solution oozes out of the pores, the sweat pores, and colours the skin from within. After one day, the hide is inverted and the process repeated for another day. This process prevents hardening and keeps the skin soft. The hides are sunned and dried for about a day or two. To flatten the swelled portions of the hide, it is hit and pressed with china plates to press it down and reduce the liquid and ooze.

There's no doubt that the emergence of factories has pushed more residents out of Bootan; some have left the leather business altogether. Khairchand's declaration that the younger generation do not want to work on raw leather or manual tanning is partially true – but it does not capture the entirety of what leather continues to mean. State investment in leather production and the export-orientation of the business tells us that leather cannot be ignored. Nevertheless, Bootan as a space of commerce has had to reboot its business and reinvent its relationship to leather. It's almost as if the neighbourhood, unable to relinquish the very thing that has given it a name, must acknowledge ties with new materials to retain a semblance of its identity. Despite the shifts and the repurposing of work, or the decline in business, the smell of curing raw hide that lingers in the air tells us most clearly that Bootan has not completely turned its back on its past, nor given up the arduous work of converting life to leather.

NOTES

1. ICSSR-ESRC Collaborative Research Programme on Urban Trasformations in India, University of Delhi and University of Edinburgh Project 'From the Margins: Exploring Low Income Migrant Workers Access to Basic Services'. I am indebted to all the members of the project. To Dr. Jeevan Sharma, PI at the University of Edinburgh, and to Prof. Anuj Kapilashrami for discussions and thought-provoking insights, and for keeping the project going with energy and imagination – and sheer hard work. I am particularly grateful to Anurag Sharma and Bharti Kumari for their detailed and meticulous fieldwork in Jalandhar. Anurita Hazarika and NEN for so sensitively highlighting the life experiences of migrant workers in Guwahati, Assam. To Patricia Jeffery for keeping all of us on track, for sharing her field notes and astute comments, and never missing that extraneous comma that slipped into careless writing!
2. In popular reference, people rarely use the full name of the neighbourhood, truncating it as a way of demonstrating their familiarity with the place, rather like shortening the name of a loved child.
3. In Punjabi usage of English words, the plural is suggested by a complicated mixture of 'loan' terms and by a process of code switching between the grammar of Punjabi and other languages. The phenomenon of code switching and code mixing with other languages 'is a natural part of the verbal behaviour of Punjabis … [though] this type of verbal behaviour makes Punjabis a subject of jokes' (Bhatia 2008: 130).
4. Rezoning resulted in a reclassification or recategorization of agrarian land within the industrial zone. This reclassified area is now a distinct and identifiable site of migrant housing, composed of structures that are custom-built to rent out to migrant families. The basic plan is a set of rooms around a common courtyard, where water and toilet facilities are shared by migrant tenants. Agriculturalists have become urban rentiers.

5. The interview was conducted by Anurag Sharma, one of the members of the collaborative project team. The names of all interviewees have been changed to ensure privacy and in keeping with traditions of the anthropological method. Interviewed 2 December 2018.
6. Babul (*Vachellia nilotica*) bark is an important tanning substance in northern India. A by-product of timber felling, the bark is separated from the logs by beating them with wooden mallets, work usually performed by migrant labour. The strips of bark are dried in the open, chipped into smaller pieces and sent to tanneries.
7. *Bhaiyye* is a generalised term for migrants from Eastern India. As a term it hovers on the edge of insult. Respected outsiders are usually referred to as *bhai*, or brother, a kin term that is extended to include people who are not kin, but included within *biraderi* or fraternal bonds. Ritual functionaries in village *gurudwaras*, for example, are referred to as *Bhai*, signalling their inclusion as esteemed 'elder brothers' and respectable members of an inclusive community. The migrants are not *bhai* but *bhaiyye*, a generic plural indicating a 'group'. The term deindividualises and depersonalises each migrant person.
8. Interviewed by Anurag Sharma 26 July 2019
9. Interview conducted by Bharati Kumari, 20 July 2019.
10. Interview conducted by Anurag Sharma, 30 November 2018.
11. Villages along the southbound highway to the south and south west of the city of Jalandhar are the primary suppliers of raw hide to Bootan Mandi and to the modern factory Leather Complex situated along the Jalandhar-Kapurthala Highway.
12. People with skin ailments bathe in the water from the *garki* . Water from *kunds* is used to treat congestion and coughs for children and cattle (Chandu, interviewed by Anurag Sharma, 2 December 2018).

REFERENCES

Aikin, A. 1830. 'On Tanning and Leather-Dressing', *Transactions of the Society, Instituted at London, for the Encouragement of Arts, Manufactures, and Commerce*, 50, 192–214 https://www.jstor.org/stable/41327305 (accessed 1 November 2020).

Akyüz, F. 2009. 'Odor: An important problem in leather industry', 32nd Congress of the International Union of Leather Technologists and Chemist Societies, https://www.researchgate.net/publication/270892028 (accessed 8 December 2020).

Ashutosh, K. 2014. 'Deras as sites of electoral mobilisation in Indian Punjab: Examining the reasons that political parties flock to the deras', *Asian Ethnicity* 15(3). DOI:10.1080/14631369.2013.878209.

Bellwinkel-Schempp, M. 1998. 'The Khatiks of Kanpur and the Bristle Trade: Towards an Anthropology of Man and Beast', *Sociological Bulletin*, 47(2), 185–206. http://www.jstor.org/stable/23620273 (accessed 9 October 2017).

Bhatia, T.K. 2008. 'Major Regional Languages', in B.B. Kachru, Y. Kachru and S.N. Sridhar (eds), *Language in South Asia*, pp 121–31. Cambridge: Cambridge University Press.

Coffey, D., J. Papp and D. Spears. 2015. 'Short-Term Labor Migration from Rural North India: Evidence from New Survey Data', *Population Research and Policy Review*, 34(3), 361–80. https://www.jstor.org/stable/43672135 (accessed 23 January 2019).

Coleho, K. and M. Vijayabhaskar. 2014. 'On the Charts, Off the Tracks: Disconnected Development in Ambur Town, Tamil Nadu', *Economic and Political Weekly*, 49(22), 101–110.

Damodaran, S. and P. Mansingh. 2008. *Leather Industry in India*, CEC Working paper, https://www.cec-india.org/libpdf/1437550410LeatherIndustryinIndia.pdf (accessed 8 December 2020).

EPW 1989. 'Unexploited Potential'. *Economic and Political Weekly*, 24(38), 2099. https://www.jstor.org/stable/4395348 (accessed 21 July 2020).

Lynch, O. 1969. *The Politics of Untouchability: Social Mobility and Social Change in a City of India*. New York: Columbia University Press.

Jeffery, P. 1979. *Frogs in a Well: Indian Women in Purdah*. London: Zed Press.

Jodhka, S.S. 2009. 'The Ravi Dasis of Punjab: Global Contours of Caste and Religious Strife', *Economic & Political Weekly*, 44(24). https://www.epw.in/journal/2009/24/special-articles/ravi-dasis-punjab-global-contours-caste-a nd-religious-strife.html (accessed 8 December 2020).

Juergensmeyer, M. 1988. *Religious Rebels in the Punjab: The Social Vision of Untouchables*. Delhi: Ajanta Publications.

Khan, S. 2020. 'Tanneries in tatters: Country's leather sector on the verge of collapse', *The Economic Times*, https://economictimes.indiatimes.com/small-biz/sme-sector/tanneries-in-tatters-countrys-leather-sector-on-the-verge-of-collapse/articleshow/76438599.cms (accessed 21 July 2020).

Ram, R. 2004. 'Untouchability, Dalit consciousness, and the Ad Dharm movement in Punjab', *Contributions to Indian Sociology*, 34. https://doi.org/10.1177/006996670403800302 (accessed 19 September 2013).

Ram, R. 2009. 'The Ravi Dasis of Punjab: Global Contours of Caste and Religious Strife', *Economic & Political Weekly*, 44(24). https://www.epw.in/journal/2009/24/special-articles/ravi-dasis-punjab-global-contours-caste-and-religious-strife.html (accessed 8 December 2020).

Saberwal, S. 1976. *Mobile Men. Limits to Social Change in Urban Punjab*. New Delhi : Vikas Publishing House.

Saglio-Yatzimirsky, M-C. 2013. *Dharavi, From Mega-Slum to Urban Paradigm*, New Delhi and Abingdon: Routledge.

Sharma, H.C. 1983. 'A Note on Urban Artisans of the British Punjab' *Proceedings of the Indian History Congress* 44, 506512. http://www.jstor.com/stable/44139894 (accessed 21 July 2020).

Singh, G. 2012. 'Transnationalism, Ravidasi Identity and the Dera Sant Sarwan Dass, Ballan', *Sikh Formations: Religion, Culture, Theory*, 8(1), 21–36.

Sujatha, V. 2002. 'Leather Processing: Role of Indigenous Technology', *Economic and Political Weekly*, 37(47), 4,672–5.

Vialles, N. (trans. J.A.Underwood). 1987/1994. *Animal to Edible*. Cambridge: Cambridge University Press.

5

Inheritance Law and Practice in a South Indian Muslim Family, 1860–1984

Sylvia Vatuk

This chapter addresses questions regarding the relationship of law and practice, with specific reference to the Islamic law of inheritance. This issue has been raised more than once by David Powers, historian of Islamic law, who has criticized scholars in his field for 'assuming that the Islamic law of inheritance is the key to understanding the intergenerational transmission of property in Muslim society' (1993a: 13). This assumption, he says, has led to their almost exclusive focus on the 'legal rules' of *shari'a*, to the neglect of 'social processes'—that is, of the many other ways in which, in societies around the Muslim world, property was—and continues to be—transmitted, *in practice,* from one generation to another.

In an earlier publication, Powers traced the development of Islamic inheritance law from the time of the Prophet through the colonial era in Algeria and India, showing that, by the first century AH, 'the law of inheritance had proved to be a serious inconvenience to Muslim proprietors' (1989: 566). Jurists were thus led to 'neutralize' its effects, by teaching that the Qur'anic rules take effect only upon the property owner's death or at the onset of his or her final illness. Thereafter, Muslims were legally free to dispose of their property in any way and to any person they chose fit, as long as they did so during their lifetime. As time went on, Muslim assets were increasingly transferred through such means as pre-mortem gifts, bequests, family endowments, dowries, fictitious sales, and so on, the Islamic laws of succession coming to play 'only a small and relatively unimportant role in the larger system of the intergenerational transmission of property' (1989: 566–67; see also Powers 1993a and 1994b).

Even earlier, J.N.D. Anderson had drawn attention to features of the Islamic Law of inheritance that, from an early period in Islam's history, had 'provoked increasing dissatisfaction' among Muslim property owners (1965: 349–50, 1959: 77–80). And Lucy Carroll has since discussed the matter at some length, with reference to the contemporary Muslim world, saying that 'however highly the [Islamic] law of succession may be eulogized' by Muslim jurists and those Western scholars who have devoted their lives to studying it, 'many are the [Muslim] individuals who feel that, in application to their particular circumstances, that law requires some adjustment' (2001: 245). They may, for example, wish to provide more generously for their wives or daughters than the Islamic rules of intestate succession allow. Or they may worry about the future financial security of an adopted child, an illegitimate child or an 'orphaned grandchild' (*ahfād yatīm*, the child of a previously deceased son or daughter)[1], none of whom is entitled, under *shari'a*, to share in his or her parent's estate (see also Carroll 1994, 1998, 2001).

Social anthropologists who have researched inheritance patterns and other forms of property transmission in Muslim countries around the world have likewise shown how a variety of religiously legitimate ways of *working around* the Islamic succession rules are routinely employed by Muslims, when trying to deal with the kinds of personal and family issues that Powers, Anderson, and Carroll discuss.[2] But these issues have received little attention in the ethnographic or historical literature on South Asia. Here, therefore, I intend to address this lacuna in the scholarly record by describing and analyzing a series of actual cases of the transmission of property within and between the generations, dating from the late nineteenth to the third quarter of the twentieth centuries in a large Muslim extended family or descent group (a *khāndān,* in Urdu), based in the south Indian cities of Madras (now Chennai) and Hyderabad.

Such a discussion seems particularly appropriate in a Festschrift honoring Patricia Jeffery, a leading ethnographer of South Asian Islam who, in the early 1970s, began doctoral research in Bristol on Pakistani migrants to the UK (1976) and then went on to carry out fieldwork among women of *pirzada* families at the shrine of Hazrat Nizamuddin Auliya in Delhi (1979). Her subsequent four decades of research on the lives of women—Hindu as well as Muslim—in rural western Uttar Pradesh has resulted in several books and a multitude of scholarly articles, in one of the more influential of which she raises an issue that underlies the work I am engaged in here, namely, 'the relationship between formal law and theology on the one hand and the lived realities' of Indian women on the other (2001: 1). Although questions of Islamic inheritance have not been one of Jeffery's main concerns, a key theme running through the cited work, as well as in most of her other publications is women's 'lack [of] entitlements to economic resources' (2001: 21), a key cause of which—as she points out in several other works, as well—is the patrilineal inheritance regime that prevails almost everywhere in South Asia among people of all religions and is inextricably connected to the way property is transferred from one generation to the next (cf. Jeffery 1979: 56–7; Jeffery, Jeffery and Lyon 1989: 62–3; Jeffery and Jeffery 1996: 10–11. See also Kozlowski 1987).

Since the main focus of this chapter is on *Muslim* inheritance practices, I begin by providing some background on the Indian system of family law, followed by a summary of the main principles of the Qur'anic laws of intestate succession and a review of recent literature on the actual practice of Muslim inheritance in South Asia, with respect to women's rights, in particular. I then introduce the *khāndān* whose inheritance practices I will examine in more detail, presenting a number of actual case examples to illustrate how, throughout the family's history, its members used both *shari'a* rules of intestate succession *and* a variety of the alternative legal devices mentioned by Powers and others, in order to ensure that their property would pass to those whom they most wished to have it. I conclude with a summary of some of my more important arguments.

The Indian System of Family/Personal Law

Like all modern countries, India has an elaborate hierarchy of courts, a cadre of officially appointed judges, and an extensive body of civil and criminal laws that are applicable to all residents of the country. However, in the area of family or—as it is called in India—'personal' law, there are distinct and separate legal codes for each of the major religious communities in the country.[3] Cases filed under these personal law codes are not, however, heard in religious courts, but in the regular civil courts or—in large cities—in specialized family courts. When presented with a personal law case, a state-appointed judge administers the relevant provisions of whichever code is applicable to those of the petitioner's faith. The judge's *own* faith is irrelevant.

MUSLIM PERSONAL LAW

Muslim personal law is based largely upon Islamic religious law, as modified by over two centuries of precedent-setting case law: decisions laid down by British courts from the late-eighteenth to the mid-twentieth centuries and thereafter by the Supreme Court of the independent Indian state. While mostly uncodified, it includes a small number of statutes, the first of which was enacted in 1913, the most recent in 2019.[4]

In practice, however, only a minority of personal law disputes, regardless of religion, ever reach the courts.[5] Muslims are even less likely than other Indians to file a civil suit when a family conflict arises. One reason is that, whereas in most cases a citizen of any other religion must go to a state court to legally dissolve his or her marriage, a Muslim man can divorce his wife unilaterally and at will (by *talāq*), and thus has no need to approach the state for the purpose. A Muslim woman also has access to an extra-judicial divorce, if she is able to get her husband's agreement to dissolve their marriage by *khulC*, in return for waiving her right to the marriage gift (*mahr*) that he promised her when they wed (see Vatuk 2019). Only if he refuses her request—or if his whereabouts are unknown—nee she resort to filing a suit for divorce under the 1939 Dissolution of Muslim Marriages Act. But relatively few Muslim divorces are handled in this way. Disputes around other personal law matters likewise seldom end up in court. Most often, one or both parties will turn for help to family elders or consult the *jama'at* (governing committee) of their local mosque or a respected religious authority—a *qāzī, muftī*, or *imam*—for advice or mediation. Filing suit in a court of law is, almost always, a last resort.[6]

Islamic Rules of Intestate Succession: The South Asian Context

The rules governing the division of the estate of a deceased Muslim are complicated and, except in the simplest of cases, calculating the proper share for each heir may require specialized expertise that few lay persons possess. In the *khāndān* discussed in this chapter, most adult men and women have at least a general understanding of its basic principles. One of these is that both sexes have inheritance rights, though a female always receives a smaller share than does a male who stands in an equivalent relationship to the deceased. For example, the share of a daughter is half that of a son, a widow's is half of a widower's and so on. In colloquial discourse, an heir's entitlements are generally spoken of in terms of an older Indian currency, in which the *rūpāī* was divided into 16 *āne*. Thus, a man's son is commonly said to inherit 1 *rūpāī* to the daughter's 8 *āne*, while his widow inherits 2 *āne*—in the presence of children—or 4 *āne*—should he have died childless.[7]

Every South Asian country today has laws giving women of any religion rights of inheritance from a parent, spouse, and other close relatives. But, as a number of anthropologists and other social scientists have learned from firsthand investigations, women in the region seldom actually avail themselves of those rights (see White 1991; Agarwal 1994: 249–91; Chowdhry 1997, 2009; Basu 1999: 117–57, 2001; Mehdi 2001; Fazalbhoy 2005, 2012; Baruah 2007, 2010: 25–31, 128–33; Sethi 2009; Arora and Singhi 2009; Deininger et al. 2013; Holden and Chaudhary 2013; Nelson 2013; Kelkar 2014; Vatuk 2022). Whereas a daughter may occasionally receive—at the time of a death or in anticipation of it—an amount of cash, jewelry, or other *movable* items of value (such as, in agricultural or pastoral communities, a cow, goat, or other livestock—see Khatana 1976: 110; Rao 1998: 197–8), she is almost never allotted a share of the deceased's *immovable* property (agricultural land, houses, commercial real estate, or a family business). When her father dies, she typically either explicitly waives her inheritance rights in favor of her brothers or silently acquiesces to their simply distributing the entire estate among themselves.[8] The most common justification for this outcome is that a woman is supported by her father until she marries, thereafter by her husband and the men of her affinal family, and, in later life, by her sons. She therefore has no need for substantial material assets of her own. It is also argued that, according to custom, she has already received—or, if still single, will eventually receive—a dowry, the substantial gift of clothing, household goods, furniture, jewelry and other valuable items (sometimes including cash) given by a woman's natal family when she marries, a portion to her and the rest to her husband and her in-laws.[9] Women themselves typically explain that they avoid claiming their entitlements out of a desire to remain on good terms with their brothers, to whom they may need to turn for help in the event of marital or other difficulties. And most also agree with the majority sentiment that, whatever the circumstances, it is only proper that a family's property remain for generations in the male line of descent.

However, almost all of the research cited above was carried out either in exclusively Hindu communities or in sites with so few Muslims that it was not possible for the researchers to control, when analysing the data, for respondents' religion. Consequently, we know little about Indian *Muslim* inheritance practices, beyond what Fazalbhoy (2005) has written regarding inheritance among elite

Shi'a women in Mumbai and my own piece on the subject, based on interviews carried out in Delhi in 2011 (Vatuk 2022). Jeffery, in her book on the women of the Nizamuddin shrine, mentions women's inheritance rights only briefly. There, in the context of a discussion of women's life-long economic dependence on men, she notes that they

> often do not receive…their entitlement, unless there are no close male relatives…A few men have insisted that their sisters take their due, but many women receive nothing…it is considered honourable for a woman to forgo her rights (1979: 56).

In a later work, she and her co-authors further remark that, in western Uttar Pradesh, '[t]hose few women who are aware of their [legal] entitlements hesitate to demand them from their brothers, their only refuge if their marriage collapses' (Jeffery, Jeffery and Lyon 1989: 62).

The ethnographic literature on Pakistani Muslims help to partially fill this unfortunate gap in our knowledge of South Asian Muslim daughters' inheritance rights and practices. Several anthropologists working in that country have found that women rarely receive what they are entitled to under *shari'a*. Donnan thus writes that, although the Dhund of Rawalpindi District 'recognize that under Muslim Personal Law (Shariat) daughters are entitled to one-half the share which a son inherits from their father, they customarily exclude women from holding land in practice' (1988: 89). More recently, Mehdi (2001) and Holden and Chaudhary (2013) have investigated the matter more thoroughly in other Pakistani settings. They provide extensive case examples and detailed analyses that similarly document women's widespread failure to benefit from *shari'a* rules of intestate inheritance.

A South Indian Sunni Muslim Extended Family

The family whose historical inheritance practices I discuss here belongs to a larger community (*qaum*) called Naiti or Nawayat, members of which are dispersed widely—though in relatively small numbers—throughout southern India. [10] They trace their descent from Arab traders and preachers who came by sea, from Basra—in what is now Iraq—to the western coast of India, as early as the 8th century c.e. (D'Souza 1955; Aziz Jang Bahadur 1976; 'Umari 1963). In the centuries that followed, some moved eastward and southward, the men finding employment in the administrations of a series of Muslim rulers of the Deccan and later in provincial outposts of the Mughal Empire. Among them were several ancestors of this particular extended family (*khāndān*) who, for many generations, had been in government employ, working either as *qāzīs* (Islamic judges), as lower-ranking judicial officers, or in non-judicial administrative or military posts.[11] Whatever they did for a living, however, many also found time to study one or more of the Islamic disciplines, a pursuit regarded as far more important to a man's self-image and social standing than how he supports his family.

This *khāndān* traces its more recent ancestry to an Islamic scholar (*'alim*, pl. *'ulama*) by the name of Muhammad Ghaus,[12] who came to Madras in 1801 from Arcot, the then seat of the Carnatic Nawabs, having been invited by Nawab Azim-ud Daula, newly installed on the Carnatic *masnad* (seat/throne) by the East India Company, to become the Diwan (Chief Minister) of his *sarkār* (government, administration).[13] Both of his sons and most of his grandsons later served, in a variety of posts, under succeeding Nawabs. His elder son, following in his footsteps, eventually became Diwan, as well, under later Nawabs, and the younger —said to have been, from an early age, an unusually brilliant scholar—held a series of junior judicial posts before being appointed in 1844 as Chief Qazi (*qāzī-ul quzāt*) in the court of the last Carnatic Nawab, Muhammad Ghulam Ghaus Khan. As such, he presided over the Nawab's court of judicature (the *mahakama*), administering Islamic law in cases involving members of the Nawab's large circle of family and staff, while also resolving disputes brought to him by other Muslim residents of Madras.

In 1855 the young Nawab unexpectedly died, whereupon the British authorities refused to recognize a successor and proceeded to dismantle the Nawabi establishment. They pensioned off his high-ranking officials—including the Diwan and the Chief Qazi—but left those of lower rank to fend for themselves. So, several younger men of the *khāndān,* having no other source of income, left Madras for Hyderabad to take up employment with the Nizam's government, where, as under the Nawabs, Persian was the official administrative language. With their wives and children they eventually formed, in that city, the core of what became a second branch of the *khāndān*. Following the 1947 partition of British India and the subsequent forceful incorporation of the princely state of Hyderabad into the Indian Union, a few *khāndān* members left for Pakistan, while others have emigrated more recently to other parts of the world, particularly Canada and the United States.[14]

Khāndān Properties

By the time the Nawabi ended, the Diwan and the Qazi had each acquired considerable property, much of it located near the late Nawab's palace on the Madras seashore, where they and their families had lived for decades. But their residences were soon confiscated by the Crown. In 1864, on the Diwan's initiative, they used the money they had received in compensation to purchase a large plot of land on the outskirts of the town. They had several one-story buildings constructed in the traditional, local style—with tile roofs, wide verandahs and enclosed open-air courtyards—to accommodate their households and those of their adult offspring. More houses were later added and, in the early twentieth century, a mosque and an Islamic school (*madrasa),* as well. Boys of the *khāndān* and from elsewhere in Madras still go there to memorize the entire Qur'an (*hifz-i Qur'an*), and thereby earn the title of Hafiz, authorizing them to teach the sacred text to others. On an adjoining site is a small library, housing family records, *fatwas* issued by generations of *qāzīs*, and tens of thousands of books and antique manuscripts, inherited over the years by various individuals from long-ago ancestors.[15]

As Madras expanded, the area in which this family enclave was located became quite central and by 1984 most of the remaining open land within its boundaries had been built upon and had increased greatly in value. These assets—combined with holdings that a few had already owned when the Nawabi was abolished or had been able to acquire more recently with funds from employment, business activities, and investments—formed the basis of whatever wealth members of the *khāndān* have been able to pass on to subsequent generations. Wealth had, of course, never been evenly distributed within the *khāndān* and the resulting variations in economic status within it are reflected in the case examples described below.

Inheritance Practices in the Khāndān

As one would expect in a family with such a strong tradition of Islamic scholarship, members of this *khāndān* regard *shari'a*—and specifically the laws of the Shāfi'ī school, to which they adhere—as binding upon them, not only in matters of inheritance but also in every other sphere of life. The government-appointed Chief Qazi of Tamil Nadu is a member of this *khāndān,* as were the three previous official government *qāzīs*, all descended from the former *qāzī-ul quzāt* in the Nawab's *sarkār.* He has both a Western-style undergraduate education and qualifications from studying Islamic Law and Arabic language at Al Azhar University in Cairo, the world's premier center of Islamic learning.[16] He is widely respected for his religious expertise by the Muslims of Madras and of Tamil Nadu more generally, and is consulted regularly by people all over the state on religio-legal matters, including those related to inheritance.[17] Members of his own *khāndān* also recognize his superior knowledge of such matters and sometimes seek his guidance when trying to decide how to properly divide an estate. However, it is apparent from the cases described below that they have not always felt it necessary to do so, relying instead upon their own or other close family members' (not always accurate) understanding of *shari'a* inheritance law.

Case Studies

The data that I draw upon here were collected by me in the course of a long-term ethnographic and archival study of the family history of the *khāndān*, that began in Hyderabad and Madras in 1983 and continued into the mid-1990s. Most of the case details presented below were shared with me in the winters of 1984 and 1993 in interviews with *khāndān* members whom I had come to know during those years (see fn. 11). Although I have no reason to doubt the accuracy of any of the information I was given, I cannot say, with certainty, that, in every one of the cases I describe, the property in question was in fact distributed precisely as I have indicated. This is, in part, because many of those to whom I spoke described inheritance transactions that had occurred many years ago, which they may not have been able to recall with exactitude. Furthermore, some of my interlocutors had been interested parties in the transactions they described; this may well have affected their perspectives on, and what they chose to tell me about, the circumstances surrounding certain past inheritance transactions. Some narratives may also have been altered because of privacy concerns and/or because of the narrator's awareness that I would be interviewing other parties to the same event at some later time. It is also very possible that I have misinterpreted some of what I was told or have inadvertently filled gaps in my fieldnotes with assumptions of my own that were not firmly based in fact. Despite these caveats, I believe that my account of these transactions is close enough to 'what really happened' to support and illustrate my main argument: namely that *shari'a* inheritance rules provide Muslims with a variety of approved means by which to transfer property to their preferred recipients, of which lay Muslims, in India as elsewhere, have made—and presumably continue to make—abundant use .

ESTATES DISTRIBUTED ACCORDING TO SHARI'A

In most of the instances I have recorded, it is important to note, the men and women of this *khāndān* divided the property of a deceased family member strictly in accordance with *shari'a* rules for intestate succession. The entitlements of female heirs were usually honored—something that is not always the case, as I have shown, in other South Asian Muslim communities. The women of this *khāndān* were thus, by comparison with the generality of Indian women—Muslim or otherwise—in a favorable position, in terms of their ability to inherit, own, and control property. The right of daughters and wives to inherit both movable property and real estate was explicitly acknowledged, and most adult women of middle age and above did, in fact, own property—including real estate—acquired through inheritance, purchase, gifts, and other means. Furthermore, throughout the *khāndān's* history, there are numerous examples of women who, despite living largely secluded lives, engaged actively in financial activities, buying and selling real estate and other goods in their own names, collecting rent, paying expenses and, in some cases, investing their profits elsewhere.

In the 1920s, for example, one woman organized the group purchase of a market in the northern part of Madras that in 1993 was still being managed by one of her male descendants, providing a regular income to 163 *khāndān* shareholders from the rents paid by its vendors. A daughter-in-law of the *khāndān's* founding ancestor is likewise described by her husband's biographer as having been an excellent money manager. Her husband, an important official in the Nawab's court, had received a large lump sum payment from the British when his position was abolished in the late 1850s. From it, he is said to have set aside 500 rupees for each child, to be given to them on their wedding day. But, since they were all still too young to marry, he entrusted the money to his wife. She, instead of buying jewelry (as, her biographer presumably believed *most* women would have done), bought real estate. Thus, after her husband's early death, she was able to educate her sons well with the income from her investments, giving them a good start on their successful adult careers ('Umari 1963: 504).

For a more recent example, in the 1950s two sisters received their prescribed Quranic shares of a large Hyderabad house that had belonged to their father. At the time, both were married and living in their marital homes, so they rented out the rooms in the house they had inherited, managed it jointly, and, after paying any expenses, divided the remaining income between them. When the elder sister passed away, her children—three daughters and a son—inherited her share, again in accordance with *shari'a.* Thereafter, the house's net rental income was divided each month among the five surviving owners, in accordance with the respective Qur'anic shares to which each was entitled.

Another Hyderabad house and its adjoining shops were distributed in a similar manner among its owner's heirs. However, before the owner died, he had written an affidavit, expressing his desire that his heirs keep the property undivided and that it never be sold, so that any of his offspring or descendants who wished to do so could live in it, free of cost. The document also provided that the income from the shops and the proceeds from any portions of the building that they might wish to let out, should be divided among his heirs according to the same Qur'anic principles: namely 1 *rūpāī* to each son; 8 *āne* to each daughter; and 2 *āne* to his wife. As it happened, his wife died before he did, so the entire estate was inherited by his children, who honored his wishes. Likewise, in accordance with *shari'a,* his orphaned grandchildren—the offspring of a son who had predeceased him—were not provided for in any way.

In whatever way a deceased person's property was transferred to his or her descendants, it often happened—as in this and other cases—that its formal division (*taqsīm*) was delayed, often for many years, sometimes even for a generation or more. The eldest son of the deceased usually acts as manager of the jointly held property. But sometimes, especially if the property includes income-producing real estate, another more competent brother, brother's wife, or even a mother or sister, will manage it for the benefit of the various shareholders (*hissedār*), distributing the proceeds on a regular basis according to their respective ownership shares. Thus, for example, an unmarried daughter of the above-mentioned man had already taken over the management of the shops that adjoined his residence and was still in this role when I met her in 1984: paying the electricity bills, the taxes and maintenance expenses and distributing the remaining profit among her siblings.

Even though women's inheritance rights were generally acknowledged by members of this *khāndān*, daughters did not always receive all that they were entitled to when their deceased parent's estate was distributed. This was usually because they had either refrained from pressing a claim or had explicitly renounced it in favor of some other member of their family. I was told by one woman that, from her early childhood, her widowed mother repeatedly impressed upon her and her sisters that, when she died, she wanted the house in which they lived to go to the orphaned children of their deceased brother. When she passed away, all three respected their mother's wishes and, instead of taking their designated shares of the inheritance, had, as she put it to me, 'sacrificed ourselves for our nephews'.

Another woman was said to have waived her right to a share of both parents' estates for a very different reason. Years before they had so strongly opposed her choice of a husband that, when she nevertheless insisted on marrying him, they had refused to host the wedding. Much earlier, a daughter of the *khāndān's* founding ancestor had still another motive for giving up her shares of her father's estate. As the story goes, when the estate was being divided, she had asked to be given a particular piece of his property. But her brothers were unwilling to part with it and offered another parcel, as a substitute. But she rejected it and, although they kept that piece of land aside for her until the end of her life—in hopes that she would change her mind—she never relented. After her death, her sons—and then their heirs—had similarly refused to take ownership of it.

ALTERNATIVE ARRANGEMENTS MADE DURING AN OWNER'S LIFETIME

Although most *khāndān* men and women left their assets to be distributed after their deaths, others made arrangements to have their possessions apportioned during their lifetime. Methods that have been employed for centuries, alone or in combination, by Muslims all over the world who find themselves in such situations, include pre-mortem gifts (*hiba*, pl. *hibāt*), family trusts or endowments (*waqf*, pl. *auqāf*), bequests (*waṣīyya*), and private agreements with prospective heirs.

Certain family situations are especially likely to lead a Muslim property owner to dispose of—or make arrangements for the future disposal of—his or her assets, before dying. The most common such situation is one in which an adult child dies during the parents' lifetime, leaving one or more surviving offspring. The issue of women's lesser inheritance rights may also come into play at such a time. For example, a childless man might wish his wife to get his entire estate, rather than the mere one-quarter that she would receive if it were left to be distributed after his death. Similarly, a man with one or more daughters but no son might want the former to have everything he owns, rather than allow a significant proportion of his estate—one-half, if he has one daughter, one-third, if there are two or more—to go to his brothers, brothers' sons, or, in their absence, a more distantly related collateral kinsman.

Pre-mortem Gifts: Hibāt (Sg. Hiba)

Islamic law allows one to make a pre-mortem gift (*hiba*), in any amount, to whomever one chooses—with the important condition that the recipient must actually take possession of the property before one dies. If the gift is only *promised*, but not formally handed over and accepted by the recipient, the transfer is invalid (on the law of *hiba*, see Fyzee 1974: 217–73; Hidayatullah and Hidayatullah 1990: 112–42; Pearl and Menski 1998: 487–93; AIMPLB 2002: 137–44). *Khāndān* property owners who wished to avoid having their estates divided after death frequently handed over some or all of their assets to a preferred recipient during their lifetime, most often by using this device.

One woman with four sons and one daughter disposed of her entire property in this way during her lifetime. She and her husband each owned separate parcels of real estate. Both of them agreed that their respective holdings should be divided among all five children, equally, rather than allowing the sons to get twice as much as the daughter—as would happen, were their estates left to be distributed after their deaths. She decided to handle this by formally gifting her entire property, as *hibāt*, to each of the five, in equal proportions.[18]

A man sometimes gave real estate, cash, or other valuables in *hiba* to his wife, so that, if widowed, she would have more than the minimal shares to which she would be entitled, were the estate left to be divided after his death.[19] In 1892, an early migrant to Hyderabad who had been able to secure a highly responsible and well-paid position in the Nizam's administration, purchased a 2½ acre plot of land on the edge of town. On the land was a mansion built in the late eighteenth century by a French general who had served for years in a previous Nizam's army.[20] Next to that structure, the new owner constructed another large residence to house his growing family, which eventually included seven children: five sons and two daughters. Some years later he legally transferred ownership of the entire property, as *hiba,* to his wife. All of his offspring were still alive when he died in 1907, but his widow lived to a very old age, during which two of her sons and both daughters passed away, three of them leaving young children. At some point, she made over a portion of the land, as *hiba,* to one of her orphaned granddaughters. Then, in 1953, when she was preparing to go to Mecca for *hajj,* she transferred the rest of the property to her three surviving sons, who did not formally divide it but kept it intact up to and even after her death in 1959 at the age of 93.

In 1965, by which time the city had begun to grow up around it and the location had become very desirable, the three brothers accepted a lucrative offer from a developer. One of the brothers was unwilling to vacate the house in which he and his family were residing, so the three agreed to leave that building, and some adjoining shops that their mother had purchased many years ago, out of the sale. They divided the proceeds of the sale evenly among them. Then, out of his share, the first brother paid the other two an agreed-upon amount for full title to his house and the adjoining shops. Although the children of their four deceased siblings had no legal claim to any part of the sales price, each of the brothers voluntarily set aside about 15 percent of what they had earned from the sale and divided it among their orphaned nephew and nieces, twice as much to the males as to the females.

The other two brothers each purchased new homes on the outskirts of Hyderabad. But in 1984 all but two of the third brother's offspring still lived with their families in the house that had been kept out of the 1965 sale. An unmarried son, a government employee serving in a rural area of the state, came back to stay there on holidays, while a married daughter, living in Madras in her husband's natal home, visited from time to time, usually for several weeks or months.

Trusts/Endowments: Auqāf (sg. Waqf)

Another way in which *khāndān* men and women transferred property without being subject to the law of intestate succession, was by setting up a trust (*waqf,* pl. *auqāf*) for the benefit of their children and future descendants (on the law of *waqf* see Fyzee 1974: 274–332; Qureshi 1990; Hidayatullah and Hidayatullah 1990: 143–202; Pearl and Menski 1998: 493–503; Hoexter 1998; Kader 1999; AIMPLB 2002: 201–16; and Abbasi 2012).[21] A number of such *auqāf* were extant in the family in 1984 and doubtless still are today. One of the earliest was set up by the sons of the *khāndān* founder, who had served as Diwan and Chief Qazi, respectively, under the last Nawab of the Carnatic. This is a relatively small *waqf,* its purpose being to pay for the recitations of the *fatiha* (the opening *sura* of the Qur'an) on the anniversaries of their deaths.

Another *waqf* was endowed by a daughter-in-law of the founding ancestor who—also in the late nineteenth century—purchased a piece of land on the then-outskirts of Madras, to be used in perpetuity as a *khāndān* cemetery. And a son of the last Nawab's Chief Qazi put a house he owned in *waqf,* so that his offspring and their future descendants could always live there, rent-free.

A much larger *waqf,* this one established by the Chief Qazi's sister, holds part of a large piece of property within the bounds of the *khāndān* enclave in Madras that her husband—a first cousin—had inherited from his father, the Diwan. He had given it to her in *hiba*, some say in recognition of the fact that she was a far better money manager than he. He is remembered as a man of great generosity who allegedly found it difficult to ignore the pleas of the many who came to importune him for loans that were seldom repaid! During her lifetime, this woman, when widowed, donated part of the property to build the *khāndān's* mosque, the *madrasa*, and the library mentioned above. She later put the rest of her holdings—a connected series of residential structures that came to be known within the *khāndān* as the Big House (*bara ghar*)—into a *waqf* for the benefit of her descendants. As donor (*wāqif*), she specified that it should never be divided or sold, but be kept for any of her descendants (*aulād*) who might wish to live there, free of charge. The rental income from several attached shops along the roadside were to be used for its upkeep and other expenses. For decades after her death the *bara ghar* was occupied by a changing series of *khāndān* families, managed by one of her daughters who also collected the rents from the shops, disbursed the excess income among the donor's heirs according to *shari'a* principles, and for some time also made arrangements for the feeding of its residents.

In a more recent generation, an unmarried, childless man put the rental income of property he had purchased with income earned from his own business into a *waqf* to provide scholarships for needy *khāndān* children. He appointed trustees to manage the trust. Later, when one of the trustees died, there was a move to have his son replace him. But other trustees objected to using a hereditary principle to fill the vacancy, starting a dispute that was still going on in the 1980s. I was told that one of the objectors regarded the *waqf's* very creation as an offense against the rule that one may not give away by will more than one-third of one's property, proposing that, to save the deceased donor from the consequences of that 'sin,' his heirs should insist upon its being divided among themselves as *shari'a* dictates. However, the heirs were not persuaded by his interpretation of the law nor of its relevance to the case at hand and declined to take such action.[22]

Bequests: waṣīt (pl. waṣītīn)

Shari'a places strict limits on a Muslim's testamentary freedom (for the law of bequests, see Coulson 1971: 213–58; Fyzee 1974: 355–74; Hidayatullah and Hidayatullah 1990: 104–8; Pearl and Menski 1998: 448–52; AIMPLB 2002: 145–61). The main limitation is that a Muslim cannot dispose of more than one-third of his or her property in a will (*waṣīyya*). The remainder must be distributed in accordance with the rules of intestate succession. Sunni law also prevents a testator from favoring one or more legal heir over others, by laying down the further condition that one may not make a bequest (*wirṣa*) to a legal heir. Furthermore, the terms of a will cannot result in the denial or diminution of a legal heir's inheritance rights—unless the latter agrees, *after* the testator's death, to waive them.

It was fairly common in this *khāndān* for men and women who wished to control the way their property would be divided after their deaths to record their wishes in a written will (*wasīyatnāma*), although they did not always observe the one-third limit on the amount bequeathed. I mentioned above the couple who agreed to divide their respective estates equally among their five children. While the wife handled the matter by making them pre-mortem gifts, the husband chose instead to write a will, in which he directed that his entire estate—most of which consisted of rental property—be divided in equal proportions among the five. To further ensure that his wishes would be carried out, he showed the document to his sons and secured their agreement to its terms. When the time came, they kept their promise to allot one-fifth of the property to their sister, as well as to themselves. However, they did not formally divide it and in 1984 were still managing it jointly, dividing the rental income each month into five equal parts and sending their sister's share to her affinal home in another city.[23]

But sometimes a testator's heirs did not honor the terms of the will. For example, one *khāndān* grandmother's desire to secure a future for the children of a deceased son was not fulfilled. Her son had died at a fairly young age, leaving two wives and several children by each. She owned a great deal of property and wanted his children to have that share of her assets that would have been his, had he survived her. She wrote a will, making them the beneficiaries, and showed it to each of her offspring, having them sign a pledge to share her estate with their fatherless nephews and nieces when she died. However, when the time came, they reneged on their promise and divided her assets entirely among themselves. Had their deceased brother's children taken the matter to court, the will might have been upheld, but they were still quite young at the time. In any case, to file a civil suit over a family matter of this kind is something that few Muslims in their position would have considered doing, even if they had help and the necessary knowledge, skills, and financial wherewithal to embark on such a time-consuming and unpredictable venture.

A Mid-Nineteenth-Century Will

Whereas members of the *khāndān* described to me the contents of several wills, often in considerable detail, I was never shown an actual copy of one. However, the full text of a nineteenth-century *wasīyatnāma,* prepared by Nawab Ghulam Ghaus Khan's Bakshi (Military Paymaster)—a grandson of the *khāndān's* founding ancestor—is translated from the original Persian and reproduced in both languages in 'Umari's account of the *khāndān*'s early history (1963: 527–31).[24] The Bakshi wrote it two months before his death in July 1866, at the age of 56, leaving two widows, three daughters and five sons by his second wife and two daughters by the third.[25] In a series of twelve clauses he makes reference to two of the most commonly used pre-mortem property-transfer devices available to a religious Muslim: the *hiba* and the *waqf.* Thus, he mentions having given (*hiba kar dīyā*) to each wife full ownership rights in her own residence and its contents, a gold watch to his eldest son and a silver one to his elder daughter's husband, a son of his mother's brother. He puts his books—to the disposal of which members of this scholarly *khāndān* always paid special attention—into a *waqf,* assigning responsibility for their care to whoever among his offspring (*aulād*) was capable of making good use of them.

He puts most of the remainder of his estate—representing the bulk of his assets—into a second *waqf* for the maintenance of a traveler's inn (*sarāī*), constructed for him several years before in a suburb northwest of the town, assigning its management to 'those of my offspring who are grown.' At the time, his oldest son was only 10 years old and, although 'Umari does not say who served as the *waqf's* trustee (*mutawalli*) until he came of age, it is likely to have been his second wife's brother (his own mother's brother's son), one of two witnesses to his signing of the *wasīyatnāma* and the one to whom, on his deathbed, he personally entrusted the document.[26]

The Bakshi explicitly notes that, because he still has the responsibility of marrying off his two youngest daughters (one by each of his surviving wives), neither of them is to share in his estate. Should they still be single when he dies, his heirs are to sell his remaining personal possessions[27] and, after paying for his funeral and other related ritual expenses, use the remaining proceeds for the girls' weddings.[28] As for his married daughter, he notes that, 'having already received her due' (presumably referring to the trousseau (*jahez*) he presented at her nuptials, two years before),[29] she will likewise have no share in his estate.

Private Agreements with Heirs

Several parents in this *khāndān,* instead of employing one of the devices described above, simply informed their children, ahead of time, that they wished them to deviate from the way in which the estate would otherwise, according to *shari'a,* be distributed upon their deaths. They often extracted from their prospective heirs a promise—either orally or in writing—to honor those wishes when the time came. On several occasions, however, their heirs reneged on those promises. See above for one example, concerning a widow's thwarted desire to provide for her orphaned grandchildren.

A particularly complicated situation, in which no agreement had been reached before the property-owner's death, involved the heirs of one of the first men to migrate to Hyderabad after the Carnatic Nawabi was dismantled. Well-educated in Persian, he had been able, upon his arrival, to secure a fairly high-ranking position in the Nizam's administration and soon purchased a substantial house in a central city location, roomy enough to accommodate not only his immediate family, but also those of several related later arrivals from Madras. He and his wife had two sons and four daughters, two of whom died in childhood. A third daughter grew to adulthood, married and had two daughters of her own, but also predeceased him. When he died, therefore, his only heirs were his wife, his two sons and one surviving daughter. It was well-understood, by all concerned, that his motherless granddaughters would not inherit and he apparently made no effort to rectify their situation.

After his death, however, but before his estate could be settled, it became known that his sons had managed to secretly take away and sell some jewelry that their deceased sister had left to her daughters when she died. Upon discovering what they had done, their surviving sister insisted that they compensate their orphaned nieces by giving them a share of their grandfather's property. They complied, signing over a portion of his dwelling to the two young women before distributing the rest of the estate in accordance with the rules of *shari'a.*

Marriage Strategies

Another way in which property owners can try to control the disposition of their assets is through the strategic arrangement of their children's marriages. Close kin marriage has a long history in Islam. The only kinsmen sexually forbidden to a Muslim woman are those in the kinship category of *maharam*—a word derived from the Arabic *harām,* meaning 'sacred,' or 'private.' They include her father and other male ascendants, her parents' brothers, her own brothers, her siblings' sons, her own sons and other male descendants. These are the only males permitted entry into the private area of her home, the only males with whom she, as a respectable woman, may freely associate. All other men, whether related or not, fall into the category of *nāmaharam* and are *potentially* marriageable. But, in practice, her spouse will be chosen from only a very limited and carefully selected segment thereof.

As is usual in South Asia, *khāndān* marriages were—and to a considerable extent, still are—arranged by the parents or other elders of the young people concerned. Until fairly recently, the young people had little or no input into the choice of a life partner. Once they had attained puberty, children of the opposite sex, even those living within the same extended family household, were prevented, as far as possible, from interacting with one another. Any attempt on a young person's part to choose his or her own mate—even one within the permitted degrees of kinship relatedness—was immediately thwarted by the parents and, should the pair nevertheless persist in pursuing their desire to wed, both would be severely punished, and the girl usually hastily married off to someone else.

The most desirable match was regarded as one that joined close kinsmen, preferably first cousins. Such matches were very common and often came about through agreements between adult siblings of the same or opposite sex to marry their respective children to one another when the latter reached marriageable age. In earlier generations such agreements were sometimes concluded when the children were very young—occasionally even before they were born, though the marriage would not be consummated until the bride had reached puberty or later. By the beginning of the twentieth century, however, parents had begun to wait until their children reached late adolescence or young adulthood before making any final decisions about their marriages (see Vatuk 2014).

In some Muslim communities the preferred marriage is between patrilateral parallel cousins (father's brother's daughter/father's brother's son—see Kressel 1986; Holy 1989), but in this *khāndān* there was no strong marriage preference for this or any other specific cousin. In fact, genealogies indicate that a woman more often married a cousin on her mother's, than on her father's side (i.e., a mother's brother's or mother's sister's son, rather than the son of a father's brother or sister). This was perhaps a consequence of the leading role that women played in the matchmaking process (cf. Vatuk 2014).

To what extent property considerations in fact entered into matchmaking decisions in this *khāndān* is impossible to say, but it is clear that in a number of instances the choices parents made for their children had the result of keeping family property from passing into other lines of descent. One example can be seen in the alliances that two sets of siblings—themselves related by marriage—contracted in the 1960s for their combined eight daughters. Two of the daughters married matrilateral cross-cousins (mother's brother's sons) and two married matrilateral parallel cousins (mother's sister's sons). A fifth was engaged to a matrilateral parallel cousin (mother's sister's son) when still a child but—for unknown reasons—was eventually wed to a more distant relative. The sixth daughter was the only one who married a cousin on her father's side, while the other two remained unmarried. Whether it was the parents' deliberate intention or not, one consequence of the way this series of marriages were arranged, is that most of the property that had originally belonged to the young women's grandparents—on both sides—came to be held exclusively by members of this close cohort of first cousins.

Mahr

Another way in which property can be taken out of an estate before a man's death is by his handing over to his wife her *mahr*, the gift of money or other valuables that a man must present—or at least *promise*—to his bride on their wedding day. The amount of the gift—agreed-upon *before* the marriage—must be entered into the marriage contract (*nikāhnāma*) at its signing, in order for the marriage to be legally valid. Whereas in much of the Muslim world the *mahr* is customarily paid at the wedding ceremony, in full or in part, either to the bride herself or to her marriage guardian (*walī*) (see, for example, Maher 1974; Moors 1995), in South Asia, however—at least among Sunnis—it is seldom handed over 'promptly' (*mu'ajjal*). More often it is simply noted in the *nikāhnāma* as 'deferred' (*muwajjal*) to some unspecified future time. In some cases, a man pays it to his wife later in the marriage. Otherwise, it becomes due upon divorce or upon the husband's death. In the latter case, it is treated as a debt, to be paid before the man's estate is distributed. In practice, however, most South Asian women—whether married, divorced, or widowed—never receive it (see, for example, Jeffery 2001: 57–9).[30]

As for *mahr* in this *khāndān*, a family biographical register (Majid 1984) details the amounts given (or promised) to every woman married from the beginning of the nineteenth century to the 1980s. It documents the fact that, unlike most other South Asian Muslims, this family has long had a practice of giving a fixed *mahr* amount, rather than negotiating it anew, before each wedding. Thus, with very few exceptions, the *mahr* was either 39 *tolās* of gold or 480 *dirhāns*—an old Arabian coin.[31] Whether or not the amounts were actually handed over—at the wedding or on some later occasion—or were simply entered into the *nikāhnāma* as 'deferred', is not indicated.

One Hyderabad member of the *khāndān*, an office worker of middling rank in the Nizam's service, died in 1965, leaving a widow and six children—three sons and three daughters. Before his death he had transferred the title of his house to his wife, specifically, according to what I was told, in lieu of the *mahr* that he had promised her when they wed. This meant that its value was not included in the estate when the remainder of his property was distributed among his heirs. I was not able to determine whether this is what he had promised her when they wed or was simply being exceptionally generous when he decided to pay.[32]

Childless Property Owners

Men and women who had no children often gifted property, during their lifetime, to the child of a deceased sibling or sometimes even to one whose parents were still alive.[33] A childless woman might have taken a major role in bringing up the child and, therefore, would have had a particularly compelling reason for wishing to provide for his or her financial future. If she did not do so during her lifetime—typically by gifting her property to the child by *hiba*—her estate would be divided, after her death, among her living siblings and their children, or among other, more distant, relatives. In one case, a childless widow gave to her *own* sisters' children (whom she had helped to raise) the jewelry she had received in her dowry, while she gave items given by her *in-laws* to the children of her late-husband's siblings.

Adopted Children

Whereas adoption is allowed in Islam, an adoptee is not entitled, under the law of intestate succession, to inherit any share of the adoptive parent's estate. In this *khāndān,* children whose mother had died were almost always raised by their mother's or father's sister or by some other close relative—even if, as in some cases, the father was still alive. But formal adoptions were not very common. I learned about only one case in which an adopted child's lack of inheritance rights became an issue. A childless couple had adopted a daughter of the husband's sister's son. The husband and his sisters had earlier inherited a building from their father, of which he had received a one-half share and each sister one-quarter. Out of concern for his adopted daughter's future, he had bought out his sisters' shares in that building with money obtained by selling another property that he owned outright. Now sole owner of the inherited building, he gave it in *hiba* to his wife, with the idea that, after his death, she would be able to comfortably support herself and the child. However, when he died, his sisters reportedly denied the existence of the *hiba* and insisted that the building be divided, along with the rest of their brother's estate, according to *shari'a*.

INHERITANCE DISPUTES IN THE COURTS

As I have indicated above, inheritance matters were almost always dealt with privately, within the *khāndān*, by the individuals and families concerned, sometimes assisted by a respected kinsman knowledgeable about Islamic jurisprudence. If a dispute could not be settled in this way, one or more of the parties might decide to explore other avenues. Occasionally they sought professional legal advice, preferably from a law graduate within the *khāndān,* but otherwise from a trusted outsider. Muhammad Hamidullah, one of the first *khāndān* men to study law, graduated from Osmania University in 1930 with a degree in International law[34] and was asked in 1948 to arbitrate between two sets of step-siblings, close relatives of his, over how to divide their father's estate between the offspring of his first and third wives. Advising them against taking the matter to the civil court, he instead engaged engineers in Madras and in Hyderabad to appraise the properties owned by the deceased in each city. On the basis of their reports, he worked out an equitable allotment of the holdings among the various heirs, taking into consideration their relationships to the deceased, their places of residence, and their genders. The deceased's first wife (who had passed away many years before) had been a Hyderabadi woman, while his third wife had been born in Madras and still lived there. She owned other properties in that city, which her children were in line to inherit upon her death. This was doubtless one of the considerations leading him to propose that the Madras properties be allotted to *her* offspring and the Hyderabad properties to those of her predecessor.

There are only a few examples in the *khāndān* of an intra-family property dispute being taken to the civil courts for adjudication. One such instance involved a man of the *khāndān*'s third generation who, in the late 19th century, while acting as manager of an undivided estate, is alleged to have contrived to do his siblings and their descendants out of a portion of their rightful shares of the jointly held property. This led to a very long-running dispute that was unresolved for more than half a century, by which time the number of shareholders had grown to over 20 individuals. At some point, a suit was filed by those who considered themselves or their ancestors to have been cheated. Finally, in the 1950s, after a lengthy series of proceedings, the case was settled out of court.

Another case taken to court also ended up with an out-of-court settlement. A widow had inherited from her late husband the house in which they lived. Early on, she had told family members that she wished it to go, after her death, to two of her daughters, to the exclusion of a third daughter and two sons. However, she never took the step of transferring the title of the house to her favored recipients. At some point, wishing to certify their responsibility for paying the annual house tax, she registered a statement to that effect with the municipal authorities. Later, needing money for repairs, she mortgaged the house to a Hindu moneylender, stating in the mortgage agreement that she was its sole owner. After her death, one of her sons brought a court case against his two sisters, questioning the significance of the municipal registration and contending that his mother had never intended to disinherit him and her two other offspring.

This case dragged on for several years before the parties reached a settlement that required selling the house, so that the proceeds could be shared among them according to *shari'a* succession rules. In part because the house had been in litigation, they had difficulty finding a buyer and were eventually forced to sell it to the mortgage holder at a reduced price. The long-running dispute created very bad relations among the siblings, who for a long time did not speak to or visit one another. Finally—as I was told by the original litigant—the husband of one of his sisters brought them all together, inviting them to share a meal at their home and, at its conclusion, having them embrace one another (*gale lagnā*) to reconcile their differences.

Conclusion

There is a massive body of literature on inheritance in Islamic law, focusing largely on describing and analyzing the legal rules of *shari'a* and some of their historical, economic and social implications over the course of its long history. Less has been written about how real Muslim men and women, throughout history and into the present, have actually proceeded, when faced with the problem that confronts not only Muslims but people of all religions, all over the world: namely, who will take possession of their belongings when they die. As a number of scholars have pointed out, whereas *shari'a* lays down strict guidelines for distributing the assets of a Muslim who has died intestate, it also provides a number of options for the religiously observant individual who, for whatever reason, wishes to make alternative arrangements for the disposal of his or her property, while he or she is still alive.

That such religiously approved devices as wills, trusts, and pre-mortem gifts have been used extensively over the course of many centuries in Muslim societies of the Middle East and elsewhere, has been abundantly documented by historians—using Ottoman and other court records from earlier centuries (e.g., Doumani 1998)—as well as by anthropologists who have conducted fieldwork in those regions and investigated *actual practices* of property transmission in the communities they studied (e.g., Maher 1974; Moors 1995; Bowen 1996).

Insofar as South Asia is concerned, the study of Muslim personal law has recently attracted the attention of a number of scholars—legal anthropologists, sociologists, and political scientists—whose work forms the core of a rich and growing body of literature exploring the ways in which its provisions impact the everyday lives of Muslims in the region. To date, they have focused primarily on issues of marriage and divorce (e.g., Subramanian 2008, 2014; Solanki 2011; Tschalaer 2017; Lemons 2018, 2019; Vatuk 2005, 2019; Redding 2020), though questions about inheritance have been raised less often. To the extent that we have any firsthand information from the region about inheritance *practices*—as distinct from inheritance *laws*—it is almost entirely in connection with the important issue of Muslim *women's* widespread inability to access the inheritance rights accorded to them by *shari'a* (see Fazalbhoy 2005, 2012; Holden and Chaudhary 2013; Mehdi 2001; Nelson 2013; Vatuk 2022).

It is in an effort to broaden our scholarly perspective on inheritance practices among Indian Muslims that I have described here and discussed some of the myriad ways in which the members of one large south Indian Muslim descent group transferred their assets from one generation to another over the course of more than a century. I have found that, in most cases, members of this religiously observant *khāndān* left it up to their heirs to distribute their estates after death and that, in doing so, almost always adhered strictly to *shari'a* rules, including recognizing the rights of female heirs. Yet, as I have also shown, there were times when property owners found Islamic succession rules to be—as Powers put it—a 'serious inconvenience' (1989: 566) to their ability to provide financially for a favored recipient. Consequently, before death, they took actions to ensure that their property was distributed differently from the way it would have been, had they died intestate. They made pre-mortem gifts or put all or a portion of their assets into a trust. Some resorted to writing a will, though that device did not always achieve its intended purpose. Individual motives for seeking an alternative arrangement for distributing property naturally varied. The most frequent recipients of premortem gifts or bequests were grandchildren whose parent had predeceased them and who therefore had no inheritance rights under *shari'a* law. Sometimes a sonless man or woman gave property to a daughter to prevent the bulk of the estate from going to more distantly related male collaterals. Men occasionally made a gift to a wife or paid her a generous *mahr,* in order to make sure that she was more generously endowed in widowhood than *shari'a* rules of intestate succession allow, or because he recognized that her superior financial management skills could be deployed for the benefit of the entire family, even during his lifetime! The writers of wills were motivated by a similar range of considerations, while the rationales behind the decisions of others to place property in trust for future generations and for specific purposes were more idiosyncratic and can only be unraveled on a case-by-case basis.

In her introduction—co-authored with Kaveri Qureshi—to a recently published collection of articles on 'the Muslim woman'—Jeffery has forcefully critiqued the 'malicious images' that have circulated for centuries and continue to 'pervade dominant discourses' about Muslim women, as—among other things—'backward, passive, mute, cloistered and victimized by Islamic precepts.' To counter these tenacious stereotypes, they urge that we seek to learn about, and to present for our readers, the diversity of women's 'everyday lives and voices, in all their richness and complexity' (Jeffery and Qureshi 2022). I have endeavored to follow their example, while applying it to the question of how Muslims are portrayed and how Muslim inheritance law, in particular, is understood—by legal scholars, as well as by members of the public—to be practiced.

There has long been a stereotype—a 'malicious image,' in Jeffery's and Qureshi's terms—of Muslims as bound so tightly by the rigid dictates of the Qur'an and the laws based upon its teaching, that they are unable to think for themselves. But, in reality, like followers of any other religion, observant Muslim men and women, while striving in their everyday lives to serve their God and act in accordance with His guidance, must, at the same time, make their way through life, as best they can, figuring out, as they go along, how to survive and how to ensure the survival of those they love. They accommodate themselves to the situations in which they find themselves, guided, on the one hand, by the ideals and the rules of proper behavior that they were taught by their elders and by the respected leaders of their community, but, on the other hand, also making use of all permissible strategies available to them, in order to achieve their personal goals.

When it comes to the disposition of their material possessions, they have options within the confines of Islamic law. The choices they make vary from one individual to another, depending upon their knowledge and experience, and on such factors as their gender, age, education, the size and demographic composition of their family, the quality of the relationships among its members, the amount of property they own, of what it consists, where it is located, and so on. Thus, the specific examples of property transmission that I have presented here, drawn from the history of a particular south Indian extended family, illustrate what previous writers on the subject have urged us to recognize: namely, that Islamic law—in addition to its widely discussed, analyzed, and debated rules for intestate succession—provides a variety of ways of passing on property, available to anyone who finds those rules inappropriate to their particular circumstances. Throughout history these options have been extensively used by men and women throughout the Muslim world, including in South Asia. In this sphere of life, the religious law, far from tying its followers' hands and preventing them from providing materially in the way that they wish for those who will succeed them, actually gives the faithful considerable freedom to do so in a manner that meets, to a considerable extent, their individual preferences, desires and needs.

NOTES

1. The English translation of this term is a bit misleading. Whereas in English an orphan is usually understood to be a child who has lost *both* parents, in Arabic it also applies to a child only *one* of whose parents is deceased.
2. In this connection, Powers (1993a) specifically cites the work in Yemen of anthropologists Martha Mundy (1979) and Tomas Gerholm (1985). Studies by Vanessa Maher (1974) in Morocco and, more recently, by Annelies Moors (1995) in Palestine, and Bowen (1996) in Indonesia provide additional evidence of the variety of on-the-ground inheritance practices to be found in Muslim cultures around the world.
3. The origins of this system date from precolonial times (see, for example, Cohn 1996; Rudolph and Rudolph 2001).
4. The relevant statutes are the Mussalman Wakf Validating Act 1913, the Muslim Personal Law (Shariat) Application Act 1937, the Dissolution of Muslim Marriages Act 1939, the Muslim Women (Protection of Rights on Divorce) Act 1986, and the Muslim Women (Protection of Rights on Marriage) Act 2019. The first two of these had certain positive implications for women's inheritance rights, though their practical impact was minimal.
5. Reasons for avoiding the courts range from the cost—in money and time—to the risk of harm to one's reputation among members of a close-knit community. Lack of knowledge of the applicable laws and of the procedures involved in obtaining 'justice' via that route is another important factor, particularly for the substantial segment of the female populace who are minimally educated, if at all.
6. Not surprisingly, a review of appellate case law shows that men or women with substantial means are those most likely to take an inheritance dispute to the courts. Furthermore, in a plurality of such cases, the deceased had numerous heirs, of both genders, often related to one another in complex ways—such as through multiple marriages, extra-marital relationships, adoptions, and so on.
7. That is, one-eighth of the estate if there are children or one-fourth in their absence. For a detailed exposition of the very complicated principles of inheritance according to Sunni law see Coulson (1971: 10-107), Fyzee (1974: 387–440), and Mundy 1988. Esposito (1982: 39-48) summarizes the main points.
8. Likewise, when a woman is widowed, she often allows her sons to take ownership of their father's entire property, rather than claiming her legal share of the estate. This practice is similarly justified in terms of women's economic dependence—in this case, on their sons.

9. There are others who counter that the cost of a daughter's dowry—at least in a family of some means—rarely approaches the value of her prospective inheritance share, and point out that, in any case, once she is married, she is unlikely to be able to retain much, if any, control over its contents.
10. The data presented here were collected in the course of a long-term ethnographic and archival study of the *khāndān*'s history, in interviews conducted in Madras and Hyderabad, primarily in the winters of 1984 and 1993 with Drs Zakira Ghouse, A.M. Shakira, A.S. Nasira, Rahat Mahmouda, Sayida Ataullah and Mr. Muhammad Ataullah, Mrs Tayyaba Qadar and Mr. Abdul Qadar, and Mr. Muhammad Ataiq. In later years, several younger members of their respective families were also helpful to me. I am very grateful to all of them for their generous assistance with this and other aspects of my research and greatly regret that it is no longer possible to thank in person those who, in the intervening years, have passed on.
11. The following sections on the early history of the *khāndān* rely heavily on the work of Muhammad Yusuf Kokan 'Umari (1963, 1974). For further details about the family's more recent history see Vatuk 1989 and 1990, and the archival sources cited therein.
12. In some earlier publications I have referred to him by the pseudonym Ghulam Mahmud.
13. Although Madras is now called Chennai, I use here the name by which it was known during the period about which I am writing.
14. In a house-to-house survey, conducted for me in 1984 by several educated young women of the *khāndān,* there were 92 *khāndān* households with 446 occupants in Madras, and 49 households with 220 occupants in Hyderabad. Two hundred or so *khāndān* members were already living outside of India at the time, about a quarter of them men working abroad temporarily—in the Gulf and Middle East—a few accompanied by their wives. Aside from a handful of young males who had emigrated permanently to North America and elsewhere, most of the rest were in Pakistan, having moved there either shortly after Partition or in later years, for marriage or other reasons (Vatuk 1989: 119-31).
15. Regarding the library, see 'Umari 1963, Gurney 1973, and Iqbal 1973.
16. In 1857, a few years after Nawab Ghulam Ghaus Khan's death, his Chief Qazi was relieved of his post by the British. However, in 1880, a newly enacted Kazi Act authorized the resumption of the appointment of *qāzīs* in localities of significant Muslim population, and one of his sons, Ubaidullah, was selected for the new position of Qazi of the Town of Madras. After Indian independence and the later 1969 reorganization of states, the official title of his successors became Government Chief Qazi of Tamil Nadu. Except for a brief interval in the late 1890s, this post has been held by men of this *khāndān,* having been passed first to Qazi Ubaidullah's son, then to the latter's daughter's husband and then to that man's wife's father's sister's son—who was also a grandson of the first official appointee. The present incumbent is his nephew.

17. Such cases represent only a very small minority of those brought to him, however, and almost always consist of enquiries about how to properly distribute an estate among multiple heirs. Most of those who approach him during the daily afternoon hearings on his household verandah come with questions related to marriage or divorce. A significant number are women, seeking his help in contacting an absent husband and/or asking him to facilitate a wife-initiated *khulC* divorce, for which the husband's consent is required.
18. Her husband, instead, wrote a will to the same effect. See below.
19. Although I have no specific examples of this from Muhamad Ghaus' *khāndān*, I know from other research of cases in which married but childless men gave substantial pre-mortem gifts to their wives, not wanting the bulk of their assets to go to their brothers or nephews, leaving the women unable to maintain their accustomed standards of living.
20. Michel Joachim Marie Raymond, 1755—98.
21. See also Kozlowski 1985, on the extended controversy that led to the passage of the 1913 Mussalman Wakf Validating Act, legitimizing this type of *waqf*.
22. In fact, this man's objection was based on an erroneous understanding of the law. The one-third limit pertains only to the amount that may be given away in a will (see below). One may place all or any proportion of one's assets in a *waqf* or gift it as *hiba*.
23. These bequests clearly far exceeded the one-third limit allowed by *shari'a,* and also, by giving the testator's daughter a full, rather than a half share, deprived the male heirs of a portion of their entitlements. But, since all of the male heirs had agreed to it and none complained, that issue was, as far as I am aware, never raised.
24. All subsequent translations of 'Umari's text into English are mine.
25. One widow was his second wife, a first cousin (mother's brother's daughter), whom he had married in 1850, ten months after his first wife passed away. In the will he refers to her by the respectful 'my *ahlīya*.' When referring to the two wives together, he uses the term *bībīyan* (sg. *bībī*). But when referring to his third wife he either uses her first name or by the term 'my *mankūha*', whose literal meaning is 'a woman married by *nikāh*', thus, 'a legally wedded wife'. In this time and place, however, the term specifically denoted a woman whose *nikāh* had taken place in private, without any of the customary several days of celebratory rituals and feasts for relatives and invited guests that accompany a complete, traditional Muslim wedding, a *shādī*. *Nikāh* marriages were almost always unions of personal choice—not arranged, in the usual way, by the elders of the two families. Furthermore, the bride was invariably a *ghair-khāndānī* (outsider) woman—in this case, a Hindu convert. It is not clear when this couple's *nikāh* was read. In his book, 'Umari almost always notes, alongside a woman's name, the date of her marriage. But, in the case of the Bakshi's *mankūha,* this information is lacking—doubtless because the wedding took place without the knowledge of his other family members and was therefore not to be found in any of the *khāndān's* records when he was doing his research.

However, based on the date of birth of their first (and his youngest) child, it seems likely that the two were probably wed sometime around 1856, several years after he took his cousin as his second wife.

26. The fact that 'Umari does not identify the second witness to the will suggests that he was probably not a close kinsman.
27. Except for the big clock that hangs in his sitting room (*diwān khāna*), his horse, and the animals that belong to his *mankūha,* his third wife.
28. One of these girls was married eight months, the other sixteen months, after the Bakshi's death. Both wed close relatives: the daughter of his second wife to her mother's father's brother's son (a classificatory maternal uncle [*māmā*]), the daughter of his third wife to her father's father's sister's son (a classificatory paternal uncle [cacā]).
29. At the time the Bakshi was writing his will, the term *jahez* signified a trousseau of jewelry and clothing given to the bride by her parents, along with a set (*joṛā*) of clothes for the groom to wear during the *nikāh* ceremony and a horse (*ghoṛā*) upon which to ride from his home to that of the bride—the two gifts combined as *ghoṛā-joṛā*. Nowadays, however, Indian Muslims, like those of other religions, have begun transferring a much more extensive 'dowry'—also called *jahez*–when a daughter marries. It typically includes the trousseau and the *joṛā* (nowadays not a readymade suit, but an amount of money sufficient to cover the cost of having one specially tailored), as well as other expensive goods—and sometimes cash, as well—for the groom and members of his household (for recent dowry practices among Indian Muslims, see Fanselow n.d.; Khan 1994; Assayag 1995; Waheed 2009; Vatuk 2007). Members of this *khāndān,* however, have generally refrained from adopting this new custom and, except when the groom belongs to a *ghair-khāndān,* and continue to practice their traditionally minimalist mode of gift-giving on such occasions.
30. In other families, it often happens that, immediately after consummation, the husband asks his new bride to permanently relieve him of the obligation to pay what he has just promised her. Later, even if she has not waived those rights, she is hesitant to demand it, for to do so suggests a lack of commitment to the marriage and raises, in his mind, the possibility that she may be planning to leave him. Since there is no enforcement mechanism for its payment—other than filing suit for breach of contract in a state court--it is almost impossible for a divorced woman or her family to compel her former husband to come up with the money. And, if she is widowed, her in-laws typically convince her not to take her *mahr* amount from his estate, as it will allegedly cause the deceased to suffer in the afterlife. The situation is complicated by the fact that men (both for prestige reasons and because the bride's family believes that it may deter him from divorcing her) often promise a *mahr* so large that they would never be in a position to come up with the money (see a discussion of my findings on *mahr* among Muslims in Chennai and Hyderabad, from research in the family courts of both cities [Vatuk 2005: 33-37]).
31. The value of these in modern Indian rupees, of course, varies over time.

32. His widow was one of the heirs, but a widow's share is such that, had the house remained in his estate, she would not have been allotted the entire structure.
33. There was an unusually large number of never-married men and women in this *khāndān*, particularly among those born in the early to mid-1900s. The reasons for this are multiple and not easy to unravel (see Vatuk 1994: 154–8 and table 6.5). For example, of the 190 females born between 1920 and 1945 who survived to age 30, 15 percent were still unmarried in 1984. A household census conducted in that year in both cities found 30 never-married women aged 30 or above—almost one-quarter of all women in that age group. There have been occasional examples in the family's history of women marrying for the first time in their thirties or early forties, but it is probable that most of the women we surveyed in 1984 remained single for the rest of their lives.
34. Already a serious student of Islam—and of Shāfi'ī jurisprudence, in particular—earned degrees in Islamic studies in subsequent years from the University of Bonn (in 1933) and from the Sorbonne (in 1935). After the 1948 military annexation of Hyderabad by the Indian Union, he settled in France, where he lived and worked for most of the rest of his life, becoming well-known as a scholar of Islam, authoring numerous books and hundreds of scholarly articles in English, Urdu, French, and other languages.

REFERENCES

Abbasi, M.Z. 2012. 'The Classical Islamic Law of Waqf: A Concise Introduction', *Arab Law Quarterly*, 26(2): 121–53.

Agarwal, B. 1994. *A Field of Her Own: Gender and Land Rights in South Asia.* Cambridge: Cambridge University Press.

All India Muslim Personal Law Board (AIMPLB). 2002. *Compendium of Islamic Laws.* 2nd edition. New Delhi: AIMPLB.

Anderson, J.N.D. 1965. 'Recent Reforms in the Islamic Law of Inheritance', *The International and Comparative Law Quarterly*, 14(2): 349–65.

Anderson, J.N.D. 1959. *Islamic Law in the Modern World.* New York: New York University Press.

Arora, S.J and L.C. Singhi. 2009. 'Women's Access and Rights to Land in Uttar Pradesh', in *Gender Discrimination in Land Ownership: Land Reforms in India,* Volume II, P. Chowdhry (ed.), pp. 244–76. New Delhi: Sage Publications.

Assayag, J. 1995. *Au Confluent de Deux Rivières: Musulmans et Hindous dans le Sud de l'Inde.* Paris: École Française d'Extrême-Orient.

Aziz Jang Bahadur. 1976 (original 1904). *Tarikh-un-Nawāyat* (*A History of the Nawayats*) [Urdu]. Hyderabad: Wala Akaidemi

Baruah, B. 2007. 'Gendered Realities: Exploring Property Ownership and Tenancy Relationships in Urban India', *World Development* 35(12): 2096–109.

Baruah, B. 2010. *Women and Property in Urban India.* Vancouver: University of British Columbia Press.

Bowen, J.R. 1996. 'Equality, Difference, and Law in Indonesian Inheritance Practices: A Sumatran Case', *Political and Legal Anthropology Review*, 19(11): 83–90.

Basu, S. 1999. *She Comes to Take her Rights: Indian Women, Property, and Propriety.* Albany: State University of New York Press.

Basu, S. 2001. 'The Personal and the Political: Indian Women and Inheritance Law', in G.J. Larson (ed.), *Religion and Personal Law in Secular India: A Call to Judgment*, pp. 163–83. Bloomington: Indiana University Press.

Carroll, L. 1994. 'Definition and Interpretation of Muslim Law in South Asia: The Case of Gifts to Minors.' *Islamic Law and Society*, 1(11): 83–115.

Carroll, L. 1998. 'Orphaned Grandchildren in Islamic Law of Succession: Reform and Islamization in Pakistan', *Islamic Law and Society*, 5(3): 409–47.

Carroll, L. 2001. 'Life Interests and Inter-Generational Transfer of Property Avoiding the Law of Succession', *Islamic Law and Society*, 8(2): 245–86.

Cohn, B.S. 1996. 'Law and the Colonial State in India,' in *Colonialism and its Forms of Knowledge: The British in India,* pp. 57–75. Princeton: Princeton University Press.

Coulson, N.J. 1971. *Succession in the Muslim Family.* Cambridge: Cambridge University Press.

Deininger, K., A. Goyal and H. Nagarajan. 2013. 'Women's Inheritance Rights and Intergenerational Transmission of Resources in India', *The Journal of Human Resources*, 48(1): 114–41.

Donnan, H. 1988. *Marriage among Muslims: Preference and Choice in Northern Pakistan*. Delhi: Hindustan Publishing Corporation.

Doumani, B. 1998. 'Endowing Family: *Waqf*, Property Devolution, and Gender in Greater Syria, 1800 to 1860', *Comparative Studies in Society and History*, 40(11): 3–41.

D'Souza, Victor S. 1955. *The Navayats of Kanara.* Dharwar: Kannada Research Institute.

Esposito, J.L. 1982. *Women in Muslim Family Law*. Syracuse: Syracuse University Press.

Fanselow, F. S. n.d. 'Dan, Dakshina and Dowry: An Analysis of the Muslim Marriage Market in Tamil Nadu.' Unpublished Manuscript.

Fazalbhoy, N. 2005. 'Muslim Women and Inheritance', in Z. Hasan and R. Menon (eds), *In a Minority: Essays on Muslim Women in India,* pp. 69–107. New Delhi: Oxford University Press.

Fazalbhoy, N. 2012. 'Negotiating Rights and Relationships: Muslim Women and Inheritance', in F. Agnes and S.V. Ghosh (eds), *Negotiating Spaces: Legal Domains, Gender Concerns, and Community Constructs* pp. 311–34. New Delhi: Oxford University Press.

Fyzee, A.A.A. 1974. *Outlines of Muhammadan Law.* Fourth Edition. Delhi: Oxford University Press.

Gerholm, T. 1985. 'Aspects of Inheritance and Marriage Payment in North Yemen', in A. E. Mayer (ed.), *Property, Social Structure, and Law in the Modern Middle East,* pp. 129–51. Albany: SUNY Press.

Gurney, J. D. 1973. 'Fresh Light on the Character of the Nawab of Arcot', in A. Whiteman, et al. (eds), *Statesmen, Scholars and Merchants.* Oxford: The Clarendon Press.

Hidayatullah, M. and A. Hidayatullah (eds). 1990. *Mulla's Principles of Mahomedan Law.* 19th edition. Bombay: N. M. Tripathi Private Ltd.

Hoexter, M. 1998. 'Waqf Studies in the Twentieth Century: The State of the Art', *Journal of the Economic and Social History of the Orient,* 41(4): 474–95.

Holden, L. and A. Chaudhary. 2013. 'Daughters' Inheritance, Legal Pluralism, and Governance in Pakistan', *The Journal of Legal Pluralism and Unofficial Law,* 45(11): 104–23.

Holy, L. 1989. *Kinship, Honour and Solidarity: Cousin Marriage in the Middle East.* Manchester: Manchester University Press.

Iqbal, M. A., (ed.) 1973. *Tazkira-ī-Saīd* (*A Biography of Saīd*) [Urdu]. Sayeedia Library and Research Institute.

Jeffery, P. 1976. *Migrants and Refugees: Muslim and Christian Pakistani Families in Bristol.* Cambridge: Cambridge University Press.

Jeffery, P. 1979. *Frogs in a Well: Indian Women in Purdah.* New Delhi: Vikas Publishing House.

Jeffery, P. 2001. 'A Uniform Customary Code? Marital Breakdown and Women's Economic Entitlements in Rural Bijnor', *Contributions to Indian Sociology,* 35(1): 1–32.

Jeffery, P. and R. Jeffery. 1996. *Don't Marry Me to a Plowman: Women's Everyday Lives in Rural North India.* Boulder, CO: Westview Press.

Jeffery, P., R. Jeffery and A. Lyon. 1989. *Labour Pains and Labour Power: Women and Childbearing in India.* New Delhi: Manohar.

Jeffery, P. and K. Qureshi. 2022. 'Muslim Woman, Muslim Women: Lived Experiences Beyond Religion and Gender in South Asia and its Diasporas', *Contemporary South Asia,* 30(1): 1-15.

Kader, S.A. 1999. *The Law of Waqfs—An Analytical and Critical Study.* Calcutta: Eastern Law House.

Khan, C.G.H. 1994. *Marriage and Kinship among Muslims in South India.* Jaipur and Delhi: Rawat Publications.

Khatana, R.P. 1976 'Marriage and Kinship among the Gujar Bakarwals of Jammu and Kashmir', in I. Ahmad (ed.), *Family, Kinship and Marriage among Muslims in India,* pp. 83–126. New Delhi: Manohar Book Service.

Kozlowski, G.C. 1985. *Muslim Endowments and Society in British India.* Cambridge: Cambridge University Press.

Kozlowski, G.C. 1987. 'Muslim Women and the Control of Property in North India', *Indian Economic & Social History Review,* 24(2): 163–81.

Kressel, G. 1986. 'Prescriptive Patrilateral Parallel Cousin Marriage: The Perspective of the Bride's Father and Brothers', *Ethnology,* 25(3): 163–80.

Lemons, K. 2018. 'Sharia Courts and Muslim Personal Law in India: Intersecting Legal Regimes', *Law and Society Review*, 52(3): 603–29.

Lemons, K. 2019. *Divorcing Traditions: Islamic Marriage Law and the Making of Indian Secularism*. Ithaca: Cornell University Press.

Maher, V. 1974. *Women and Property in Morocco*. Cambridge: Cambridge University Press.

Majid, A. 1984. *Taẓkira-ī Khāndān* (*Family Biographical Register*) [Urdu]. Unpublished Manuscript.

Mehdi, R. 2001. *Gender and Property Law in Pakistan*. Copenhagen: DJØF Publishing.

Moors, A. 1995. *Women, Property and Islam: Palestinian Experiences 1920–1990*. Cambridge: Cambridge University Press.

Mundy, M. 1988. 'Family, Inheritance, and Islam: A Re-examination of the Sociology of *Fara'id* Law', in A. al-Azmeh (ed.), *Islamic Law: Social and Historical Contexts*, pp. 1–123. London: Routledge.

Mundy, M. 1979. 'Women's Inheritance of Land in Highland Yemen', *Arabian Studies*, 5: 161–88.

Nelson, M.J. 2013. 'Inheritance Unbound: The Politics of Personal Law Reform in Pakistan and India', in S. Khilnani, V. Raghavan and A.K. Thiruvengadam (eds), *Comparative Constitutionalism in South Asia*, pp. 219–46. New Delhi: Oxford University Press.

Pearl, D. and W. Menski. 1998. *Muslim Family Law*. 3rd ed. London: Sweet and Maxwell.

Powers, D.S. 1989. 'Orientalism, Colonialism, and Legal History: The Attack on Muslim Family Endowments in Algeria and India', *Comparative Studies in Society and History*, 31(3): 535–71.

Powers, D.S. 1993a. 'The Islamic Inheritance System: A Socio-Historical Approach', *Arab Law Quarterly*, 8(11): 13–29.

Powers, D.S. 1993b. 'The Maliki Family Endowment: Legal Norms and Social Practices', *International Journal of Middle East Studies*, 25(3):379–406.

Qureshi, M.A. 1990. *Waqfs in India: A Study of Administrative and Statutory Control*. New Delhi: Gian Publishing House.

Rao, A. 1998. *Autonomy: Life Cycle, Gender and Status among Himalayan Pastoralists*. New York: Berghahn Books.

Redding, J.A. 2020. *A Secular Need: Islamic Law and State Governance in Contemporary India*. Seattle: University of Washington Press.

Rudolph, S.H. and L.I. Rudolph. 2001. 'Living with Difference in India', in G.J. Larson (ed.), *Religion and Personal Law in Secular India: A Call to Judgment*, pp. 36–65. Bloomington: Indiana University Press.

Solanki, G. 2011. *Adjudication in Religious Family Laws: Cultural Accommodation, Legal Pluralism, and Gender Equality in India*. Cambridge: Cambridge University Press.

Subramanian, N. 2008. 'Legal Change and Gender Inequality: Changes in Muslim Family Law in India', *Law and Social Inquiry*, 33(3): 631–72.

Subramanian, N. 2014. *Nation and Family: Personal Law, Cultural Pluralism, and Gendered Citizenship in India.* Stanford: Stanford University Press.

Tschalaer, M.H. 2017. *Muslim Women's Quest for Justice: Gender, Law and Activism in India.* Cambridge: Cambridge University Press.

'Umari, M.Y.K. 1963. *Khānwāda-ī Qāzī Badr-ud Daula* (*The Family of Qazi Badr-ud Daula*) [Urdu]. Madras: Dar-ul Tasnif.

'Umari, M.Y.K. 1974. *Arabic and Persian in Carnatic, 1710–1960.* Madras: Printed at Ameera & Co.

Vatuk, S. 1989. 'Household Form and Formation: Variability and Social Change among South Indian Muslims', in J.N. Gray and D.J. Mearns (eds), *Society from the Inside Out: Anthropological Perspectives on the South Asian Household,* pp. 107–39. New Delhi: Sage Publications.

Vatuk, S. 1990. 'The Cultural Construction of Shared Identity: A South Indian Muslim Family History', *Social Analysis,* 28: 114–31.

Vatuk, S. 1994. 'Schooling for What? The Cultural and Social Context of Women's Education in a South Indian Muslim Family,' in C.C. Mukhopadhyay and S. Seymour (eds), *Women, Education, and Family Structure in India,* pp. 135–64. Boulder: Westview Press.

Vatuk, S. 2005. 'Muslim Women and Personal Law', in Z. Hasan and R. Menon (eds), *In a Minority: Essays on Muslim Women in India,* pp. 18–68. New Delhi: Oxford University Press (reprinted in *Marriage and its Discontents: Women, Islam and the Law in India,* pp. 29–92. New Delhi: Women Unlimited 2017).

Vatuk, S. 2007. 'The "Cancer of Dowry" in Indian Muslim Marriages: Themes in the Popular Rhetoric from the South Indian Muslim Press', in M. Hasan (ed), *Living With Secularism: The Destiny of India's Muslims,* pp. 155–76. New Delhi: Manohar Publishers (reprinted in *Marriage and its Discontents: Women, Islam and the Law in India,* pp. 93–115. New Delhi: Women Unlimited 2017).

Vatuk, S. 2014. 'Change and Continuity in Marital Alliance Patterns: Muslims in South India, 1800–2012', in R. Kaur and R. Palriwala (eds), *Marrying in South Asia: Shifting Concepts and Changing Practices in a Globalising World,* pp. 28–48. New Delhi: Orient Black Swan.

Vatuk, S. 2019. 'Extra-Judicial *KhulC* Divorce in India's Muslim Personal Law', *Islamic Law and Society* 26(11): 111–48.

Vatuk, S. 2022. 'Muslim Daughters and Inheritance in India: *Shari'at,* Custom and Practice', In P. Jeffery and K. Qureshi. Muslim Woman/Muslim women: lived experiences beyond religion and gender in South Asia and its diasporas. *Contemporary South Asia,* 30(1): 16-29.

Waheed, A. 2009. 'Dowry among Indian Muslims: Ideals and Practices', *Indian Journal of Gender Studies,* 16(11): 47–75.

White, S.C. 1991. *Arguing with the Crocodile: Gender and Class in Bangladesh.* London: Zed Books Ltd.

6

From Plowmen to Freshies

Writing About Gender, Kinship and Migration

Katharine Charsley

Don't marry me to a plowman!

O, mother, marry me to a man in service,
Don't marry me to a plowman!

When a plowman returns from his plowing,
A revolting stench comes from afar.
When an office worker returns from his office,
A sweet perfume comes from afar.
O, mother marry me to a man in service,
Don't marry me to a plowman!

When a plowman returns from his plowing,
He eats a dozen or so pieces of thick griddle bread,
When an office worker returns from his office,
He eats just a couple of little puffed fried breads.
O, mother, marry me to a man in service,
Don't marry me to a plowman!

When a plowman returns from his plowing,
His goad shows up from afar.
When an office worker returns from his office,
Wads of hundred rupee bank notes show up from afar.

O, mother marry me to a man in service,
Don't marry me to a plowman!

(in Jeffery and Jeffery 1996)

Being a Freshie's Cool

CHORUS:

All my life I've been a Freshie
My Mum and Dad are Freshies too
Join my gang of Freshies
It's time to know – being a Freshie is cool

Fresh off the boat with a student visa
Work in a chicken shop on Green Lane
Came to the country in a silk *kurta*
Exchanged that in for a chav's gold chain

In my car, a gold and red tissue box
Perving on young girls on the bus
They all run away
Why they run away?

Import, export, socks with flip flops
Hairy arms, hairy brow, curry house, sweet shop
Yes I am a bad man, rasta man, blood clot
Rollin' in my Honda blasting Indian hip hop – yaar

CHORUS

Giving wrong change in my corner shop
Charming the White girls with my swagger on lock
Side parting with the greasy top
Olive oil in my hair and popping them spots

Playing Jay Sean on my speaker phone
Keeping plastic on my remote control
Walking round town taking tourist photos
To show my village children London life back at home.
Cleaning my ears with my set of car keys
Picking my nose while I'm walking down the street

Wearing fake Armani
And yes I voted BNP – No way!

CHORUS

Being a Freshie is Cool (repeat to end)

(Mawaan Rizwan 2012, in Charsley and Bolognani 2017)

These two songs appear in the openings of academic works. The first is from *Don't Marry me to a Plowman! Women's Everyday Lives in Rural North India* (Jeffery and Jeffery 1996). The second is from an article I wrote with Marta Bolognani called 'Being a Freshie is (not) Cool: stigma, capital and disgust in British Pakistani stereotypes of new subcontinental migrants' (2017). The first is a wedding song sung by a bride's relatives before she departs for her husband's home, while the second is from a YouTube skit by Mawaan Rizwan, a Pakistan-born British actor, director and comedian. The two appear to be very different genres, composed in very different contexts, but this chapter draws connections between the two – not just on the themes of disgust and, I would argue, marriageability, which feature in both, but also the impact of *Plowman,* and Patricia Jeffery's wider work, on the intellectual trajectory which led me to the Freshie article.

In many ways, this chapter is an academic 'thank you' letter to Tricia who, a few years after *Plowman* was published, became an enormously inspiring and supportive supervisor for my PhD on transnational Pakistani marriages. It is also an opportunity for reflection on one strand of my own work – that of Pakistani men migrating to Britain through marriage.

(British) Pakistani transnational marriages

As an undergraduate fresh from travelling in South India to visit the region where my family had lived for a year when I was a baby, I gravitated increasingly to focusing my studies on South Asia. I was lucky to have selected the University of Edinburgh for my degree, without being aware of the thriving South Asian Studies community there. Meeting Tricia in person and reading her earlier classic, *Frogs in a Well* (1979), on Pirzada Muslim women in North India, stimulated my interest in South Asian Muslims, kinship and gender. So, when I became fascinated by marriages between British Pakistanis and partners from Pakistan during a research post in Bristol, after graduating with my Edinburgh MA, Tricia was the obvious person to approach to be my supervisor. She had, coincidentally, also undertaken her doctoral research in Bristol – published as the book *Migrants and Refugees: Muslim and Christian Pakistani Families in Bristol* (1976) – so I followed in her footsteps in carrying out ethnographic research with Pakistanis in Bristol, combined with a spell in Pakistan.

The parallels between our work did not stop there. First, I was very much inspired by the kind of 'person-centred ethnography' in *Don't Marry me to a Plowman!*, where accounts of individual people and relationships form the centre of the exploration of gender roles and kinship.[1] The style of my ethnographic writing bears a strong imprint of this influence, using frequent and often extended interview narratives to communicate the individual experiences of gendered family dynamics. Like Tricia, I was motivated to avoid my participants appearing as culturally determined 'others', or 'rule-bound automata' (Jeffery and Jeffery 1996: 14). The introduction to *Plowman* sets out the hope that the use of biographical narratives will allow a more nuanced portrayal of individuality and agency, so that 'the women who feature in this account should not be read as ciphers for "The Third World woman."' (1996: 3). In my doctoral work with British Pakistanis and spousal migrants from Pakistan, I similarly hoped to counter the parallel British stereotypes of 'Muslim women' (a passive figure quite different from the engaged and engaging Bristolian Pakistani women I met in the course of my research), and the accounts of Pakistani arranged marriage practices as primarily a matter of marriage rules/cultural preferences, or of family strategy (e.g. Ballard 1987, 1990; Donnan 1988). My own fieldwork, in contrast, was rich with tales of emotion accompanying marriage arrangements: love between siblings, parents and children; concern over the risks of getting a match wrong; and, not infrequently, attraction between the young people whose marriages were being arranged (Charsley 2013; Charsley et al. 2020).

Although Tricia's research over the last few decades has centred on North India, while my own concerns the Pakistani diaspora, the many similarities between North Indian Muslim and Pakistani gender and kinship conventions meant that her work (sole or co-authored) has been an invaluable source of inspiration, insight and comparison. The vulnerability of women in a patrilocal system, in which the norm is for a bride to live with her husband's relatives, as is documented so clearly in *Plowman* for example, may be amplified in transnational marriage where women travel not to the next village, but to a distant continent, far from recourse to their natal family for support (Charsley 2005a; Jeffery and Jeffery 1996). The detailed ethnography in books such as *Labour Pains and Labour Power* (1989) and *Plowman* were also valuable, however, in reducing the likelihood of misattributions of risks to the transnational nature of the marriages I studied – as when one Pakistani woman in Bristol told me of her family's shock in learning only after the wedding had taken place that the British groom had a serious disability. My initial assumption that the fact that the families lived in different countries facilitated this concealment was tempered by reading of a family in *Plowman* who turned up for their son's wedding to find that the bride was not the young woman they had inspected on their visit to her family's village before agreeing to the match.

Migrant husbands

At the time of my doctoral fieldwork, up to 10,000 spouses from Pakistan were being granted entry to the UK each year.[2] Despite the significant numbers involved, spousal migration from Pakistan to Britain was not the subject of a great deal of academic or political attention.[3] What attention there was usually focused on the wives who had long accounted for the majority of such migrants – such women, far from their natal families and often without a strong grasp of English, were seen as vulnerable to isolation and mistreatment (e.g. Fenton and Sadiq 1993). In the late 1990s, when I was developing an interest in the topic, the Primary Purpose Rule (PPR) was abolished. Under the PPR, those seeking to enter the UK as spouses of British citizens had to prove that the primary purpose of their marriage was not to gain entry to Britain – something that was rather challenging for men (who were under greater suspicion of an economic motivation) in arranged marriages, without a romantic history of coupledom to display to immigration officials (Menski 1999; Sachdeva 1993). In response to the abolition of the PPR, the number of husbands arriving in the UK from Pakistan increased dramatically, so that when I first did ethnographic research on the topic, around half of the grants of settlement to spouses from Pakistan were to men. Hence, I encountered many British Pakistani women with recently arrived Pakistani husbands during my fieldwork.

While the potential risks to women of transnational marriage were often discussed by those I met in Bristol and in academic literature – vulnerabilities for migrant wives, and for British Pakistani women the dangers of being deserted by husbands interested only in passports, or being left as 'immigration widows' if their husband is denied a visa (Menski 1999) – the experiences of migrant husbands were largely missing from these discussions.

So, in my doctoral research, I attempted an exploration of migrant husbands' positions as lone incomers in their wife's family – a reversal of the conventional position of the new bride – and the consequences for some in terms of a weak position in domestic power relations, having to 'adjust' to their wife's family's ways, and the prospect of children being raised in an unfamiliar family culture. This position could challenge the taken-for-granted assumptions about a masculine life course with which they may have grown up. And all of this happened at the same time as such men were often experiencing migration to a new country, with the loss of social networks, downward mobility and low-skilled employment that often accompanies it. Not all migrant husbands suffer from all of these elements (something I'll elaborate on), but these kinds of combinations of factors featured as sources of considerable stress for some of the men I dealt with (Charsley 2005b).

Given the lack of academic attention to the issue at this time – and indeed a wider neglect in migration studies of the task of approaching the experience of migrant men with a gendered lens (Charsley and Wray 2015) – what literature could I draw on to make sense of this situation? Once again, *Plowman* and *Labour Pains and Labour Power* provided key insights. These volumes centred on the lives of South Asian women, but men also appeared as fathers, husbands and brothers and, tantalisingly, in the figure of the *ghar-jamai* (or in-living son-in-law):

> a somewhat derogatory term for a man living in his wife's village. This usually happened only when a woman had no brothers capable of farming her father's land and caring for her parents. The in-living son-in-law would expect to be accused of taking land from his wife's cousins, and he would have no ready allies. (Jeffery and Jeffery 1996: 115)

In *Labour Pains and Labour Power* (Jeffery, Jeffery and Lyon 1989), I found more detail on men's own perspectives on this position:

> While granting the attractions of inheriting more land, none was prepared to concede that being a *ghar-jamai* had any other benefits. The *ghar-jamai* is virtually a mirror image of the normal *bahu* [daughter-in-law], precisely the grounds for men's objections. Being a *ghar-jamai* undermines a man's ability to retain control over his wife. She has constant protection from her natal kin … But her husband lacks both his normal back-up from his kin and freedom from interference from his in-laws. He may have problems retaining his position as master of the house. Men talked about ceasing to be their own man, even on brief visits to their *susral* [in-laws' place] when they must abide by the eating and sleeping times of their in-laws and behave meekly in their father-in-law's presence. These difficulties may be exacerbated by a *ghar-jamai*'s in-laws. Instead of respecting their 'guest' … they may jibe and insult him. He loses face for scrounging and may become enmeshed in tussles with his wife's hostile cousins and uncles over possession of the house and land. (p. 37)

Men migrating as husbands from Pakistan to Britain move in a similarly culturally unusual direction – towards their wife's family rather than vice versa. Many initially live with, or at least very near to, their in-laws, and are dependent on their wives and families for accommodation and help in finding work (Charsley 2005b; Charsley et al. 2020). Structurally then, they appear to be in a similar position to the *ghar-jamai*, but although the term (or the synonym *ghar-damad)* was familiar to my Bristolian participants, they did not use it to refer to husbands arriving from Pakistan.

Nevertheless, interviews suggested that some aspects of the *ghar-jamai* position found parallels in the situations of some of these men. Far from their own natal family, while their wife had hers close at hand, some appeared in weak positions in household power dynamics. One man, Tahir, spoke of his frustration in having to adjust his behaviour and of raising his children in his in-law's orbit, and his yearning to move the family to Pakistan and re-establish the patrilocal norms which conventionally can provide generational continuity in family culture for men:

> It's been the opposite way round – usually girls make adjustments [when they move to their in-law's house]. Some things I can't change like certain habits of mine. I've changed most of them – I don't smoke inside, I smoke always outside now … I think it's more comfortable [since we have moved out of the extended family home]. We have our own privacy. Secondly, the lifestyle we want to develop for our own selves, we can. That's most important to me – I can grow my children the way I want to. Teach them the things I want … [But still …] before they are ten years old, I would like them to go back [to Pakistan] … [If] my parents had children like Asma's family, there were a lot of things they couldn't have tolerated. Like if we talk rude to our parents … I would love to go, we'd all like to live with our parents all together. My father he said, 'All right – I'll grow your children up for you'. I said, 'That's very nice.' (in Charsley 2013: 161).[4]

In *Plowman,* another North Indian wedding song depicts the tearful farewell (*ruhksati*) of a bride on her wedding day, no longer belonging with her natal kin:

> The darling bride's huge eyes are brimming with tears.
> Just as she's leaving, the girl says this:
> "Father, don't get me married,
> My life with be afflicted by calamities."

"Child, you'll be left alone in this house,
Your mother will taunt you, she'll make you cry."

(in Jeffery and Jeffery 1996, p112)

In a direct reversal of this convention, in my own fieldnotes, Tahir's wife Asma seemed to foretell her husband's position in comments to her relatives at her own *ruhksati*:

> I didn't even cry on my wedding day. Everybody said, 'Why didn't you cry?' I said I was going to come back to England. He should be crying – he's leaving his house.
>
> (Asma, in Charsley 2005b: 91)

Migration, masculinity, agency and the Freshie stereotype

As a body of literature on masculinity and migration has (rather belatedly) developed,[5] the challenges migration may pose for aspirations to hegemonic masculinities – through downward mobility in the labour market and/or the necessity to take on employment in feminised sectors – has developed as a key theme (Charsley and Wray 2015). In a step away from a tendency to universalise heteronormative 'breadwinner masculinities' in portrayals of migrant men (Donaldson et al. 2009), Batnizky and colleagues (2009) suggested that migrants' classed positionalities could correlate with differing strategies in the face of migration challenges – compensating for potential indignities by being 'flexible' or 'strategic' with their gendered and classed identities, to reap other benefits (such as status in sending countries, or control over performance of gender identities in countries of migration). Migrant husbands may, at least initially, be limited in their ability to make such 'trade-offs' – focus group participants reported that not only were they dependent on their wives and in-laws, but also their low wages precluded sending remittances to family in Pakistan, while their marital commitment to a UK spouse restricted their options for change (Charsley and Ersanilli 2019).

Ali Nobil Ahmad (2008) notes that the routes to home ownership and secure employment available to an earlier generation of migrants are no longer so accessible in an era of inflated property prices and casualised service sector employment. In other words, attention to the gendered and kinship positions of these migrant men, and changes over migrant generations, alert us to a range of potential constraints to their agency.

In developing my work on migrant husbands, a collaboration with Danish colleague Anika Liversage uncovered striking parallels between Turkish husbands in Denmark and Pakistani husbands in the UK. We worked together on papers about how such men's particular intersectional positions may reduce their ability to seek support in the challenges they faced (Charsley and Liversage 2015), and on transnational polygamy (marrying again in Pakistan/Turkey) as one (uncommon) strategy of compensation for loss of status abroad (Charsley and Liversage 2013).

The most recent step in my exploration of migrant husbands, however, has brought my work back into dialogue with *Plowman* in a new way – bringing in cultural representations in the form of song (Charsley and Bolognani 2017). Wedding songs are a particular feature of *Plowman*, often sung by women as commentaries on gendered power, or to poke fun at the groom (as in the titular 'Don't Marry me to a Plowman') in ways that might not be acceptable in normal discourse. These, the introduction suggests, could be seen as 'weapons of the weak' (Scott 1985), as small acts of resistance to gendered subordination.

In my article with Marta Bolognani, on the other hand, we explore a common British Pakistani stereotype of new migrants from the subcontinent as Freshies – a variation of the 'fresh off the boat' or 'FOB' terminology found among a variety of ethnic and migrant groups in English-speaking contexts (Pyke and Dang 2003). In a whole genre of YouTube comedy clips by British Pakistanis (and other British South Asians), these new arrivals, almost universally men, are portrayed as ridiculous in their lack of linguistic proficiency (Rizwan's song is sung with a marked accent and the Freshie's attempts at Jamaican-infused street-talk are ridiculed) and inability to display locally acceptable tastes (either carrying over such subcontinental styles as the gold and red tissue box or dressing like a 'chav' – a British stereotype of a cultural underclass) and their lowly employment profiles (curry house, chicken shop). They are depicted as untrustworthy (breaching visa conditions, swindling customers), but also as viscerally disgusting (body hair, nose-picking, spot-popping) and as sexually inappropriate (perving on young girls).[6]

This final element of revulsion is particularly interesting considering the frequency of marriages between British Pakistanis and spouses from Pakistan. Just as disgust at the plowman as a potential marriage partner actually speaks to the likelihood of just such a marriage for a girl in rural Uttar Pradesh (Jeffery and Jeffery 1996: 1), the commonality of transnational marriage among British Pakistanis means that British Pakistani young people viewing these videos or using the image of the Freshie are fairly likely to find themselves presented with potential marriage partners from Pakistan, or to encounter them as the spouses of friends and relatives. Indeed, the term *mangetar* (fiancé) or 'mango' (for short) is not infrequently used as a synonym for Freshie. And, while North Indian women singing of the stench of the plowman coming home from the fields are likely to have just such men as fathers, uncles and brothers, the stereotype of the Freshie conceals migration histories and contemporary transnationalism which blur the boundaries between insider and other (Charsley and Bolognani 1996). So, just as the Indian wedding song appears to contest the definition of a suitable husband, our suggestion is that contestations over marriageability are central to understanding 'Being a Freshie's Cool' and wider depictions of Pakistani Freshies.

We might even, as suggested of the wedding songs in *Plowman,* view these depictions as, in part, 'weapons of the weak'. Although the British partner in a transnational marriage is often conceptualised as benefiting from power in relation to their migrant spouse, derived from their citizenship of a desirable destination country (Liversage 2012), young British Pakistanis whose marriages are being discussed may not perceive themselves to be in a position of strength in generational terms, and (particularly British Pakistani women) may wrestle with concerns over the trustworthiness of a potential Pakistani partner (Charsley 2020).

Finally, stereotypes of Freshies can have real-world consequences for those characterised in this way. In my project on 'Marriage Migration and Integration' (Charsley et al. 2020) we picked up ways in which these kinds of representation can form part of social barriers between Pakistani migrants and British Pakistanis. One focus group participant complained that British Pakistanis looked down on poorer recent migrants like him, while a British Pakistani woman reported that her children had started calling their Pakistani father 'Freshie':

> Keenly aware of being ridiculed by some British Pakistanis as *mangetars* (or 'freshies') recently arrived focus group participants were often reluctant to practice their accented English with their wife's relatives, and had generally not developed friendships with British Pakistanis. (Charsley and Ersanilli 2019)

This is not to say that all migrant husbands from Pakistan face a miserable life of downward mobility, domestic disempowerment and ridicule. My notes from various periods of research are peppered with more positive accounts of men forging positive relations with in-laws and eventually developing careers and status in the UK (Charsley 2013: 173–4). One man in the same focus group as above described his wife's parents as very supportive, encouraging him to take a while on arrival to spend time with his wife, explore his surroundings and improve his English, before finding him a job (Charsley and Ersanilli 2019). As Chopra notes, after an initial period of dependency, migrant husbands may gain status as independent heads of households (2009). Jafar described his long route to improving his situation from overworked new migrant with limited English language skills and social networks – whose English tutor told him that there was no point in him even coming to class as he was too tired to learn – to self-employment in the building industry:

> I was working very hard, but I always got the same money, regardless of the amount of the hours. My English was very poor, but I did not need much English for a packing job. I don't know if my English

> was too poor, but the new supervisor … started to give me problems. So I started working on building sites. I learnt all building work here – I was only a farmer in Pakistan. Slowly, slowly, I built up work. Some weeks I would work one day, some weeks four days. I learnt how to do central heating, tiles, bathrooms … I learnt my English from my friends. In Pakistan I knew a little, but from school. I have English friends from work. English people talk to me about plastering, and I understand quickly, but if they talk about different things, it is difficult for me. I have had a friend from Ghana for a long time, another Jamaican … After 2 or 3 years I started to be self-employed and I am still self-employed. I do plastering and I am taking a course on plastering and decorating. I am also doing a course to get a certificate to do central heating and then I will be paid more money … It has been easy for me to make friends and now I make new friends at college, it is easier because I speak more English. (in Charsley et al. 2020: 142–3)

One older man, Ghalib, recounted his arrival in Bristol as a young groom from Pakistan:

> It was very difficult. But I remember one thing my father said to me, like they say to girls … 'Your in-laws are your father and mother and you should respect them' … That's what my father [had] given me, the last lesson, in airport. And believe you me, I'm not trying to blow my own trumpet, as they say in English, [but] if my father-in-law comes here and you ask him, 'How do you find Ghalib here as in-law?' he will say 'I personally think he's not my in-law, he's my son.' And that's the way he treated me, all the way. He was there for me financially, physically – in every way and I admire him …. He says to me, 'Daytime is night', I say, 'Yes, it is night', even [though] I knew it is daytime and I can say to him, 'It's wrong, it's daytime' – I never say to him. At that time I agree, but then quietly, politely, I say to him 'What do you think if we just go outside and see if it's day or night?' Then he say 'Yeah, yeah'. So that's why I think we had a relationship between ourselves very successful. I'm never, never outspoken in front of them. That's the key for success I think. (in Charsley 2013: 172)

These parallels with the position of the in-marrying bride are depicted not as a humiliation, but as an opportunity for a young man to respectfully exercise his diplomatic skills for the benefit of both himself and his father-in-law (even though a footnote reports Tricia's observation that the same 'day is night' formulation is advice given to women as to how they can influence their husbands).

Even Junaid, who described interference from his in-laws as leading to his marriage ending in a divorce in which he lost his home and access to his children (his wife, he said, had told the court that Junaid would murder them in an honour killing and flee to Pakistan), narrated a possible positive future. He hoped to be able to save for a property, marry again in Pakistan and bring his wife to join him in the UK, so that the family court judge will see him as a stable family man, rather than as a stereotypical dangerous Muslim patriarch, and allow him to see his children once more (Charsley 2013: 175–80).

Conclusion

Just as *Plowman* sets out to nuance the 'cipher' of 'the Indian woman' (Jeffery and Jeffery 1996), by bringing my work together with that text, it is clear that I have been undertaking a similar project with regard to Pakistani men migrating to the UK through marriage. However, rather than addressing concealed forms of agency, a key thread in my work on migrant husbands has been to expose the vulnerabilities (or potential vulnerabilities) masked by portrayals of hyper-agentic Muslim men as powerful and oppressive patriarchs (Lutz 2010). Neither does the stereotypical depiction of a pathetic Freshie portray a relatable human being, negotiating challenging situations. A combination of empirical research and analysis of these cultural representations reveals the migrant husband as a gendered kinship position, which can nuance our understanding of such men's experience and behaviour. In this light, even contracting a second marriage in Pakistan may be revealed as a complex response to layered challenges rather than a sign that the first marriage was likely a 'sham', as suggested in a 2011 Home Office public consultation on proposed restrictions to spousal immigration.

In a final echo of *Don't Marry me to a Plowman!*, I bring this chapter to a close with another song; this time, a response from

Pakistani singer Shaukat Ali to the potential gendered indignities of the transnational *mangetar*.

Mangeteran di Mat Wat Gai (Mangetars have gone mad)

(Migrant) fiancés have gone mad
Women are robust and lone men are feeble
Fiancés have gone mad
Women are robust and lone men are feeble
Fiancés have gone mad

Initially they invite (sponsor for entry visa) boys from their native land
Then they put them in trouble for the whole life
Initially they invite (sponsor for entry visa) boys from their native land
Then they put them in trouble for the whole life
Then they (fiancés) forget the grandeur of the homeland
Then they (fiancés) forget the grandeur of the homeland
Fiancés have gone mad

Women are robust and lone men are feeble
Fiancés have gone mad
Women are robust and lone men are feeble
Fiancés have gone mad

They keep men on a tight rein (exercise strict control over men)
They fly these helpless men like a kite
They keep men on a tight rein (exercise strict control over men)
They fly these helpless men like a kite
They pull the strings whenever they want
They pull the strings whenever they want
Fiancés have gone mad

Women are robust and lone men are feeble
Fiancés have gone mad
Women are robust and lone men are feeble
Fiancés have gone mad

There was a hue and cry in London and America
Fiancés have gone mad
There was a hue and cry in London and America
Fiancés have gone mad

Women are robust and lone men are feeble
Fiancés have gone mad
Women are robust and lone men are feeble
Fiancés have gone mad
Fiancés have gone mad

(Shaukat Ali, translated for the 'Marriage Migration and Integration' project by Waqas Butt).

NOTES

1. Here I use the term in the basic sense of learning from people about their lives within a socio-cultural context, rather than approaching them for information on general principles of their society and culture – what Levy and Hollan call (in now somewhat dated terminology) a shift from interviewee as 'informant' to 'respondent' – rather than the specific methodology and psychological flavour sometimes associated with the term (Levy and Hollan 2014).
2. Analysis of Labour Force Survey data established that rates of transnational marriage have declined since this period (Charsley et al. 2020).
3. Something that was to change a few years later with renewed political focus on restricting spousal immigration (e.g. Wilson 2007).
4. In more a recent research project, we encountered some British Pakistani women who described the benefits of bringing a husband from Pakistan – avoiding the subordinate daughter-in-law role and tempering the conventional gendered authority of a husband – so that one family of sisters with a variety of marriages suggested that a marriage to a migrant was easier than one with a British co-ethnic (Charsley et al. 2020).
5. Along with work on South Asian masculinities (Chopra et al. 2004).
6. For further exploration of these themes in YouTube videos, see Charsley and Bolognani 2017.

REFERENCES

Ahmad, A.N. 2008. Gender and Generation in Pakistani Migration. in *Gendering Migration* edited by L. Ryan and W. Webster, 155–70. Aldershot: Ashgate.

Ballard, R. 1987. The political economy of migration: Pakistan, Britain, and the Middle East. In *Migrants, Workers, and the Social Order.* (ed.) J. Eades. London: Tavistock.

Ballard, R. 1990. Migration and kinship: The differential effect of marriage rules on the processes of Punjabi migration to Britain. In *South Asians Overseas* (eds) C. Clarke, C. Peach and S. Vertovec. Cambridge: Cambridge University Press.

Batnitzky, A., McDowell, L., and Dyer, S. (2009). Flexible and strategic masculinities: The working lives and gendered identities of male migrants in London. *Journal of Ethnic and Migration Studies*, *35*(8), 1275–93.

Charsley, K. 2005a. Vulnerable brides and transnational Ghar Damads: Gender, risk and 'adjustment' among Pakistani marriage migrants to Britain. *Indian Journal of Gender Studies*, *12*(2–3), 381–406.

Charsley, K. 2005b. Unhappy husbands: Masculinity and migration in transnational Pakistani marriages. *Journal of the Royal Anthropological Institute*, *11*(1), 85–105.

Charsley, K. 2013. *Transnational Pakistani connections: marrying 'back home'.* London: Routledge.

Charsley, K., and Bolognani, M. 2017. Being a Freshie is (not) cool: stigma, capital and disgust in British Pakistani stereotypes of new subcontinental migrants. *Ethnic and Racial Studies*, *40*(1), 43–62.

Charsley, K., and Ersanilli, E. 2019. The 'Mangetar Trap'? Work, family and Pakistani migrant husbands. *NORMA*, *14*(2), 128–45.

Charsley, K., and Liversage, A. 2013. Transforming polygamy: migration, transnationalism and multiple marriages among Muslim minorities. *Global Networks*, *13*(1), 60–78.

Charsley, K., and Liversage, A. 2015. Silenced husbands: Muslim marriage migration and masculinity. *Men and Masculinities*, *18*(4), 489–508.

Charsley, K., Bolognani, M., Ersanilli, E. and Spencer, S. 2020 *Marriage Migration and Integration.* London: Palgrave.

Chopra, R., C. Osella and F. Osella (eds) 2004. *South Asian Masculinities: Contexts of change, sites of continuities.* Delhi: Kali for Women.

Chopra, R. 2009. Ghar Jawai (Househusband): a note on mis-translation. *Culture, Society and Masculinity* 1(1): 96–105.

Donnan, H. 1988. *Marriage among Muslims: Preference and Choice in Northern Pakistan.* Delhi: Hindustan Publishing Corporation.

Donaldson, M., R. Hibbins, R. Howson and B. Pease. 2009. *Migrant Men.* London: Routledge.

Fenton, S. and A. Sadiq 1993. *The sorrow in my heart . . .: sixteen Asian women speak about depression.* London: Centre for Racial Equality.

Jeffery, P. 1976. *Migrants and Refugees: Muslim and Christian Pakistani Families in Bristol.* Cambridge: Cambridge University Press.

Jeffery, P. 1979. *Frogs in a Well: Indian Women in Purdah.* London: Zed Books.

Jeffery, P., R. Jeffery and A. Lyon. 1989. *Labour pains and labour power: Women and childbearing in India.* London: Zed Books.

Jeffery, P. and R. Jeffery. 1996. *Don't Marry Me to a Plowman!.* Oxford: Westview.

Home Office. 2011. *Family Migration: evidence and analysis.* Home Office Research Report 94 http://www.homeoffice.gov.uk/publications/science-research-statistics/research-statistics/immigration-asylum-research/occ94/occ94?view=Binary accessed on 7 March 2011.

Levy, R. and D. Hollan. 2014. Person-centered interviewing and observation in anthropology. In. H.R. Bernard (ed) *Handbook of methods in cultural anthropology*, 2nd Edition. London and Maryland: Rowman and Littlefields, pp. 333–64.

Liversage, A. 2012. Transnational Families Breaking Up: Divorce among Turkish Immigrants in Denmark. In *Transnational Families: New Perspectives from Europe and Beyond.* K. Charsley (ed). London: Routledge.

Lutz, H. 2010. Gender in the Migratory Process. *Journal of Ethnic and Migration Studies* 36(1): 1,647–63.

Menski, W. 1999. South Asian Women in Britain, Family Integrity and the Primary Purpose Rule. In *Ethnicity, Gender and Social Change* (eds) R. Barot, H.Bradley and S. Fenton. London: MacMillan.

Pyke, K. and Dang, T. 2003. 'FOB' and 'Whitewashed': identity and internalized racism among second generation Asian Americans, *Qualitative Sociology* 26(2): 147–72.

Sachdeva, S. 1993. *The Primary Purpose Rule in British Immigration Law.* Stoke-on-Trent: Trentham Books.

Scott. J.C. 1985. *Weapons of the Weak: Everyday Forms of Peasant Resistance.* Yale: Yale University Press.

Wilson, A. 2007. The Forced Marriage Debate and the British State. *Race & Class* 49(1): 25–38.

7

'A Uniform Customary Code' Transposed

Family, Community and Religious Mediation in British South Asian Marriages

Kaveri Qureshi

Introduction

In a very important paper from 2001, Patricia Jeffery intervened critically in feminist debates over personal law, religious freedom and gender inequality in India, in ways that proved prescient, not only for Indian but also for South Asian contexts elsewhere in the world. At the time, Indian feminism was reeling from the controversial Shah Bano case. In this famous case, an elderly Muslim woman appealed to the courts, through Section 125 of the Indian Criminal Procedure Code, for maintenance from her ex-husband. He contested that it would be un-Islamic for him to provide for his wife beyond the *iddat* (roughly three or four months of seclusion that a woman must observe after divorce or her husband's death, during which she may not remarry). The Supreme Court upheld Shah Bano's right to lifelong maintenance under Section 125. However, public protests against the judgement by conservative Muslims across India led the

Congress party to respond with the Muslim Women (Protection of Rights on Divorce) Act in 1986, to exclude Muslim divorcees from Section 125, and attempt to quiet the uproar. Troublingly, the fallout from Shah Bano folded into the communal politics of the late 1980s and early 1990s, with the Hindu Right accusing Congress of appeasing the Muslim vote by giving them more rights than the Hindu majority, and taking the conservative Muslim stance as confirmation that Muslim women are oppressed and need to be protected from Muslim men. As Jeffery surmises, this produced a thorny feminist dilemma: to call for a Uniform Civil Code would mean playing into the hands of the Hindu Right, yet failure to demand gender equality in family law would leave personal laws unchallenged.

At this point, Jeffery intervened with her own field material from Bijnor, which showed that the commonalities between Hindu and Muslim women in their responses to marital breakdown were far greater than their differences because neither were able to survive economically outside of marriage. In neither community could women rely upon their natal kin to support them in ending their marriages or to sustain them economically at the natal home in the long term. Jeffery ended with some thoughts about Indian feminist strategies, advocating a broadening of struggle for gender justice beyond the purview of the law. In a dominant feminist strategy centred on legal reform, Jeffery saw 'the trap of framing issues of gender equity solely in terms of women's position in the "private" sphere of the family' and suggested that 'maybe the emphasis should be on enabling women to attain economic viability outside marriage that would be a better long-term remedy for their disempowering dependency within marriage' (Jeffery 2001: 22–3).

Fast-forward two decades, and Jeffery's analysis continues to resonate with feminist debates over personal law in India. The Hindu Right continued to conduct a highly politicised campaign against Muslim personal law, particularly over the oral unilateral triple *talaaq* which was presented as a particular sign of Muslim backwardness and from which Muslim women needed to be saved. In this volume, Zoya Hasan documents the divisions among feminists over the Bharatiya Janata Party's (BJP) Muslim Women (Protection of Rights on Marriage) Bill, which was passed as an Act in 2019. This Act was triggered by a Supreme Court case filed in 2016 by a woman named Shayara Bano, who had been subject to the triple *talaaq*, tagged alongside similar petitions by a handful of other Muslim women, and supported by the Bharatiya Muslim Mahila Andolan and the Bebaak Collective. While the Supreme Court judgement ruled only that the triple *talaaq* was unconstitutional, the BJP followed with an Act that criminalised the practice, leading to challenges from Muslim religious organisations, some other Muslim women's organisations, and secular feminist legal experts.

Moving across oceans, a very similar dilemma has also been witnessed in the UK, where Islamic family law has become the centre of another political maelstrom. In the UK, the alliances made to demonise or defend practices of Islamic family law are as complex as in India. There has been an uneasy coming together of right-wing Islamophobic groups, such as the UK Independence Party and the English Defence League, of Christian organisations, of the National Secular Society and even a black feminist organisation, the Southall Black Sisters, calling – for different reasons – for closer governmental oversight of Muslim family law (Grillo 2015). Most prominent, indeed a lightning rod for concerns about Islamic family law, have been the UK's sharia councils, which have been increasingly closely scrutinised since Archbishop Rowan Williams' notorious sharia lecture in 2008 (Bano 2008). Repeatedly since 2011, Christian peer Baroness Cox has proposed an Arbitration and Mediation Services (Equality) Bill to the UK parliament, with the stated remit of outlawing gender discrimination in all arbitration organisations – but sharia councils are the real target of the Bill. Cox has stated that they regularly provide 'illegal' advice on marriage and divorce, ruling on questions of child custody and domestic violence, and violating human rights among women compelled to return to abusive husbands, or to give up children and property (McVeigh and Hill 2011). Subsequently, the government announced two public reviews of sharia councils, with a Home Affairs Select Committee formed in 2016, and the Siddiqui Review published in 2018 (Grillo 2018).

Not only have sharia councils been problematised, but so has the underlying process of informal mediation that happens in families before couples end up at a sharia council. Socio-legal scholars have expressed concerns that family mediation is a pressure on British Muslim women to stay in unhappy marriages and to accept the status quo (Shah-Kazemi 2001; Nunnerley 2003. The British Muslim women interviewed by Bano (2012) expected and claimed family mediation as one of the benefits of an arranged marriage. Yet equally, they reported pressure from their families to stay in the marriage, and thus 'what at first seemed like a new space of dialogue and autonomy in the family could, in some cases, still depend upon the traditional framework of power' (Bano 2012 p. 198).

Valuably, legal scholar Maliha Malik (2012) has tried to de-exoticise the UK sharia debate by drawing parallels with other ethnic and religious 'minority legal orders'. Whereas Muslim families have become a flashpoint for bitter debate about the tensions between multiculturalism, minority rights and women's rights, the situation in other 'minority legal orders' has elicited little attention and scrutiny. Sikhs, by contrast, have been politically positioned – and have been actively positioning themselves – as a 'model minority' (Sian 2013). Existing work on informal marriage mediation among Sikhs documents that women's voices may also be overruled by male-dominated, informal mediation in families and with community and religious authorities (Jhutti-Johal 2013).

Again there are parallels with the Indian situation, as Rajeswari Sundar Rajan (2003) observes, there are personal laws for four religious communities – the majority Hindu, and the minority Christian, Parsee and Muslim communities – all of which disadvantage women, and the reform or removal of which becomes a threat to community identity and/or established patriarchal arrangements – and yet, it is only Muslim personal law that has become 'an issue of moment' (p. 148). These parallels are unsurprising given that both polities are marked by deeply shared, right-wing, Islamophobic discourse (Friedrichs 2018). The images of 'imperilled' Muslim women (Razack 2004) that are circulating in Western countries, recently invigorated by the war on terror, draw a direct line back to colonial discourse (Abu-Lughod 2002; Bhattacharyya 2009). The same is true of the Hindu Right's images of the 'plight' of Muslim women in India, which track back to militant Hindu revivalist representations fomented in the late colonial period (Sarkar 1998; 2002), kindled by the provocation of 'white men saving brown women from brown men' (Spivak 1985) and the nationalist resolution of the 'woman question' (Chatterjee 1993). Due to this shared colonial legacy, images of Muslim women as backward, oppressed, passive and victimised became constitutive of projects of civilisational self-assurance for Hindu nationalists and for colonial powers (Sarkar 2017).

In this chapter, I attempt a comparative ethnography, analogous to Jeffery's (2001) earlier work, based on a UK context. Jeffery (2001) contrasted the predicament of the Muslim minority with the Hindu majority in North India, to dispel political myths exceptionalising the 'plight' of Muslim women's journeys through marital breakdown, divorce and post-separation destitution. I compare the British Pakistani Muslim minority with the British Sikh minority in the UK and attempt to dispel similar political myths, identifying overarching similarities in structures of family, community and religious mediation, despite sometimes slightly different forms, levels of institutionalisation and scrutiny. In the discussion and conclusion, like Jeffery but in the British context, I end with some reflections about the implications of this ethnography for strategies of feminist mobilising over the problem of 'minority legal orders'. I elaborate upon this approach in the following section, which provides a brief introduction to the research setting and methods.

Research setting

This chapter draws upon a study of marital breakdown conducted among British South Asians in East London and Peterborough between 2012–14, which set out to explore the processes undergirding the increasing prevalence of marital breakdown in these minority populations. The project was located partly as a contribution to the sociology of families and relationships in the UK, in which divorce in South Asian minorities had been little commented upon, except for Berthoud's (2000) work based on a quantitative analysis of surveys from the mid-1990s. This identified British South Asians as having relatively low rates of separation and divorce and saw them as flying the flag for the traditional family, at the still old-fashioned end of an inevitable process of individualisation. As Smart and Shipman (2004) argued, this perspective on minorised families was lamentable, as they are not static and the terms of their change may not even relate to the teleologies of individualisation theory: they 'do not necessarily fall into step with the march of many American or English families (assuming for a moment that these families are homogeneous and increasingly individualized)' (p. 506). Rejoining British family sociology's 'vision in monochrome' (Smart and Shipman 2004: 491), I redid the statistical analysis, using data from the Labour Force Survey, and found that by 2012–14, some 10% of ever-married Pakistani Muslim and Indian Sikh adults were separated or divorced, a rise from the 4% documented by Berthoud in 2000, and higher than in other British South Asian ethno-religious groups.

The project was equally a contribution to research on marriage and divorce in South Asian contexts. This was not to assume that the same practices of marriage and divorce would be straightforwardly transplanted from the diasporic homelands to the UK. Rather, as Werbner (2002) explicates, we should assume complex cultural transpositions. Nor was this method of locating the project intended primarily to draw out transnational connections (Palriwala and Uberoi 2008; Charsley 2013). It was because work on marriage and intimacy in South Asia has been richly generative, and I sought to import these insights, in conversation, into my work (e.g. John and Nair 1998; Grover 2011; Sen et al. 2011; Kaur and Palriwala 2014; Basu and Ramberg 2015; Vatuk 2017; Lemons 2019; Chaudhry 2021).

The project was initially conceived as a systematic comparison of Pakistani Muslim and Indian Sikh marriage breakdowns, taking the same model as Jeffery's (2001) comparative ethnography. I believed that the comparison would be illuminating. While Pakistani Muslims and Indian Sikhs share a common practice of transnational marriage, albeit to a lesser extent for Indian Sikhs (Dale and Ahmed 2011), differences in migratory histories and socioeconomic trajectories (Modood et al. 1997), marriage patterns (Ballard 1990), religions and their recognition by the British state and politics of multiculturalism (Grillo 2007; 2015) lent a relevance to comparative work. Unfortunately, the project did not materialise in that way, as the research with Pakistani Muslim families took off while that with Sikhs did not, for reasons that warrant discussion.

During the research, interlocutors often questioned my logic of comparing across the Pakistani Muslim and Indian Sikh cases, for different reasons on the Pakistani Muslim to the Indian Sikh sides of the study. To the sheikh at the sharia council where I conducted fieldwork, the comparison seemed unwarranted because of the entirely different levels of institutionalisation of religious mediation. Whereas in the Muslim case there is a highly legalistic body of theology and jurisprudence relating to marriage breakdown, embodied by the tomes of *fiqh* on the bookshelves behind him, and to which he pointed, in the Sikh case he saw it as 'only cultural'. When I tried to suggest that the underlying structures of community and religious mediation might be similar, he waved his arms around the room and quizzed, 'Do you see any organisation such as this one among the Sikh case?'

On the Sikh side of the study, many community spokespersons – such as gurdwara volunteers and committee members – offered a narrative of legal observance by Sikhs in distinction to a narrative of British Muslims subversively following a parallel law. Mr Balbir, for example, insisted that 'the majority of Sikhs just follow British law, they take it to court, they don't take it into their own hands'. He continued with a diatribe about:

> the problem with Muslims in this country … their sharia law just wants to produce as many children as they can, whether with one wife or four wives if they can. Every single Muslim man in this country, he sets out to get four wives, it's called 'mass production'.

He segued into the topic of sexual grooming of Sikh girls by Muslim men, which he saw as part of the purposive mass production strategy linked to forced religious conversion. Mr Balbir's views were echoed so routinely by Sikh interlocutors that I regretfully let that side of the study slip because I had recently married into a Pakistani Muslim family and was at the time of fieldwork increasingly visibly pregnant, and thus found it particularly difficult to absorb the level of scrutiny of my marriage and reproductive life.

Clearly, my own sociality and embodiment was a provocation for this relentless topic of conversation. But it was not the only provocation, as witnessed by Katy Sian's (2013) extensive work on the pervasiveness of forced conversion narratives, their significance in British Sikh–Muslim tensions. Sian describes Islamophobia as 'hegemonic' in the Sikh diaspora, which she traces to a colonial history of fomenting communal identities and casting Sikhs as a martial race worthy of respect from the British. This has been reworked in the UK context as discourse on Sikhs as a 'model minority' – an identity formation accelerated by the post-9/11 context of fear surrounding British Muslims and the repudiation of any notion of shared heritage. At the heart of this conflict lie the rumours of sexual 'grooming' and 'forced conversions', which have also been written about in India, in the context of the BJP's ascendancy (Gupta 2009; 2018). For Sian, these narratives represent a cautionary tale, providing British Sikhs with an evil villain with which to disidentify, and which also necessitate the policing of young Sikh women, whose growing agency and independence threatens the security of the community. Sian argues that Sikh Islamophobias represent 'a means of articulating the aspirations of a Western identity through their exclusion and dismissal of the "non-Western", that is, the Muslim subject' (Sian 2013, p. 102). The only political response, she proposes, is a wholesale decolonisation of British Sikhs, implying 'a means of elaborating Sikhness in its own terms' (p. 113). More recently, Sian and Dhamoon (2020) have offered an agenda for a decolonial feminist Sikh studies, which would problematise the policing of interfaith and interracial marriages in UK gurdwaras, both analytically and in actuality, alongside the policing of same-sex desires and LGBT identities, and take these intimacies as 'markers of choice about the body and sexuality … [which can] open the opportunity to educate communities on how struggles of justice are interconnected' (p. 49). I offer this chapter in this spirit of the praxis they outline, of 'locat[ing] the lived and embodied experiences of Sikh women beyond the constraining narratives generated on the one hand by western discourse and on the other by sexist Sikh discourse' (p. 48), as part of a project 'to document, disrupt, and dislocate gender hierarchies that violently exclude' (p. 49).

This chapter therefore focuses on my early-stage work with Indian Sikhs, unlike my wider work, which focuses on Pakistani Muslim divorces (Qureshi 2016). It does not draw in detail on the ethnographic material on which I reported in that wider work, which was based on interviews with 61 British Muslims, mostly British Pakistani Muslims, in East London and Peterborough – 41 women and 20 men – plus key informant interviews with solicitors, women's refuge workers, imams, spiritual healers, sheikhs at the sharia council, and observations in these and other community settings. Instead, it draws on interviews I conducted with 13 separated or divorced Sikhs in the same localities – 10 women and 3 men – and from some 10 key informants from Sikh community organisations and gurdwaras. My approach is to briefly recapitulate the findings on the Pakistani Muslim side of the study, which are reported in more detail elsewhere (Qureshi 2016), and provide details regarding the observations from the Indian Sikh side of the study. All participants have been anonymised and given pseudonyms.

My research indicated strong commonalities between British Pakistani Muslim and Indian Sikh families in the cultural elaboration of informal family mediation, which typically charts a course that begins with sounding-out with parents and in-laws, and escalates to the convening of family meetings and appointing of mediators, at which point community and religious authorities may also be approached. I briefly work through these three stages and in the concluding discussion, I consider the Muslim exceptionalism evident in the UK and India and think about the implications of this ethnography for feminist strategies, returning to Jeffery (2001).

Family, community and religious mediation

While affirming that there is no prescriptive course to informal family mediation, my wider work (Qureshi 2016, p. 124) argues that family mediation follows a 'kinscript' (Stack and Burton 1994), albeit with the proviso that these are scripts that are not read out so much as worked out – analogous to Finch and Mason (1993) on the working out, rather than following family responsibilities.

In their descriptions of an initial sounding-out with, or protest to, parents, the commonalities between British Pakistani Muslim and Indian Sikh 'kinscripts' are reflected in shared oral traditions reminiscent of those that Jeffery (2001) also heard in Bijnor, where parents insisted that 'a married daughter is in "her own" house and is expected to deal with her own difficulties' (p. 14). I heard many Urdu and Punjabi oral traditions to the effect that when the daughter leaves her parents' home on her *doli* (wedding palanquin) the parents say this is your dead body leaving the house, so that she never thinks to return (Qureshi 2016, p. 111; p. 127). On both sides of the study, I did many interviews with women who abided by this logic and did not divorce, or remained in intolerable marriages for extended periods of time, due to pressure from their natal families to remain in the marriage.

On the Indian Sikh side of the study, there were similar axes that differentiated recourse to natal kin support from the responses from natal kin and women's responses to these responses. Generation and migration status were important in differentiating trajectories. Older women described meeting with severe responses from natal kin decades previously. Sixty-five year old Mrs Parkasho from Jalandhar endured decades of domestic abuse at the hand of her husband, whom she described as an alcoholic. She raised six children by working in a factory as a hand-presser, with such meagre financial contributions from her husband that they could be regarded as economic violence (Chowbey 2017). Her brother, who had also migrated to the UK and lived nearby, told her that their parents in India would die of shame were she to leave the marriage. Tragically, Mrs Parkasho described his death from liver disease some years previously, in his 50s, as a weight lifting off her.

Younger women who had migrated recently to the UK described similar responses by their natal families. Although communication with family in South Asia was cheaper and technologically easier than in the early years of Mrs Parkasho's marriage, husbands and in-laws often conspired to prevent migrant women from speaking to their families, for example, blocking access to phone cards and mobile phones. Recourse to natal family support was particularly difficult for marriage migrants, as also seen in the Pakistani Muslim case (Qureshi 2016). Amarjit's in-laws confiscated her passport and refused to apply for her 'Indefinite Leave' once she had completed her stay on the probationary spouse visa. After being forced to stay beyond her visa's validity, and enduring years of domestic abuse and economic violence, Amarjit left her in-laws' home and became what she called a fugitive. She slept on the bedroom floors and couches of women she had befriended while working in *desi* shops for rates well below the minimum wage because she did not have her passport. Her parents in India were broadly supportive, but they too instructed her to stay in the UK until she became *pukki* (permanent). Eventually, one of Amarjit's acquaintances introduced her to a lawyer, who informed her that she was eligible to apply for asylum on the grounds of domestic abuse and that her staying on in the UK, despite her visa expiring, was legitimate because her in-laws had wilfully allowed the spouse visa to lapse (Mirza 2016). When I interviewed her, Amarjit was planning to visit her parents in India for the first time in six and a half years:

> I used to think about India a lot. My sisters, two of my sisters got married and I couldn't go because of my papers. I missed them too, too much. I don't have any brothers and sisters in England, they're all in India. I don't have anyone over here. If any of my own relatives had been here then, perhaps, my in-laws would not have treated me like that.

Simran, now in her 30s, had a similar narrative. She had arrived in the UK aged 18 to endure an abusive marriage, economic violence and patterns of close control by her husband and mother-in-law for more than a decade:

> I waited 11 years. Afterwards, wished I'd done it sooner, but my parents didn't support me to leave because of the shame. They said 'stay, no, give it a try' but in the end I said I can't live like this. They didn't talk to me for two years after I divorced him.

She tried to protest to her mother-in-law but:

> my mother-in-law brainwashed me. Three months in, he was already raising his hand to me but she told me I had to stay. 'Think what people will say, that you're burdening your brothers', cause my dad died when I was only just married and my brothers are younger and not working yet. So she brainwashed me like that, like I'll be bringing disrespect.

Without any natal family in the UK, and without the support of her family in India, when she finally left the marriage, she described two years 'neither here nor there, moving from pillar to post'.

By contrast, younger, British-born and British-educated women had greater ease of access to support from their natal families, and were more likely to report that their parents were supportive – partly relating to the greater vulnerability of women in transnational marriages (Mirza 2016), but also with some lessening of stigma as people take on board the fragility of marriage and the possibility of divorce, changing the interiority of family life (Qureshi 2016). Raj, now aged 32, exited from her marriage after discovering that her husband was having another affair, a third time, after only four and a half years of marriage. At first, she said her parents had insisted that she work on the marriage:

> they prevented me from leaving originally, when I found out about the affair two years prior to that, because I left a couple of times because I felt that I couldn't cope. And at that point, on that third occasion I think they thought, 'you know what? Just let her go'.

She gushed:

> my parents were amazing – like, unbelievably amazing, they just said look you know, 'don't let it get you down', you know, 'so many people go through this nowadays, don't think that you're the only woman'.

Significant in Raj's predicament was that hers had been a love-cum-arranged marriage, to a British Sikh man she met while working as a media intern in London. They dated for three years before the relationship was folded into a more conventional mode of arranged marriage after his parents approached hers for a proposal. She said her parents originally presented her marriage to the rest of the world as arranged:

> it all came out because of the whole divorce really, because my mum was like 'well you know', she just kind-of let everybody know that we had split up, you know 'at the end of the day we didn't find him and it just didn't work out'.

In the Pakistani Muslim case, in keeping with Shalini Grover's (2011) work on marital instability and kinship support in Delhi slums, I have drawn out how women in love marriages often felt less entitled to support from their parents in the event of the marriage not working out, and how natal kin may feel less motivated to save the marriage (Qureshi 2016, p. 119–23). The extract from Raj suggests much the same for Indian Sikhs. On the Pakistani Muslim side I identified further differences among the British-born and British-educated women I interviewed according to *biradari* membership, among women from high-ranked *biradaris*, such as Sayyad *biradaris* or high-ranked landowning *biradaris* such as Chaudhary described, there is more pressure to stay in the marriage for fear of reputational damage (Qureshi 2016, p. 110–11). On the Indian Sikh side of the study parallel caste particularities were expressed, especially in relation to Bhatra families, who were described as particularly traditional and controlling of women. Parminder, who married at 16 and divorced in her mid-20s, said that her father had refused to speak to her since her divorce eight years previously, 'we're Bhatra Sikhs you know, it's a very traditional community, my dad is proper old school'.

Escalating from sounding-out parents or reaching out to natal kin for support, in situations where a wife or husband insisted that the marriage was irreparable, or where natal kin proved impotent in influencing or prevailing over the other party, more formal meetings are convened with intermediaries. There were differences between the communities in the 'kinscripts' of intermediation;

in the Pakistani Muslim case, where marriages frequently took place within extended families, with cousins for example, influential elders connected to both husband and wife would be approached for this role – as one woman put it, 'my big people in the family' (Qureshi 2016, p. 122). Frequently, these would be uncles (p. 114–16) but sometimes also aunts (p. 117–18). By contrast, among Indian Sikhs, the *vichola* or *vicholan* – the intermediary who arranged the marriage – was widely acknowledged to have a customary or conventional role in meeting with couples experiencing marital difficulties and trying to help them to reconcile their difficulties.

Suman, then 49, had married unusually late at 36, to a divorced man who, she insisted, turned out to be gay – an explanation she presented as self-explanatory, invoking the bounds of compulsory heterosexuality, which are policed to such a degree that queer British South Asians may experience pressure to marry irrespective, or feel unable to articulate their queer orientation with parents (Mody 2014; Basi and Qureshi 2018). The marriage had come about through 'a middleman' from the temple [the gurdwara] who was acquainted with her sister. 'He was a contact of my sister's, a temple man – he often introduces couples'. She rued that her sister hadn't done her homework properly:

> my dad had passed way a few years before. He would have found out more, but mum, she was elderly, she couldn't. We didn't know the family, that was it. We just left that to the middleman who said, 'he's so nice, he just had bad luck before'. I thought 'fair enough', you take your chances and get married.

Problems became apparent very early on. The story of informal mediation followed the course outlined above: first she protested to her sisters, and then to her brother.

> I realised, after two or three months. Of course, I prayed. I told my sister, 'I've made a mistake'. My sister said 'don't worry, you'll make it work, they're all like that, at that stage'. I used to say 'ok', but then I realised he wasn't ok. I told mum too, but that worried her more and my brother told me off, 'why are you telling mum things and making her worry'. [Her siblings advised] 'talk to him, work at it'.

> They tried talking to his sisters, to my *saas* (mother-in-law) but they just blamed me.

When she left for a B&B, the marriage difficulties became impossible for Suman's siblings to ignore, and her sister notified the middleman. He met with Suman and heard her side of the story, and then 'went to their house and told him everything to discuss. He tried to help, but my *saas* just said "it's nothing to do with you, you've done your bit"'.

Jhutti-Johal (2013) depicts the process of intermediation by a *vichola/vicholan* as male-dominated, but according to my early-stage interviews this is not necessarily the case. Guddu, aged 28, a male migrant student from India, married at 24 to a British-born woman in an arranged marriage where the intermediary was his wife's *maasi* (mother's sister) whom a friend of Guddu's mother knew from the gurdwara. His wife's *maasi* had matched them on the basis of their educated status – both having degrees – and because their Jat *gots* did not match for several generations back, on either their mother's or their fathers' sides. Guddu blamed everything that went wrong in the marriage on his wife's parents. He had wanted to live separately, but his wife insisted that they stay at her parents' house so that they could save money; he had felt extremely uncomfortable living as a *ghar jawai* (live-in son-in-law) at his wife's parents' house. In keeping with his marginalised power as a migrant man married to a British-born woman (see Charsley 2013; Bi 2020; Charsley et al. 2020) it is notable that he was the one turning repeatedly to his wife's *maasi* for help in the marriage:

> I said '*maasi*', I said, 'look *maasi*, she said to me this, I didn't like it' and then she explained to mama [his mother-in-law] 'look it's not good, you're talking to your son-in-law like that'. She did help a lot. Then after when we were separate, even then she still try to make us get together, but then my wife didn't because she was all pumped up from her mum. And her *maasi*, she told her, 'look, one day your brother, he's going to get married and he's going to move; you're going to be living with your mum, and then one day you're going to think, what have I done? … Don't run for your mum and then leave your husband behind, it's not fair, it's not good to make'.

While intermediation by a *vichola/vicholan* might not always be as male-elder-dominated as Jhutti-Johal (2013) suggests, it is evident that the marital wisdom dispensed falls into the established patriarchal cultural logics of gendered marital roles.

Finally, where intermediation through formal family meetings did not work, in both contexts a process of approaching community or religious authorities for mediation was described. On the Pakistani Muslim side, this was institutionalised to differing extents, ranging from, in one case, a 'skype *maulvi*' – one woman's son's Arabic teacher, a student from Islamabad earning some money to augment his tuition fees by teaching Quran to British school children – to local mosque volunteers and imams, and at the most formalised end, to the aforementioned sharia councils (Qureshi 2016, p. 167–76). While Islamic jurisprudence or *fiqh* lays down elaborate rules surrounding divorce, in the British context it is crucial to note that the proscriptions of *fiqh* are not imposed through a strictly legal register because English law governs the family and the sharia exists only as a quasi-official legal order. Consequently, even in the most formal setting of the sharia council, jurists prevail over the men and women who approach them for intermediation or release from marriage in a moral-ethical register and through communal claims (Qureshi 2016; 2022).

Briefly, on the Indian Sikh side of the study, men and women similarly approached gurdwara volunteers and committee members in their capacity as wise and influential figures, either to attempt at intermediation or to justify a discontented wife or husband's desire to leave.

While much concern has been expressed over Islamic jurists' moral obligation to assist couples to reconcile, ahead of enabling them to leave marriages (see Shah-Kazemi 2001; Bano 2012) it is notable that the Sikh religious leaders I interviewed expressed much the same views. Bhai Narinder, a religious teacher based at a gurdwara, cited verses from the Guru Granth Sahib and went very deep into an exegesis of the *anand karaj* (the Sikh marriage ceremony, meaning 'Act towards happiness' or 'Act towards happy life') in order to stress the sanctity of marriage from the perspective of Sikhism. Contrasting it unfavourably with Islamic law, under which marriage may be seen as a contract, he said:

> I've never been able to understand that, about Islam – that how marriage can be a contract. If you hold a woman's arm, she becomes your wife; this is the hadith. A court marriage, that might be a contract too. But the *anand karaj* is not.

He gave the analogy of cutting a wedding cake and sharing sweetmeats, as wedding rituals, to distinguish the *anand karaj* from mere ritual or ceremony:

> The *anand karaj* is not a ritual. When you go four times around the Guru Granth Sahib, that's not a ritual. If you go out for takeaway once a week, that's a ritual, but we don't eat food as a ritual: we eat food as a *need.*

Given this emphasis on the transcendence and sanctity of the *anand karaj* is it not surprising that he had dim views about divorce from a Sikh perspective: 'Sikhism doesn't have a place for divorce'. This isn't to say that divorce is not permissible under Sikhism:

> If you lead your marriage for materialistic reasons, you should get divorced. To get rid of your evil, the evil you commit is not a sin. So that's why Sikhs can divorce, Guruji won't say it's a sin. But what's wrong is your understanding, your understanding of marriage, and why you're doing it.

While this deep theological account of divorce and sin was not shared by other gurdwara volunteers and committee members, others did explain to me that much of their work in relation to marriage mediation was that of attempting to reconcile estranged spouses. So, Bhai Satinder at a gurdwara in East London told me of a choice example:

> One girl, she called the gurdwara because she wanted to split. I listened to the mum and then to the girl and the boy. The girl and the boy, they didn't want to split but they wanted to go separately. The boy's father had died young so there was a very strong bond between the boy and his mum. I sided with the boy and the girl, I said, 'they're married, they need to leave, you can't spoil their lives because of emotional blackmail'. Bitter words were exchanged on

> both sides, the boy refused to step foot in the house but today thank goodness, they're back all together and the boy is back too.

In another example, Bhai Satinder continued:

> there was one in Southall where a husband found messages on his wife's mobile phone. He wouldn't give it back to her and she started screaming. The boy said, 'I want to divorce' but I told him 'marriage doesn't come with no guarantees'. Her parents took her home and stood up to his accusations. I agreed with the parents, sometimes people do send cheeky texts, you need to take it with a pinch of salt. The boy realised in hindsight that the problems won't go away by divorcing. This is just the British way of life, for Asians it's a bit hard because they haven't seen it before.

It was striking how readily and consistently gurdwara volunteers seemed to elaborate on the established patriarchal logics of marriage. So, Mr Balbir told me:

> like the Christians have their ten commandments, in Sikhism there are 10 gurus and each of the 10 gurus has lessons on *grehasti* (domesticity). In this matter our Sikh community is walking away from the religious understandings. They're very advanced in Britishness but they lose touch with their own Sikhism.

Mrs Satnam told me 'in our culture the wife's job is to endure and compromise but that thing is lacking these days'.

One last observation is the reticence of gurdwara volunteers towards marriage mediation work. As Bhai Satinder explained:

> at the gurdwara we're not always keen to get involved. Sometimes people are not willing. It could be politically – that we'd be seen as interfering in people's personal life. It's difficult if it's a well-known family that's often in the gurdwara. Or, it can be that it's difficult to be neutral because one party often comes to the gurdwara, so you're seen as becoming involved, sometimes people don't appreciate that. So, it's an unsatisfactory system we've got at the gurudwara.

The level of institutionalisation in the Muslim case does seem to be a significant point of contrast. As institutions designated for marriage mediation, the sharia council staff fully *expect* to interfere in a personal life, and show no such reticence or reserve.

Concluding discussion

Patricia Jeffery (2001) argued, in relation to Bijnor, that there are more commonalities than differences across communities in the structures of family and community/religious mediation. In the UK, in both Indian Sikh and Pakistani Muslim cases, informal family mediation is marked by similar gender inequalities, as well as by differentiation along the lines of generation, migration status, education and also, seemingly, by *biradari*/caste background. When it comes to community and religious mediation, there are similar compulsions to pursue reconciliation wherever possible. What seems significantly different are the levels of institutionalisation of community and religious mediation, with the sharia councils a far more formal, designated, legalistic institution and also, therefore, a sitting duck for public and political scrutiny. By contrast, the mediations by Sikh community and religious institutions are far more low-key. Nonetheless, an interesting point of contact and a point to pursue with respect to arguments about 'cultural voluntarism' (Malik 2013) is that even in the case of sharia councils, jurists may prevail over litigants not only through proclamations of law but also by making moral and communal claims. This suggests the need for further research to explore how community claims may be made upon those undergoing marriage breakdown through a discourse of living up to what it means to be a good Muslim or a good Sikh.

Based upon this material, I would like to end by going back to Jeffery's work two decades earlier, and think about the implications of this material for feminist strategising with an analogous argument. Clearly, the solution is not to call for similar levels of public and political scrutiny to other 'minority legal orders', such as those of British Sikhs. There are plenty of earlier flashpoints – such as that over the *Behzti* play (Grillo 2007) – and broader racialised discourses of backwardness and authoritarianism in South Asian families that would make this extremely unhelpful and take the discussion back several decades. Absolutely, we must push back to discourses of Muslim exceptionalism, but by tracking the historical roots of these distinct Islamophobias to colonial projects of civilisational self-assurance staked on the repudiation of images of Muslims (Sarkar 2017; and as explicated in the case of British Sikhs, by Sian 2013). In particular, we need to be cognizant of how long-standing visions of Muslim women and their plight came to the fore from the crucible of colonial attempts to uplift Indian women, which triggered preoccupations with nationalist and communal identity productions staked on women's comportment and sexuality (Sarkar 2008). Because of these same preoccupations with controlling women as emblems of communities and nations, the East India Company was able to manufacture consent to the project of colonial rule by relegating 'private' matters of the family from the state to communities, inaugurating the troublesome edifice of the 'religious legal adjudication of kinship' (Lemons 2019, p. 8). Fundamentally, the pitting of multiculturalism and minority rights against women's rights is the long-standing problem of the colonial settlement.

Writing about the Shah Bano controversy in India, Rajeswari Sundar Rajan (2003) argued that the one promising way for women to break out of the 'aporetic shuttle between community and state in any struggle' was for women to occupy their own space within civil society, where they might 'push the debate on personal law beyond the dispute between the state and the rights of religious communities' and become 'not merely the subjects but the rightful agents of change' (pp. 168, 173). Surely it follows that our strategy should not remain within the trap of 'framing issues of gender equity solely in terms of women's position in the "private" sphere of the family', and that a broader emphasis on critiquing the 'disempowering dependency' of women within marriage is needed (see Jeffery 2001, p. 22–3). Hence I see my work as one of standing shoulder-to-shoulder with all those embracing 'the possibilities and pleasures of conjugal trouble and troubling conjugality' (Basu and Ramberg 2015, p. vii).

REFERENCES

Abu-Lughod, L. 2002. 'Do Muslim women really need saving? Anthropological reflections on cultural relativism and its others', *American Anthropologist*, 104(3): 783–90.

Ballard, R. 1990. 'Migration and Kinship: The Differential Effect of Marriage Rules on the Processes of Punjabi Migration to Britain', in C. Clarke, C. Peach and S. Vertovec (eds), *South Asians Overseas,* pp. 219–49. Cambridge: Cambridge University Press.

Bano, S. 2008. 'In pursuit of religious and legal diversity: A response to the Archbishop of Canterbury and the "Sharia debate" in Britain', *Ecclesiastical Law Journal,* 10(3): 283–309.

Bano, S. 2012. *Muslim women and Shari'ah councils: Transcending the boundaries of community and law*. London: Palgrave.

Basi, C.S. and K. Qureshi. 2018. 'Homing desires: Queer young Asian men in London', in *Travelling Towards Home: Mobilities and Homemaking*. Berghahn Books.

Basu, R. and L. Ramberg (eds). 2015. *Conjugality Unbound: Sexual Economies, State Regulation and the Marital Form in India.* New Delhi: Women Unlimited.

Berthoud, R. 2000. *Family Formation in Multi-Cultural Britain: Three Patterns of Diversity.* University of Essex: Institute of Social and Economic Research.

Bhattacharyya, G. 2009. *Dangerous brown men: Exploiting sex, violence and feminism in the 'war on terror'.* London: Bloomsbury.

Bi, S. 2020. 'Marriage and masculinities in motion: Examining the migrant husband's experience in Birmingham's British Pakistani community', Unpublished doctoral dissertation, UCL.

Charsley, K. 2013. *Transnational Pakistani Connections: Marrying 'Back Home'.* London: Routledge.

Charsley, K., M. Bolognani, E. Ersanilli and S. Spencer. 2020. *Marriage migration and integration.* London: Palgrave.

Chatterjee, P. 1993. *The nation and its fragments.* Princeton: Princeton University Press.

Chaudhry, S. 2021. *Moving for Marriage: Inequalities, Intimacy, and Women's Lives in Rural North India.* New York: SUNY Press.

Chowbey, P. 2017. 'Women's narratives of economic abuse and financial strategies in Britain and South Asia', *Psychology of Violence,* 7(3): 459.

Dale, A. and S. Ahmed. 2011. 'Marriage and employment patterns amongst UK-raised Indian, Pakistani, and Bangladeshi women', *Ethnic and Racial Studies,* 34(6): 902–24.

Finch, J. and J. Mason. 1993. *Negotiating Family Responsibilities.* London: Routledge.

Friedrichs, J. 2018. *Hindu–Muslim Relations: What Europe Might Learn from India.* New Delhi: Routledge India.

Grillo, R.D. 2007. 'Licence to offend? The Behzti affair', *Ethnicities,* 7(1): 5–29.

Grillo, R. 2015. *Muslim families, politics and the law: A legal industry in multicultural Britain.* Aldershot: Ashgate.

Grillo, R. 2018. 'Comment on the Report of the Siddiqui Review Panel, 2018', *Journal of Muslims in Europe,* 7(3): 283–308.

Grover, S. 2011. *Marriage, Love, Caste and Kinship Support: Lived Experiences of the Urban Poor in India.* New Delhi: Social Science Press.

Gupta, C. 2009. 'Hindu Women, Muslim Men: Love Jihad and Conversions', *Economic and Political Weekly,* 44(51): 13–15.

Gupta, C. 2018. 'Allegories of "love *jihad*" and *ghar wapsi*: Interlocking the socio-religious with the political', in M. Rehman (ed.) *Rise of Saffron Power: Reflections on Indian Politics*, pp. 84–110. London and New York: Routledge.

Jeffery, P. 2001. 'A Uniform Customary Code? Marital breakdown and women's economic entitlements in rural Bijnor', *Contributions to Indian Sociology*, 35(1): 132.

Jhutti-Johal, J. 2013. 'How Parties to Sikh Marriages Use and Are Influenced by the Norms of Their Religion and Culture When Engaging with Mediation', in M. MacLean and J. Eekelaar (eds), *Managing Family Justice in Diverse Societies*, pp. 203–19. Oxford: Hart.

John, M.E. and J. Nair (eds). 1998. *A Question of Silence?: The Sexual Economies of Modern India.* New Delhi: Kali for Women.

Kaur, R. and R. Palriwala (eds). 2014. *Marrying in South Asia: Shifting Concepts, Changing Practices in a Globalising World.* New Delhi: Orient Blackswan.

Lemons, K. 2019. *Divorcing Traditions*. Cornell: Cornell University Press.

Malik, M. 2012. *Minority Legal Orders in the UK: Minorities, Pluralism and the Law.* London, British Academy.

Malik, M. 2013. 'Islam and English Law', *Prospect Magazine*, June 19.

McVeigh, K. and A. Hill. 2011. 'Bill limiting sharia law is motivated by "concern for Muslim women"', *The Guardian,* June 8.

Mirza, N. 2016. 'The UK government's conflicting agendas and "harmful" immigration policies: Shaping South Asian women's experiences of abuse and "exit"', *Critical Social Policy*, 36(4): 592–609.

Modood, T., R. Berthoud, J. Lakey, J. Nazroo, P. Smith, S. Virdee and S. Beishon. 1997. *Ethnic minorities in Britain: diversity and disadvantage*. Bristol: Policy Studies Institute.

Mody, P. 2014. 'Marriages of Convenience and Capitulation: South Asian marriage, family and intimacy in the diaspora', in J. Chatterji and D. Washbrook (eds), *Routledge Handbook of the South Asian Diaspora*, pp. 374–87. Routledge.

Nunnerley, M.L. 2003. 'A study of family mediation during divorce in the Pakistani Muslim community in Bradford. Some observations on the implications for the theory and practice of conflict resolution', Unpublished doctoral dissertation, University of Bradford.

Palriwala, R. and P. Uberoi (eds). 2008. *Marriage, migration and gender*. New Delhi: Sage.

Qureshi, K. 2016. *Marital breakdown among British Asians: Conjugality, legal pluralism and new kinship.* London: Palgrave.

Qureshi, K. 2022. 'Courting agency: gender and divorce in an English sharia council', *Contemporary South Asia*, 30(1): 30–43.

Rajan, R.S. 2003. *The scandal of the state: women, law, and citizenship in postcolonial India*. New Delhi: Permanent Black.

Razack, S.H. 2004. 'Imperilled Muslim women, dangerous Muslim men and civilised Europeans: Legal and social responses to forced marriages', *Feminist Legal Studies*, 12(2): 129–74.

Sarkar, T. 1998. 'Woman, Community, and Nation', in P. Jeffery and A. Basu (eds), *Appropriating Gender: Women's Activism and Politicized Religion in South Asia*, pp. 89–104. New York and London: Routledge.

Sarkar, T. 2002. 'Semiotics of Terror: Muslim Children and Women in Hindu Rashtra', *Economic and Political Weekly*, 37(28): 2,872–76.

Sarkar, M. 2008. *Visible Histories/Disappearing Women: Producing Muslim Womanhood in late Colonial Bengal*. Durham: Duke University Press.

Sarkar, M. 2017. 'Why Does the West Need to Save Muslim Women?' *Cultural Critique*, 95: 244–62.

Sen, S., R. Biswas and N. Dhawan (eds). 2011. *Intimate Others: Marriage and Sexualities in India*. Kolkata: Stree; Bhatkal and Sen.

Shah-Kazemi, S.N. 2001. *Untying the Knot: Muslim Women, Divorce and the Sharia*. London: Nuffield Foundation.

Sian, K.P. 2013. *Unsettling Sikh and Muslim Conflict: Mistaken Identities, Forced Conversions, and Postcolonial Formations*. London: Lexington Books.

Sian, K.P. and R.K. Dhamoon. 2020. 'Decolonizing Sikh Studies: A Feminist Manifesto', *Journal of World Philosophies*, 5(2): 43–60.

Smart, C. and B. Shipman. 2004. 'Visions in Monochrome: Families, Marriage and the Individualization Thesis', *The British Journal of Sociology*, 55(4): 491–509.

Spivak, G.C. 1985. 'Can the Subaltern Speak? Speculations on Widow Sacrifice', *Wedge* 7/8: 120–30.

Stack, C. and L. Burton. 1994. 'Kinscripts', *Journal of Comparative Family Studies*, 24(2): 157–70.

Vatuk, S. 2017. *Marriage and its Discontents: Women, Islam and the Law in India*. New Delhi: Women Unlimited.

Werbner, P. 2002. *Imagined diasporas among Manchester Muslims: The public performance of Pakistani transnational identity politics*. London: James Currey.

8

Gender Imbalance, Bride Shortage and Marriage Migration in Uttar Pradesh

An Exploration

Ravinder Kaur

Introduction

Patricia Jeffery's lifelong, ongoing work, based on her studies in Hindu and Muslim villages in the Bijnor district of Uttar Pradesh, is grounded in feminist and gender perspectives. She has explored many themes in her work – fertility, sex ratios, marriage, women's work, and the role of factors such as education and religion in shaping gendered practices and outcomes. She has also engaged in debates around women's status and the shaping of their agency. Patricia's extensive work in Bijnor highlighted how the demographic characteristics of a population that contribute to shaping gender relations and the status of women can only be understood contextually, considering levels of development, cultural factors, the political environment and people's aspirations around family-building, marriage, education, and work (1996, 1997).

I thought a fitting tribute to her vast scholarship would be to attempt a piece on Uttar Pradesh (UP), on matters of mutual interest. This chapter delves into how the state's demography, shaped by an ongoing fertility transition, is impacting its skewed sex ratio that in turn is re-shaping marriage practices. UP's large size, encompassing 75 districts, with a population totalling 235 million in 2021, implies that demographic shifts in the state are likely to have a nationwide impact. It comes as no surprise that as the state undergoes a demographic transition, accompanied by a resilient son preference and sex selection, it is contributing the largest number of girls 'missing at birth' (30% to 40%) to India's total (Kulkarni 2020; Chao et al. 2020; author calculations for this paper). While the alarming extent of sex-selective abortion and persistent neglect of girl children is of great concern in itself, the missing female births will also have a significant impact on the ongoing marriage squeeze, exacerbating the already existing bride shortage. UP, like several other northern states such as Punjab, Haryana and Rajasthan, has been importing brides from other states as one solution to address the bride shortage.

In this paper, I argue that the large size of UP, with its regionally divergent sex ratios and socioeconomic characteristics, results in multiple patterns of bride import and marriage migration. I hypothesize that there is an intra-state pattern in which men from richer districts of western UP, characterised by a higher deficit of females, draw local women from eastern UP and an inter-state pattern in which men from the less female deficient but poorer districts of eastern UP are forced into drawing brides from states such as West Bengal, Bihar and Jharkhand.[1] Primary data collected by the author on migrant brides in two districts, Etah in western UP and Basti in the east, suggests that brides move from east to west within UP and into UP from states lying to the east of UP. I demonstrate that these two movements of migrant brides conform to patterns of spatial hypergamy identified in several studies of marriage migration (Lavely cited in Constable 2005; Davin 2005; Kaur 2012).

Son preference, fertility decline and missing girls

While Amartya Sen's iconic 1990 essay 'More than 100 million women are missing' brought worldwide attention to the problem of missing women in Asia, the Indian censuses of 2001 and 2011 pointed to the emergence of a new dimension of this problem – that of missing daughters - referring to the fewer girls being born due to sex-selective abortion. Several data sources show that this phenomenon has also taken hold in UP where a large number of girls are being lost through a combination of sex-selective abortions and post-birth neglect. Thus, Kulkarni (2020) estimates over 679,000 missing female births in UP between 2004 and 2011, with very high levels of under-five female mortality. Results from a National Family Health Survey (NFHS) show that the child sex ratio (CSR – number of girls to 1000 boys in the 0-6 age group) was a low 904 in 2015–16, while the sex ratio at birth (SRB) declined from 915 in 2005–6 to 896 in 2015–16 (Kumari and Goli 2021).[2] SRS data show that the SRB has been below 900 since 1982. Calculations show that the percentage of girls missing at birth has steadily gone up from 30% in 1997 to 41% in 2017 (SRS, Various years). Given UP's large population size (17.35% of India's population), the state is at present contributing more than 40% of the missing girls in India, an alarming figure to say the least.[3]

As demographers have shown, apart from the impact of sex selection technologies on female births, fertility decline also plays a role in skewing sex ratios in son-preference societies. Das Gupta and Mari Bhat (1997) note the 'intensification effect', whereby discrimination against girls intensifies during the fertility transition towards smaller families. According to them, fertility declines faster than son preference as a result of which girls get squeezed out of the family. Further nuancing this process, Bhalla et al. 2012 show that in many states couples attempt to ensure, at first, two sons and later, at least one son during the process of fertility decline. Positing a zig-zag relationship between fertility and sex ratio trends, these authors show that at different transitions in the fertility rate (for example from five to four children, four to three and three to two and finally to one), the transition to odd numbers worsens the sex ratio, while the approach to an even number of children improves the sex ratio. The decline in fertility rates in UP since the early 1980s has been slow, with a steady reduction in fertility rates from nearly six children per couple in 1982 to three in 2016.[4] The movement towards a preferred family size of three children, with a continuing desire for more sons than daughters, thus accounts for the large rise in sex-selective abortions. The latest NFHS survey (2020–21) shows that fertility in the state is declining at a very fast pace, having fallen to 2.4, accompanied by an improvement in the SRB.

Persistence of strong son preference

Several studies, historical and contemporary, have shown that UP, like several other north Indian states has been characterized by strong son preference. Miller (1987: 54) noted that UP was one of the northern states with a high prevalence of son preference and where the use of female infanticide was common among the upper castes. Oldenburg (1992) called west-central UP the 'Bermuda Triangle for girls' and hypothesized that the violent nature of the society necessitated that families have more sons in order to defend themselves. Dreze and Khera (2000) show that murder rates were higher in Indian districts with low female-male ratios; to illustrate, they contrast female-male ratios in two districts of undivided UP – Pilibhit and Garhwal – the former has low sex ratios and higher murder rates and vice-versa. Commenting on the fertility choices of women in the Bijnor villages they studied, Jeffery and Jeffery stated, 'Women with daughters but no son tend to refuse to consider family planning until they have a son' (1997: 33). Chaudhry (2018: 86–7) mentioned that in the village she studied (Barampur, in Baghpat district of western UP), son preference and daughter aversion were widespread, although they varied among the different castes. She quotes a respondent as saying, 'No one desires a daughter because of increasing expenses. You can neither educate them nor get them married. Boys will earn and bring money into the family and then they will get married and their wives will bring a dowry' (Chaudhry 2021: 57).

Several other studies document ongoing son preference and sex selection in the state; especially in its western districts. Srivastav et al. (2011) interviewed 317 rural women in the reproductive age group in Bareilly district and found that, despite a lack of literacy, there was a high level of awareness of prenatal sex determination technologies but not of the PCPNDT Act.[5] A substantial proportion of the women felt that prenatal sex determination was justified and 20% justified sex-selective abortion. In a study of masculinity and sex ratios, across several states, researchers at the International Centre of Research on Women (ICRW) showed that rigid masculinity was highest in UP at 64%, and intimate partner violence in the year before the survey was also the highest in UP, at 49% (Nanda et al. 2013).[6] According to the ICRW, men who are 'rigidly masculine' are likely to have a high preference for sons.

Those migrating from UP carry son preference to their destinations. Thus, a study of migrants to Ludhiana district of Punjab (a state well known for its extreme son preference) showed that of 1,000 respondents who were interviewed, 92.80% felt that a male child was necessary for the family (Nag and Singhal 2013). The CSR among this group was 884, indicating active sex selection or fatal girl child neglect. The authors found that 9.75% of couples had aborted female foetuses, which is likely to be an underestimation since people hesitate to report sex selection.

Longitudinal sex ratio data for UP reflect that the preference for sons has remained resilient for over a century; however, as John et al. (2008) point out, the reasons for the persistence of son preference and daughter aversion change over time. While daughters have long been considered a burden in India's northwestern region (Miller 1997), different aspects of unwantedness weigh on parents at different points in time. While the inability of daughters to contribute to natal households remains a central reason for the preference for sons who live patrilocally and support elderly parents, the reasons for which daughters are devaluated shift in different historical, socio-economic and political contexts.

Scholars have pointed out that improvements in economic development indicators do not necessarily signal an automatic improvement in women's status and that the opposite has often been the case with sex ratios (John et al. 2008; Gooch 2014; Kumari and Goli 2021). Thus, even as UP has shown improvements in its economy (it is the third-largest in the country and the percentage of poor in the state declined from 48% to 29% between 1994 and 2012) (World Bank 2016), the sex ratio has continued to worsen, and sex-selective abortion has taken hold in the state. Analysing data between 1970 and 2010, Dubuc and Sivia (2018) demonstrate that UP is among the northern states with a very high propensity for sex selection.

Kaur et al. (2016a) point out that as families become more educated and prosperous they tend to opt for lower fertility and take advantage of sex determination technologies to 'rationally' plan small, but son-biased families, lowering the SRB. John et al. (2008) also argued that with the rise in age at marriage, the need for an appropriate amount of education for daughters to find good matches and the responsibility for securing their sexual safety for a longer period reinforces the notion of daughters as a burden, even under modernising conditions. Ensuring more sons than daughters is also an important family mobility strategy, as Kaur and Kapoor argue (2021).

Skewed sex ratio, bride shortage and marriage migration

An outcome of sex ratios skewed against females is a surplus of marriageable men and a shortage of marriageable women. As a state with a long-standing skewed sex ratio, documented since the colonial period, UP has been experiencing varying degrees of bride shortage. It is expected that with the current and worsening deficit of girls in UP, the marriage squeeze will deepen and continue well into the future. In their study on marriage squeeze in female deficit states, Kaur et al. (2016b) showed that in UP there were 10% unmarried men in the marriageable age group in 2012, which is expected to rise to 17% by 2050. This calculation considers both the age gap and the educational gap between spouses, two important determinants of marriage availability. The authors show that Haryana and Punjab states were at the peak of the marriage squeeze in 2012, by 2050 Rajasthan and UP will experience the worst bride shortage.

The remainder of this chapter discusses how UP has been coping with the marriage squeeze and how its large and heterogeneous character is shaping marriage patterns across the state. The excess of males resulting in bride shortages is not necessarily new; there is historical evidence of disadvantaged men in various castes being forced to remain bachelors or acquire brides in non-normative ways or from elsewhere. Jeffery and Jeffery (1996: 76) pointed to 'bought brides' in Bijnor in the 1970s and 1980s. Kalpagam (2008) also mentions the phenomenon of 'bought brides' in eastern UP. While bought brides might be from within the same community but from a different caste or class, many brides are brought from outside the cultural region. Such marriages have come to be studied as cross-regional marriages in which couples do not share region, language, culture and very often even caste and religion (Kaur 2004). UP too has plenty of evidence of cross-regional brides. Thus, Chaudhry and Mohan (2011) discuss brides from West Bengal and Bihar who married men in Badaun district and Chaudhry (2021) studies such brides in Barampur village of Baghpat district. Blanchet (2005) documents women from West Bengal and Bangladesh who are marriage migrants in Basti and Gonda districts. Kaur (2004, 2012) documents the presence of Bengali brides in Etah and Basti districts of the state.

Cross-region marriage as spatial hypergamy

A well-identified pattern in Indian society is that of hypergamous marriage, in which parents seek to marry their daughters to grooms of higher status, on several matchmaking criteria, including caste, education and land ownership. Studies of marriage patterns in India also yield directionality as an important characteristic of the geographical flows of brides and grooms (Libbee 1975: 80, cited in Kaur 2004). These flows are often unidirectional, with brides being brought from one direction and given in another. A well-known pattern in northern India is men in the plains of Punjab and UP bringing in brides from the northern hills of Himachal Pradesh and Uttarakhand (Darling 1977, Mishra 2018).

Lavely (1991, cited in Constable 2005) named one such variant of hypergamous marriage as 'spatial hypergamy', proposing the concept in the Chinese context to describe a phenomenon in which women move to more favoured geographic locations to achieve greater economic security or upward mobility through marriage (see Fan and Li 2002). Such a pattern is also evident in cross-border and cross-regional marriages documented in the context of several Asian countries characterised by demographic imbalances. The large literature on such marriages shows that women move from poorer countries/states and districts, to richer countries/regions with a female deficit (Davin 2005; Constable 2005; Yang and Lu 2010; Kaur 2004, 2012; Williams 2010). India and China have both recorded cross-border and cross-regional flows of brides in response to bride shortages. Chinese men have imported brides from countries such as Vietnam and North Korea; while within China, there are flows of brides from poorer, mountainous regions to the richer coastal areas, where sex ratios are more skewed and the demographic deficit of women is larger (Davin 2007; Das Gupta, Ebenstein and Sharygin 2010). In India, women from Nepal and Bangladesh have married men in bride-deficit areas of the north, while within the country brides flow from poorer eastern regions to richer regions in the north that have worse sex ratios and fewer marriageable women (Kaur 2004, 2012). Thus, men respond to bride shortages by looking for wives in other regions (within or outside their own countries), while women generally respond to such marriage opportunities due to various reasons, socio-economic mobility through marriage being one (Palriwala and Uberoi 2008).

Studies on cross-regional marriage in India show that the women are mostly from poorer eastern states, including Bihar, West Bengal, Assam and Odisha. They are generally from families with several daughters, in which the parents are willing to marry off daughters into faraway, culturally alien regions to grooms who do not demand dowries and take care of marriage expenses. Some parents might even receive money from grooms. Grooms are generally men who are disadvantaged in the local marriage market due to landlessness, lack of employment, being 'overage' by local standards, one of several unmarried brothers, being widowers or being tainted by alcoholism or some other character blemish (Blanchet 2005; Kaur 2004, 2012, 2016b; Chaudhry and Mohan 2011; Chaudhry 2018, 2021; Mishra, 2013, 2018; Kukreja 2018; Srinivasan 2017).

Some women migrate into bride-deficit regions from relatively prosperous states, such as Kerala, Maharashtra and Tamil Nadu. They have generally been left out of the marriage market for diverse reasons and are seeking to marry (Mishra 2021). Women's experiences in cross-regional marriages are embedded in and framed by local enactments of caste, class, gender, kinship and regional imaginaries. It is important to note that it is not only the migrant women who might be at the receiving end in cross-region marriages; men facing marriage difficulties also find themselves in stigmatised positions (Mishra 2018; Chaudhry 2018).

Several authors, including Kaur (2004), Chaudhry and Mohan (2011) and Mishra (2013) have pointed out common factors in such long-distance, cross-region marriages – skewed sex ratios and bride shortages in the receiving areas, and poverty and demand for a dowry in the bride-sending regions. Kaur (2004) notes another aspect of spatial hypergamy and unidirectionality, that women in deficit regions are not given in marriage into states from which the brides are brought. Thus, through their relative economic superiority and the unidirectional aspect of taking and not giving brides, the bride-takers (men in deficit areas) reproduce gendered geographies and unequal marriage patterns.

Region, demography, and marriage patterns in UP

To understand the patterns of marriage migration that have evolved in response to the marriage squeeze in UP, it is important to understand the immense variation in the state's demographic, socioeconomic and cultural characteristics, which often remain concealed behind its characterisation as a populous and poor state. Sharp differences exist between the western and eastern districts of the large state. Thus, western UP, with its fertile agriculture, high per capita income and urbanisation levels, and the dominance of rich farmers (Jats or Chaudhrys) is closer to Punjab and Haryana in character. Similar to these states, western UP districts have worse sex ratios than districts in the central and eastern regions. In comparison, the eastern districts are generally poorer, with better sex ratios and a less daughter unfriendly culture.

The percentage of the population below the poverty line varies widely across the state. In the western districts, it ranges between 2% and 18%, while in the central and eastern districts it is as high as 30% to 60% (World Bank 2016). According to the 2011 census, the worst sex ratios were in the better-off western districts, including Etah, Baghpat, Badaun, Mathura and Agra. Gautam Budh Nagar, a newly created district in the northwest, closest to Delhi, has the worst sex ratio in the state.[7] In contrast, the best overall sex ratios were in the poorer eastern districts of Jaunpur, Azamgarh and Deoria (above 1,000, which are as good as in Kerala, the state with the best overall sex ratio in India). The map of district sex ratios, available through the link in the footnote, immediately makes clear the east-west divergence in sex ratios in the state.[8]

This variation in prosperity and sex ratios between the western and eastern districts has resulted in an interesting dual pattern of spatial and socio-economic hypergamy, in which brides flow westwards within and into the state. In the first pattern, needy men in female deficit regions of western UP might be bringing 'eligible' local central and eastern UP women in marriage and, in turn, creating a shortage of brides for men in these districts. I hypothesise that the shortage created by women who marry in western UP is probably being filled by brides drawn from poorer states east of UP, such as West Bengal, Bihar, Jharkhand and Assam, with some marriage migrants from Bangladesh. Among these, the largest percentage of migrant brides is from West Bengal (see Kaur 2010).

Intra- and inter-state bride flows: Evidence from Etah and Basti districts

A survey of cross-regional brides in villages of two districts of UP, Etah (in 2003) and Basti (in 2012), hints at evidence for these two patterns. Data from Etah is based on a questionnaire plus interviews with cross-region brides in one village and scattered interviews with such brides in Delhi who were married in Etah district. I met the latter brides in Delhi through one Bengali bride I knew very well. Data on 90 cross-region brides in villages in Basti district was collected through a questionnaire.[9] Although such survey-based data coupled with a few interviews has its limitations, it did confirm the prevalence of cross-regional marriage in the district and provides a basis for the hypothesis offered in the paper.

Etah district lies in the western part of UP (close to Agra) and the sex ratio documented for the district ranged between 824 and 870 (between 1901 and 2011). The overall sex ratio was 873 in 2011 and the CSR was 879.[10] The latest sex ratio data, from NFHS (2015–16), shows that the SRB was 881 and the CSR was 860. However, an even stronger indicator of the strength of son preference and the degree of daughter elimination is the sex ratio at last birth (SRLB), which is shockingly low at 641. Ongoing bride shortages are, therefore, likely to deepen further in this district as a result of this trend.

Basti district lies in the eastern part of the state; the overall sex ratio improved from 938 in 2001 to 963 in 2011. However, the CSR declined from 938 to 929 between 2001 and 2011.[11] The latest NFHS data (2015–16) shows that the SRB is 881 and the CSR is even lower at 860 (indicating girl child mortality due to neglect, apart from sex selection at birth) and the SRLB goes down further to 708.

Both districts import brides from nearby states, such as West Bengal, Assam and Jharkhand. What is curious about Basti is that there is an inflow of brides despite the district's robust overall sex ratio. The low CSR implies that there might be a future demographic shortage of women, but why are men in this district currently bringing in brides from elsewhere? The paper hypothesises that the shortage of local brides faced by disadvantaged men could be caused by local women moving in hypergamous marriages to western UP or other preferred destinations (including urban locations).

ETAH

There were ten cross-region brides in the village of Amroli-Ratanpur in Etah district, when data on marriage patterns and cross-region marriage was gathered in 2003. The village is dominated by an OBC caste, the Lodhis, with other castes also being present (nine of the grooms were from this caste while one was from an SC caste, Jatav). In regional marriages, traditionally daughters of the village were married west of Etah, into the districts of Mainpuri, Aligarh, Agra and Mathura; while the men generally acquired brides east of Etah, from Farrukhabad, Badayun, Etawah and Kanpur districts. Thus, marriages of women from Etah and those who married into Etah followed a spatial hypergamy pattern. Most women were married within a radius of 15–120 kilometres, while the men had to go farther afield to search for a bride. Villagers stated that the marriage distance had been increasing over time, with men being affected by a scarcity of women, while the women's parents looked for 'suitable grooms' to conform to hypergamous marriage aspirations.

Etah and several other western UP districts also bring in brides from other states, the cross-regional marriage distance stretching to 1,000 kilometres or more. Among the ten brides in the village, nine were from West Bengal and one was from Chattisgarh, confirming a spatially hypergamous pattern for the in-migrating brides, while needy men are forced to marry outside their cultural region. The phenomenon of chain marriage migration of brides noted earlier could be facilitated either by men or women (Kaur 2004; Davin 2007). In-married women and men who married out often became conduits for arranging marriages. Thus, a Jatav (SC) man from the village, who had brought a bride from West Bengal, regularly arranged marriages of UP men with West Bengal women. The resulting chain marriage migration of in-marrying women can have some positive implications for the migrant brides, who generally face isolation and lack of acceptance due to cultural differences and the tag of being a 'bought bride'.

Basti

I unpack the Basti data a little more to discuss the *inter-state* pattern of spatial hypergamy. All the cross-region brides in Basti were drawn from states east of UP. Of the 90 brides on whom data was procured, 76%–84.4% came from West Bengal, followed by 12% from Assam and Bihar, while one bride was from Jharkhand and one admitted to being from Bangladesh. The brides from West Bengal were referred to as Kalkatahi (from Kolkata) or as Bangalan (from Bengal), while the few from Bihar were referred to as Bihariya.

The needy grooms who brought in these brides were spread across the caste spectrum of high, middle and low castes. Choudhary's stood out at 31%, followed by SCs who self-identified as Harijans, at 15%. They were followed by Brahmins, Nais, Prajapatis and Yadavs, with the remainder distributed in very small percentages over 18 other named castes. A few of the grooms came from Muslim castes. Chaudhry (2021), in her work in Baghpat district in western UP, notes that although sex ratios are masculine among both upper and lower castes, men of different castes face different problems getting married. She notes that the employment of SCs at brick kilns was a dampener on finding local brides, a reason why many of them had to seek brides from other states. Upper-caste landed men found it difficult to get local brides due to criteria for desirable grooms also requiring education and salaried employment, apart from land ownership (see Jeffery and Jeffery 1996).

Cross-region marriage was considered less prestigious and, among the men, seen as a last resort after the search for a local bride did not yield results. The brides and grooms surveyed were asked why they had to marry far away and into culturally alien states, instead of marrying locally as would normally be the case. Table 8.1 provides an insight into their perceived reasons for doing so.

Table 8.1 Stated Reasons for Marrying Out

Variable	Number		Percent	
	Brides	**Grooms**	**Brides**	**Grooms**
Poverty	85	72	59.4	43.4
Dowry	48	-	33.6	-
Bride's sister married in that village	4	1	2.8	0.6
Bride's father died	2	-	1.4	-
No job	1	43	0.7	25.9
Handicapped	1	1	0.7	0.6
Good match	1	1	0.7	0.6
Other	1	4	0.7	2.4
Death of wife	-	19		11.4
No land	-	17		10.2
Divorce/ Desertion by wife	-	8		4.8
Total	143	166	100	100

Source: Author data on cross-region couples in Basti villages

We found that more brides than grooms cited poverty as a major reason for not being able to marry locally. Nearly 34% of brides also cited dowry as a major reason.[12] Not having a job appears to be correlated to having lesser means and thereby lower social status for 26% of the grooms. Around 10% of the grooms cited landlessness as a reason. Around 12% of grooms were seeking to marry again after the death of their first wife, a common reason in patriarchal societies where it is expected that a widowed man will remarry in order to have a woman who will do household chores and take care of his children.

It is unsurprising that the shortage of brides does not come up as a reason for men marrying out of state and their cultural community. The underlying reality of a demographic imbalance is not experienced directly and is overshadowed by more intimately experienced hurdles in the search for a local match, such as joblessness, landlessness or the need for a second wife. However, the deepening marriage squeeze in UP will reach a 17% surplus of unmarried men by 2050, which might force an acknowledgement of bride shortage as one of the reasons men find it hard to get local brides (Kaur et al. 2016b), as has happened in the case of Haryana recently.

We found that the largest proportion of brides in both districts was from West Bengal (as in other states with cross-region marriage), leading one to query why Bengali daughters, although not unwanted as progeny (unlike in the north) are pushed out at the time of marriage (Kaur 2010). In West Bengal, family poverty, the inability to provide a dowry and the presence of several daughters in a family were significant reasons for out-marriage. A visit to a family in Dhaniakhali village, Hooghly district of West Bengal, where daughters of several families were married to men in UP, revealed other reasons for out-marriage of daughters, such as grooms demanding a cash dowry or the inability to find grooms who were employed or addiction-free and who could support a family. The family we spoke to mentioned that their locally married daughter was dependent upon her natal family for subsistence, while the cross-regionally married daughter was not.

In a paper in 2010, I argued that for families of brides, cross-regional out-marriage is a livelihood strategy that reduces the burden on her natal family in several ways - one less mouth to feed, daughter's marriage accomplished, and parents relieved of paying dowry or incurring expenditure on marriage ceremonies. An important factor driving out-marriage is the number of daughters in a family; most brides had more than two and up to seven sisters. Similarly, many men had more than two brothers, the highest number being five. Thus, the micro-demography of the families, combined with other factors, drove individual cross-region marriages.

Conclusion

This chapter explored some aspects of the intersection of demography and marriage patterns in UP. Pointing towards the worrying trend of a large number of girls going missing at birth and post-birth, it argues that the reasons for this lie in the contemporary phase of a fertility transition, fuelled by the desire for a small family. Resilient son preference, combined with the accelerated use of ultrasound for sex determination, followed by sex-selective abortion of female foetuses, ensures that couples can shape smaller but son-biased families.

A commonly identified effect of the male-biased sex ratio is a male marriage squeeze, resulting in local bride shortages. Men fill these bride shortages by seeking brides from elsewhere, usually from less economically advantaged geographical locations. In UP, this appears to have resulted in a dual pattern of intra- and inter-state marriages, characterised by spatial hypergamy. The intra-state, spatially hypergamous marriage migration of eastern UP women is into richer western UP districts facing an acute bride shortage. Their departure probably creates a shortage for eastern UP men that is in turn being filled by these men drawing brides from poorer states that lie further east of UP – West Bengal, Bihar, Jharkhand, Assam and so on. A discussion of survey data gathered from two districts of UP, Etah and Basti, supports this hypothesis, but to fully substantiate it would require further data collection and ethnographic research of marriage patterns and gender norms within UP, of the kind carried out in Patricia Jeffery's vast body of work.

NOTES

1. Western UP men receive migrant brides from other states also and do not rely exclusively on local brides drawn from other parts of the state. Patterns of marriage migration of women from hills to plains of undivided UP are also well known in the literature.
2. The latest NFHS data (2020–21) show an unexpected and welcome improvement of the SRB to 941. However, this number still has to be verified by demographers after unit level data is released.
3. https://statisticstimes.com/demographics/india/indian-states-population.php (accessed on 20/11/2021).
4. The decline has been comparatively much faster in other states with Haryana, Punjab and West Bengal all halving their levels since the mid-1990s (latest data for 2018) with Delhi and West Bengal having the lowest fertility rate (1.5) in 2018. Among the major states, only Bihar, Madhya Pradesh, Odisha and UP now have a fertility level above the replacement level of 2.1.

5. The PCPNDT Act (1994, 2003) regulates the use of preconception and prenatal sex determination technologies and is intended to discourage prenatal sex selection.
6. The survey defines 'rigidly masculine men' as those who have weak attitudes to gender equality and are highly controlling. Such men believe that women need to be bounded by the more traditional and accepted norms around gender relations. The states surveyed were Uttar Pradesh, Madhya Pradesh, Odisha, Punjab, Haryana, Maharashtra and Rajasthan.
7. https://www.indiacensus.net/states/uttar-pradesh (accessed 28 November 2021).
8. https://www.mapsofindia.com/census2011/uttar-pradesh-sex-ratio.html.
9. The data was collected under my supervision by a research assistant, Jagram, who belonged to the district and was therefore familiar with the local dialect. The questionnaire was prepared by me; data was processed and analysed by me with the research assistance of Prasanthi Ramakrishnan.
10. Census of India 2011, https://censusindia.gov.in/2011census/dchb/DCHB_A/09/0970_PART_A_DCHB_ETAH.pdf (accessed 10 January 2022).
11. https://www.census2011.co.in/census/district/556-basti.html (accessed on 30/3/2022)
12. Patricia Jeffery (2014) argues that the shortage of women does not necessarily lead to a reduction in dowry for local brides. Due to segmented marriage markets and changing matchmaking criteria, dowries still have be paid for desirable grooms. Only cross-region marriages are generally dowry-less.

REFERENCES

Bhalla, S., Kaur, R., Agrawal, M. 2012. 'Son Preference, Fertility Decline and the Future of the Sex Ratio at Birth', https://papers.ssrn.com/sol3/cf_dev/AbsByAuth.cfm?per_id=2141423

Blanchet, T. 2008, 'Bangladeshi Girls Sold as Wives in North India' in Palriwala, R. and Patricia Uberoi (ed.), *Marriage, Migration and Gender* New Delhi: Sage Publications, 152–79.

Boserup, E. 1970. *Woman's role in economic development*. New York: St. Martins Press

Census of India. Various years. Sample Registration System Statistical Reports from various years. Office of the Registrar General and Census Commissioner, India. New Delhi: Ministry of Home Affairs. https://censusindia.gov.in/vital_statistics/SRS_Statistical_Report.html (accessed 10 January 2022).

Census of India. 2011. Executive Summary. https://censusindia.gov.in/2011census/PCA/PCA_Highlights/pca_highlights_file/UP/45Executive_Summary.pdf (accessed 10 January 2022).

Chao, F. Guilmoto, C.Z. Samir K. C., Ombao, H. 2020, Probabilistic projection of the sex ratio at birth and missing female births by State and Union Territory in India, in PLOS, Published: August 19, 2020, https://doi.org/10.1371/journal.pone.0236673

Chaudhry, S. 2018. '"Now It Is Difficult to Get Married": Contextualising Cross-Regional Marriage and Bachelorhood in a North Indian Village', in S. Srinivasan, S. Li (eds.), *Scarce Women and Surplus Men in China and India*, vol. 8 in Demographic Transformation and Socio-Economic Development series. Springer.

Chaudhry, S. 2021. *Moving for marriage: inequalities, intimacy and women's lives in North India*. Albany, NY: SUNY Press.

Chaudhry, S. and T. Mohan. 2011. 'Of Marriage and Migration: Bengali and Bihari Brides in a UP Village', *Indian Journal of Gender Studies*, 18(3), pp. 311–40.

Constable, N. (ed.). 2005. *Cross-border Marriages: Gender and Mobility in Transnational Asia*. Philadelphia: University of Pennsylvania Press.

Darling, Malcolm Lyall. 1925. *The Punjab Peasant in Prosperity and Debt* (London: Oxford University Press).

Das Gupta, M. and P.N. Mari Bhat. 1997. 'Fertility Decline and Increased Manifestation of Sex Bias in India', *Population Studies* 51(3), pp. 307–15.

Das Gupta, M., A. Ebenstein and E. Sharygin. 2016. 'China's Marriage Market and Upcoming Challenges for Elderly Men' in R. Kaur (ed.) *Too Many Men, Too Few Women: Social Consequences of Gender Imbalance in India and China*. New Delhi: Orient Blackswan, pp. 89–117.

Davin, D. 2005. 'Marriage Migration in China: The Enlargement of Marriage Markets in the Era of Market Reform', *Indian Journal of Gender Studies*, 12(2–3), 173–88.

Davin, D. 2007. 'Marriage Migration in China and East Asia', *Journal of Contemporary China*, 16(50): 83–95, DOI: 10.1080/10670560601026827.

Dreze, J. and R. Khera. 2000. 'Crime, Gender, and Society in India: Insights from Homicide Data', *Population and Development Review*, 26(2): 335–52.

Dubuc, S. and D.S. Sivia. 2018. 'Is sex ratio at birth an appropriate measure of prenatal sex selection? Findings of a theoretical model and its application to India', *BMJ Glob Health*, 3:e000675

Fan, C.C. and L. Li. 2002. 'Marriage and migration in transitional China: a field study of Gaozhou, western Guangdong', *Environment and Planning A: Economy and Space* 34(4): 619–38. doi:10.1068/a34116.

Gooch, P. 2014. 'Daughters of the Hills: Gendered Agricultural Production, Modernisation, and Declining Child Sex Ratios in the Indian Central Himalayas' in M. Fischer-Kowalski, A. Reenberg, A. Schaffartzik and A. Mayer (eds) *Ester Boserup's Legacy on Sustainability: Orientations for Contemporary Research*. Springer.

Jeffery, P. and R. Jeffery. 1996. *Don't Marry Me to a Plowman! Women's Everyday Lives in Rural North India*. Boulder, Colorado: Westview Press.

Jeffery, P. and R. Jeffery. 1997. *Population, Gender and Politics: Demographic Change in Rural India* Cambridge: Cambridge University Press.

Jeffery, P. 2014. 'Supply-and-demand demographics: dowry, daughter aversion and marriage markets in contemporary north India', *Contemporary South Asia*, 22(2): 171–88, DOI: 10.1080/09584935.2014.899982.

John, Mary, R. Kaur, R. Palriwala, S. Raju, A. Sagar, A. 2008. Planning families, planning gender: The adverse child sex ratio in selected districts of Madhya Pradesh, Rajasthan, Himachal Pradesh, Haryana and Punjabhttps://idl-bnc-idrc.dspacedirect.org/handle/10625/39996 (Accessed 15 June 2023

Kalpagam, U. 2008. 'Marriage Norms, Choice and Aspirations of Rural Women', *Economic and Political Weekly*, 43(21): 53–63.

Kaur, R. 2004. 'Across Region Marriages: Poverty, Female Migration and the Sex Ratio', *Economic & Political Weekly*, 39(25): 2,595–2,603.

Kaur, R. 2008. 'Dispensable Daughters and Bachelor Sons: Sex Discrimination in North India', *Economic & Political Weekly*, 43(30): 109–14.

Kaur, R. 2010. 'Bengali Brides Diaspora: Cross-region, Cross-culture Marriage as a Livelihood Strategy', *Economic & Political Weekly*, 45(5).

Kaur, R. 2012. 'Marriage and Migration: Citizenship and Marital Experience in Cross-border Marriages between Uttar Pradesh, West Bengal and Bangladesh', *Economic and Political Weekly*, 47 (43)

Kaur, R. 2013. 'Mapping the adverse consequences of sex selection and gender imbalance in India and China.' *Economic & Political Weekly*, 158(35): 37–44.

Kaur, R., S. Bhalla, M. Kumar and P. Ramakrishnan. 2016a. 'Sex Ratio at Birth – The Role of Class and Education', Technical Paper, UNFPA, India.

Kaur, R., S. Bhalla, M. Kumar and P. Ramakrishnan. 2016b. 'Sex Ratio Imbalances and Marriage Squeeze in India: 2000–2050', Technical Paper, UNFPA, India.

Kaur, R. and T. Kapoor. 2021. 'The Gendered Biopolitics of Sex Selection in India.' *Asian Bioethics Review*, 13: 111–27. https://doi.org/10.1007/s41649-020-00159-7

Kukreja, R. 2018. 'Caste and Cross-region Marriages in Haryana, India: Experience of Dalit cross-region brides in Jat households', *Modern Asian Studies*, 52(2): 492–531 doi:10.1017/S0026749X16000391.

Kulkarni, P.M. 2020. *Sex ratio at birth in India: Recent trends and patterns*. India: UNFPA. https://india.unfpa.org/en/publications/sex-ratio-birth-india-recent-trends-and-patterns (accessed 10 January 2022).

Kumari, A. and S. Goli. 2021. 'Skewed Child Sex Ratios in India: A Revisit to Geographical patterns and Socio-economic correlates', *Journal of Population Research*, online, DOI 10.1007/s12546-021-09277-x (accessed 10 January 2022).

Libbee, Michael (1980): 'Territorial Endogamy and the Spatial Structure of Marriage in Rural India' in D.E. Sopher (ed), *An Exploration of India: Geographical Perspectives on Society and Culture*, Cornell University Press, Ithaca, NY.

Miller, B.D. 1987. 'Female Infanticide and Child Neglect in Rural North India', in: Scheper-Hughes, N. (eds) *Child Survival. Culture, Illness and Healing*, vol 11. Springer, Dordrecht

Mishra, P. 2013. 'Sex Ratios, Cross-Region Marriages and the Challenge to Caste Endogamy in Haryana', *Economic & Political Weekly*, 158(35): 70–78.

Mishra, P. 2018. 'Being "Bare Branches": Demographic Imbalance, Marriage Exclusion and Masculinity in North India', in S. Srinivasan, S. Li (eds.), *Scarce Women and Surplus Men in China and India*, vol. 8 in Demographic Transformation and Socio-Economic Development series. Springer.

Mishra, P. 2021. 'When South Meets North: Interrogating Agency and Marital Mobility in Kerala-Haryana Marriages', in S. Mani and C.G. Iyer (eds.), *India's Economy and Society. India Studies in Business and Economics*. Singapore: Springer. https://doi.org/10.1007/978-981-16-0869-8_14

Nag, N. and Singhal, P. 2013. 'Gender Preference towards Male Child among Uttar Pradesh Migrants in Ludhiana, Punjab, India', The Anthropologist, 15:2, 219 223, DOI: 10.1080/09720073.2013.11891309

Nanda, P., A. Gautam, R. Verma, S. Kumar and D. Brahme. 2013. 'Masculinity, Son Preference and Intimate Partner Violence', *ICRW*. https://www.icrw.org/publications/masculinity-son-preference-intimate-partner-violence/ (accessed 10 January 2022).

Oldenburg, P. 1992. 'Sex Ratio, Son Preference and Violence in India, A Research Note', *Economic & Political Weekly*, 27(49–50): 2,657–62.

Palriwala, R. and P. Uberoi. 2008. *Marriage, Migration and Gender*. New Delhi: Sage Publications.

Srinivasan, S. 2017. 'Cross-region migration of brides and gender relations in a daughter deficit context'. *Migration and Development*, 6(1): 123–43, DOI: 10.1080/21632324.2015.1083723

Srivastav, S, Kairwal, P, Kapilasrami MC. 2011. A community-based study on awareness and perception on gender discrimination and sex preference among married women (in reproductive age-group) in a rural population of district bareilly Uttar-Pradesh, National Journal of Community Medicine. 2 (2) July-Sept 2011

Williams, L., 2010. *Global marriage: Cross-border marriage migration in global context*. Springer.

World Bank. 2016. 'Uttar Pradesh: Poverty, Growth and Inequality', Uttar Pradesh - World Bank Documents, https://documents1.worldbank.org › curated › pdf

Yang, W.-S. and Lu, M.C.-W. (eds.). 2010. *Asian Cross-border Marriage Migration: Demographic Patterns and Social Issues*. Amsterdam University Press. http://www.jstor.org/stable/j.ctt45kfn7 (accessed 10 January 2022).

9

'Love Unturned'

Female Solidarity and Friendships among Lower-Caste Middle-Aged Women in India

Shalini Grover

> Omvati: 'People (*gali ke loog*) have said all kinds of bad things to me about Radha and likewise they have bad-mouthed Radha about me. We have never terminated our friendship or stopped supporting each other. We continue to remain loyal as we are *dharam behen* or blood sisters.'

Introduction

This quote is a useful preliminary to this chapter, which foregrounds friendship and gender-caste solidarity in urban north India, in which I revisit my doctoral fieldwork material (2000–01) and add certain observations from follow-up research (Grover 2018) on urban sweeper caste women.[1] I highlight the camaraderie between three middle-aged women in their forties and fifties. I argue that these friendships enabled women to deal with male desertion, the validation of consensual love, transgressions, stark discrimination from upper-castes, familial crisis and domestic violence. My interest lies in exploring the depth of female solidarity during these crises and the problems faced by middle-aged women. Are the accentuated loyalties in the introductory quotation as strong and viable as women claim they are and where do the limitations lie? In other words, to what extent does loyalty translate into action?

For this chapter, I discuss how female friendships are based on practices of solidarity. Unequivocally we need more insights into what constitutes friendship and the depth of these very personalised relationships in the Indian milieu. For a largely kin-based nation, friendship seems remiss and understated in anthropological monographs. We are still less informed about varied class and caste practices of gendered friendships. The sociology and anthropology of friendship is more developed and expansive for western societies (Allan 1989; Bell and Coleman 1999; Giddens 1993), in which the meanings of friendship are examined in western contexts. Yet even here, anthropologists have noted the neglect of friendship to the privileging of kinship (e.g., Bell and Coleman 1999; Desai and Killick 2010). Dyson (2010) articulates how scholars have been more concerned with hierarchical familial relations than with other social bonds that have affirmative dimensions. Her work portrays how friendships based on the labour of leaf collection in a remote part of the Indian Himalayas had contradictory implications for marginalised sections of society. Hence, female friendships in the Himalayas between the ages of 10 to 14, offered opportunities for everyday solidarity and yet they also further entrenched dominant norms. Analogously, Bunnell et al (2011: 6) tell us that while friendships connote a relation to others, they always involve racial, class, sexual and gender dynamics, creating what is acceptable and what is not. Equally, other strands of scholarship in India, such as 'youth culture', have opened the doors for the comprehensive detailing of young people's sociability and friendship outside the framework of conventional kinship (Abraham 2001; 2002; Chakraborty 2016; Dyson 2010; Nisbett 2007).

This chapter draws on ethnographic fieldwork to delineate the nature of friendships between middle-aged women. Such friendships are not an entirely separate universe from fictive kin bonds and concepts of relatedness (Lambert 2000; Raheja and Gold 1994).

As Desai and Killick (2010: 1) note, 'friendship is interesting because it evades definition'. Both anthropologists emphasise the close interweaving and, at times, the inseparability of friendship and kinship. Nevertheless, they saliently underscore (2010: 2) how it is imperative to retain the distinction between friendship and kinship, 'since it is this aspect that appears to be of crucial importance in giving friendship its moral force in many societies around the world'. These reflections are of import to this chapter.

To comprehend practices of solidarity, I turn to the emerging literature on global informality that stresses how 'informal ties' constitute an imaginative approach to sharing and giving in modern societies (Ledeneva 2018). Ledeneva explicates how informal ties with godfathers in Montenegro, 'dear brothers' in Finland and 'little cousins' in Switzerland, can make a world of difference to your well-being. She explores whether certain types of friendships are defined by regimes of affection, regimes of status, or regimes of equivalence, and asks what kinds of favours are involved, at whose expense and in which context? (2018: 18).

For the Delhi milieu, I argue that the caste-based friendships under scrutiny are about 'regimes of affection' that are interlaced with abetting structural constraints in women's lives. This resonates with the work of Raheja and Gold (1994) on how married women carve ties with other women in their conjugal villages, when natal kin support is not forthcoming. Likewise, Qureshi (2016) portrays how divorced women form strong friendship networks that are based on solace and common lived experiences, especially when they have felt let down by natal kin. This chapter makes four key points:

1. That low-caste friendships facilitate women to moderate power and prejudice with those in close proximity, such as lovers, partners, affinal kin and neighbours.
2. These close friendships are linked to the alienation of a particular stigmatised and abhorred caste group, regarded as the lowest caste in Delhi.
3. Such friendships that are elevated on par with agnatic bonds are carved out by women at a later stage in their life (at 40–50 years of age) so as to substitute for deceased natal kin.

4. Certain limitations within these friendships are linked with structural constraints.

This chapter draws inspiration from Patricia Jeffery's extensive contributions on gender and kinship for the north Indian region (e.g. 1996; 2001). Jeffery was the external examiner for my doctoral thesis and remains a long-standing mentor and collaborator. Her influence on how I view women's marital and labour market experiences, especially the critical interrogation of sweeper caste women as having abundant economic independence and sexual autonomy as portrayed in the social sciences literature has again been crucial in revisiting of this chapter. Through her rich analysis of domestic arena politics Patricia has inspired many scholars like myself by augmenting simplified marriage narratives accessible to a wider audience. The 'Don't Marry Me to a Plowman' (1996) trajectory of both mundane and dramatic events 'that are still unfolding in the lives of women' or 'plots can take on courses that may astonish us' (Jeffery and Jeffery 1996: 28), remain relevant to ongoing investigations of modern-day marriage and intimate relationships. So do her reflections on women's relationships of disunity and conflict and their supportive relationships that vary across the life-course.

BACKDROP TO DHARAM BEHEN BONDS: GENDER, CASTE AND KINSHIP

The friendships among sweeper-caste women that feature in this chapter are of the *dharam behen* (honorary sister or sister-friend) variety, which means that while the bond is a fictive kin one, this type of relationship cannot be taken casually. As Desai and Killick (2010: 2) ask, 'what does friendship do differently from kinship?' I follow these anthropologists in illustrating that the force of friendship may at times (depending on the age-group and circumstances) be stronger than conventional kinship ties. Furthermore, in my fieldwork setting, the sweeper castes, known as *Balmikis* were positioned as the lowest castes. Most other castes refused to eat with them, and preferred to limit any type of sociality. Balmikis were constantly subjected to upper-caste derision and discrimination. As a caste, they relied extensively on each other for mutual assistance. Given the overlapping hierarchies of caste and gender, Balimiki women were more disadvantaged than their male counterparts. For the former and other resource-poor married women in Mohini Nagar I demonstrated the closeness of post-marital bonds with natal kin, especially the ties between mothers and daughters and the nature of everyday intergenerational reliance (Grover 2009, 2011a, 2011b, 2018). The depth and endurance of such ties was conditional on whether a married woman had opted for a family-arranged marriage, a love marriage or a remarriage.

In conventional family-arranged marriages, natal families played a more significant role in their daughters' marital trajectories. Natal kin support structures nonetheless had a notable time shelf in a woman's life cycle; typically such support was unsustainable when parents grew old and brothers decided to form nuclear units. Consequently, after a certain stage in a woman's life cycle, the natal unit's active engagement and interest may begin to decline. As a caveat, even when levels of kin support seem munificent (e.g. in the nascent years of marriage), not all women invest completely in their natal families. The nature of kin support may have been double-edged and disruptive, such as the constant use of a married daughter's labour that plunged them into a precarious future (Grover 2009; Grover 2011a). Accordingly, *dharam behen* bonds that augmented and offered other levels of care and trust were cultivated by these women at a particular stage in their life cycle.

In what follows, I begin by foregrounding notions of female solidarity through the binary of 'us versus them' and I elucidate the distinction between 'neighbours' and 'friends' and how (assumed) shared locality and space is not always indicative of a deep friendship. I describe how a young couple's love marriage was strictly opposed on account of their mothers having established a *dharam behen* bond and I illustrate practices of solidarity building when *dharam behen* faced major crises in their lives. Finally, I present a detailed romantic biography and case study of domestic violence that allows me to assess female solidarity (*sath dena*) that is central to the *dharam behen* ideology.

Notions of Solidarity and Friendship

US VERSUS THEM

My fieldwork was conducted in Mohini Nagar, which is south of the capital of the New Delhi. The area comprises resettlement colonies and *bastis* (shanty settlements or slums) with a dense population. Residents of all ages lived in narrow and congested *galis* (by-lanes or alleyways). The term *gali ke loog* (literally, 'people who live in the by-lane') often denoted immediate neighbours and even epitomised the wider *basti* population. Given the close physical proximity of neighbours in *galis*, at a quotidian level they were perennially competing over resources such as water, electricity and space. Simultaneously, in times of familial crisis, neighbours were expected to support each other, invoking the aphorism 'neighbours are family'. Cooperation from neighbours was anticipated during celebratory events such as weddings, illnesses and childbirth. These ideals of cooperation were forthcoming at times, but they were also at odds with the competition over resources that neighbours faced. Given the spatial frictions, anxieties and lack of privacy in *galis*, neighbours often experienced ambivalence in these locality-based relationships. The neighbour aphorism thus portended paradoxical subject positions. Even if female neighbours gathered routinely in groups to sympathise over drunken spouses, domestic violence, affinal dominance woes and troublesome children, they were also at times in opposition. The vibrant socialising and collective sympathising that I witnessed in Mohini Nagar for over a decade was not always representative of deep friendships between women, even if they had spent 20–30 years in the same *gali* or residential area. The collective sympathising did every now and then manifest female solidarity and alliances, but equally at times it did not. A mixed picture of support, conflict, ambivalence and unity characterised relationships between neighbours.

If neighbours became 'friends' there was more at stake. They had to overlook the politics and skirmishes that enmeshed them in relations of conflict within their *galis*. Allegiance to a friend meant continuous socialising and support, even if this required overturning the judgemental views of senior affines and male folks. For example, signs of solidarity included shielding a friend from reputational damage. These were not easy gestures, as affines and spouses would get offended and gossip would be generated. There were women who conveyed how they preferred not to make friends in their *galis* and neighbourhoods. Many were also dismissive of a friendship ideology (e.g. *saheli*),[2] conveying that betrayals and break-ups among women were common.

A notable separation was 'us versus them' (i.e. friends versus others), as conveyed by Radha and Omvathi. The 'us' connoted loyalty, whereby even if women were neighbours there was an altogether different understanding of what grounded their friendship. Radha and Omvathi lived in adjoining *galis* and characterised their friendship by accentuating 'us versus them'. Resisting the onslaught of jealousy, spousal objections and vicious gossip by the majoritarian *gali ke loog*, their meaning of friendship was to boldly exhibit loyalty.

DHARAM BEHEN BONDS

Radha and Omvathi belonged to the Balmiki caste and had become *dharam behen* or honorary sisters. I came across at least eight *dharam behen* bonds, during my fieldwork, where all the women were from the Balmiki caste. While cross-caste fictive relationships did exist (cf. Lambert 2000), most castes tried to avoid the company of Balmikis. During my fieldwork, I tried to understand the distinctions between *behen* (which means sister) and *dharam behen* (honorary sister). The former denoted agnatic ties or a blood sister (*sagi behen*) and was also generically used for conferring respect on young girls and women in many Indian contexts. On the other hand, while *dharam behen* was synonymous with fictive kin, for my female respondents this honorary bond was on a par with agnatic relationships.

To reiterate, the key friendships in this chapter were of the *dharam behen* variety, which were not meant to be taken nonchalantly. In the following abridged case study, Sushma and Sangeeta were faced with an awkward situation that had implications for their *dharam behen* status. Their children were in love and attempted recurring elopements. The mothers managed to stall their children's love marriage by underscoring the idiom of their *dharam behen* bond.

KHUN KE RISTHE: OPPOSING A LOVE MARRIAGE

In the events that unfolded, Sushma's son Raj was in love with Sangeeta's daughter Hema.[3] The *dharam behen* relationship between Sushma and Sangeeta meant that the younger generation was allowed to socialise and have close contact with each other. Like many young couples who had grown up as neighbours, Raj described their love as, *bachpan ka pyar* (love that grew from childhood):

> Our love blossomed during childhood. Not only were we neighbours, but our mothers were always catching up and helping each other. Then my entire family moved to another part of Delhi, a different neighbourhood (Area X) about forty minutes away from where we first lived (Area Y). By the stroke of luck, I was given permission to continue residing in Area Y, as I was learning to drive an auto-rickshaw for a living. My association with Hema's family continued unabated because of the *dharam behen* connection between our mothers. Hema and I were attracted to each other and began meeting secretly in private. We would meet in the public toilets and then she got pregnant. She was 15 and I was 17 and we managed to have her foetus aborted. All our attempts to get married were severed because of our mothers' *dharam behen* connection. We were told the bond is sacred and marriage should be avoided at all costs. Hema's brothers began beating me up and Hema was under duress to terminate the relationship.

As Raj's mother, Sushma stressed, the marriage was impeded and the fact that the couple were not at the legal age of marriage was also used as a justification to separate them. However, the underlying objection and contestation was the *dharam behen* connection, which meant that a marriage between the couple was tantamount to a violation of blood ties. Raj and Hema's relationship created acute tensions for their mothers, who were faced with the test of retaining their *dharam behen* bond. The mothers began to avoid each other and Sushma mentioned that their friendship would only mend once their children were secure in new arranged marriages and when the matter was well past them.

Challenging Power Relations

Patrilineal norms may position middle-aged women more favourably than younger women. In the middle-aged phase of a woman's life she may no longer be just a wife, sister or daughter, but also a new mother-in-law. Jeffery and Jeffery (1996) discussed how age can impact on women's shifting power positions in households. When married women are forty to fifty years of age or more, or have acquired a different status (e.g. the role of a mother-in-law), they may face fewer questions over their freedom of movement. Depending on their socio-economic circumstances, the middle-aged phase in the life cycle may allow for more leisure time with friends, especially if they live close by. I was fortunate to partake in several informal conversations among middle-aged Balmiki women where laughter, solidarity, trust, advice and companionship went hand in hand.

An overt trait of solidarity among my *dharam behen* respondents was the act of confidence building, which required they remain non-judgemental towards each other. In one encounter, Omvathi and Radha met their third *dharam behen*, Basanti, to help sort out a pressing and rather delicate confidential matter. Basanti's daughter had got pregnant before marriage with an adolescent boy she was attracted to. Reacting to this pre-marital transgression, Basanti immediately prompted a 'quick-fix' family-arranged marriage for her daughter, with a groom who belonged to an entirely different region of India. After Basanti's daughter gave birth, the paternity of her baby was questioned with animosity and contempt by her affines. While the tensions unfolded for Basanti's daughter, Radha and Omvathi not only intervened but also offered advice, which I am told worked in their sister-friend's favour.

> We urged Basanti to confront her daughter in-law's affines (*sasural*). We asked her to threaten them by invoking the courts and police stations. With Basanti appearing bold and fearless, thereby provoking

> the affinal unit, they stopped troubling her daughter. She needed that confidence to challenge them outright.

With regard to confidential matters, *dharam behen* did invest trust in each other. Instances of trust were further endorsed when these women's lives were affected in traumatic ways. In Mohini Nagar I observed distinguishable patterns of serial monogamy and how men and women were searching for love, romance and companionship. There was also a prevalence of male desertions and betrayals in consensual unions (*doosri shaadi*), which are also known in the literature as secondary unions (Dumont 1964), a type of informal remarriage that may have happened on account of extra-marital affairs and romantic elopements (Grover 2011a; 2011b; 2018).[4] They may have a risky element as natal families may not be in favour of daughters dissolving their primary marriages. *Dharam behen* bonds, such as those between Radha, Omvathi and Basanti, were crucial for validating and countering emotional distress in consensual unions. These middle-aged women, whose natal kin members were no longer alive, had established durable alliances and social arrangements of support via their sister-friends that enabled them to challenge power relations.

Radha's account of her betrayal by her lover Subhash, illustrates the depth and closeness of *dharam behen* bonds. For instance, Radha conveyed that after she was jilted by her lover, her *dharam behen* cluster equally felt her anger, pain and hurt. Radha portrayed Subhash's betrayal as a notably shared experience with her *dharam behen* trio:

> After Subhash, who was from my caste, ended the relationship, he immediately found a new wife. I was heartbroken and my life was in turmoil. Omvathi and Basanti came along with me to berate Subhash, yelling abuses in front of his new wife and warning her of his disloyal nature. They complained to his and my other family members, who knew only too well about our torrid love affair but now seemed indifferent to my pain.

This narrative reveals that levels of intervention and solidarity were poignant and entirely different from the normative judgements being articulated by other neighbours (*gali ke loog*) and kin members who were familiar with Radha's and Subhash's fraught relationship. The help of sister-friends was stronger and more effective compared to the mild (and judgemental) advice of kin members. Radha, Omvati and Basanti supported each other unconditionally and expressed their own experiences of sorrow and difficult relationships. Their solidarity in berating Subhash publicly and warning his new wife led me to interrogate whether there were limits to caste-gender unity that I was witnessing throughout my fieldwork. What role did the *dharam behen* play when domestic violence and bodily hurt were routine or intermittent in a sister-friend's life?

The Extremity of Domestic Violence: Does the sisterhood work to protect women?

A large number of women in Mohini Nagar were at the receiving end of domestic violence.[5] Physical abuse was also common in those consensual unions that were exalted as being uniquely happy. I have discussed (Grover 2011a; 2011b; 2018) how, in consensual unions, women have to renegotiate the terms and conditions of their domestic lives in more drastic, complicated and unequal ways. Such unions reproduce the conflict, violence and inequalities that were visible in primary marriages. This brings me to Omvathi's circulated love story with her upper-caste partner, Prem Singh, and their consensual union that was hailed as 'legendary'. After hearing Omvathi and Prem Singh's romantic biography from Radha, I was told that such coupledom was rare and that their love endured the test of time. All the same, the sentimentalised myth of an everlasting romantic dyad was shattered the day I walked past her *gali* and found he had beaten her severely. The image of Omvathi haunts me to this day; she was lying in the corner of her *gali*, shrunken and unrecognisable, with scratch marks all over her arms and face. On seeing me, tears flowed down her cheeks and she clung to me. Omvathi was alone, no neighbour had passed by to offer their sympathies or a glass of water. I asked myself where Omvathi's *dharam behen* were in this critical hour? Where was Radha, her immediate neighbour and most loyal friend?

The isolation that Omvathi faced led me to probe Radha, Prem Singh and the latter's children. Why was Prem Singh so vocal about his true love for Omvathi? Did their children not care about their mother, who had lain alone for hours, like a corpse? Did *dharam behen* bonds not matter in such distressing moments? After all, given the state Omvathi was in, she should have been taken to a hospital emergency unit or a domestic violence women's shelter. Were these *dharam behen* bonds based on a camaraderie as strong as Balmiki women had been portraying them? This incident allowed me to re-assess the solidarity that *dharam behen* bonds invoked. Radha reacted calmly by revealing that what I had witnessed was indeed disturbing, but this was certainly not the first time that Prem Singh had bashed her up. Her rejoinder was:

> Given that we are her *dharam behen*, we do care. We feel her pain and hurt the same way as you do. Her natal kin are no longer alive and she is in a consensual relationship (*doosri shaadi*) with Prem Singh, with whom she has two children. Where will she go and who will look after her children? Her health is frail and she is underweight. Either she should leave Prem Singh or otherwise she has no choice but to endure his volatile nature. By the way, Prem Singh, is completely fearless. Everyone in Mohini Nagar is scared of him, even the police. If Omvathi were to threaten him by using the trope of Domestic Violence Laws and the support of NGOs, he may just beat her to death. Omvathi feeds her entire family with her Municipal Corporation Salary (MCD). Even in her frail state, she hands over her entire salary to Prem Singh, who just gambles away the money. After bouts of drinking and gambling, he then beats her up whenever he wants to. She is my friend and there is so much love between us. But beyond a point I am helpless and can only comfort her.

Undeniably, domestic violence prompted sympathy from women but it also drew ambivalent reactions and non-interference practices from *gali ke loog*. In most domestic violence situations, women tended to seek succour from their natal kin, women's NGOs and police authorities in the vicinity. With Omvathi, her conglomerate of *dharam behen* had long concluded that she had no choice but to continue living with Prem Singh. Omvathi's natal kin were no longer alive and she had lost contact with her brother. After hearing Radha's version, I got the sense that concrete interventions on behalf of close friends had limitations. As Radha reminded me: 'If I had taken Omvathi home or given her shelter for the night, Prem Singh may have walked in and killed us both.' As it stands, in cases of extreme domestic violence, friends may not always be in a position to offer immediate care or shelter. They would need to find tactful ways to handle volatile, upper-caste men like Prem Singh and thus they have constraints of their own. I have argued (Grover 2011a; 2018) that to achieve far-reaching changes in women's lives, more effective and gender-sensitive legal systems, alternatives to the institution of marriage (i.e. the societal acceptance of living as single women) and extensive material transformations are necessary.

On the other hand, Prem Singh's rejoinders regarding Omvathi's beatings prompted the phrase, 'no conflict is ever one-sided or there are two sides to a story' ('*tali dono hath se bajti hai*') (see Grover 2018: 41). By using this phrase Omvathi was made to feel responsible for the domestic violence she encountered. By citing this phrase, Prem Singh justified his physical beatings and his children exonerated their father's violent behaviour. The *dharam behen* did not concur with Prem Singh's justifications, as echoed through the phrase 'no conflict is ever one-sided'. This is not to say that in other situations involving different women from the locality, they would not invoke this phrase. There are many complex rejoinders to domestic violence that prompt an outright condemnation of tolerance. Prem Singh thereafter avoided the subject of violence with me, while signalling I should stop asking any further questions. I found the family slowly coming together again after this painful incident. A week later they were sitting outside in the winter sunshine eating peanuts. Omvathi's courage and strength lasted only a few more months and then she died. As a reaction to her death, Prem Singh took once again to heavy drinking. While Omvathi had always been a frail woman, in response to her weak physical constitution, Prem Singh would mention to me and to the *gali ka loog* that she had a terminal illness. This narrative of a terminal illness constructed by Prem Singh was no longer a convincing one for me. What led to Omvathi's ill health and her ultimate death were the routine beatings she endured in a consensual union that was symbolised as being exceptionally romantic.

Conclusion

The age-old question of the ethics of intervention or non-intervention that anthropologists grapple with came up time and again in my fieldwork. Should I have taken Omvathi to a hospital? Should I have reported the incident to a Woman's NGO or the neighbourhood police? As anthropologists we are cautioned against meddling in everyday social relations beyond a certain point. The politics of saving other women was not my intention, for in this context we are reminded of the words of Abu-Lughod (2002: 789):

> Where we seek to be active in the affairs of distant places, can we do so in the spirit of support for those within those communities whose goals are to make women's and men's lives better? Can we use a more egalitarian language of alliances, coalitions, and solidarity, instead of salvation?

My outrage at that time resulted in several discussions with Radha and Basanti over Prem Singh's actions. Whatever their justifications were for Omvathi having to remain in a consensual union, we seemed in agreement about the need to rally around her even more.

This chapter has signposted that *dharam behen* bonds exemplify practices of solidarity 'that can make a world of difference to your well-being' (Ledeneva 2018). These highly personalised friendships had subversive elements. While these *dharam behen* bonds did not cut across caste boundaries, the *dharam behen* trio under discussion did somewhat challenge the power relations of inter-caste intimacies. From transgressions to male betrayals to countering vicious gossip in *galis*, all this required courage and imagination on their part. These middle-aged *dharam behen* were a 'force to reckon with' in their neighbourhood. Nevertheless, there were times when the *dharam behen* trio did not question idealised notions of love or the romantic cultural narratives of consensual unions. They were also unable to assist practically in situations when a *dharam behen* really needed their help. As I have illustrated, their inability to assist in situations of extreme domestic violence was because of wider constraints, such as their particular caste-class location and other patriarchal gender and community norms that could put them in jeopardy. As Bunnell et al (2011) remind us, there are lines drawn in friendships (based on race, class, gender and so on) as to what is acceptable and what is not.

Acknowledgements

I am very grateful to Shruti Chaudhry and Radhika Govinda for their valuable suggestions and detailed reading of the paper.

NOTES

1. The new research was conducted in short intervals during 2016–17 for the revised edition of my book (2018). These were recurring visits to meet key respondents I have known for several years, combining unstructured interviews with participant observation. The research questions were aimed at capturing dimensions of change and continuity since 2000–01. However, this chapter still draws largely from the doctoral fieldwork I conducted in 2000.
2. The Hindi term *saheli* means friend (the literal translation being a 'non-kin' oriented friend). Many women, especially young women, use the *saheli* terminology. My respondents used *behen*, hyphenating their relationship as 'sister-friend'.
3. Parts of this narrative that focus on the love relationship between Hema and Raj have appeared in Grover (2011a and 2018), but the *dharam behen* angle did not appear in these previous works.
4. As I have written quite extensively (2011a; 2011b) consensual and secondary unions that permit greater emotional and sexual freedom also have a purposeful role, as they serve as critical exit options or survival mechanisms for poor women.
5. It is equally the case that domestic violence prevails among the Indian middle-classes and affluent families. In the higher echelons it is simply more hidden and less discussed (See Grover forthcoming 2022 for a detailed account).

REFERENCES

Abraham, L. 2001. 'Redrawing the Lakshman Rekha: Gender difference and cultural constructions in youth sexuality in urban India', *South Asia*, 24: 133–56.

Abraham, L. 2002. 'Bhai-Behen, True Love, Time Pass: Friendships and sexual partnerships among youth in an Indian metropolis', *Culture, Health, Sexuality*, 4(3): 337–53.

Abu-Lughod, L. 2002. 'Do Muslim Women Really Need Saving? Anthropological reflections on cultural relativism and its others', *American Ethnologist*, 104(3): 783–90.

Allan, G. 1989. *Friendship: Developing a Sociological Perspective*. Boulder, Co: Westview Press.

Bell, S. and S. Coleman. 1999. *The Anthropology of Friendship*. Oxford: Berg.

Bunnell, T., S. Yea, L. Peake, T. Skelton and M. Smith. 2011. 'Geographies of Friendship', *Progress in Human Geography*, 36(4): 490–507.

Chakraborty, K. 2016. *Young Muslim Women in India: Bollywood, Identity and Changing Youth Culture*. London and New York: Routledge.

Desai, A. and E. Killick (eds.) 2010. *The Ways of Friendship: Anthropological Perspectives*. United States: Berghahn.

Dumont, L. 1964. 'Marriage in India, the Present State of the Question: postscript to Part I. Part II: Marriage and Status, Nayar and Newar'. *Contributions to Indian Sociology*, 7: 77–98.

Dyson, J. 2010. 'Friendship in Practice: Girls' Work in the Indian Himalayas', *American Ethnologist*, 37–93: 482–98.

Giddens, A. 1993. *The Transformation of Intimacy: Sexuality, love and eroticism in modern societies*. Stanford, CA: Stanford University Press.

Grover, S. 2009. 'Lived Experiences: Marriage, notions of love and kinship support among poor women in Delhi', *Contributions to Indian Sociology*, 43(1): 1–33.

Grover, S. 2011a. *Marriage, Love, Caste, and Kinship Support: Lived experiences of the urban poor in India*. New Delhi: Social Science Press.

Grover, S. 2011b. ' "*Purani Aur Nai Shaadi*": Separation, divorce, and remarriage in the lives of the urban poor in New Delhi', *Asian Journal of Women's Studies*, (17)1: 67–99.

Grover, S. 2017. 'Jural Relations of Middle-Class Marriage and Women as Legal Subjects in the Imaginary of "new India"', *The Australian Journal of Anthropology (TAJA)*, 28(3): 249–393.

Grover, S. 2018 (revised new edition). *Marriage, Love, Caste, and Kinship Support: Lived experiences of the urban poor in India*. London: Routledge.

Grover, S. 2022 (forthcoming). 'Family-Arranged Marriages in Globalizing India: Shifting Scripts of Desire, Infidelity and Emotional Compatibility', in P. Betra (ed.), *Title in progress*. USA: Rutgers University Press.

Jeffery, P. 2001. 'A Uniform Civil Code? Marital breakdown and women's economic entitlement in rural Bijnor', *Contributions to Indian Sociology*, 35(1): 1–32.

Jeffery, P. and R. Jeffery. 1996. *Don't Marry Me to a Plowman. Women's Everyday Lived in Rural North India*. New Delhi: Vistaar.

Lambert, H. 2000. 'Sentiment and Substance in North Indian Forms of Relatedness', in J. Carsten (ed.), *Cultures of Relatedness: New Approaches to the Study of Kinship*. Cambridge: Cambridge University Press.

Ledeneva, A. 2018. *The Global Encyclopedia of Informality*. London: UCL Press.
Nisbett, N. 2007. 'Friendship, Consumption, Morality: Practicing identity, negotiating hierarchy in middle class Bangalore', *Journal of the Royal Anthropological Institute*, 13(4): 935–50.
Qureshi, K. 2016. *Marital Breakdown Among British Asians: Conjugality, legal pluralism and new kinship*. London: Palgrave.
Raheja, G.G. and A.G. Gold. 1994. *Listen to the Heron's Words: Reimagining gender and kinship in North India*. Berkeley: University of California Press.

10

Exploring Trajectories of Being Single

Questions of Never-married Women in Delhi

Rajni Palriwala

A bulb lights up – or not

We met Indira on the main road as we were leaving, disappointed after the daughters-in-law of a woman we had spoken with at length refused to be interviewed. Their husbands had told them not to. It was difficult to assess her age, she was dressed well in a *salwar kameez*, with dyed black hair, a sprightly stance and a clear voice. She stopped us and asked aggressively what we were doing.[1] I elaborated that we were documenting life histories of senior women selected from an earlier survey. 'Oh, a survey. I have done many. I am a retired school teacher,' was her response. I explained that this was not a survey, and that we hoped to hear the little-heard life stories of women. She then said that she would not tell us her story as she had to think of her sister and other kin who lived in the same neighbourhood as her. However, she kept us talking and told us that she was unmarried and lived alone, and narrated much of her life, family problems, her work and daily routine. Finally, she gave us her phone number and invited us to come over for more chats.

Neither in age nor in marital status was Indira among those we were focusing on (women aged 70 plus, who lived in households or houses where there was at least one other adult kinswoman of a junior generation).[2] We had selected them from a large survey on family values and inter-generational care practices (2011–12).[3] Yet, after being turned away by some before or after the first conversation, finding that other selected households had moved since the original survey and were 'missing', or that the elderly woman in the household was no more, we were ready to broaden our field. Indira was one of only two women we met and conversed with at length, who lived in a single person household. In thinking about a theme for a paper in a volume honouring Patricia, I first thought of struggles in family life in women-only households, overlaid by the theme of social change that framed our focus on life narratives. I soon realised that one of the households I was thinking of was not a women-only household. It had seemed it was, as we had only met the women, true of much of this fieldwork. Later, I was struck by the common difference in three of these households: they were the only ones we spent time with in which the not-yet-married women were likely to remain never-married. Not a small number relative to the small sample of households (16) in which we interacted with women, at length, in 2013 and 2015.[4]

In thinking about a theme for this chapter, I had been going back to Patricia's ethnographies and it struck me that even in their richness we heard little of or from adult never-married women, whether in Delhi or Bijnor. Never-married females figure in ethnographic work mostly as not-yet-married adolescents, around issues of education, match-making, labour and concerns about sexuality/chastity. Other than these glimmerings, including in my own work in/on India, the unmarried women were largely once-married, mostly middle-aged and elderly, living in joint households or in adjunct dwellings or alone. Never-married men have been discussed more, largely in the context of preventing the fragmentation of land holdings among poor farmers and the marriage squeeze following the worsening adverse sex ratio (Jeffery and Jeffery 1997; Kaur 2008). It is not that there is no writing or discussion of never-married women in South Asia. There has been work on female religious ascetics (Babb 1984, 1987; Phillimore 1991). There is an emerging body of writing on women who have rejected heterosexuality, for whom the possibility of same-sex marriage is fraught, who may or may not critique marriage itself and may or may not marry (Biswas 2011; Sharma 2006). I wondered if I had overlooked the adult, never-married woman, whether my research questions had made them invisible, or if they were truly absent in the settings in which I had earlier conducted fieldwork (such as rural Rajasthan) or been engaged with as an activist (Delhi working-class neighbourhoods in the 1980s). Thus, one question troubled me – a matter of clearing the underbrush: had never-married adult women been absent or been made invisible by the hegemonic value of compulsory, heterosexual marriage? Had these values indeed translated into universal practices of gender, marriage, and familial life or had they formed a screen of anthropological 'truths' that hid the never-married?' A second question was: what can one learn in terms of trends and questions in social relations, gender and social change through an initial exploration of the lives of single women?

Who is the single woman?

The term 'single woman' has been postulated as a break from defining women through their relationship with a male spouse (Ellison 2003, cited in Lamb 2018).[5] Pappu indicates the complexity of this term in India in its 'host of inchoate meanings that drive from the diverse discourses of the family, free market, developmental economics, behavioural psychology, feminist and queer movements among others' (2011: 370). The thread running through them all, she asserts, is the absence of a legitimate male sexual partner. But there is more. The term suggests that women (and men) are not meant to be alone. The continuing reality of compulsory and well-nigh universal heterosexual marriage as practice and value in India, and the disregard of those who do not conform, cannot be denied by juggling with words, even as this value may place a smokescreen around them. True, the many women who join such sects as the Brahmakumaris, Buddhist nunneries, or the *sidhin* of Kangra discussed by Phillimore (1991), are respected, even revered, in their celibacy and asceticism. This may be the case even when they do not live in sectarian communities, but rather, like the *sidhin* of Kangra and Buddhist nuns in Ladakh (Brown 1998),[6] remain in familial life and households. Indeed, they are hardly thought of as 'single women', although they are pledged to celibacy.

Lamb's studies (2018, 2021) are one of the few ethnographic accounts of never-married women. She tells us that '"single" has been emerging as an emic, local category in India to refer to adult women and men who are not (yet) married' (2018: 51). As indicated above, the focus in academic and lay writings and activism in South Asia has been on the once-married, elderly (women and men), widows, divorcees and abandoned women.[7] Like them, the 'secular' never-married men and women (having crossed a certain age) are spoken of as 'tragic' or, if they are women, they are stigmatised.[8] Unlike them, they remain invisible, unless they claim a spiritual community. Conceivably, this is because the never-married view their single status as temporary and do not have or seem to desire the collective voice evident in the emerging and hard-won groups and networks of the once-married or of LGBTQIA+ networks. The Ekal Nari Shakti Sangathan (ENSS) and other similarly named groups fostered by NGOs may mention and carry never-married women over 35 as within their writ (Chen 1998; ENSS 2011; Habazaki 2013; Lamb 2018; Pappu 2011; Salve 2015). However, their documentation, activities and the support they receive is shaped primarily by the violence, cultural stigma, social ostracism, economic stress and poverty experienced by the once-married, though many never-marrieds also face this . The once married are both confronted by community and family marginalisations and denials of resources (Singh 2013) and perceived as tragic in upper-caste, middle class assumptions that they will now remain alone and single. A very small proportion live independently (Srivastava 2020). Much of this has been elaborated through micro-studies (Chen 1998), quantitative data (Chen and Dreze 1992), and literature reviews (Palriwala 1994).

Anderson and Ray write that it has been well documented that 'unmarried individuals die at a faster rate than married individuals at all ages' (2019: 1,585) and that mortality rates are higher for unmarried than married women. They find 'that unmarried adults are typically widowed' (p. 1,586), that the largest proportion of such 'missing' adult unmarried women are in India, and that, due to the nature of data, they are unable to separate widowed, divorced and never-married in their calculations and analysis.[9] It seems there is a reason that we anthropologists rarely meet the never-married. The counted unmarried were mostly not the never-married, especially in rural areas. Not surprisingly, welfare assistance to elderly and once-married women appears to be directed to them if they remain in their current relational/marital situation. The never-married are not only about half as many, they are '**not yet**' married; the bulk of the never-married in both 2001 and 2011 were under-30 (see below). The answer to their social, cultural, economic and personal difficulties lies in marriage and assistance is directed to finding them marriage partners and arranging the wedding, dowry and trousseau.

The lack of attention is reason enough to focus on the never-married and, like Lamb, I deliberately do so in this chapter. I present aspects of the lives of three single women through their narratives: a permanent status of never-married was imminent or taken as given; they were aged 30 and older; one claimed 'waithood'; one was said to be too old for a marriage to be arranged; and the most senior simply said that she was unmarried. Their lives and concerns tell us much about family and kinship relations, the gendering of opportunity and choice, and the manner in which the flow of life happens with more or less volition on their part.

Rising age at marriage or increasing non-marriage?

Singerman (2007, cited in Inhorn and Smith-Hefne 2021) coined the term waithood to refer to an unintentional delay in marriage and childbearing and, hence, social adulthood. This is particularly a feature where social adulthood is linked to those two life events and when childbearing without marriage is beyond thought and social acceptance. For girls and women in India an idea of waithood is compelling in many ways. Waiting for marriage marks women's lives from birth and the wait has extended, given growing secondary education for girls in urban locations and rising age at marriage. Especially in the patri-virilocal, hypergamous and dowry marriage that marks Hindu North India, extended families, parents, and even daughters, keep reiterating that the girl is a temporary resident, being brought up and waiting for her true destiny – with her husband and his family.[10] This is true among Muslims too, although hypergamy is more of a value than a category and dowry has spread among them more recently.[11] Norms of a marriageable age (to do with nubility and reproductive years) and a socially appropriate match can work against each other given the assumption that there is something 'wrong' with the woman or her natal family if she is unmarried beyond an implicit age bar for women. Parents are also reminded of their duty to sons – to settle them not only by enabling work and income, but also by getting them married and ensuring a grandson. Making a match and delaying marriage is a worry not just for the 'not yet' married, those waiting, but also for their family, and is a matter of gossip among neighbours and kin.

Much of the work on the never-married arises from a concern with child marriage and the hope for a rising age at marriage, in which expanding education has been postulated as playing a major role. Srinivasan and James (2015) looked at census data between 1961 and 2001 and SRS data for 2011 at the all-India level, the two states of Bihar and Uttar Pradesh (UP) in the north and Kerala and Tamil Nadu in the south. They calculated that the pan-Indian singulate mean age at marriage for the age group 15–49 rose from 16.84 to 22.22 in this period, with a striking rise in Bihar and UP, coming close to that in Kerala, which was overtaken by Tamil Nadu. In Bihar and UP, the numbers of never-married women by the age of 34 were so few that the percentages rounded to zero. Such states shaped the all-India figure of nil for age groups 45 and above. In 2001, the all-India percentage for unmarried men over the age of 54 came to nil, but for UP it was near to 4%. Thus, marriage is well-nigh universal for women, other than in outlier states such as Kerala, while non-marriage is a small but growing possibility in the lives of men (Kaur et al. 2016). After analysing NFHS-3 data, Srinivasan and James found that age was the most significant factor in shifts in marital status, that is, a rise in age at marriage does not mean non-marriage. Caste/community endogamy remains strong. Caste and religion have more effect on the likelihood of marriage, particularly for OBC Hindus, after controlling for rural/urban residence, education of women and household wealth.[12] They argue that 'the maximum probability of marriage is among rural, illiterate, and poor women' (Srinivasan and James 2015: 43).

Choices, desires, questions among the single

It is not surprising then, that the few writings on adult never-married women are largely on urban, educated, middle-class women. These include writings in English-language media (Bhandare 2017; Kuriakose 2014, Lawrence 2014, and Sinha 2019, cited in Lamb 2021), collections of personal narratives of urban, middle-class, cosmopolitan women (Sharma 2019; Bose 2014) and elite men (Patel 2006),[13] and 'Do-It-Yourself-Books' for unmarried women (Singh 2000, cited in Pappu 2014). Pappu draws attention to contemporary literary representations in languages other than English (Vaidehi writing in Kannada). All tend towards the celebratory and suggest a 'new', modern Indian woman.

The very title of Sharma's anthology – *Single by Choice: Happily Unmarried Women* – suggests its argument. These adult never-married women are exceptions across Indian society and do not see their situation as tragic. The 'choice' to not marry may have been more happenstance and an outcome of a conscious delay, rather than a decision against marriage to start with. An age bar to marriage, albeit hazy, operates. The rebellion was often against the marriage 'choices' allowed and/or against the structure of marriage and the nature of the conjugal contract extant in India. In fact, many studies suggest that the broad brushstrokes of the latter appear frighteningly common to the many diverse communities and classes. English news reporting also indicates this thread (Bhandare 2017; Kuriakose 2014, Lawrence 2014, and Sinha 2019 as cited in Lamb 2021).

Many of the women had supportive parents and friends, and only a few lived alone (Sharma 2019). They had created families of choice, akin to but different from the chosen families of Weston's (1997) gay interlocutors. All were in paid professions that they enjoyed. As many commentaries and studies indicate, 'social freedom for women seems mainly dependent on their ability to be economically independent' and '[t]he situation for unmarried village women is very different from my own effortless journey. Few can escape from the prejudice and stigma attached to being unmarried, the inevitability to becoming unwanted, unpaid, unvalued domestic labour' (Tyabji in Sharma 2019: 34). The narratives I present of lower middle-class, urban women nuance the last and complicate the resistance, agency and denial of victimhood that the above writings emphasise. 'The political and academic desire to make feminine agency and resistance visible as against passivity or victimhood can, however, make these women invisible.' Economic dependence and/or lack of volition in remaining single are evident in the lives of at least two of interviewees. They did not have 'freedom', but did not always seem to desire it – or at least not in the frame of much feminist writing.

Simultaneously, some of the writings advise that remaining single is not easy, whether for women or men (Patel 2006). There is an element of ambivalence, even regret, as non-marriage within Indian modernity seems also to be a denial of romantic love and sexual desires (Pappu 2011). Not only does this intertwine with, and even undercut, the enviable freedom of the single person (Patel 2006), Singh notes that despite 'optimism and a variety of coping skills, a great number of single Indian women continue to feel isolated' (2000, as cited in Pappu ibid.: 386). In some of the writings and exhortations, passionate desire appears as absent or suppressed; the single woman emerges as asexual, motivated by education, career or a cause beyond her personal life, moving close to the religious, who avow a spiritual life and ascetic chastity in attaining a semblance of respectability. Desire for marriage or a barely evinced regret at being unmarried emerged in what I heard from the women whose stories I narrate, although there was no allusion to sexuality. Its absence may have been because of the situations in which our conversations took place; I was not able to spend sufficient time alone with them for them to be comfortable speaking of suppressed desires – sexuality or marriage – unlike the married women who did talk of what they expected and accepted in that domain.

As I continue, my attention is not to personhood, but to non-sexual intimacy and homosociality, observed among and spoken of by my interlocutors, and seen in Patricia's discussions of the domestic community of women who work together, in Nizamuddin (Jeffery 1979) and Bijnor (Jeffery and Jeffery 1996). The ties with natal kin were often viewed as the only surety in women's lives, and the desire to maintain them, which Lamb also finds, and the kinwork this entails was significant. Given the overall ethos of consanguineal and immediate kin as being the first circle of support and responsibility and only then affinal and lastly conjugal ties, one may wonder that there are not more women who take this seriously enough to opt to remain with natal kin. The reason, of course, ties into the gendering of family, kinship and social values and relations across patrilineal, patri-virilocal north India and in other parts of the sub-continent, even if they had the choice.

As women grow up they hear that a daughter is a guest in her natal home (Dube 1988); that she is destined to move to her 'real' home with her marital/conjugal family and should never forget it. She is trained and monitored in her interactions towards that transfer, even if she is pampered in the years prior. The possibilities and paths of arranging a match define the process from 'not yet' to 'never-married'. True, daughters have important ritual roles and labour contributions to make, the last enhanced by their greater physical mobility than in-married daughters-in-law; they are also recognised as more caring of parents than their brothers and their wives. This should, however, be as visiting married daughters, whatever the limitations, rather than as co-resident unmarried women. Thus, among other themes, the narratives I turn to speak of the relational world in which single women live and make or do not make claims, the different tenors of incorporation and belonging in natal families and familial life.

Family trajectories and lives of the 'never-married'

The women I conversed with resided in two neighbourhoods in West Delhi, a couple of kilometres distant from each other. Indira and Meena lived in RB, in which migrants after partition and later and people of varied ethnic origins (largely from northern parts) resided. Market hubs and residential areas, schools and small businesses are interspersed. Its inhabitants are diverse in class – new and old middle-class, those who have been on the upward ladder for some time, those who remain there by the skin of their teeth, small business owners, mechanics and technicians, secure government employees, aspiring entrepreneurs, unemployed men, long-settled house owners and recently arrived tenants, who are largely working class. Houses have been gradually built up over many floors and rooms, with little care for the foundations.[14]

This diversity was not unusual in such areas. The markets in the second neighbourhood, S'pur, were oriented to the local residents; it was relatively more lower middle and working class in composition than RB. Though overall more diverse in ethnicity, individual blocks/lanes were less so in ethnicity, caste and religion. It had begun as a resettlement colony where people from slums and hutment dwellings across Delhi were forcibly moved as communities in 1976.[15] Over 40 years, it too had seen tremendous upwards construction. Many of the original allottees had sold their small plots and moved to new unauthorised neighbourhoods of hutments. Some of the construction was as families expanded, but much was for rental income from new migrants looking for cheap accommodation.

NEELU

Neelu, aged 29 when I first met her, and her widowed mother, Laxmi, lived on the ground floor of one such four-storey house, which they owned. Laxmi's parents and in-laws had migrated from eastern Rajasthan, where they had been weavers and agricultural labourers. In Delhi they worked as construction labourers. Laxmi described the long hours that her own mother had laboured, work that became the life of her and her siblings and, after marriage, that of her and her husband. After they were displaced to S'pur, she took to vegetable vending, first selling from a mat on the pavement and then from a stall they were allotted, while her husband continued in construction. They built two floors of their house with their savings and their own labour. Her husband fell ill and it was not possible both to care for him and to run her stall. On his suggestion, they sold it, used some of the money to build more floors, which could be rented out, and some for his treatment. He did not survive the long illness. They now lived off the rental income and Laxmi's small public pension for widows. Neelu claimed that relative to their neighbours, they had below average income. Their living conditions and standards were fairly simple, but comfortable, far removed from the construction work and huts of Laxmi's youth.

Neelu was a precious only child, born after many years and, unusually for their class in that period, in hospital. Her labouring parents earned enough to ensure that she enrolled and continued in school, completing her secondary education, rather than joining in the family enterprise. One birthday, when entering her teens, she was given a television, a family set, but in their eyes bought as a gift for her from her father. Schooling and birthday gifts for daughters were new trajectories and rituals – of the urban, modern, upwardly mobile – as was her attire and language, very distant from the villages of her parents' origins. The question of why Neelu was unmarried constantly niggled – was she 'not yet' or 'never' to be married? This was a sensitive and personal topic and, as it was rare that others were not present when we talked, I could not ask outright. Long-standing neighbours, often distant kin, and visiting relatives were in and out of the house, constantly ready to help in illness and keeping an eye on their home when they were away. Presumably they were also ready 'to talk', they were people in front of whom face would have to be maintained.

Was Neelu unmarried because her parents could not pay attention to arranging a match during her father's long illness? Was there 'no man' to take on the responsibility after his death, a view I had heard in other contexts? When we met, Laxmi was not well, she was finding it difficult to walk and had been advised very expensive injections/ operation for her joints. One time when I called to say I would like to visit, Neelu told me that they were in Laxmi's natal village, for naturopathy/allopathic treatment for her mother. Another time, they were with Neelu's maternal cousins (mama) in another part of Delhi, again for treatment. On the one hand, this could mean that Laxmi was not strong enough to undertake the search for the right husband for her dear daughter. On the other hand, they were embedded in a network of kin, who were often the persons through whom a match would be found. Finally, when I dropped in over a year after I first met her, Neelu was alone. Her mother was still away for treatment, but Neelu had joined computer classes nearby and came and went – she was about to leave for a session. As the conversation flowed, I commented that she was not married. Was she going to remain so? 'No,' she said, 'my mother is trying. The search has been on for many years, from when my father was alive. A suitable match is not turning up. In our community, mostly they are drinkers, not much educated, so no suitable match has been found. And there is another thing. When they get to know that I am an only child, they fear that their son has to come and live here. This is making it difficult.' Neelu did not explicitly express a desire to marry, but the eagerness with which she spoke of an ongoing and complicated search made it evident that she wished for it. Even as she appeared on the verge of the age bar, she made it clear that she was depending on her mother to 'find' a match; she would not think of doing it herself. Their mutual responsibilities and closeness to each other, and the love with which she had grown up, shaped a faith in her mother and an inability to abandon her.

INDIRA

Indira was nearing 60, a retired and unmarried school teacher. It was unlikely that she would move out of the never-married group. Her parents had been Partition refugees and built the family house in RB, which she and her siblings now owned. She was the most educated of four siblings and the only one in paid, public employment. We never got to talk of how and why she had not married, but she spoke of the details of her current family difficulties without any prompting. Her married sister and two brothers tapped her for support and financial help. She had given loans to her brothers to buy the buses they operated, loans they had returned. They had been doing well until new fuel and environmental regulations required further investment, after which one brother was in trouble. Indira narrated an oft-heard theme of family troubles over property and between women,[16] in particular between her and a brother's wife, who she said had taken over the entire house. Indira accused the wife of locking her out and threatening her with a knife, such that she did not dare go back for two months. She accused her sister-in-law of continuing to trouble her in various ways, like purposely throwing garbage in her path.

Some years ago, her sister had come to her door on the morning of the first day of the year, crying. Her sister's husband had two married brothers and they all shared one house with a single toilet. There were constant fights because of this and she was scared that there would be violence between her son and his younger uncle. Indira sent her home, saying do not start the new year with such a story, come back later. She spent the next three days of the school vacation searching for and buying a flat. She moved there and her sister joined her with her nuclear unit and stayed for two years. It was only after the latter's marital home was formally and clearly divided that she moved back and Indira returned to the family home.

Due to troubles with her sister-in-law, Indira said she spent as little time as she could at home, returning for matters of daily self-care, to cook, eat and sleep. In the mornings she went to a centre owned by a well-known religious sect that was influential in the area, where she volunteered in managing their sewing classes. After lunch she would go to her sister's or some other place. Indira was not a single woman turning to religion, but a retired school teacher who wanted to remain busy and wanted social interaction, yet did not want to work under anybody or be tied down. Undoubtedly, she was no lamb and, by her own account, could stand up for herself – whether in her job or at the charity centre. Her education and employment had given her financial and social freedom. 'You must spend money on yourself, look after yourself, your health,' she advised me and said that because she did so, she did not look her age. Yet, in the stories she narrated, her earnings were not just for herself. Her natal family was very important, evident in her refusal to move away, even when it meant losing a promotion to be school principal, and in the loans she gave her brothers and how she had supported her sister. Even now, Indira would drop whatever she was doing if her sister called.

MEENA

Meena was 36 years old and lived with two brothers (one unmarried), two sisters-in-law (one a widow), a sister who was separated – all older than her – and two nephews and a niece. Her mother had died after the time of our survey and before we visited them three years later. As one talked about marriage and kin, Meena's singleness appeared to be part of a family marked by sorrow, failed marriages and failures in arranging matches. Meena's elder sister, Chandrakala, had walked out of her own marriage after a couple of years because, she said, her husband was mentally challenged and 'did no work'. Her maternal grandfather, a house priest in the town, had arranged it; he was a *seedha* man and had gone by the boy's appearance. Her marriage had been rushed as her father had died. A couple of years later, her eldest married brother and a second unmarried brother also died. Their mother was distraught and took to her bed, unable to do anything. Their economic condition deteriorated. Talking of Meena, Chandrakala said, 'it was just like that, her marriage talks did not work out anywhere and now is she past the age'. However, they were still searching for a match for the youngest brother, older than her at about 38. Coincidently or in a pattern, two of the four brothers of Aarti, the wife of the one married, living brother, were also unmarried; one was said to be physically challenged.

Aarti, Chandrakala and Meena appeared to have a harmonious relationship, unlike that between Indira and her sister-in-law. Was that because the two sisters were dependent on the goodwill of their brother and his wife and made no claims? Or because they had no property to share? Or it was merely their personality? In answering questions during the survey, Aarti had not listed Chandrakala, Meena, her widowed sister-in-law (*jethani*) and nephew, or her younger brother-in-law as household members. Other than her own nuclear unit, she had mentioned only her mother-in-law. It could have been a misunderstanding on her part or, more likely, an assertion of property rights as she had claimed her husband owned the house. It must be noted that she left out not only the unmarried sisters of her husband but also his brother, nephew and sister-in-law. The last was in paid public employment, in the place of her deceased husband, and was absent on weekdays.

Aarti insisted that they did not just share a house, but were a single household with a shared kitchen, although they lived and slept on different floors of the three-storey house. According to her, all domestic work was undertaken jointly or divided among the four women, whether it was the daily cleaning or cooking three fresh meals. Indeed, it appeared to be so. Aarti and Chandrakala made a huge batch of dried snacks, after the cleaning had been completed as we talked. Then, Chandrakala extracted butter from the curds they had collected over a few days, while Aarti cooked and Meena served lunch to her nephew and niece who had returned from school. Grocery shopping was done by Chandrakala and Meena, but for other shopping all three would go together, with a brother. Undoubtedly, the three women were company for each other and worked together. Chandrakala and Aarti equally took the lead in conversations. However, Meena was the least heard, finishing off cleaning tasks and remaining in the background unless directly spoken to, but with questions about why somebody was unmarried. It could have been her age – she was the youngest – it could have been the shyness of an unmarried woman who had not moved socially beyond her own family, or it could be because she was expected not to put herself forward due to her singleness.

Concluding remarks

As with the middle-class, cosmopolitan women in Sharma's anthology, the singleness of Neelu, Indira and Meena appeared as more happenstance than choice. In contrast, their desire and choice was clearly to marry, despite the narrations of the many difficulties in marriage, between spouses and in the affinal home. There was a conscious search for a marital match, at least for Neelu and Meena. The inability to find a suitable match hit the age bar and defined their trajectory.

The difficulties were partly due to life events in their natal families – illness and death of male and senior members of the family. The extended kin, who could be expected to pitch in here, would do so only to some extent; the urgency they would feel for their own daughters or co-resident nieces was absent. Extended families were important, but concern and kinwork attenuated with kinship distance. The gendering of kinship belonging was also evident. Being an only child who would inherit some property did not make Neelu more eligible in a patri-virilocal context. Other families did not want to lose a son; being an in-married son-in-law was considered undignified; and a mother could not stay with her married daughter except in her own home. As a woman who would inherit property, Neelu was worth more than many men in her community, again upsetting the gender balance.

There was a complex of factors, structural and individual, that came into play; incompatibilities between economic condition, caste status, family history and women's education within a continuing emphasis on caste endogamy. Given the levels of education in her community, Neelu's education made a match difficult. With Indira too, education and her secure employment would not have added to her eligibility. From her own family history it appeared that higher education and employment were not pervasive when she was younger. The economic status of Meena's family was poor when they were searching for a groom, while caste status was high; the family history of failed marriages/unmarried members could have had added deleterious effects.

For all three women, the choice seemed to have been made against a poor marriage, both socially and considering the daughter's well-being. Neelu refused to exercise individual choice, while Meena went with the flow in her natal family. Indira may not have exercised a choice for self-arranged or family-arranged marriage, but she chose for her natal family as against her own career. For all three, their life as a single woman was embedded within family life, as Lamb (2021) found among her interlocutors, whether by choice or through the unfolding of life events not made through their own volition, and by the social environment in which they remained. Indira was proud of a career that gave her social adulthood, although she was 'never-married'. She was 'social', an extrovert who fostered her social relations, but she was ready to breach social norms to a limited extent. Despite the quarrels with kin and living alone, single life for her was entwined with family. Neelu and Indira were in control of their domestic spheres; Neelu may have been unvalued outside her home, but not within it. Meena appeared as an invisible worker, both within the home and for people beyond, but perhaps the presence of her strong, once-married, elder sister ensured that she was not devalued, even if somewhat silent. Their singleness was lived in a familial co-habitation. Neelu, who hoped still to marry, and Meena, who was not to be married now, did not resist the social norms. These demanded that they comport themselves with the reticence expected of single women, a readiness to defer to family elders. Singleness meant that they remained within the known and comforting environment of the natal home, but did not achieve social adulthood. For all three, desires which social norms tied to marriage remained unsaid and suppressed.

NOTES

1. Prof. Fumiko Oshikawa of Kyoto University and me.
2. This was a collaboration between five researchers on life histories of elderly women, living in rural and urban Varanasi, Pune city and Delhi. It was sponsored by the Japanese Society for the Promotion of Science (JSPS). I conducted the Delhi interviews, many with Prof. Oshikawa, the grant applicant.
3. The Indian component of the Asian Family Survey, which was modelled on the East Asian Social Survey (EASS) family module and was an initiative of the Kyoto University Global COE on 'Reconstruction of Intimate and Public Spheres in 21st Century Asia'. It covered 1,030 households in Delhi,

270 households in Rohtak, Haryana, and 1,096 households in Chennai over 2011–12.

4. In-depth interviews were conducted and recorded during one to three visits to a household, each visit ranging from one to four hours. In 10 cases, we spoke with at least two women members of a household/family separately, at times with other family members present.
5. This article was written when most libraries were closed due to the pandemic. The collections in those that were open did not include all the books that I wished to refer to. Hence, I have occasionally been dependent on others' takes on them.
6. My own fieldwork in Leh in 1987.
7. In 2011, approximately 12% of the female population was listed as single, a 39% increase from 2001 (Salve 2015).
8. In a conversation, Ravinder Kaur observed that single women are dealt with more in the pages of medical and psychology journals, which suggests that they are not seen as 'normal'.
9. Never-married women were approximately 36% of the single in rural and urban combined, as against 60% who were widowed, but only 18% in rural areas (Salve 2015). Most would be not-yet-married.
10. The three sisters who committed suicide in Kanpur in the late 1980s and young women at a conference on dowry organised by AIDWA in the early 2000s, wrote/spoke of how they refused dowry marriage as a devaluation of their personhood and a burden on their parents. The former chose to die as they would not be allowed to remain single, while the latter asked for solidarity/support groups in their singleness.
11. Seen in Patricia's discussions (1979) of Nizamuddin.
12. They undertook a binomial logit regression using age, rural/urban, education level, household wealth and a religio-caste variable to examine never married, ever-married and once-married women.
13. This anthology includes the once-married and 'almost' single, married, but living apart.
14. Soon after one of my visits, continuous rain through the afternoon and evening flooded the roads and two houses collapsed.
15. Between 1975–77, Internal Emergency and an abrogation of democratic rights was declared by the Indira Gandhi government. These displacements were conducted in the name of beautification of the city. Poor people were moved to 'resettlement colonies' which, at that time, were on the outskirts of the city and beyond (Tarlo 1995).
16. The daily domestic hassles and the quarrels they can give rise to are faced by women. Simultaneously, a married woman may often be her husband's proxy in disputes.

REFERENCES

Anderson, S. and D. Ray. 2019. 'Missing Unmarried Women', *Journal of the European Economic Association*, 17(5): 1,585–1,616 DOI: 10.1093/jeea/jvy027 (accessed 25 March 2021).

Babb, L.A. 1984. 'Indigenous Feminism in a Modern Hindu Sect'. *Signs: Journal of Women, Culture and Society*, 9: 399–416.

Babb, L.A. 1987. *Redemptive Encounters. Three Modern Styles in the Hindu Tradition*. Berkeley: University of California Press.

Bhandare, N. 2017. 'All the single women', *Mint*, 05 Apr, https://www.livemint.com/Opinion/IHwr81o7BBoNL0ggJlIl9N/All-the-single-women.html

Biswas, R. 2011. 'Of Love, Marriage and Kinship: Queering the Family', in S. Sen, R. Biswas, N. Dhawan (eds.) *Intimate Others: Marriage and Sexualities in India*, pp. 414–35. Kolkata: Stree.

Bose, S. 2014. *Single in the City*. New Delhi: Om Books International.

Brown, D. 1998. 'Buddhist Nuns Putting Equality into Practice', *Herizons*, 2(3): 12.

Chen, M.A. 1998. *Widow in India: Social Neglect and Public Action*. New Delhi: Sage Publications.

Chen, M.A. and J. Dreze. 1992. *Widows and Well-being in Rural North India. Development Economics Research Programme Discussion Paper Series*, No. 40. Suntory-Toyota International Centre for Economics and Related Disciplines, London School of Economics.

Dube, L. 1988 'On the construction of gender: Socialization of Hindu girls in Patrilineal India', *Economic and Political Weekly*, 23(18): WS-11–19.

ENSS. 2011. *Are We Forgotten Women? A Study on the Status of Low-income Single Women in India*. National Forum for Single Women's Rights.

Habazaki, M. 2013. 'Widowhood, Socio-cultural Practices, and collective action: A Study of Survival Strategies of Single Women in Nepal', in R. Kaur and R. Palriwala (eds.) *Marrying in South Asia: Shifting concepts, Changing Practices in a Globalised World*. Delhi: Orient BlackSwan.

Inhorn, M.C. and N.J. Smith-Hefne (eds). 2021. *Waithood: Gender, Education, and Global Delays in Marriage and Childbearing*. Berghahn Books.

Jeffery, P. 1979. *Frogs in a Well: Indian Women in Purdah*. London: Zed Books.

Jeffery, P. and R. Jeffery. 1996. *Don't Marry Me To A Plowman! Women's Everyday Lives In Rural North India*. Boulder, Colorado: Westview Press.

Jeffery, R. and P. Jeffery. 1997. *Population, Gender and Politics: Demographic Change in Rural North India*. Cambridge: Cambridge University Press. (Ch. 6)

Kaur, R. 2008. 'Dispensable Daughters and Bachelor Sons: Sex Discrimination in North India.' *Economic and Political Weekly*, 43(30): 109–114.

Kaur, R., S.S. Bhalla, M.K. Agarwal and P. Ramakrishnan. 2016. *Sex Ratio Imbalances and Marriage Squeeze in India: 2000–2050*. Delhi: UNFPA.

Lamb, S. 2018. 'Being Single in India: Gendered Identities, Class Mobilities, and Personhoods in Flux', *Ethos*, 46(1): 49–69.

Lamb, S. 2021. 'Never-married women in India: Gendered Life Courses, Desires, and Identities in Flux', in M.C. Inhorn and N.J. Smith-Hefne (eds), *Waithood: Gender, Education, and Global Delays in Marriage and Childbearing*. Berghahn Books.

Palriwala, R. 1994. *Changing kinship, family, and gender relations in South Asia: Processes, trends and issues*. Leiden: Women and Autonomy Centre, University of Leiden.

Pappu, R. 2011. 'Reconsidering Romance and Intimacy: The Case of the Single Unmarried Woman', in S. Sen, R. Biswas, N. Dhawan (eds), *Intimate Others: Marriage and Sexualities in India*, pp. 370–90. Kolkata: Stree.

Patel, B. 2006. *Chasing the Good Life: On Being Single*. Delhi: Viking.

Phillimore, P. 1991. 'Unmarried Women of the Dhaula Dhar: Celibacy and Social Control in Northwest India', *Journal of Anthropological Research*, 47(3): 331–50.

Salve, P. 2015. '71 Million Single Women, 39% Rise Over A Decade', *The Wire*, 14 November. https://thewire.in/gender/71-million-single-women-39-rise-over-a-decade (accessed 7 June 2021).

Sharma, M. 2006. *Loving Women: Being Lesbian in Unprivileged India*. Delhi: Yoda Press.

Sharma, K. (ed.). 2019. *Single by Choice: Happily Unmarried Women!* New Delhi: Women Unlimited.

Singh, K. 2013. *Separated and Divorced Women in India: Economic Rights and Entitlements*. New Delhi: Sage Publications, International Development Research Institute.

Srinivasan, K. and K.S. James. 2015. 'The Golden Cage: Stability of the Institution of Marriage in India', *Economic and Political Weekly*, 50(13): 38–45.

Srivastava, A. 2020. 'Kerala Tamil Nadu Have Highest Number Of Single Women Living Independently In India: Report'. July 6. https://www.shethepeople.tv/news/single-women-living-alone-india/ (accessed 19 March 2021).

Tarlo, E. 1995. 'From Victim to Agent: Memories of Emergency from a Resettlement Colony in Delhi', *Economic and Political Weekly* 30(46): 2,921–28.

Weston, K. 1997. *Families We Choose: Lesbians, Gays, Kinship* (revised edition). New York: Columbia University Press.

11

Saving Mothers' and Children's Lives

Reflections on Gender and Healthcare in Nepal

Jeevan R Sharma

Introduction

Saving mothers' and children's lives is one of the key challenges in global health. Over the decades, global health institutions and governments have mobilised considerable resources, expertise, metrics and interventions, all in the name of a future free from maternal and child morbidity and mortality (Brunson and Suh 2019; Starrs 2006; Campbell and Graham 2006; Wendland 2016). Innovative interventions have included: the mobilisation of unpaid or underpaid female community health volunteers; a range of safe motherhood initiatives; a push toward institutional delivery and skilled birth attendants; and new norms of results-based programming.

Patricia Jeffery's extensive work on gender and healthcare in North India has consistently criticised medical and healthcare services for failing to take into account the social, political and economic context of childbearing women's lives (Jeffery et al. 1989: 221; Jeffery and Jeffery 2008, 2010). As she often reiterates in her writings and presentations, 'context matters' (Jeffery, forthcoming). More specifically, her work has shown that poor maternal health and mortality do not emanate just from broader structural factors – such as underinvestment in healthcare provision, an exclusionary state and widespread poverty – they also reflect the status of women, including the value attached to women's work more generally and the problem facing daughters-in-law in the South Asian context more specifically (Jeffery et al. 1989, 221). Jeffery et. al write:

> in most WHO documents, sociological explanations of women's position are reduced to socio-economic indicators such as age, parity, social class, housing quality, and location. The problem is seen as merely one of attitudes and motivation, not something constantly established and reinforced through systems of kinship, marriage and property, and class relationships, which are all shot through with gender differentiation. (1989: 222)

Women's needs concerning childbearing are rarely given priority and they have very little control over decisions on the type, cost and timing of access to healthcare (Jeffery et al. 1989; Jeffery and Jeffery 2010). Jeffery's work also examined the impact of India's economic liberalisation on people's access to healthcare through key developments that include: a) the expansion of private medical practice in the context of widespread poverty and the state's failure to provide a 'safety net'; b) the inability of the state and citizens to regulate the healthcare market; and c) the impact of these on undermining the Indian state's legitimacy (Jeffery and Jeffery 2008: 81).

By drawing inspiration from Patricia Jeffery's work on gender and access to healthcare services in the context of South Asia, this chapter critically reflects on two aspects of maternal and child healthcare in Nepal, just across the border from North India. Unlike Patricia Jeffery's rich and vivid ethnographic accounts based on long-term fieldwork, I am only able to offer a brief reflective account based on a patchwork of my research and observation in this field since 2001.

First, I draw on the mobilisation of unpaid female community health volunteers (FCHVs) in Nepal, and reflect on how this 'unpaid free labour' is caught between the policymakers' political justification of empowerment and the gendered exploitation of female labour in the name of volunteerism.

Second, I reflect on the widespread push for institutional delivery in the contexts of underresourced public health institutions and of gendered access to healthcare in Nepal. The rapid expansion of birthing centres in remote parts of the country, and in other parts of South Asia, has not been met by the provision of quality services. Instead, an unregulated and profit-seeking private sector has filled the gap for institutional delivery, as well as for caesarean section delivery, with significant financial costs for the poor.

Additionally, I reflect on new norms of results-based programmes that have been introduced in the field of maternal and child health since around 2005, particularly in institutional delivery. This is seen as a way to make services more effective, in other words, to make a more explicit link between investment in healthcare and subsequent outputs, within the broader framework of upward accountability. Results-based programmes for institutional delivery had not made an impact when Patricia Jeffery started fieldwork in North India in the 1980s, although the people she worked with had been exposed to India's coercive family planning programmes and their attached targets and incentives. She writes that the introduction of Janani Suraksha Yojana made institutional deliveries more common and more normalised in the North Indian villagers' understandings and, by 2018, every baby born to a woman married into the village was born in an institution (Jeffery, forthcoming).

My reflections on these two specific issues are inspired by Patricia Jeffery's long-standing concern with women's subordination and their health, particularly in the context of the value attached to women's work, as well as the influence of the broader political-economic context and far-reaching webs of relations (including household, state and market) on maternal and child health. Women's work has been consistently undervalued, partly due to the overpowering image of Nepali women in religious and ritual practices, which relegates them to the domestic and reproductive sphere. This undervaluing of women's work is visible in the mobilisation of unpaid FCHVs by the Nepali State and by development donors for the altruistic motive of saving mothers' and children's lives. As in North India, Nepali women's access to healthcare is highly gendered and they have little control over the timing, cost and type of access, which directly impacts the visible indicators of women's health and mortality. Thus, the introduction of safe motherhood initiatives and specific interventions, such as incentivising institutional delivery, that do not address the political problem of gendered access to healthcare are unlikely to lead to a long-term, sustainable, positive change in maternal health and mortality. Furthermore, the uncritical acceptance of results-based financing programmes to increase institutional healthcare delivery that make explicit links between the investment and the outputs – within the broader framework of upward accountability alongside the expansion of the private sector in the context of underresourced state healthcare institutions – have major implications for the poor and for state legitimacy. I discuss the two examples of FCHVs and a widespread push for institutional delivery using the underlying neoliberal logics of development policy and practice: resting on individuals; scaling back state provision; erasing the context; introducing metrics; and increasing privatisation. This chapter indicates the rich possibilities for sociological and anthropological inquiries into maternal and child health in Nepal, rather than reporting on findings from new research.

The next section offers a brief contextual background on maternal health in Nepal before reflecting on each aspect in a little more detail.

Nepal context

Nepal has been undergoing turbulent sociopolitical and economic transformations since the 1950s. Sociopolitically, it has transformed from a feudal, hierarchical monarchy to a republican order that has attempted to ingrain ideas of human rights, equality and inclusive citizenship. Economically, there has been a gradual shift in the political economy of rural livelihoods with: the commodification of land and labour; the widespread flows of cash and financialisation; and an extensive outmigration of men and women, with significant costs for those left behind. The countryside has been deeply penetrated by the ideas and the material aspects of development, market and modernity (Sharma 2021). At the macro level, Nepal has experienced a profound and impressive social change in just one generation. There has been a notable shift from a deeply hierarchical social order, where gender differences were enforced through social norms, supported by a combination of religious ritual, legal provision, political economy and state bureaucracy, to one where the call for gender equality and social inclusion is widespread.

While significant differences exist between the situation of women based on the intersections of caste, ethnicity, class and religion, Nepali women have been stereotypically represented within development discourses as a homogenous group without agency and voice, subjugated by the dominant Hindu patriarchal social order. 'In the context of Nepal, the effacement of ethnic, religious and thus gendered differences among heterogenous communities not only ensured an easy target population for development but legitimized the creation of the single national culture based on Hindu norms extolled by the Pànchayat regime' (Tamang 2002: 317). Accordingly, gender has been seen largely as a residual issue of religion and culture, to be dealt with through remedial provisions, rather than as a dynamic relational problem that needs to address wider issues of economic and social inequality.

A major demographic transition from a high-mortality, high-fertility society to a low-mortality, low-fertility society within a relatively short period has significant consequences for gender, generation and the economy. The fertility rate, which measures the average number of children per couple, decreased from 6.68 in 1977 to 2.3 in 2016 (MoH, New Era and ICF 2017). The widespread push for institutional delivery and skilled birth attendants meant that more than half of the births (57 per cent) took place in health facilities in 2016, compared to only 8 per cent in 1996 in Nepal. Skilled assistance during childbirth has increased from 9 per cent in 1996 to 58 per cent in 2016 (MoH, New Era and ICF 2017). Although statistics on maternal mortality ratio are contentious in Nepal (Sharma 2016), authoritative statistics that shape policymaking and the design and delivery of programmatic interventions show that Nepal has made significant progress in saving mother's and children's lives since around 2000. Demographic and Health Survey (DHS) data show that maternal mortality decreased from 539 in

1996 to 239 in 2016 (MoH, New Era and ICF 2017). Despite this, poor maternal and child health remain major concerns in Nepal, as indicated by the widespread prevalence of home births and the lack of skilled birth attendants, especially for the poor. Brunson (2010) found that women in a semi-urban area in Kathmandu city were not receiving obstetric care, not because it was not available within commuting distance, but because women do not have the power to demand biomedical services or emergency care, and men still viewed birth as the domain of women and remained mostly uninvolved in the process. DHS data show high levels of disparity in terms of educational status, that is, 85 per cent of births among women with at least a school leaving certificate (SLC) were delivered in a health facility, compared with only 36 per cent for women with no education. Births among women in the highest wealth quintile were more likely (90 per cent) to occur at a health facility than among women in the lowest quintile (34 per cent).

The history of modern maternal and child health services in Nepal is closely associated with the entry of foreign aid in 1950. The initial focus was influenced by the neo-Malthusian idea of population growth and the priority was to reduce the size of the family by offering permanent and temporary contraceptives (Thapa 1989). Following the idea of Health for All by 2000, Nepal's first Long-Term Health Plan (1975–90) led to the establishment of maternal and child health services in six districts, which was later expanded to all 75 districts. Based on the spirit of community participation and women's empowerment, Nepal started a FCHV programme in 1988 with the support of USAID, UNFPA and UNICEF, which was expanded to cover the whole of Nepal by 1995 (Glenton et. al 2010). Like many other developing countries, Nepal has been experimenting with several innovations in the field of maternal and child health, with the support of bilateral and multilateral donors. The National Safe Motherhood Policy, formulated by the Government in 1998, emphasised strengthening maternity services (including family planning), enhancing the technical skills of healthcare providers at all levels, and strengthening referral services for basic emergency obstetric care. The National Safe Motherhood and Newborn Health

Long Term Plan (2006–17) emphasised institutional birth and focused particularly on the development of functioning birthing centres with basic emergency obstetric care across the country. Along with bilateral agencies such as USAID and DfID, UN agencies such as UNICEF, the World Health Organisation and UNFPA have been major players in providing technical assistance in maternal and child health service provision in Nepal, ranging from community-based interventions to results-based financing for promoting institutional delivery (Sharma and Adhikari 2021). I/NGOs and private sector organisations – such as Save the Children, Care Nepal, Hellen Keller International, John Snow Inc, Research Triangle International, Plan and JHPIEGO, among others – have worked with donors, local implementing partner NGOs, networks and the Government of Nepal to manage and provide managerial and technical assistance to realise these interventions (Sharma, Khatri and Harper 2018). All these actors and different interventions have shaped the ideas and practices of maternal health in Nepal, although there has been very little ethnographic scrutiny of this issue in the country. Below, I discuss how policymakers use the language of empowerment as a justification for the mobilisation of unpaid FCHVs in Nepal, ironically this exploits poor women's labour in the name of saving mothers' and children's lives.

Female community health volunteers (FCHVs)

Recent estimates suggest that there are around 52,000 FCHVs in Nepal, who have been a key pillar of Nepal's healthcare delivery system, with a primary focus on maternal and child health, and family planning. A key feature of Nepal's FCHV programme, which started in 1988, is that FCHVs are not paid a salary but they are expected to voluntarily assist other paid community health workers. The stated objective of the FCHV programme was to increase community participation in basic primary healthcare. In the minds of the architects of the programme, it had the 'double-win' or 'win-win' of extending community-level healthcare services in rural Nepal and empowering Nepali women.

FCHVs are local women, mostly over the age of 25. Almost all (95 per cent) live in the ward where they performed FCHV functions. One survey showed their average age as 41.3, with only 4 per cent under 25 years (GoN 2015). Almost 90 per cent are married. They are selected by the mother's groups or nominated by their community. One FCHV is selected per ward, although some areas have more than one FCHV per ward, based on population coverage. Although literacy is not a requirement, FCHV literacy rates are estimated at 83 per cent, and 67 per cent of FCHVs had been to school.

Although FCHVs are unpaid volunteers, the government has given them an extensive job description. Initially, their role covered family planning education and the distribution of birth control pills and condoms. Over the years, this expanded significantly, to focus on the promotion of safe motherhood, child care, community health and family planning. FCHVs are also expected to motivate community members to use health services and to communicate the community's demand for services to health workers. Each FCHV is provided with some basic knowledge of first aid and a small drug kit containing basic medication. They are expected to conduct mother's group meetings and to present health education on such topics as safe motherhood, immunisation, family planning, nutrition, sanitation, diarrhoea, acute respiratory infection, communicable diseases and so on.

In a more visible form, FCHVs are mobilised in the national programmes for National Immunization Days for polio eradication and vitamin A capsule distribution. They prepare lists of eligible children, make home visits and give considerable time to preparing local people for children's immunisation. Paid health workers with responsibility for immunisation or other national health programmes always rely on FCHVs for their knowledge and community mobilisation. FCHVs have considerable authority because of their proximity to the community they serve. They play a key role in other interventions, such as the community-based treatment of acute respiratory infection and diarrhoea, and in providing community-based health services to mothers and newborns, using a birth preparedness package, and other activities, including distributing iron folate. FCHVs are also mobilised to support other pilot interventions aimed at generating evidence, such as misoprostol distribution to prevent post-partum haemorrhage (Sharma, Khatri and Harper 2018).

Over the years, FCHVs have been involved in major health programmes, which has increased their workload, visibility and expectations. Also, FCHVs have become a default point of contact at ward level for any development intervention beyond health initiated by NGOs and the Government of Nepal, which has expanded their networks and visibility but it has also meant an increased workload and their expectations of incentives and salaries. They are also frequently approached by neighbours and community members for help, such as accompanying pregnant women to the health facility for delivery.

FCHVs receive 18 days of initial training and then refresher training in aspects of maternal and child health services. They are expected to be part-time and surveys indicate that, on average, they work around five to six hours a week. Although many FCHVs I have met spend a considerable time in their role, especially during vaccination, distribution of vitamin A or other public health campaigns, including when they were mobilised for contact tracing during the coronavirus pandemic in 2020–21.

They receive incentives in the form of an 'allowance' of Nepali Rs. 400 per day from the government or non-governmental providers during training or during the days of mobilisation. The government also gives each FCHV a sign to display at her home, a cloth bag, a badge, an identity card and a certificate. In many areas, local governments offer further incentives, such as bicycles, bags and umbrellas. While the issue of remuneration has been raised since 1988, the government and the donors supporting the programme have refrained from paying a regular salary as they consider it undermines the voluntary nature of the FCHV role. Interestingly, the retention rate is very high (around 96 per cent) and people mostly leave the role when they become too old to work, die, become ill or migrate.

The success of the programme has meant additional responsibilities for FCHVs. While this has increased their visibility, especially when they are tasked with distributing medicines (or other tangible services), the responsibility to assist other healthcare workers raises doubts about the voluntary nature of their work. As more public health tasks are shifted to FCHVs, such increasing reliance on unpaid female volunteers raises obvious questions about the exploitation of female labour.

It is clear that FCHVs do not just view their role in terms of community service and empowerment, as envisaged by the architects of the programme. During my fieldwork in Nepal, FCHVs have spoken, both individually and collectively, about the difficulties and challenges that come with additional labour demands without proper compensation. Such unpaid work amounts to female exploitation. Although volunteerism is usually associated with actions arising from free will or spontaneity of choice and without formal or legal obligation, FCHVs do not have an obvious choice to avoid the ever-increasing responsibility together with other regular labour demands at home.

Policymakers and planners use the language of empowerment to justify women's mobilisation as unpaid volunteers and as a part of a broader project to bring them from their domestic sphere into a public sphere. Yet, questions remain about why poor women are chosen to be unpaid volunteers who are expected to assist paid health workers; whether volunteers from poor communities should be properly remunerated beyond an intermittent allowance and an honorarium; and, what are appropriate expectations in terms of time and activities for FCHVs? Similar to Aradhana Sharma's argument in the context of the Mahila Samakhya (MS) programme in North India, it is possible that conceiving poor rural women's labour as altruistic empowerment (and therefore either non-remunerative or low paid) ended up reproducing gender, class and caste-based norms that it otherwise set out to challenge (Sharma 2006). Shifting critical public health work from paid health workers to unpaid FCHVs, and justifying this under the name of empowerment, alerts us to the ironic project of empowerment that ends up exploiting poor women.

Institutional delivery

In 2009, the Government of Nepal introduced the Aama Programme to reduce financial barriers to women seeking institutional delivery, in order to reduce maternal morbidity and mortality. The programme evolved from the DfID funded interventions of Nepal Safe Motherhood Project (NSMP) and Support for Safe Motherhood Programme (SSMP). NSMP ran from 1997 to 2004 and piloted interventions on the role of skilled birth attendants and emergency obstetric care in nine districts. The follow-up SSMP programme ran from 2005–10 and supported the delivery of and access to quality maternal and newborn health services, including human resources, infrastructure investments, equipment and supplies, and comprehensive abortion care.

A Maternity Incentive Scheme was launched in 2005 under SSMP, to help mitigate the high financial cost of childbirth (transport, loss of earnings, support and medical costs) so that poor women, many of them in remote rural areas, could reach health facilities (Bhandari et al. 2011). This was designed to ensure that there was no cost to childbirth in the institution (waiver of any fee) and that other costs associated with travel and purchasing materials needed for childbirth were compensated through incentives. In 2007, a provision was added to offer incentives to health workers/health facilities offering childbirth services.

The Aama Programme has three components. First, it offers transport incentives to all women who deliver in an institution: Nepali Rs. 1,500 in the mountain region, Rs. 1,000 in the hill region, and Rs. 500 in the Terai region. Also, women are given Rs. 400 for making antenatal visits. Second, health institutions are provided with incentives per delivery: Nepali Rs. 1,000 for normal delivery at a health facility with fewer than 25 beds, Rs. 1,500 for normal delivery at a health facility with more than 25 beds, Rs. 3,000 for complicated delivery, and Rs. 7,000 for C-section delivery. Third, a health worker is given Nepali Rs. 300 for institutional delivery and Rs. 100 for home delivery.

According to DHS 2016 data, the push for institutional delivery and skilled birth attendants meant that more than half of births in Nepal (57 per cent) took place in health facilities in 2016, compared to only 8 per cent in 1996. Skilled assistance during childbirth has increased from 9 per cent in 1996 to 58 per cent in 2016 (MoH, New Era and ICF 2017). Yet, despite a significant push for institutional delivery and skilled birth attendants, 43 per cent of childbirths took place at home and 42 per cent are not attended by skilled birth attendants. DHS 2016 data shows that when asked why women did not give birth in the facility, the most commonly reported reason was that it was not necessary to deliver in a health facility (56 per cent), followed by the birth taking place before reaching the facility (18 per cent) and the facility being too far away or not having transportation (17 per cent). DHS data shows high levels of disparity in terms of educational status: 85 per cent of births for women with at least an SLC were delivered in a health facility, compared with only 36 per cent for women with no education. Births among women in the highest wealth quintile were more likely (90 per cent) to occur at a health facility than among women in the lowest quintile (34 per cent). Similarly, the proportion of births attended by skilled providers increases with the mother's educational attainment and wealth quintile.

On the supply side, apart from the physical building, birthing centres in rural remote villages rarely have the equipment, staffing or facilities required for childbirth. Thus, it appears that the push for institutional delivery, in the context of poor availability of childbirth facilities in government health facilities, has created a lucrative opportunity for the private sector and its expansion in childbirth in Nepal. DHS data for 2016 showed that: 10 per cent of births in the five years preceding the survey were delivered in private health facilities; the proportion of births by caesarean section had almost doubled, from 5 per cent in 2011 to 9 per cent in 2016. The caesarean section delivery rate is considerably higher for births in expensive private facilities (35 per cent) than in government health facilities (12 per cent). The rapid expansion of the expensive private sector in childbirth services in the context of the weak regulatory capacity of the state has major implications for the poor.

Nepal's Aama Programme reflects the neoliberal norms of targets and incentives framed by results-based programmes in global health. This is linked to profound political pressure to demonstrate the impact of interventions in terms of the disbursement of resources tied to measurable results. Projects and programme objectives are organised as a set of measurable results; activity costs are directly linked to results through recording and tools such as log frame. Programmes are organised around the generation of evidence through monitoring and evaluation systems and a results framework. The direct implication is that health workers spend considerable time documenting and recording, as reward and accountability are tied to these. The influence of a broader political-economic context and such critical questions as gendered access to healthcare gets ignored under a pressure to demonstrate achievements circumscribed by measurable results. Furthermore, there are open questions on whether and how the push for institutional delivery may be contributing to the expansion of the private sector with a disproportionate impact on the poor.

Conclusion

This chapter is inspired by Patricia Jeffery's empirically grounded and accessible work on gender and healthcare and shows the rich possibilities for a sociological examination of the unpaid work done by FCHVs and the consequences of the push for institutional delivery in the context of poor state healthcare services and household gender dynamics. Both of which indicate the paradoxical nature of a neoliberal logic of development policy and practice.

First, policymakers use the language of empowerment to mobilise large numbers of poor women as unpaid community health volunteers, which ends up exploiting poor rural women.

This is made possible by the overpowering image of Nepali women within religious and ritual practices, which relegates their position within the domestic and reproductive sphere and thus undervalues women's work. Second, the pressure to demonstrate achievements circumscribed by measurable results ignores critical political questions on gendered access to healthcare that directly shape the visible indicators of women's health and mortality. A long-term, sustainable, positive change in maternal health and mortality must address gendered access to healthcare. Third, the expansion of the private sector in caesarean section delivery, in the context of a weak regulatory capacity of the state, which has coincided with the push for institutional delivery that seeks to secure upward accountability through quantitative metrics, raises critical questions on the neoliberal logic of development, particularly impacting the poor and their citizenship.

Patricia Jeffery's work has taught us that context matters. So why is it that planners and policymakers do not make use of available contextual knowledge in the design and delivery of healthcare programmes? It is not because sociocultural knowledge does not exist. The evidence on is widely available and government agencies and international organisations frequently consult and/or hire social scientists and experts with technical and contextual knowledge to help design healthcare policies and programmes. The problem does not appear to lie in the lack of sociocultural knowledge or expertise. The failure to account for contextual sociocultural knowledge is not a technical problem but a political one, since it has been rendered invisible through a neoliberal logic and programmes of development.

REFERENCES

Bhandari, A., M. Gordon and G. Shakya. 2011. 'Reducing maternal mortality in Nepal', *BJOG,* 118 (Suppl.2): 26-30.

Brunson, J. 2010. 'Confronting maternal mortality, controlling birth in Nepal: The gendered politics of receiving biomedical care at birth', *Social Science & Medicine,* 71(10): 1,719–27.

Brunson, J. and S. Suh. 2019. 'Behind the measures of maternal and reproductive health: Ethnographic accounts of inventory and intervention', *Social Science & Medicine,* 254. doi.org/10.1016/j.socscimed.2019.112730.

Campbell, O.M.R. and W.J. Graham. 2006. 'Strategies for reducing maternal mortality: getting on with what works', *The Lancet*, 368(9542): 1,284–99.

Glenton, C., I.B. Scheel, S. Pradhan, S. Lewin, S. Hodgins and V. Shrestha. 2010. 'The female community health volunteer programme in Nepal: decision makers' perceptions of volunteerism, payment and other incentives'. *Social Science & Medicine*. 70(12): 1,920–27.

Government of Nepal (GoN). 2015. National Female Community Health Volunteers Survey 2014.

Jeffery, P. Forthcoming. *Muslim villagers, child survival and fertility in north India: Contextualising the demographic transition* (Routledge)

Jeffery, P. and R. Jeffery. 2008. 'Money itself discriminates: Obstetric emergencies in the time of liberalisation', *Contributions to Indian Sociology* 42(1): 61–93

Jeffery, P. and R. Jeffery. 2010. 'Only when the boat has started sinking: a maternal death in rural north India' (special issue on Loss in Childbearing), *Social Science and Medicine* 71(10): 1,711–18

Jeffery, P., R. Jeffery and A. Lyon. 1989. *Labour Pains and Labour Power: Women and Childbearing in India*. London & Manohar, New Delhi: Zed Books.

Ministry of Health Nepal, New ERA, and ICF. 2017. Nepal Demographic and Health Survey 2016. Kathmandu, Nepal: Ministry of Health, Nepal

Sharma, A. 2006. 'Crossbreeding Institutions, Breeding Struggle: Women's Empowerment, Neoliberal Governmentality, and State (Re)Formation in India', *Cultural Anthropology*, 21: 60–95

Sharma, J.R. 2016. Looking beyond Maternal Mortality Rates in maternal health interventions: Lessons from Nepal. LSE South Asia Blog. https://blogs.lse.ac.uk/southasia/2016/07/20/looking-beyond-maternal-mortality-rates-in-maternal-health-interventions-lessons-from-nepal/ (accessed 12 December 2020).

Sharma, J.R. 2021. *Political Economy of Social Change and Development in Nepal*, New Delhi: Bloomsbury.

Sharma, J.R. and R. Adhikari. 2021. 'Politics of Childbirth in Nepal: The case of the maternal mortality ratio', in C. Jullien and R. Jeffery (eds) *Childbirth in South Asia: old challenges and new paradoxes*. New Delhi: Oxford University Press.

Sharma, J.R., R. Khatri and I. Harper. 2018. 'Accountability and generating evidence for global health interventions: The case of misoprostol in Nepal', *IDS Bulletin* 49(2): 49–64.

Starrs, A.M. 2006. 'Safe motherhood initiative: 20 years and counting', *The Lancet*, 368(9542): 1,130–32.

Tamang, S. 2002. 'Dis-embedding the Sexual/Social Contract: Citizenship and Gender in Nepal', *Citizenship Studies*, 6(3): 309–24.

Thapa, S. 1989. 'A Decade of Nepal's Family Planning Program: Achievements and Prospects', *Studies in Family Planning*, 20(1): 38–52.

Wendland, C. 2016. 'Estimating death: a close reading of maternal mortality metrics in Malawi', in V. Adams (ed.) *Metrics: What Counts in Global Health*, pp. 57–81. Durham, NC: Duke University Press.

12

Taking Dung-Work Seriously

Women's Shit-Work in Waste

Barbara Harriss-White[1]

1. Introduction

In 1989, Patricia Jeffery and her research colleagues published a paper about the significance of animal waste for women's productive and reproductive work called 'Taking dung-work seriously' (DW89). Although the role of dung in the rural economy is now much diminished, the DW89 has stood the test of time.[2]

By way of a tribute to an intellectual courage that has foregrounded the often hidden background of social life, this chapter is a response to DW89, over three decades later. Waste, including waste from all the substitutes for dung, has become one of the fastest-growing sectors of India's now much bigger economy. Yet, as we will show, women's work is still shit-work, literally and figuratively. It involves human as well as animal waste and is defined, as in DW89, as low-status menial work with no control over resources. Waste work is still invisibilised, despite taking place in public spaces. And the congruence between waste and stigma is unchanged.

First, to contextualise this response, is a summary of the lasting significance of DW89.

1.1. DUNG WORK

In DW89, cow dung, a form of waste from the expenditure of animal energy in agriculture and from the production of milk, is conceived as raw material: for cooking (cakes, 'peat'); for agriculture (composted mulch and manure); and for home maintenance and construction (mud 'plaster').

Much labour is applied to this animal 'waste'; labour that is overwhelmingly female and non-monetised. When money values were imputed to it, the product of an example of women's dung-work amounted to an income stream equivalent to over half a year's agricultural wages.

Further, dung-work is 'invisibilised': it is heavy and tiring, and it takes place in private and public spaces that are female gendered. Despite its drudgery and potential economic value, this female work is regarded as non-economic, ignored by village men and development experts alike.

In DW89, practices of handling dung were mobilised to interrogate concepts in the study of development. First, the tendency for binaries in fundamental concepts of feminist analysis in social science: in this case, production and reproduction (although public and private, male and female also suggest themselves). As an input, cow dung straddles both productive and reproductive work. Second, the category of 'shit-work', meaning low status work that is undervalued by the men who actually own the cattle and by others, who privatise, degrade and encroach upon the common property resources which provide cattle with feed.

DW89 called for further research. To do this, we fast-forward to the present era, researching waste in South rather than North India, in a small town rather than in two villages, with a workforce which is both male and female, in monetised as well as non-monetised waste practices, which cover the entire local economy and – despite the importance of cow waste to Hindutva-blessed agriculture (Smith et al. 2020) – in an urban economy in which the cow has a much diminished role.

But in this different context, what is waste?

1.2. SOCIAL MEANINGS OF URBAN WASTE

As Valerian Rodrigues explained (2009), Indian society shears itself between those entitled to throw waste into impure, caste-cosmopolitan public space and those obliged to remove it. For the former it is invisibilised, while for the latter, men as well as women, waste is visibly the raw material of their work in the urban economy. While waste behaviour is a material expression of caste relations, these socioecological waste-scapes map onto a remarkably differentiated sector in terms of business organisation, assets and ownership. They are not significantly different from the urban economy as a whole (see Appendix 1 and Harriss-White 2016).

Locally, high-status, high-caste municipal officials who are formally in charge of waste, marginalise it in their burden of responsibilities, dispute the size and material content of the 'problem', do not care to learn the geography of waste in their current posting or to speak to, let alone consult, the municipal waste workforce. Meanwhile, we estimated through fieldwork that, for every municipal waste worker, between 10–15 are deployed in the informal economy. Despite the growing workforce, the town's waste was hardly under control. By afternoon waste engulfed all open spaces, irrespective of property rights – a public health threat in the course of unprecedently rapid development.

The town's waste is understood incoherently: through colloquial labels specific to the workers involved; through local and central government terms of art; through engineering sub-fields; and through academic categories. Together, these multiple systems of classification render the knowledge-field of waste peculiarly hard to navigate. Further, waste studies have been distinctively focused on certain kinds of work (e.g. manual scavenging, rag picking), certain kinds of site and space (e.g. leather streets in Hyderabad, dumpyards, e-waste yards) and certain kinds of waste (e.g. plastic, shipbreaking) (Harriss-White 2018). We chose a town.

1.3. PLACE AND METHODS

The nameless South Indian urban waste economy which I studied through three field visits between 2015 and 2019 is a one-lakh town, spilling over into surrounding villages. A central place for administration, construction, wholesale and retail trade, and its finance; it is a hub for communications, public and private healthcare, school and college education, religion and culture (from temples, churches and marriage halls to cinemas).

1.3.1. Research design

While DW89 cast the analytical categories of production and reproduction as a problem for the feminist analysis of dung-work, in the research reported here, these spheres were developed as the means to finding analytical order in the urban waste economy. From political ecology and economy, we examined the social relations of urban waste generation and disposal throughout the circuits of capital (Harriss-White 2019). The circuits are:

1. production (in this town, urban industrial production: liquor, rice milling and garment accessories)
2. distribution (the production and disposal of waste in the distribution of people [Indian Railways] and of commodities [the wholesale vegetable market])
3. waste practices of consumption (involving the municipality and its permanent sanitation workforce, the wage workers in private companies contracted to the municipality, plus self-employed unregistered waste workers)
4. waste in the production of urban labour (the generation and disposal of human body-waste which, in our case, is often merged with consumption waste)
5. waste generation in the reproduction of urban society (first, of waste in liquor consumption, without which the waste labour forces themselves would not go to work; and second, of the production and disposal of waste in public and private medicine, which ensures the health of society).

1.3.2. Case studies

Judgements grounded in experience were involved both in the selection of the town and in the choices through which over 150 interviews are summarised. As Flyvbjerg (2006) observes in his refutation of five myths about case studies, context–dependent knowledge is as important as theory in public policy and deliberation. And, as in DW89, the former can be used to critique the latter. Case studies do not simply validate theories and accepted generalisations, they also produce surprises. The most memorable surprises in the fieldwork reported here were the agency of animals and the dehumanising as animals of some of the waste workers by others.

In DW89, case studies were used to engage with the abstract (theories of production and reproduction) and with concrete questions in development policy and practice (unvalued women's work, the erosion of the commons). Patricia Jeffery's life work also confirmed that the case study is a lens through which society may be glimpsed.

This chapter assembles case studies niched in the circuits of capital and representing different scales and positions – the town, sectors, firms and workers. It is a long way from cow dung. It introduces the five circuits of urban waste production and lets waste workers explain their life-worlds. Following DW89 so far as is possible, it focuses on what they teach us about substances, organisation and tasks, commodification and earnings, women–men relations at work, and political and social visibility, particularly as they pertain to the biodegradable waste which, until recently, dominated urban and village waste.

2. Gendered livelihoods in waste

2.1. LIVELIHOODS IN WASTE CREATED BY INDUSTRIAL PRODUCTION

The town is poorly industrialised, with a small factory sector operating on non-local raw materials. An alcohol industry uses molasses from sugar cane, water and fossil-fuel energy to generate industrial alcohol and liquid waste – in principle it is non-toxic and biodegradable, in practice it is neither. Untreated molasses sludge has been piped to a river bed from where evaporation solidifies the waste and percolation contaminates the water table, while unattended blockages and leaks pollute nearby *Dalit* farmland and water.[3] Both the factory and the village it pollutes have histories of caste conflict. Dalits have been evicted from factory land and, according to the Panchayat President, Mrs E., a feisty Dalit woman, are being 'constantly sacked' from the factory's casual labour force – down from 50% at the start, to 12% in 2015 – and disproportionately concentrated in dealing with the physical tasks of effluent management and paid 'rock bottom rates' of about Rs. 6,000 a month. Mrs E. attributed the pay levels of factory waste workers not to supply and demand but to caste-based contempt.

However, most of the town's factories are rice mills.

2.1.1. Rice mills

Substances and processes: The 50 rice mills ringing the town produce rice from paddy, plus a series of solids as waste (husk, bran, broken-rice and ash, all theoretically biodegradable). Depending on the season, these are recycled, generating value as raw materials and sold through a small army of local wholesalers. Husk is used as fuel on site and dry-season surplus is sold to 'factories with boilers' – dyers, distilleries and sugar factories – from which burnt husk ash is abandoned in piles outside the factory compounds, free for farmers in dry seasons. In the monsoon, the mill-owners pay to have damp, decomposing husk ash taken to the town's dumpyard. Bran generates edible oil, soap and paint in a solvent extraction process, the waste from which is sold as cattle cake. In the wider region some rice-waste cattle cake is even exported to Europe. Black and broken grains are traded long distances to supply an intensive chicken industry. These systematic activities urge caution in taking for granted UN agencies' high estimates of food system loss and waste (FAO 2019).

Men–women work relations and earnings: While the means of subsistence have been commodified, while household labour rarely involves de-husking grain and while the rice mill labour force is masculinising, waste work in rice processing remains one of the several tasks of a casual migrant labour force (approximately 10–15 per mill). Gagged and disempowered by their lack of local language, these menial workers get about Rs. 6,000 per month on a daily rate, most of which is remitted home. Daily (food) allowances and discretionary perks underwrite their pauperised day-to-day existence. Identifying as Dalit on casual contracts, labourers may also be attached by custom (as well as by debt) to a mill.

Mill waste is swept by local Dalit women in three shifts. There is a big pay gap between them and the men. 'I'm paid Rs. 3,000 a month' said one of a modern rice mill's three sweepers. The women sweepers are from asset-less labouring households. 'We have no land. My sister's husband works in a labour gang, loading and unloading husk and bran on paddy lorries. His pay has gone to piece rate. He gets about Rs. 6,000 (per month)'.

The women sweepers are *Irular* – a scheduled tribe whose people are feared and despised – constantly being evicted from workplaces and campsites. (We will learn more from them later.) One explained: 'There used to be more tribal women working on the mill's drying yard but they were laid off when husk-fired driers were installed.' Her throwaway remark confirms how the sun-drying on huge cement yards of moist paddy, prior to milling, was female-labour intensive. In recent decades, it has been replaced by capital-intensive technology, which displaces not the costliest labour (as in economic theory) but the labour with lowest social status – low-caste women.

Political visibility: The state permits these unregistered workers to survive, not through any interventions in work conditions but through what it provides outside work, based on peoples' eligibility as poor citizens. 'The rice ration is vital to keep us alive,' said the rice-waste sweeper – and this was a comment frequently heard in fieldwork. Subsidised rice from the public distribution system (PDS) reduces pressure on employers' wage bills. In 2015, the poverty line was Rs. 1,400 per person and the minimum wage for a month was Rs. 5,000, so it was tough to maintain a family with dependents on incomes like those of rice mill waste workers without economic transfers.

2.2. LIVELIHOODS IN URBAN CIRCUITS OF DISTRIBUTION

Between production and consumption lies a complex circuit through which commodities and labour are organised over time and space. These processes of distribution generate waste. Our case studies involve the railway that serves the town by distributing people (and cargo) and the marketplace that supplies the town with vegetables for consumption and onward distribution throughout the region.

The transport of freight and passengers by rail generates solid and liquid consumption waste, as well as human waste, much of it combined at its spaces of generation – dropped on the tracks and strewn at stations. Just as Rodrigues theorised (2009), users of Indian Railways feel entitled to cast their waste and shit into these impure public spaces. 'Even educated people use the station as a dustbin,' complained a Railways Health Inspector. That the two sites, track and station, are managed by different departments of Indian Railways illustrates another general point, that waste management has non-trivial coordination problems. And the medical department in charge of stations has many other responsibilities, including food standards. Station waste is a chore combining high physical visibility and low social status.

Indian Railways' waste workforce also embodies a dramatic story of neoliberalisation found in other branches of government, such as hospitals and colleges. From 2008, under orders from a United Progressive Alliance/Congress government keen on shrinking the state, Indian Railways rolled out a nationwide subcontracting of waste management to private companies. With private rates of return on capital of up to 33%, the workforce, laid off by state agencies and re-hired by private companies, experienced a catastrophic pay crash. From about Rs. 15,000 per month, with work-related social security entitlements, the women's wages plummeted to Rs. 210 per day (approximately Rs. 5,250 per month, with severely compromised social security rights). To make ends meet, the now semi-formal working shift is lengthened by extra hours spent informally self-employed separating paper, plastic, card and glass, bagging and hauling station waste to sell, unreceipted, to small private wholesalers. The average extra daily income of Rs. 50 raises their total monthly earnings to perhaps Rs. 6–8,000. Trade unions find the organisation of informal/unregistered workers and workers in fly-by-night private companies much more difficult than in the public sector workforce. While DW89 showed how standard economic accounting invisibilises women's domestic waste work, the employment practices of Indian Railways shows how its waste labour has even been made invisible in the public sector of the economy.

2.2.1. Livelihoods in the distribution of commodities: the fruit and vegetable (F&V) markets.

Substances and organisation: The town has two wholesale markets for vegetables. One marketplace site is auctioned privately, a swathe of land for 10 F&V wholesalers and about 400 illegal retailers and their artistic displays. The second is a less frequented, periodic, municipal 'farmers' market', where small traders from surrounding villages sell produce they have previously purchased and so already in the circuit of distribution. Tucked in the suburbs you can also find cramped and makeshift, fly-blown places selling meat and fish.

General waste from these marketplaces overflows the municipal skips. F&V waste (currently estimated at as much as 40%[4] the reduction of which is used as the justification for new cold-stores and hi-tech infrastructure [Pandya et al. 2016]) consists of cuttings, perished F&V, bruised vegetables, vegetables speared by hooks during loading and unloading, vegetable matter used in packaging, and fungi and mushrooms.

Since, regardless of its proportion, the absolute amount of F&V waste far exceeds the disposal capacity of the town's waste workforce, much marketplace waste is fly-tipped onto common land from lorries supplying F&V on their return journeys to their villages of origin.

Vegetable waste is also generated by the hundreds of 'meals hotels' in town.[5] Sometimes a milk-cow is tethered outside a meals-hotel to deal directly with banana leaves. By dusk, biodegradable waste forms huge piles on which packs of feral dogs, privately-owned pigs and goats are to be found foraging under streetlights. 'It is truly disgusting,' declared a wholesaler of this common property resource.

As we saw for rice, so with F&V. A significant amount is recycled as raw material – in this case for informal urban dairies and for pigs. Down confined alleys teeming with chickens and goats, cleaned by water from private handpumps, at the back of narrow but deep, tile-roofed terrace houses, complete with storerooms for fodder and recycled plastic milk bottles, are dozens of very small family businesses in byres holding – say – four cows and three calves.[6] Cattle feed isn't confined to vegetable waste and pasture but is residually commodified, consisting of unwanted ration rice and waste husk from rice, dhal and gram milling.

Mostly penned in backyards, 500–750 pigs also flourish on food waste, while a further 1,000 forage and roam the forested peri-urban hills.

Tasks and agency: F&V – and meat/fish waste – provide the raw material for an extraordinary amount of non-human agency (Kumar et al. 2019). Between 10–15 flocks of goats and herds of stray cattle (let loose by poor citizens) feed, even on the burning surface of the dumpyard. 'Though plastic waste is an ever-present danger, all the cows know very well how to graze this town,' a pig-rearer explained.

Human agency in the F&V market is structured by gender – mostly male – and caste – mostly Backward. Few women own either vegetable market resources or the animals reared on vegetable waste. Just 7% of the hundreds of retailers are women. One *Naicker*[7] clan owns half the wholesale vegetable firms (with portfolios in transport, rabbits, cattle and land). The largest local firm is globalised and exports okra, brinjal and ginger by air to Europe and imports garlic and cardamom from China.

Men–women work relations and earnings: Urban dairying is gendered. Boys and men gather the edible waste, retail the milk, manage grazing and dispose of cow dung, urine and waste water onto the local peri-urban water-meadows (common land used for pasture). All the other work of cleaning empty bottles, rearing and milking cows and rolling credit and debt is done by women. Rural–urban marriage migrants, they learnt the physically hard work of dairying in their villages of origin. 'If you rear a cow you have to work like a cow,' a dairywoman told us, grimacing and grinning.

Despite low cash input costs, totalling on average Rs. 10,000 a month, they explained, 'we hardly break even'. I calculated a monthly net income of about Rs. 2,000. Debt penetrates dairying lives. 'Banks, no way! One month's default and they would confiscate our cattle ... We would rather live slightly bonded to our loyal consumers than disgraced by the banks.'

Visibility: The petty commodity production of milk faces stiff price competition from adulterated supplies from larger dairies. To avoid inspection, their milk is not branded, their cows are uninsured and they have no collective representation. This backstreet waste-dairy economy depends on cross-subsidies from diversified household income streams. One example involved a storeroom with machines for sewing and tailoring. More women's work.

2.3 THE CIRCUIT OF CONSUMPTION: LIVELIHOODS IN CONSUMPTION WASTE

Visible waste on verges and spare urban land (whatever its tenurial status) is mostly thrown out as the by-product of consumption. In the 1970s, urban consumption waste was biodegradable and recycled through composting pits auctioned as agricultural manure. Over the last five decades of rapid urbanisation the proportion of non-biodegradable consumption waste has risen to equal or exceed that of biodegradable waste (Ahluwalia and Patel 2018).

This waste is formally the responsibility of a municipality that relies on revenue from property and professional taxes to pay a directly-employed labour force of 115 municipal sanitation workers (MSWs) – the labour aristocracy of waste. As with Indian Railways – but due to tax evasion which thins the revenue stream – the municipality is being forced to privatise its workforce incrementally. By 2015–16 it had auctioned one-third of its streets to private bidders. The need to make a profit from a successful low bid eats into the wage component. So the company employs debt-bonded, long-distance, migrant-labouring couples on deteriorating pay, with no benefits except for slum housing, outside which piles of segregated materials betray the lengthening working day. Such is the strain on public finance that one ward was given over for free to tribal collectors.

About half of urban consumption waste is currently recycled. Alongside the MSWs and the private subcontracters, there are about 50 unregistered buyers and bulkers of card, paper, metal, glass and plastic. This unregistered wholesale system, a fortress of the *Nadar* caste, supplies a joint family business.[8] In a seven-acre depot, plus three satellite sites, over 200 raw materials are segregated for reprocessing in Chennai by a labour force of 75 local low-caste women and about 50 migrant men from Bihar and Orissa. An unknown-sized army of unregistered, self-employed collectors gathers and sorts waste and supplies this system; some with trikes or bikes, many on foot, some migrants, a few vagrants. Supplies are supplemented by wage workers on shifts clearing waste in schools, colleges, office complexes, hospitals and the bus and railway stations, who work extra hours as self-employed segregators of the waste piles they are employed to gather.

2.3.1. Municipal sanitation work

Here we shift the style of this storytelling for a reason Patricia Jeffery may appreciate. The experience of two municipal sanitation workers and trade union leaders needs telling rather as they themselves told it – intertwined with one another. On each field visit, we met in the CITU office under posters of Lenin, Mao and local labour leaders.[9] 'Please use our names. We want the Chief Minister to know'. Illiterate, articulate, militant, streetwise, one a *Paraiyar* and one an *Arundathiar*, they wear their gold as a symbol of their pride and the respect they feel they deserve but do not get for work that is an essential service.[10]

Fig. 12.1 Municipal Sanitation Workers T and K with Barbara Harriss-White. Source: Barbara Harriss-White

It is midday, late September 2019, T and K have eaten but are between shifts, having washed and changed for our meeting behind a fish market shop because the municipality has no changing rooms or washrooms for the labour force cleaning the town. 'Yes, we remove their shit from the drains but while we work we ourselves have to shit on the verges. That is why most of us don't eat or drink until after the first shift. We have to control our bodies.'

Substances, tasks and technology: The municipal labour force is responsible for clearing all waste thrown from shops, offices, public buildings and homes onto verges, into drains or heaped in big roadside bins. The town's consumption waste is unknown – estimated by engineering officials at anywhere between 25 and 60 tonnes a day. About half is non-recyclable, while another half is non-biodegradable.

Despite lady 'animators', whose families have exchanged a Rs. 3 lakh bribe for municipal salaries to teach households to segregate waste, only a quarter of the people of this town comply. There are no fines for those who don't segregate domestic waste.

> More and more waste is complicated, horrible and jumbled up in drains. It's new – the sanitary napkins, tampons and incontinence pads, muddled with used plastic, glass, metals, paper and cardboard and food waste … We have to collect and segregate by hand. Yes, we now have equipment, unlike when you first met us four years ago, but it isn't suitable for our work. We're sometimes given masks but they are too hot for our weather. Rubber gloves are supplied once a year but they are flabby so we work without them. Sandals pick up mud and shit and rot like cardboard and galoshes are useless in the monsoon.
>
> While 20 years back there used to be 250 workers for a quarter of the present waste, the municipality now has difficulty paying 60 women and 55 men. Even with machines there should be at least 300 of us. Our work contracts are becoming extinct. Don't talk about inheriting our jobs: 25 of us have died or retired in the last four years and have not been replaced. Workers and workloads don't add up – or they do add up and they crush us. Population and infilling means that the material we have to pick up has increased to four times what the municipality calculates. The shifts are growing longer. They are incompatible with housework.

To compensate, they have been allowed to segregate and sell the waste they collect, but that lengthens a working day already stretched way beyond official timing.

> Perhaps we get Rs. 30 extra a day. … We've also been given so-called ecological battery-operated trucks to carry the waste we collect to the dumpyard. But there are few charging points in the municipal yards, the trucks break down and their skips are too small – half the size of the tractor-trailer. We need two circuits to replace what one sweep of waste did before. There is not enough room for a team of three – a man and two women – to sit on them and they have no protection from rain/sun.

Men–women work relations and earnings: Formally, the municipal labour force receives equal pay. But ad hoc and casual contracts are rapidly increasing in prevalence and these can vary between men and women. Average monthly salaries for women are declining; said to be Rs. 15,000 in 2015, now few exceed Rs. 12,000.

> Sure, we also get benefits but they are also deteriorating: a medical card with lots of exemptions (the 6 monthly check-ups have stopped), pensions but increasingly unreliable, taking years to start arriving. We have torn nails (look …), skin allergies, URT infections, urinary infections and our children will have to look after us in old age. This will get worse because we now have to work in competition with unregistered labour working longer hours for far less pay [reported at Rs. 8,000 per month for the men and women working for the private company]. We are supposed to work in teams but men control the machinery and they also take more time off. Sometimes we have to substitute for them.

Promised housing, men are now seizing the municipality's rented accommodation for their families and resisting its demolition.

Visibility: By the afternoon the visibility of household waste strewn throughout the town contrasts sharply with the invisibility of the workforce handling it. Local government officials never consult the labour force they pay, relying on the understaffed supervisors, who themselves are mostly unfamiliar with the town's layout. We ascertained that officials who are mostly trained engineers know nothing about the unregistered workforce, regardless of whether employed by a private subcontracted company – communication with whom is further obstructed by language – or whether self-employed or wage workers for wholesalers operating in the informal economy.

Trade union CITU trained T and K and raised the problems of deteriorating terms and conditions, of pay levels and precarity in state-level fora, but to no avail. CITU succeeded in organising a protest, which wrung from the municipality a meagre death compensation for a migrant contract waste labourer killed by a tractor-trailer negotiating a pothole. CITU officials acknowledge that the union is mostly mobilised around sectors other than waste.

2.3.2. Recyclers of plastic waste

Substances: Segregated recyclable waste is sold to an 'apex' depot, where it is crudely transferred to specialist satellite hangars. Plastics, for instance, go for fine-grained classifications, underground storage, shredding into chips (when the electricity works) and stacking in gunnies on an old drying yard.

Tasks, labour relations and incomes: A mountain of jumbled plastic objects (including obsolescent TVs and mixies provided free by the government[11]) is dismantled to fill winnowing trays, which then feed a production line. Instead of sitting on stools and working on a bench, six local women of all ages and four young migrant men, sit cross-legged on the floor, in segregated groups, picking four each of 40 kinds of plastic from the trays passed down the line and throwing them in 41 bins.[12] At the end is a special skip for the waste-waste, incudings bits of metal they have to disentangle from plastic objects and which is thrown to the verge to be collected for the dumpyard. The pace is fast, the waste is dirty, some components (used syringes) are potentially infectious, the work requires intense 'eye-brain-hand' concentration and coordination, workers' bodies are crunched painfully and shifts are nine hours long, counting toilet breaks.

'I've sat in this position on this concrete for 10 years,' says one woman recycler. 'Every so often, after several weeks, we change positions and categories to stop being bored.'

'As we are all SCs and BCs, we are not under pressure at home to conform. This work gets us out of our homes and gives us incomes.'[13] It is regular, while agricultural work and NREGA is unpredictable.[14] 'We are paid weekly, and get about Rs. 4,800 a month. There is no paid leave, no sick leave but our employer pays to treat accidents.'

Men are paid much more (Rs. 7,200), which is justified because their work is considered heavier and dirtier and their shifts extend into the night.

In this part of the waste economy, punishing work conditions and low pay are compensated for by a sense of personal freedom and autonomy. 'But you don't age gracefully in this job.'

2.3.3. Consumption waste work on the edge of humanity

With waves of evictions, social oppression and marginalisation, tribal Irulars work in rice mills (with paddy still protected by its husk), in brick kilns (often as bonded labour), clearing waste in wedding halls – and on consumption waste. In 2015 the municipal labour force informally allowed them to make a dawn sweep of the town's heaps of waste before the official round of daily collections moved into gear, but by 2019 the MSW was compelled to top up its wages – like the Indian Railway workers – and turfed them off.

Substances and tasks: 'My family used to scour the dumpyard, fish and wash in the river and live in a hut nearby,' explains an Irular woman. 'Even though our children didn't go to school and the dumpyard and its smoke are dangerous, it was a living.' Sand mining has messed with the water table and dried up the water in the river (Jeyaranjan 2019). The municipality cleared part of the dumpyard and, with central government funds from Swachh Bharat, built a go-down for composting.

> Now, new diggers pack the dumpyard waste to treble the old height and we cannot walk on the top. We have moved back to the forest where we have to make homes of leaves and branches because it is protected land and we can be chased out any time by government. The only *pukka* house on *poromboke* land in our place belongs to Pentecostal missionaries. We stay clear of them.

Men–women work relations and earnings: Irulars prefer to gather waste in mixed-sex couples, for safety. Murugan explains:

> in waste there are always new sites, like behind the Girls' College. When thrown off the dumpyard, we used to work very early shifts around the edge of town for three hours as the sun rises and before anyone else arrived to collect glass, milk sachets, cardboard boxes and plastic littered the evening before. We share routes and finds. I had a gunny bag and worked with my son. When our bags got heavy, we would segregate our things and my son would sell them to our wholesaler. There are just two wholesalers in town who allow our people to trade with them. They also lend us gunnies, small loans and sometimes bikes but we get half the price others get elsewhere.

> We don't write or know numbers and are easily fooled. On a good day we might get Rs. 200. NREGA also gives us Rs. 150. [In a good month he might get Rs. 4,000, more often Rs. 3,000.] We all have bank accounts now but others use them for us! Kamala in our village, who has a mobile, helps us get work and pay but it is often delayed.
>
> My wife who worked with me died. Now I feel I'm going blind (yes, I drank alcohol) and I have stomach and back pain. New gangs of outsiders are being brought here and kept by our wholesaler. They're men with wrist watches and chains who take our routes. They have been agricultural labourers. They have cycles and can search further than we can by foot. I fear them and I can't work. Most of my family has gone from the village: it is ration rice and sugar which keeps me alive. Without it I am doomed. I have a hut next to my son, who assists a bricklayer, and his family share their ration.

Visibility: These tribal gatherers are shunned. 'They are not really humans,' a self-employed female Paraiyar waste-collector confided to us. 'We are treated like animals,' admitted a self-employed Irular. Paraiyars and people from scheduled tribes refer to them as 'beggars' and 'drunkards'. Of Irulars, they told us, 'A dog is still a dog even if you bathe it.'

There is a difference between feeling like a machine and being treated like – and feeling like – an animal. While the former is due to oppressive work, the latter is due to social discrimination. Irular waste gatherers experience both. Irulars have a unique permutation of attributes, many of which are individually associated with other groups of Dalits, *Adivasis* or low-paid workers (Charsley 1997).[15] Their closeness to nature emerged from their past association with catching rats and snakes, their knowledge of forest habitats and their encroachment with makeshift settlements without land titles on forest sites or hilltops. 'We have been temporary for three generations.' Their combination of fluent oral expression but extensive lack of formal education (with only a few of their children going to school, even today) is unusual among local Dalits and Adivasis. And the relative independence of their women, and the routine consumption of alcohol by almost every adult, marks them out from the others. But not one of these attributes is unique to them.

Regardless of whether their 'marginalised humanity' is cause or effect in the eyes of others, those who most need their entitlements, such as ration cards and ST certificates, to gain access to basic utilities, education and employment are by far the least enfranchised as citizens. An addiction to alcohol eats into budgets and, unable to afford rice at market rates, the few ration cards available have to be circulated between households. Discriminated against, ignored and shunned by others in the waste economy, Irulars are not so much socially excluded as socially expelled, and are often treated with brutality by the state.

2.4.WASTE LIVELIHOODS IN THE PRODUCTION OF LABOUR

The production and reproduction of labour cannot avoid the daily production of human waste – prominent among which are urine, faeces and menstrual waste. Disposing of which is, literally and figuratively, shit-work.

Substances, organisation and tasks: While a large literature condemns the persistence of open defecation in India, in this region the abolition of manual scavenging in the early 1990s brought about the abolition of public sector jobs reserved for female manual scavengers. The de-reservation and disinheriting of sanitation work now means these dangerous but comparatively well-paid jobs depend on official patronage and discretion. The municipal labour force is being masculinised and the disposal of 'wet waste', in which semi-solid human waste drains from latrines (or is thrown), to be mixed with general consumption waste in open drains and urban gullies is now men's rather than women's work.

Where it is impossible to separate, it is transported with other non-recyclable consumption waste to the dumpyard. The Irular families who survived by sifting the putrid surface that others rejected because of faecal contamination, were evicted in 2019. The fetid mass is contained by systematically setting fire to quarters of it, week by week, a practice which is illegal. While firing was widely blamed on Irulars, they clearly had no interest in increasing the danger of their work environment and the practice has continued after their eviction.

'Meals hotels have a bad habit of draining shit directly into the surface mains,' said a local Paraiyar politician. But by 2019 half the town's houses and most public buildings and offices had septic tanks. The Paraiyar and *Kattunaicker* owner of two small fleets, who took over in 2005 when the municipality stopped voiding septic tanks as a public service, report that many tanks are corruptly built to half the correct size. Very few households or organisations void them regularly and the Rs. 1,200 fee is considered an avoidable cost. The Paraiyar tanker-owner explained: 'They might be cleared once in a generation or when they break down … The removal of shit is the last thing people in this town think about … Some replaced dry latrines 30 years ago, have never been cleaned and are now rock solid.'

There is no infrastructure for the treatment of faecal sludge when it is pumped out, so, operating at night or bribing the police by day, septic tanker crews dump half the town's faeces and toxic sludge in a nearby lake, which is turning anoxic, and in the riverbed, deformed by sand mining.

Labour and earnings: In local terms, septic tankering is big business. The portfolio of the Kattunaicker owner comprises a fleet of tankers, other trucks, a large piggery and an agency for TV advertising.

While manual scavenging was, and domestic toilet cleaning is, women's work, the septic tank-clearing labour force is entirely male, young, local, Dalit or tribal. Voiding large septic tanks is filthy and dangerous work – cleaning labourers knew of suffocation deaths in nearby towns and cities. Daily wages pay small premiums to reflect this danger, monthly incomes vary from Rs. 7,000–10,000 but with 'no perks', no labour or social security rights. Labour turnover is high. The Kattunaicker tanker-owner said: 'This is essential work but there is no social respect. People in the neighbourhood ridicule the wives of my labourers and call their men shit carriers.'

Visibility: 'This is not a progressive occupation. And what with maintenance and competition our profits are declining.' Both competing fleet-owners have strong political connections outside the town and one is a local politician. Monetised connections with the police are essential, although, 'we pay them to clear their shit! They require us to empty their septic tanks for free, over above the bribes they extort from us' (Kattunaicker tanker-owner). Referring to under-payments by officials in the engineering college and the fire station, the Paraiyar tanker-owner explained, 'We are not well educated … We know knowledge is power. We want the next generation to have more power.'

2.5. WASTE LIVELIHOODS IN THE REPRODUCTION OF LOCAL URBAN SOCIETY

An unhealthy society cannot reproduce in a way that moves towards human development. India's social system reproduces itself through relationships of health and disease that are locked into several dynamic transitions (developing between social classes and sometimes inside a given household): from high to low birth and death rates; from diseases of poverty (under-nutrition and high infant mortality) to non-communicable diseases of affluence (obesity and lengthening life expectation).

One neglected transition affecting household health and expenditure and urban waste is a liquor transition, in which toddy and arrack is replaced by a vastly expanded and socially cosmopolitanised consumption of commercialised and state-regulated alcohol: beer, rum, brandy and whisky.

In our case-study town, drinkers range from lawyers and policemen to construction, brick, timber, sex and waste workers. Commonly dismissed as drunkards by waste-throwers, many waste workers, women and men, drink before they work in psychological preparation for the offensive sights, substances and smells they know they will encounter. 'Alcoholism is almost normal – such a horrible job handling stinking, maggoty waste,' explained a woman municipal worker, who reckoned Rs. 200–250 could be spent daily on an individual's liquor; by drinking after work to wind down, physically and emotionally, and for pain relief, an addict's life expectancy is compromised (Human Rights Watch 2014; Harriss-White 2017).

The waste from alcohol is not just costed in wasted and shortened lives, in this town it also generates a guesstimated million bottles a month as raw material for recycling or, if broken (a further hazard on urban streets), for collection and deposition with waste-waste in the dumpyard. While the tax on alcohol subtracts from the subsidy on PDS rice in poor households, the health hazards of waste workers' alcohol consumption are another human subsidy to the state, necessary for the cleanliness of urban public spaces.

India spends one of the lowest proportions of GDP on health in the world.[16] Its several health systems are also some of the most privatised and informalised (Brhlikova et al. 2009). In our case-study town there is an allopathic healthcare cluster, with one large government hospital, six large private ones and about 50 private clinics – all formally registered.

2.5.1 Healthcare waste

Substances and tasks: The waste generated by health institutions is mainly handled as general 'consumption' waste (e.g. food and human waste). The productive-therapeutic aspects of healthcare vary greatly in their generation of waste – operating theatres, maternity and labour wards and diagnostic labs generate most, while paediatrics generates little.

A small proportion of this waste is infectious or otherwise dangerous to health (needles and sharps; plastic syringes; blood transfusion, blood products and bloody waste; soiled cotton and cloth; drug bottles; saline and glucose bottles; body parts). It is termed medical waste and strictly regulated in a separate system of segregation, collection, incineration and burial (Hodges 2017). While the medical waste of the public and larger private hospitals is recorded, segregated and sent for burial – after the region's incinerator was closed following a public outcry about its polluting effects on local villages, that of the smaller private hospitals and clinics is segregated inside the campus. However, once outside, its classifications unravel as it enters the system of general consumption waste and heads for unregistered segregation or for the dumpyard.

Medical waste workers are euphemised as 'housekeepers'.

We are in S's tiny, ramshackle, two-room house, with a gaping hole in the roof where tiles have been ripped off by monkeys.

> My life has always been hard … My son bought the place cheaply from my daughter because my son-in-law had died there after falling from a tree. I fear harassment, living alone and use this place as a cupboard. I sleep next door, where I watch TV.

S is about 50, Muslim, with no education, orphaned early, brought up by relatives and deserted by her husband, who left her with three children and without financial support. In 1990, after years with a petty snack shop and then working as a washerwoman (*dhobi*), S was recommended to a small private clinic in need of a cleaner and general factotum. The place grew: from 2 to 45 beds; from a focus on childbirth to general medicine, surgery and intensive care; from a single owner to a partnership of three – two of whom are supplementing their work in the public hospital. Many of the skilled paramedic and nursing labour force are retired pensioners from the state health system.

> Waste is segregated in buckets and housekeepers empty them into metal skips outside. Food waste is then collected by the municipal sanitation workers. Medical waste is packaged and collected separately. Human waste and bedpans are cleaned by a separate labour force of scheduled caste 'bathroom cleaners'. Our own needs are met by sneaking into the labour ward staff toilets.
>
> After washing soiled material for a year, I then worked as a helper in the operating theatre and the maternity ward before entering and later managing the teams of women housekeepers. As well as cleaning wards and segregating waste, I still work in theatre. I wash equipment and I nurse post-operative patients, washing them, cleaning their teeth and dressing wounds. I work a seven-day week on 12-hour shifts: this work is not compatible with family life or other work at home. Housekeepers cannot supplement this work with side jobs. There is no time for worship. I don't go to the mosque – it is too exhausting after work. I also can't afford the cost of cloth to cover my head nor do I want to draw attention to my religion.

Men–women work relations and earnings: 'We are essential but we are paid low wages.' Many housekeepers confirmed that men and women were paid equal wages in clinics. In some cases, men do 'high work' (fans and doors), while women do stooping work, collecting 'low waste'.

S has worked for 20 years on a verbal contract, for a monthly salary worth Rs. 7,500 in 2019, with an annual festival bonus of Rs. 3,000, loans of up to a month's salary (deducted from her pay over five monthly instalments) and a provident fund that has been paid, S thinks, for the last 10 years, but 'there is no retirement age'. Uniforms, gloves and masks are provided. All leave, for whatever purpose, is discretionary and unpaid, except for illness, when S receives free treatment.

Visibility: None of the housekeeping labour is unionised in the town.

> In place of a union, once a month in this clinic there's a staff meeting for grievances: the demands are about shift length, better uniforms, overtime, breaks. About salaries, we talk privately.
>
> My relatives ask me why I do a filthy job. I get much mockery for this filthy job. But this hospital is my 'parent-home' ... Okay, so it is dirty work, but I'm proud of my reputation for being a good cleaner, and I am grateful to my patron.
>
> I also suffer for my lack of education. My son taught me my signature. I can't read and don't know English and both are important in the hospital. For drug bottles, other people have described the label to me and now I know their contents. Otherwise doctors and nurses use English and I have made mistakes in my daily work, like when someone asked for a lavatory and I took them to the laboratory. I have learned English numbers through the wards: 'Go to ward 14 or 21' etc. I get used to it ... I learned counting when I worked in a grocer's shop before I came here. I counted and separated coins in the evening. That is how I came to know numbers.

This glimpse of private medicine also reveals a very physically strenuous, grindingly poor livelihood, with responsibilities incommensurate with her education, which S makes sense of in terms of patronage, flexibility and discretion. 'In future, shit workers will be Dalit drop-outs from far-off villages.'

3. Conclusions

'Why learn about us? India is a country where knowledge can lead to inaction with impunity,' said K.

3.1 RURAL–URBAN COMPARISONS

Like rural dung in DW89, urban waste has many uses. We found it as free, common property to be gathered as raw materials – both biodegradable and non-biodegradable – for small-scale production (dairying, piggeries, second-hand repaired goods), for some composting for agriculture and for considerable recycling for reprocessing. Unlike DW89, in the town we studied, waste is not yet used for fuel/energy and waste-waste is a growing category. Half the town's waste goes to landfill. Waste-waste could be reduced, especially if human and animal shit were disposed of separately from other urban consumption waste. At best, animal waste is recycled privately on pastures, at worst (and mostly) it enters the stream of consumption waste.

3.2 MONETISATION AND COMMODIFICATION

Whereas in DW89, dung was hardly commodified and prices and earnings were imputed, these days urban waste has two pathways of commodification: first, about half the waste material is commodified into fine-grained categories for reprocessing; and second, work gathering and segregating both recyclable and non-recyclable waste-waste is being commodified through wages paid directly and indirectly from the public purse, or directly by independent private firms.

Labour is being aggressively commodified in forms ranging from salaries paid from revenue-strapped public agencies, through wages in private capitalist enterprises (in turn, ranging from corporates to small family firms), to returns to self-employment. Self-employment varies from small-scale independent livelihoods, through disguised wage work controlled through debt (including 'kind bondage' using, for example, cycle trailers), to the monetised pickings of destitute vagrants. In this wide range of forms, waste labour is no different from sectors in India's semi-registered capitalist economy.

As a consequence of new public management practices and of more or less neoliberal cost-cutting by the Indian state, the terms and conditions of work in the public sector of the waste economy have deteriorated markedly, in particular: levels of pay; the increasing length of working day needed to get a subsistence income, which is now widely reported to eat into reproductive labour hours; the precarity of contracts; the extinguishing of rights to workplace equipment and social security benefits. In private companies, waste work is at the least entitled end of a continuum of contractual forms, in which 'formal' and 'informal' are at extremes. 'Privatisation is killing us,' said a government hospital cleaner.

In the informal waste economy, mechanisation is not reducing the demand for work because the production of waste is increasing at a rate far outstripping that of labour displacement, and because the capital-biased technologies introduced are unreliable and often inappropriate. Whether as unregistered wage workers or as self-employed, the earnings of waste gatherers are a half to a third of those of the municipal labour they threaten. Any benefit other than the wage has always been exiguous and discretionary. Many have no work rights and receive state support only through transfers, such as PDS rice, which are based on citizenship below the poverty line.

3.3 GENDER IN THE URBAN WASTE ECONOMY

While not overwhelmingly female, like dung-work, and while the male waste work force is considerable and sectors such as septic tank voiding are entirely male, the urban waste economy nevertheless appears to be disproportionately feminised. Women get livelihoods from working in a vast range of waste substances, some disgusting, often toxic. Not always Dalit, the female workforce in waste is highly differentiated by: tasks and niches in the urban waste ecosystem; income; precarity; contact with filth; and degree of organisation. Women occupy the kinds of fractured niches that Kapadia evoked for Dalit women's work in general (2017). Local women are often forced to work alongside migrant men whose language they cannot understand.

Despite the entire waste economy being stigmatised, the terms and conditions of women's work are clearly more oppressive than those for men. When men and women work together, the terms subordinate women. Women tend to work harder for longer hours, lower pay, fewer discretionary perks and fewer social entitlements. More so than men, women have to control bodily functions at work, to meld their bodies to physically punitive tasks, to avoid the threats to health from filthy, toxic and physical dangerous substances and gases, and to cope with premature ageing and a life cycle shortened by shit-work.

Whereas DW89 reports even rural public space as gendered, our urban fieldwork found the gendering of space confined to sites of work rather than being expressed in the public domain – except at night, when urban public space is male space.

3.4 CASTE AND SHIT-WORK

DW89 was researched at a time when the changing role of caste in the economy was being hotly debated. While Béteille could write that 'caste is no longer an important agent of either placement or social control' (1997, p. 450), Cadène and Holmstrom concluded that caste continued to play a major 'continuity' role as a social allocator of occupations, even as the economy diversified (1998). In striking ways, waste shows both this continuity and this change. In DW89, while some *chamar* and other low-caste women used to carry out dung-work for clean-caste Hindus and high-status Muslim households, by 1989 dung-work had become domestic work for women of all castes. By contrast, in our 21st-century urban case, waste reproduces the social order and waste work is deeply, though not completely, embedded in caste. Hierarchies of stigma pervade substances, just as they do the identities of workers. Human and animal wastes are most stigmatised, paper and metals are least.

While the municipal workforce faces deteriorating conditions and accelerating contractual ad hoccery, it is also cosmopolitanising. Ten per cent are non-Dalit: 'only very poor Naickers and *Naidus* are willing to do this work.' Yet a Dalit MSW put it this way: 'Outside work we are called *kuppaikaran* (trashman) and scavengers. This is India! But non-Dalit sanitation workers are called municipal staff and they soon take the jobs in lorry driving and supervising.'

The most extreme social stigma is attached to Irular tribal people, whom other waste workers do not consider (fully) human and who are subject not so much to social exclusion as to active social expulsion, both in and out of work.

Easier to enter than to exit, the informal waste economy, labour-absorber of last resort, is work for Scheduled Castes and Scheduled Tribes. Educating the next generation is key to mobility, but access to schools and colleges faces stigmatising discrimination and exclusion (Rodrigo and Harriss-White 2016).

Deliege's paradox of marginality developed for 'untouchables' covers the low-caste informal labour force – socially marginalised but materially essential (2001). While they work unregistered and without rights to work, rights at work and rights to social security, without them the urban economy would not function and its population would fall sick.

3.5 DEVELOPMENT CONCEPTS

3.5.1. Waste as a sub-field

In the decades since DW89 reflected on the low status of waste work as a research and policy field – 'beneath contempt of development specialists' (Jeffery et al. 1989, p 36) – a sizeable sub-field has been created.[17] Yet, while waste itself has exploded in volume and diversified in composition, it remains of low status both as a zone of policy and practice and as a research sub-field. While shit has its own sub-sub field (Doron and Raja 2015), dung and other biodegradable waste is overlooked in the literature on urban waste, a neglect we have tried to repair here.[18]

In the work of recognition, it does not help that waste is a concept beset by a multitude of classifications – with no consensus on terms. Despite this epistemological incoherence, but as was found in DW89, the trajectories of waste still straddle major conceptual binaries in development thought. The economic relations of waste not ending-up in landfill, mesh circuits of capital usually theorised as distinct. While DW89 followed waste in routes transcending production and reproduction, here we see waste generated throughout the **circuits of production–distribution–consumption–the production of labour and the reproduction of society**. In the circuit of social reproduction we also identified an **'alcohol transition'** from evidence for a rapid social increase in the consumption of alcohol not just for recreation but as therapy for offensive work conditions.

While male and female work is often mapped onto distinct tasks, in waste the **gendered divisions of labour** are further structured through gender-diverse couples and teams as work units, and through other gendered binaries, such as wet and dry waste, respectively men's and women's waste material.

Even the concept of **shit-work** – readily volunteered and recognised in Tamil – developed depths hitherto unappreciated. First, the stuff of shit-work aggregated human and animal shit and animal carcasses, it aggregated faecal substances with other human waste secreted into soiled padding. Second, the mixing of shit with other consumption waste in drains and gullies greatly expands the composition of shit-stuff and its work. Third, shit-work also involves the work of shitting in public spaces, for which municipal workers, forced by the humiliating lack of municipal 'conveniences', are mocked and stigmatised. Yet fourth, while shit-work is low-paid, dirty and low status – as a sector it is not a barrier to accumulation. The state has few difficulties subcontracting this work to private and corporate capital.

The case of waste teaches us that conceptual categories should not be taken for granted and need interrogation.

3.5.2.Development policy

As in DW89, which took dung seriously, urban waste is an ever-increasing development problem. Waste is launched on a higher growth rate than most economic sectors and one destined to last the entire 21st century (Hoornweg et al. 2013). While food loss and waste has excited UN attention, the uptake of technologies to reduce it is sparse and slow (FAO 2019). And, despite Swachh Bharat, waste is hardly visible as a policy field for the local state (Doron and Raja 2015; Mander 2019). Solid waste management – a category mistake for the composition that actually exists – is a low status, residual techno-engineering field for high-status officials inside state bureaucracies. Since waste behaviour is an expression of caste norms, policies for waste which privilege technology and ignore the work conditions and social problems of the workforce reinforce the caste order.

Waste and social inclusion are two substantially separate policy fields, while the social relations of waste are not bound by the classifications of the state. Public policy analysis needs to understand better the (lack of) intersections of policy discourse and actual existing policy practice – in the case considered here, for waste, work, environment, identity and welfare/inclusion.

The Indian state requires the informal sector which operates outside its reach to organise the disposal of waste. The local state allows unregistered self-employment for essential activity it chooses not to fund. The state does nothing to discourage the deployment of casual labour in private firms to which it subcontracts waste in order to undercut the costs of municipal labour. And by reducing and precaritising their earnings, it forces municipal workers themselves to prolong their working day informally to supplement them.

In addition, if in capitulating to tax evasion the state lacks the fiscal resources to pay for waste disposal as a public service, it perpetuates the survival of this low-paid, unregistered labour force through subsidies transferred not through work but through the PDS's ration books. PDS rice was widely credited as a life-support for waste workers. While the PDS is being threatened through undebated legislative reform to the Essential Commodities Act, the object of unprecedented farmers' protests in 2020–21, the vital support role of subsidised food is confirmed by Azim Premji University's 2020 pan-Indian field evidence during the Covid-19 epidemic.

Appendix 1: Differentiated business models in a small-town waste economy

With indicative examples sourced from the author's field survey, 2015.

1. Public sector labour force (UC officials; SC/ST workforce)
   i) large labour force (130+), full rights at work, unionised (e.g. Municipal Sanitation Workers, MSW)
   ii) small labour force (<5), variable work rights – some permanently casualised (e.g. government liquor shops and glass bottle recycling)
2. Private business (Nadar owners; instead of: Nadar and SC/ST workforce)
   i) registered joint family with 10–500 wage workers – local and migrant (e.g. scrap yards; medical waste; gunny bag depot)
   ii) private companies subcontracted to state (30–300 wage workers) – local and migrant labour, no union, no work rights, side jobs (e.g. urban consumption waste and 'municipal' rubbish; hospital cleaning and security; railway sanitation)
3. Waste 'departments' inside big companies (Dalit workforce)
   i) specialised labour (3–40) to clean-up, segregate, pack – disproportionately Dalit/*Adivasi* (e.g. clothing accessories, industrial alcohol, paddy milling, wedding halls, private hospitals, big meals hotels)
4. Own account enterprise (OBCs/SCs/STs)

   i) family labour with 1–2 wage labourers and more or less tied suppliers, some with bikes/vans (e.g. general waste wholesalers; second-hand goods; septic tankers)
5. Self-employed agent (various low castes)
   i) as in reprocessing; vehicle/two-wheeler scrap; glass bottle recycling
6. Self-employed – barter (various low castes)
   i) with cart or scooter (e.g. cloth for plastic kitchenware, iron waste for salt, dates, turmeric, onion and tomatoes)
7. Self-employed individual (SC/ST)
   i) gathering on foot, with bike or cycle cart (e.g. hundreds in general waste – gathering before and after the MSW; scores on the dumpyard; scores in the vegetable market; clearing up slaughter and sales).

NOTES

1. With thanks to Gilbert Rodrigo with whom I did the fieldwork and to Hugo Gorringe for very constructive responses to the draft.
2. Jeffery R., P. Jeffery and A. Lyon (1989).
3. Dalit is an identity meaning oppressed (as in the Dalit Panthers movement, which is active in the region) and it covers several scheduled castes and tribes working in waste. In this chapter it is applied as an overarching concept – as used by our respondents.
4. https://www.ft.com/content/c1f2856e-a518-11e3-8988-00144feab7de
5. Vegetarian eating places where *sappadu* (a meal with six tastes in lentil and vegetable dishes and rice on a banana leaf) is served at lunch, while *tiffin* (a vast and eloquent array of snacks) is served at other times of day.
6. Male calves are still reared for ploughing and for slaughter. Tamil Nadu permits cow slaughter but two dairy women told us 'there is no slaughterhouse here'. Since we saw a slaughterhouse for cows in action during fieldwork as we walked up the railway line, we affirm DW89's warning that 'we do not have to accept our informants' explanations'. While cows and their milk are sacred to Hindus, their inevitable slaughter is profane and being criminalised (Narayanan 2019). No wonder the practice of slaughter, legal in Tamil Nadu, is denied by urban backstreet dairy farmers.
7. Naickers, originally Telugu-speaking warrior castes who had migrated from what is now Andhra Pradesh by the mid-17th century, compete with Mudaliars for dominance in the local urban economy.

8. Nadars, originally said to be toddy tappers, are an upwardly mobile, entrepreneurial caste from southern Tamil Nadu.
9. The Centre of India Trade Union, founded in 1970, is one of India's biggest multi-sector trade unions, with a membership of over 6 million workers in 2015.
10. Paraiyars are former untouchables, now classified as Scheduled Castes. Arundathiars are Scheduled Castes, formerly named *Chakkliyars* who migrated south from Andhra.
11. Mixies are domestic electric food grinders.
12. For instance, a woman in position 10 selects plastic thread, water cups, larger cans and toothbrushes.
13. The recycler used the English acronyms SC and BC to refer to Scheduled Castes and Backward Castes.
14. NREGA = National Rural Employment Guarantee Act
15. Adivasis are tribal people considered indigenous to South India. Kattunaickers (self-identified as pigmen [rearers] and migrants from Andhra to the north) are one such 'forest people'. Irulars are another.
16. On a par with Congo and Fiji at 4% in 2013 (IBRD, 2015)
17. See the reviews in Harriss-White 2018 and in Doron and Jeffrey 2018.
18. See Kumar et al. 2019 for a development of the human–animal nexus around urban waste.

REFERENCES

Ahluwalia, I. and U. Patel. 2018. 'Solid Waste Management in India: An assessment of resource recovery and environmental impact', *ICRIER Working Paper 365*, Indian Council for Research on International Economic Relations, New Delhi https://icrier.org/pdf/Working_Paper_356.pdf (accessed 10 January 2022).

Azim Premji University 2020. *Covid-19 Rural Livelihoods Survey* https://cse.azimpremjiuniversity.edu.in/.

Béteille, A. 1996. 'Caste in Contemporary India', in (ed.) C. Fuller *Caste Today*, New Delhi: Oxford University Press.

Brhlikova, P., P. Jeffery, G. Bhatia and S.I. Khurana. 2009. 'Intrapartum Oxytocin (Mis)use in South Asia', *Journal of Health Studies*, 2(1–3): 33–50.

Cadène, P. and M. Holmstrom (eds). 1998. *Decentralised Production in India: Industrial Districts, Flexible Specialisation and Employment.* Sage: New Delhi/London.

Charsley, K. 1997. '"Children of the Forest" or "Backwards Communities"? The Ideology of Tribal Development', *Edinburgh Papers in South Asian Studies Number 7,* School of Social and Political Studies, Edinburgh University. https://www.csas.ed.ac.uk/sites/csas/files/assets/pdf/WP07_CHARSLEY.pdf (accessed 10 January 2022).

Deliege, R. (trans. N. Scott) 2001. *The Untouchables of India*. London: Bloomsbury.

Doron, A. and R. Jeffrey. 2018. *Waste of a Nation: Garbage and Growth in India*. Boston: Harvard University Press.

Doron, A. and I. Raja. 2015. 'The cultural politics of shit: class, gender and public space in India', Postcolonial Studies, 18(2): 189–207.

FAO (Food and Agriculture Organisation) 2019, *The State of Food and Agriculture: Moving Forward on Food Loss and Waste Reduction*. Rome: FAO

Flyvbjerg, B. 2006. 'Five Misunderstandings About Case-Study Research,' *Qualitative Inquiry*, 12(2): 219–45.

Harriss-White, B. (ed). 2016. *Middle India and urban-rural development: Four decades of change*. New Delhi: Springer.

Harriss-White, B. 2017, 'Formality and informality in an Indian urban waste-economy', *International Journal of Sociology and Social Policy*, 37(7/8): 417–34.

Harriss-White, B. 2018. 'India's informal waste economy and urban informality: an illustrated tour of the epistemological horizon', Work in Progress Paper 23, Contemporary South Asian Studies Programme, School of Interdisciplinary Area Studies, Oxford University https://www.southasia.ox.ac.uk/sites/default/files/southasia/documents/media/bhw_waste_rev_lit_2018.pdf

Harriss-White, B. 2019.'Waste, social order and physical disorder in small-town India', *Journal of Development Studies* 56(2): 239–58. https://doi.org/10.1080/00220388.2019.1577386

Hodges, S. 2017. 'Hospitals as factories of medical garbage', *Anthropology and Medicine*, 24: 319–33

Hoornweg, D., P. Bhada-Tata and C. Kennedy. 2013. 'Waste production must peak this century', *Nature* 502: 615–17.

Human Rights Watch. 2014. *Cleaning Human Waste: 'Manual Scavenging,' Caste, and Discrimination in India*, https://www.hrw.org/report/2014/08/25/cleaning-human-waste/manual-scavenging-caste-and-discrimination-india (accessed 10 January 2022).

IBRD. 2015. *Current Health Expenditure (as percent of GDP)* https://data.worldbank.org/indicator/SH.XPD.CHEX.GD.ZS (accessed 10 January 2022).

Jeffery R., P. Jeffery and A. Lyon. 1989. 'Taking Dung-Work Seriously: Women's Work and Rural Development in North India', *Economic and Political Weekly*, 24(17): WS32-WS37.

Jeyaranjan, J. 2019. 'Sand and the Politics of Plunder in Tamil Nadu', in B. Harriss-White and L. Michelutti (eds), *The Wild East*, pp. 92–114. London: UCL Press.

Kapadia, K. 2017. 'We ask you to rethink: different Dalit women and their subaltern politics', in S. Anandhi and K. Kapadia (eds), *Dalit Women: Vanguard of an Alternative Politics in India*, ch. 1. London and New Delhi: Routledge.

Kumar, N., B. Harriss-White and A. Singh. 2019, 'Urban waste and the human-animal interface in Delhi', *Economic and Political Weekly*, 54(47).

Mander, H. (ed). 2019. *India Exclusion Report 2018–19*, New Delhi: Three Essays Collective.

Narayanan, Y. 2019, '*Jugaad* and informality as drivers of India's cow slaughter economy', *Economy and Space*, 51(7) 1516–35.

Pandya, S., S. Mishra, E. Kayitesi and R. Ray. 2016. 'Microbial-processing of fruit and vegetable wastes for production of vital enzymes and organic acids: Biotechnology and scopes', *Environmental Research* 146: 161–72. https://doi.org/10.1016/j.envres.2015.12.035.

Rodrigo, G. and B. Harriss-White. 2016. 'Discrimination in the waste economy: Narratives from the waste-workers of a small town', *Journal of Social Inclusion Studies*, 2(2): 3–29.

Rodrigues, V. 2009. 'Untouchability, filth, and the public domain' in G. Guru (ed) *Humiliation: Claims and context,* pp. 108–23. New Delhi: Oxford University Press.

Smith, J., J. Yeluripati, P. Smith and D. Nayak. 2020. 'Potential yield challenges to scale-up of zero budget natural farming', *Nature – Sustainability* 3: 247–52 https://www.nature.com/natsustain/ https://doi.org/10.1038/s41893-019-0469-x.

13

Mithila Painters Respond to Covid-19

Susan Wadley

In this painting made in the spring of 2020, Mithila artist Shalini Karn portrays the changes wrought in her rural society by the Covid-19 virus. Along with other Mithila artists from northern India, her art reflects on the chaos created by Covid-19 amid the human response. To the left, she has captured the corona warriors, those fighting the virus, including television reporters (upper left) interviewing street

Figure 13.1 *Faces of Corona*, Shalini Karn, 2020. Graphic Arts Collection, Firestone Library, Princeton University

cleaners, below which doctors treat patients. In the bottom left, a man isolates in his middle-class home watching an episode of the serial *The Ramayana*, replayed on the government television station to entertain those locked inside. The right side portrays the situation among the poor—the top image shows disinfecting fluids being sprayed on the homeless, "spraying the deplorables" as one artist calls it. Below are two groups of migrants trying to get home after India's Prime Minister, Narendra Modi, imposed a total lockdown on the country on March 24, 2020. Next to those walking, a woman stands waiting for a train, her child asleep on their suitcase at her feet.

In the center, Shalini features the blooming of nature, as the lockdown cut pollution. The rivers, no longer filled with industrial pollutants, are swarming with wildlife and turtles are found on a beach. The tree is filled with birds, revived by the clean air. Meanwhile, the red virus seeks to penetrate anyone who is susceptible. She portrays those situations hurt by Covid-19 in gray, and the blooming of nature in bright greens and blues.

Using Shalini's complex painting as a guide, I explore the dominant responses of Mithila artists to a pandemic that left many without a livelihood and challenged their society. Using mostly photos of their art contributed to an on-line SU exhibition of Mithila art about Covid-19, I explore the messages that the artists portrayed about the changes in their world and their views on those changes.[1] Art is often a response to social crisis: the Covid-19 pandemic exposed fault lines in societies around the world, unveiling fractures in the social fabric that became more visible in this time of crisis. The Mithila artists captured many points of stress exposed by the pandemic in Indian society, particularly points of structural violence directed at the poor and those marginalized by caste and gender, resulting in such acts such as spraying disinfectant on the homeless or the forced migration of millions back to their rural villages, and the breakdown of health care. The artists also celebrated the human "warriors" against the virus, and especially the women who fought against it in a variety of ways.

These are issues that are a focus of much of the work of Patricia Jeffery, who has focused extensively on issues of health, gender, and those marginalized in Indian society. While the artists explore issues such as the resurgence of nature during the lockdown, I touch on those topics only briefly and retain a focus on issues most relevant to Patricia's work—gender, health, and the marginalized. Further, her love of Mithila art is visible in her home office, in a painting by renowned artist Rani Jha of an abortion clinic ruled by a female doctor, said by Rani to be more potent than a cobra.

Covid Comes to India

In January 2020, Covid-19 arrived in Kerala, India, with a student who had been studying in Wuhan, China. In early March, tourists from Italy brought it with them. And by mid-March it was in Kolkata, arriving with an Indian student who had been studying in England. On March 24 with only four hours' notice, Prime Minister Modi announced a nationwide lockdown, mandating that everyone stay inside, wear a mask, and celebrate health care workers every evening. By March 25, all public transport, and much private, had ended and everything was closed, from schools, factories and malls to local stores and banks. Modi had implemented a total lockdown that reached into every city, town, and village. India, like the rest of the world, began its fight against the virus. Sadly, a year later, India's confirmed Covid-19 cases hit almost 30 million, with close to 400,000 dead—daily cases in June reached an all-time high of more than 80,000.[2]

Introducing Mithila Art

Located in the Mithila region of northern India, on the Bihar–Nepali border, Mithila art is thought to be hundreds of years old. The earliest documentation of the style is by the British administrator William Archer. In 1934, after the region was hit by a massive earthquake, Archer, as the British sub-divisional officer, set out on horseback to examine the destruction. Many village mud houses were heavily damaged, and he was astonished to find colorful paintings still visible on the broken inner walls. Painted by the households' women, this artistic tradition had been hidden from the gaze of outsiders and ignored by local male elites. Several years later, Archer returned to the Mithila region to photograph this tradition and in 1949 he published an article on Mithila painting which helped to expand awareness of the paintings beyond India.[3]

Caste plays an important role in Mithila painting, as social interactions across caste boundaries, especially for women, were rare in rural India—even now, most women socialize primarily with those of their own caste group. The two highest castes of the region—the Brahmin, or priestly, caste and the slightly lower ranking Kayastha, or accountant/scribe, caste—were the only ones whose paintings Archer photographed or wrote about. Both castes were landowners and the majority of their members were comparatively well-off. All of Archer's photographs were taken in Brahmin or Kayastha houses, although it is not known whether this was due to his limited access or to the strong likelihood that these paintings were made only in high-caste households.[4]

Mithila painting on paper was introduced by the government as a famine relief program in the late 1960s. Notably, when painting on paper became prominent, the two groups painted in distinct styles: the Brahmin in a style known as *bharni*, meaning filled, that is, with color; and the Kayastha in a style known as *kachni*, meaning linear, with line drawings primarily in black and red. Some have suggested that the Kayastha style on paper is related to their men's role as accountants and the availability of red and black pens.

The *bharni* style initially dominated in the Delhi markets as the colorful gods and goddesses captured the imaginations of the mid-to-late twentieth century urban and tourist audiences who were easily able to appreciate its imagery through their personal knowledge of Hindu deities and religious epics known across India. Nowadays, upper-caste differences in painting style have all but disappeared, with the linear style of the Kayastha community dominating in the early twenty-first century. Shalini's painting in Figure 13.1 draws heavily on the *kachni* style though, like many modern artists, her work draws from both traditions.

There is also a group of Dusadh, Dalit, painters working in Madhubani. They often employ a unique style, developed in the 1970s under the influence of the German artist Erika Moser. However, the only paintings in the Covid-19 exhibition by a Dalit painter are those of Naresh Kumar Paswan, who employs his own style of black and white drawings, related to the *kachni* style but uniquely his own (see Figure 13.2).[5]

The Mithila style has garnered admiration beyond that usually reserved for folk art, challenging the arbitrary split between folk and fine art. While the booths at the Dilli Haat folk market in Delhi are filled with paintings selling for Rs. 100 up, fine art galleries across the globe are selling Mithila paintings for thousands of dollars. In 2020, a piece by Avinash Karn went at auction for Rs. 2.48 lakhs (more than $3,000)[6]. More and more artists are receiving better training and working as professionals, exploring their own Mithila style—see, for example, the pieces in the exhibition by the young women Amrita Jha and Shalinee Kumari who have each developed distinct styles that merge *bharni* and *kachni*.

The Initial Months

With the lockdown imposed on India, the early messages were clear: "Stay Home, Wear a Mask, Keep Socially Distanced". Vinita Jha, in *Corona and Our Society, 2020,7* captures the need to mask and stay home, as well as the result of not obeying these strictures, also focusing on women as both the warriors and those ignoring the rules. Her painting also celebrates the police warriors. Vinita's horizontal piece shows a policeman on the left, masked and (apparently) enforcing the rules. His mask is green as are all the other masks. Above is a village house with a woman and child inside, both masked. Two elephants stand in the doorway, signs of auspiciousness in Mithila culture and hence marking the blessings brought due to the household's careful masking and seclusion. In the upper left corner is a crying virus, defeated by its victims' careful tactics. Toward the far right, a masked woman, who has been to market, or perhaps the fields, returns to her home with a headload of goods. Above her is another thwarted crying virus. But the center image is of a young maskless girl, purse in hand, wandering down a path. She is surrounded by four bright red viruses, the only color aside from the green masks in this otherwise black and white painting. The message is clear: wear a mask and stay home or the virus will attack you—obey our Covid warriors.

The next two images in the exhibition reiterate this "masking" message. Amrita Jha, a woman in her early 30s, used her distinct style in *Masked Mithila* to fill a woman's head with masks. While Pritee Kumari uses a traditional Mithila *kachni* style in black and white with minor red additions to show two masked teachers, holding books that are titled "stay home," with a masked student standing between them.

Marking the Fault Lines

Shalini portrays several recurring images of a fractured Indian society in Figure 13.1, as do several other Mithila artists in paintings that capture the tragedy and harshness of the lockdown on March 24, and the extreme fear of the virus. An Indian news article sums up the brutal result:

> With the nationwide lockdown, declared at four hours' notice on March 24, the government drew a cordon around the bodies it wished to protect. It halted trains and public transport, pulling up the drawbridges to guard the chosen—those who could afford to stay in. On the bodies of those outside this charmed circle, the lockdown wrought havoc.[8]

While many were affected by the Modi's lockdown of the country, those most challenged were the millions of migrant laborers who had left their rural villages for employment as construction workers, daily wage laborers, street vendors, rickshaw drivers, and domestic help in urban areas, often hundreds of miles from their home villages.

Primarily men, these laborers often came from the poorer eastern regions of India to the big cities in the west and south. Living on daily wages, frequently less than Rs. 300 (about $4) a day, most had no savings and very quickly had no food or a place to stay. Their only choice was to try to get home, but for many weeks the trains and buses were canceled, so many walked, some more than 500 miles. As one man said as he began the trek home, "It is better than living here with nothing and starving to death."[9]

Some government programs and NGOs and others eventually began to provide food and water along the way. By mid-May, some irregularly scheduled trains began to bring migrants home. But some never made it, dying on the road, while others reached their home villages only to die upon arrival. The images on both Indian news stations and international television and newspapers were vivid: hordes of mostly men attempting to get on to a bus or train. Groups of men were photographed walking down highways with their belongings in a cloth bag. Many had little to no food to bring with them, yet getting home seemed the only option. Some were actually sprayed with disinfectant at bus stops and state boundaries. State boundaries were closed so that those coming from urban areas could not bring the virus into new territories. The cordon was severe, and the poor had no recourse.

This story is most effectively painted by the Dalit male painter Naresh Kumar Paswan, who tells the story of the migrants' journey of "getting home" in a complex painting, *"Getting Home during Modi's Lockdown, 2020"* (Figure 13.2)[10]. Naresh is a largely self-taught painter from the Dalit caste known as Paswan. His father left the family of seven children when Naresh was a child and Naresh ended his schooling to go to work as a laborer to help feed his siblings. His brother-in-law from a nearby village taught him some painting, and by 2010, when in his mid-20s, he had developed his own clear style of black and white line drawings, an aesthetic that he says he likes.

I first met Naresh in 2011 in the lobby of the only viable hotel in Madhubani, where painters often arrived every morning to sell their wares to visiting tourists and scholars. In the summer of 2020, he brought his distinct style to the story of migrant laborers caught by the pandemic in several paintings. Figure 13.2 is the most elaborate of these and was bought by Princeton University, finished after the SU exhibition went on-line. It is a highly effective rendering of the challenges facing India's millions of migrant laborers. Sadly, since the markets for paintings have dried up due to Covid-19, leading to the closure of international tourism, Naresh left India in the fall of 2020 for Oman, where he is working as a day laborer and still painting when he has time.[11]

Naresh uses intersecting roads as the basis of his design, allowing him to tell different stories on each road segment. In the center, five roads intersect, with a policeman directing traffic. In the top left corner is a masked cowherd, possibly reminding us that the goals of those on the road are rural villages, as well as of the many rural areas they must cross to get home. Angling across the top is a train filled with passengers. Below the train is a road filled with travelers. Two men ride a motorcycle, while behind them is a large group of men, women, and children, most carrying bags or suitcases on their heads. One woman drags a suitcase by a rope with a sleeping child draped

Figure 13.2 *"Getting Home during Modi's Lockdown, 2020".* Naresh Kumar Paswan, 2020. Graphic Arts Collection, Firestone Library, Princeton University.

over it, repeating an image found in Figure 13.1.[12] Behind the crowd is a lorry with passengers clinging to the roof and one perched on the side waiting for a lift to the top. Carefully drawn trees show two travelers entangled in them, pulled off the off the lorry roof by the low-lying trees, an occurrence all too familiar to those traveling India's highways for free.

On the roads at the bottom are several buses and more crowds of travelers. One traveler near the bottom left is carrying a child, while another child walks with adults near the center. Another filled train runs across the bottom.

Two images demand more attention. First, next to the policeman in the center is a girl on a bicycle with her father seated behind her, holding a small bag with their belongings. This references one of the most famous "getting home stories" of the Indian lockdown, that of Jyoti Kumari, who had to bring her father 700 miles home seated on the back of a girl's pink bicycle that she bought for $20 when they were stranded outside of Delhi. In January 2020, Jyoti's father was injured in an accident while driving his tuk-tuk when working in a suburb of Delhi.[13] Sixteen-year-old Jyoti and her mother traveled from Darbhanga, in the Mithila region, to care for him, but her mother had to return shortly thereafter to keep her own job in their home village. By early May, with no income and no money for rent or food, Jyoti felt her only recourse was to get her father home. She cycled the 700 miles, at the rate of about 100 km (60 miles) a day. Her story soon hit the news and she returned home a heroine, with offers for a starring role in a Bollywood film of her story. This was the "hard luck" story that caught the attention not only of the Indian public, but also the world, with features on both NPR and the BBC. This event reappears in Puja Jha's "A Brave Cycle Girl." Puja wrote:

> Courage is the most important attribute of humans. During the Covid-19 lockdown when the entire world is fighting the Pandemic, a young brave girl stood firm for her family and carried her injured father on bicycle for more than 700 miles to their home village.

Returning to Naresh's painting, a second compelling image is the figure at the far bottom left which references the well-known Hindu story of Sravan Kumar, the son who would do anything for his parents. Filled with filial devotion, Sravan Kumar is held up as the best of sons. When his blind elderly parents, crippled and unable to walk, wanted to go on a pilgrimage, he seated them in baskets on either end of a pole and walked across India fulfilling their wishes. Sadly, Sravan Kumar's parents are later killed by King Dasharath, father of the god Rama. The father's act was ultimately responsible for the exile of Rama and his wife Sita, and her abduction by Ravana, king of Lanka. This mythological reference balances the "real life" reference to Jyoti Kumari. Both Jyoti and Sravan Kumar remind the viewer of the value of a child's devotion to their parents. They also reference a common theme in the Covid-19 paintings, examined here: we must hold hands and fight the virus together.

Most important are the ways in which Naresh captures two key fracture lines in Indian society—being a migrant laborer and class difference. As the quote above notes, the Indian government drew a line around the bodies that it wished to protect, and "discarded" the rest. Naresh's painting focuses on those discarded.

Naresh's exhibition piece (*Getting home*), completed in June 2020, has several elements not found in the larger one, which was not completed until sometime in late August. To the upper right, a policeman is chastising two boys who are traveling without masks. And in a typical Indian gesture of guilt, a third boy sits on the ground holding his ears. Naresh also shows people offering food to the travelers, a key element in their survival. Jyoti Kumari, in fact, reported that when she and her father stopped for the night at petrol stations, other travelers stranded there would give them food and drink. Throughout both of Naresh's paintings, the police are shown as hero-warriors.

Another now-famous migrant story is found in the painting "*Shakuntala*" (Figure 13.3) by Shalini Karn. Now in her early 30s, Shalini is an educated upper-caste woman from a well-known painting family. In 2013 she received an award from the Government of India for training in Mithila art and she worked primarily with Santosh Kumar Das, an older, highly regarded, male Mithila painter with professional training in Baroda. She was able to use her connections to travel more widely in India, doing workshops and eventually

Fig. 13.3 *Shakuntala*. Shalini Karn, 2020.Private Collection.

presenting in exhibitions in Delhi and beyond. She currently lives in the nearby state of Jharkhand. Much of her work has a feminist angle, focusing on issues facing women in India. And in the piece in Figure 13.3, gender and the treatment of women is the focus, more than class.

Shakuntala is based on another story widely reported in the Indian and international press in mid-May 2020. Again, it puts a real human face on the travails of those "going home." Shakuntala and her husband had been working in the industrial town of Nasik, Maharashtra. But by early May, some six to seven weeks into the lockdown, they had no food left so they and some 15 others, including their own young children, started the more than 600-mile journey to their home village in Madhya Pradesh, despite Shakuntala's advanced pregnancy. Some 70 km (40 miles) into the journey, Shakuntala went into labor and the group stopped at the edge of the road, where she gave birth with the help of four other women. After one to two hours' rest, the group began walking again, with the mother clasping her newborn. Some 160 km (99 miles) and four days later, a female police inspector noticed mother and newborn as they crossed into Madhya Pradesh. As the inspector put it, I "was moved beyond words." Food and water were provided and eventually the family was bused to their destination. Notably, the news through May frequently reported similar births on the roads traveled by migrants.

In Shalini's painting, a group of women on the left are walking home from city to village. But Shakuntala, carefully highlighted with a red aura, is pregnant. In the center, we see her giving birth, surrounded by four women helpers. Below, the mother holds her newborn, while on the right she walks onward, baby in hand. When queried about the use of black and red in this painting, in contrast to *Faces of Covid* and most of her other work, Shalini responded that she painted in black and red because she wanted to tell two stories: one about the failures of government and the other about the powers of women. The red marking Shakuntala in each portion represents female power, while the black represents the failure of government. She also wrote, "This true story of a daring woman was shocking for everyone and I think only a mother power or a goddess can do this kind of miracle."[14]

Other artists also express gender and feminist concerns. The young artist and new mother Mahalaxmi captures a similar theme in her "*Mother Train,*" when she addresses not those women walking home, but a female-run bus load of migrants. She honors those praying that their menfolk will safely return. The effects of the lockdown were many and pervasive. And human and mother power prevailed.

Lalita Dutta's "*Impact of Corona Virus, 2020*" reiterates many of these messages of gender and class, from the woman giving birth with her husband's help in the top left, to the disinfectant being sprayed in the top right, and the many migrants on the road. She also contrasts those not behaving (shaking hands in lower right) with those following the rules, in the center circle. Avinash Karn's "*Disinfecting the Vulnerables*" also directly tackles the government's treatment of the poor.

Yet few Mithila painters directly address issues facing the poor, especially outside of the Covid-19 crisis.[15] One exception is Dulari Devi who is well-known for her paintings of the poor versus the rich. Her work regularly features stories of poverty, whether it is women sent away from a children's inoculation clinic because they lack the necessary bribe, or the rich locking their doors and fleeing the effects of floods, while the poor are left behind to retrieve the dead (human or animal). Dulari is from a poor caste of fishermen and, with her marriage ended, she lived for years with her brother's family and worked at a nearby Kayastha house as a maidservant, where she also learned to paint. In 2021, she became the first Mithila non-high-caste winner of the Padma Shri, India's highest honor for artists of all kinds. In her painting of *Corona Effects in Patna*, 2020 (Figure 13.4), her concern for those at the bottom resurfaces as the fractures in Indian society are presented from her "bottom up" viewpoint.

Fig. 13.4 *Corona Effect in Patna, 2020.* Dulari Devi, 2020. Graphic Arts Collection, Firestone Library, Princeton University.

In the upper left is the hospital with patients littering the floor, without adequate care for those being carried in. Elsewhere: women are being offered food packets; a "warrior" policeman passes out masks; migrants are attempting to get home in a bus, which a worker is spraying with disinfectant; a wealthy woman, marked by her heavy jewelry, and her children flee by boat, with a low-caste, dark-skinned boatman (some say the fisherman caste god) rowing them across the Ganges. It is important to note that Dulari carefully portrays her humans with different colored skins, a code understood across India that supposedly marks caste status (as color also marks race and class in the USA). If you examine the bus carefully, you'll see that the man grabbing on to the back (and hence not paying for a ticket) is quite dark, while the passengers inside are very light-skinned. The bus driver's skin is somewhere in between. The hospital patients and caretakers also have different colored skins, marking class and possibly health. Dulari is pointing out an inadequate health care system, the plight of migrants, and the options that let the rich flee comfortably while the poor walk or maybe take a free ride on a bus home. For Dulari, being poor dominates gender issues, unlike the high-caste female painters for whom gender issues are a main concern.

Humans, Nature, and Societal Changes

The virus brought many changes for both humans and non-humans. One prime example, noted around the world, was that with closed factories and empty roads, the skies began to clear and the rivers ran cleaner. Residents of the Mithila region on the Nepal border could see Mount Everest for the first time in decades, far away in Nepal. In Delhi, the Yamuna River cleansed itself and migratory birds once again flocked to its waters and feasted on fish.[16] As one woman commented, "nature is balancing itself."

In a telling comment on the consequences of the lockdown on mental health tied to the resurgence of nature, Amrita Jha portrays a woman's head filled with birds representing the human wish to fly after months of lockdown—outside and away. Nature enters the paintings in other ways. Rani Jha captures a similar idea in her split painting with humans locked down but the animals and birds in the forest even freer than normal.[17] Shalinee Kumari's brilliant painting focuses on the opportunity for change: the Yamuna River running through Delhi is noted for its white foam but here it is clear and clean, animals run freely and the Himalayas are visible in the distance. Shalinee leaves Mother Nature undefined, "as she has begun healing, but we don't know the result."

All these painters are making strong statements, perhaps somewhat unconsciously, about the effects of industrialization and development.[18]

Battling the Virus

Numerous warriors and heroes joined forces to battle the virus, including the goddess herself by fall 2020, using the human-manufactured vaccine. Recall that Shalini in Figure 13.1 highlighted several hero-warriors: street cleaners, reporters, and doctors. One painter explained that the response to Covid-19 lay with the humans who fought it. Notably, in the view of these Mithila painters, the goddesses (usually those deities called upon to cure illnesses—Sitala the goddess of smallpox being the best known in northern India) are not brought into the Covid-19 story until mid-fall, when vaccines appear as a cure. Until then the human warriors and heroes battled on, including those heroes who merely wore masks and stayed inside.

Not surprisingly, doctors are frequently featured. Two paintings in the exhibition focus on a dominant doctor image, by Prerna Jha and Nisha Kumari. Nisha's comes closest to invoking a goddess, for here she uses the Ardhanarishvara figure of a single deity conveying two characteristics (most frequently the god Shiva and his consort) to present the goddess as a doctor, for it is the human doctor who will ultimately win against Covid. Note too that her doctor is female, on the left in traditional clothing and then on the right as a doctor. Even Shalinee Kumari's painting of the god Shiva has him playing the role of protector; as she notes, "We are waiting for the Covid miracle."

Police and cleaners are also frequently pictured as warriors. The other heroes are varied, from those practicing yoga, to the role of the media, or, like the artists themselves, those who make masks (see Chandrakant Kumar Bari's *Corona Warriors, 2020*). Some, like the women in Madhuri Jha's *Human Lives Matter*, can only cheer on the doctors and nurses with their banging pots, but each bit helps in this fight.

In Hindu ritual and mythology, the goddess is usually the one who cures illnesses and, as described in "The Goddess and the Virus", various images of the goddess fighting the virus emerged early in the pandemic, although not in Mithila art.[19] Kanchan Jha makes the Frontline Corona Warrior a doctor fighting the virus, while Kanchan Kumari uses the image of the god Shiva dancing the *rudra tandava*, the dance of destruction, while the virus dances its new Covid-19 dance of worldly destruction.[20]

Months before the vaccine, a few reports emerged of the goddess working against the virus. In one, as reported by anthropologist Tulasi Srinivas, a priest in Kerala created an image of the Corona Devi:

> While controversies over temples reopening dominates the news, a new deity, crafted from polystyrene and called "Corona Devi" has been installed in a [Kerala] temple dedicated to the pox goddess. Mr. Anilan, the priest and single devotee, says he will offer worship for "Corona Warriors"—health care workers, firefighters, and other frontline personnel. Here science and faith are not seen as inimical to one another, but as working together, hand-in-glove.[21]

Other reports mentioned new goddesses being worshipped, mostly by women, over the summer.[22]

I asked several artists about the absence of deities in the fight against Covid-19 and all responded that "it is on us," or some such phrase. "It was the work that we did, it was our efforts, that would win this battle, not the goddess. We were the warriors." And for close to a year, it was indeed the efforts of millions and billions of humans who wore masks, washed their hands, stayed inside, or made it home, who really won the battle. Humans indeed were the warriors and heroes.

In late October 2020, an email brought "*The Goddess Killing the Virus,*" painted by Nisha Jha, with the help of her mother Vinita Jha (Figure 13.5). Armed with a long syringe, the goddess is killing the

Fig. 13.5 *Corona-Asur-Mardini [The Conqueror of the Covid Demon],* Nisha Jha, 2020. Private collection.

green virus. The painting was accompanied with a long message of explanation from Nisha:

> Corona-Asur-Mardini [The Conqueror of the Covid Demon]. The incarnation of goddess as Doctor on The Earth. Here the goddess has been incarnated in form of Corona Asur Mardini, This means she has been incarnated to conquer over this corona-virus, here she is adorned with the most powerful & advanced weapons on her hands, that is sufficient and enough to kill the most dangerous Demon (Nobel [sic] corona virus) all over the world.
>
> The Lion represents the other frontier corona- warriors, who have worked very hard to minimize the bad impact of corona virus in our society, and reduce the death rate by controlling the corona-positive cases in a well-defined manner. The flooring pattern (white box & black box) is the representation of population of the earth. and as you can see the corona virus is wandering outside, and looking for the innocent people who are unaware about this dangerous virus. And if the people ignore the precautions, they must be caught by the devil in form of corona-virus. The goddess has ten hands, that work all together simultaneously in [a] multidirectional way.

Nisha then goes on to explain that the right side represents the dark side of the pandemic while the left is a new day of hope, with the rays of the sun bringing opportunity, good health and more. The right border is dark with virus while to the left it contains the lotus and conch of the gods. Likewise, in her right hands the goddess holds the weapons of the dark—the sanitizer, tracking reports, and such. In her left hands, she holds the stronger implements to fight the virus—stethoscope, masks, and medicines. As she kills the virus with the vaccine, her vehicle the lion—representing all the front-line warriors, such as doctors, sanitary workers, police, and so on—devours the virus. Nisha concludes her lengthy explanation with, "Now the corona virus is completely exhausted, tired, crying, defeated and waiting for its final time by vaccination through the mercy of goddess (Doctors) and team (other corona warriors)."[23] Nisha and her family call not only on the stories of Hindu deities and their ability to become incarnations to help the gods defeat demons but also on those in her community in 2020 who are battling the Covid-19 virus.

Sadly, in June 2021, the pandemic in India had worsened, though the lockdown had been lifted. While many worldwide initially saw the virus as an equalizer, across all social groups and borders, it clearly has only exacerbated inequalities between and within nations. In India, the heralded vaccine arrived too late, without widespread inoculation plans and with an inability to counter the virus's new variant. Further, the government failed completely, both in health care preparations and by encouraging large spreading events in the spring of 2021, such as the Kumbh Mela and political rallies, while the messages of masking and social distancing were lost. Even in the fall of 2020, religious events in Madhubani were filled with unmasked participants.

As deaths rose and hospitals were overwhelmed, the message of government failure, captured by paintings such as Shalini Karn's *Shakuntala* and Dulari Devi's *Corona Effects in Patna*, became more potent. Evidence also rose of the death toll borne by women versus men as, once again, Indian families and the medical system favored males over females and women faced increased domestic violence as families struggled to combat hunger and joblessness, issues all too familiar to scholars like Patricia.[24] Whether showing the effects of the lockdown on nature or on laborers stranded in cities or the aid given by various warriors, Mithila painters illustrated aspects of the fault lines present in their society, especially those based on class, gender, or caste. Mithila artists evocatively portrayed the social chaos resulting from Covid-19 playing havoc with the already existing fractures in India's social fabric.

NOTES

1. Mithila Art in the Time of Covid, Syracuse University Art Museum, curated by Susan S. Wadley, October 2020. https://indd.adobe.com/view/b42ffd50-92eb-4c53-b8be-cad71851cee7 (accessed January 17, 2022). Readers will need to refer to this SU exhibition to understand the references in this chapter.
2. Most non-official reports believe that the true numbers are at least double these.
3. Archer, W.G. 1949. "Maithil Painting," Marg 3(3): 24–33.
4. Rani Jha, one of the best-known current artists, only recently realized that Archer had photographed paintings in her grandmother's house on his 1937 excursion.

5. For more on the tradition and its history, see Wadley, S.S. 2014. "*Likhiyā*: Paintings Women's Live in Rural Northern India", in S. Wadley (ed.), *South Asia in the World*. NY: M.S. Sharpe, pp. 241–60.
6. See https://www.mutualart.com/Artist/Avinash-Karn/CED066019226CA96
7. For images not present here, see the exhibition *Mithila Art in the Time of Covid*.
8. Chakravarty, I. 2020. "A story of swollen feet: The physical toll of walking home during lockdown." June 20, https://scroll.in/article/963641/a-story-of-swollen-feet-the-physical-toll-of-walking-home-during-lockdown (accessed March 26, 2021).
9. Sur, P. and B. Westcott. 2020. "Desperate to go Home, Indian migrant workers face tough choice amid world's largest Lockdown." March 28. https://www.cnn.com/2020/03/27/india/coronavirus-covid-19-india-2703-intl-hnk/index.html (accessed February 21, 2021).
10. The image presented in this chapter is different to the one listed as "Getting Home" in the online exhibition.
11. A staggering 174 million travel and tourism jobs were threatened by the Covid-19 related barriers to global travel. Read more at: https://economictimes.indiatimes.com/jobs/174-million-travel-and-tourism-jobs-could-be-lost-in-2020-due-to-covid-19-and-travel-restrictions-wttc/articleshow/78948740.cms?utm_source=contentofinterest&utm_medium=text&utm_campaign=cppst. Accessed on Feb. 1, 2021.
12. 'Boy Sleeps On Suitcase Wheeled By Mother: Video Tells Migrants' Plight'. https://www.ndtv.com/india-news/coronavirus-india-lockdown-child-sleeps-on-suitcase-dragged-by-mother-migrants-tragedy-continues-2228557 (accessed March 26, 2021).
13. Ray, U.K. 2020. "From Gurgaon to Bihar, 15-Year-Old Girl Cycles 1,200 km With Injured Father." The Wire, 21 May. https://thewire.in/rights/jyoti-kumari-bihar-gurgaon-cycle-covid-19-lockdown (accessed March 2, 2021). Frayer, L. 2020. "Indian Teen Bikes 700 Miles With Injured Dad, Gets Movie Deal—And Sparks Debate." NPR, 20 July. https://www.npr.org/sections/goatsandsoda/2020/06/02/866952444/indian-teen-bikes-700-miles-with-injured-dad-is-hailed-as-hero-and-sparks-debate (accessed March 2, 2021).
14. 2020. "Migrant Worker Delivers Baby on Road, Walks Another 150 KM to Get Help." Outlook, May 13. https://www.outlookindia.com/website/story/india-news-migrant-worker-delivers-baby-on-road-walks-another-150-km-to-get-help/352658 (accessed February 10, 2021). Jain, A. 2020. "Madhya Pradesh: woman give birth on roadside, and marches on for 160km." Times of India, May 10. https://timesofindia.indiatimes.com/city/indore/madhya-pradesh-woman-gives-birth-on-roadside-and-marches-on-for-160km/articleshow/75654249.cms (accessed February 10, 2021).
15. I would argue that Shalini's painting of Shakuntala draws on her feminist leanings rather than as a story of poverty. While women's issues are a frequent

focus of upper-caste Mithila paintings, issues around caste or poverty are almost absent.

16. https://www.ndtv.com/india-news/coronavirus-lockdown-yamuna-cleanest-in-30-years-as-industrial-dumping-halts-2234790 (accessed March 2, 2021).
17. n.a. 2020. "How the Coronavirus Lockdown helped nature to heal even if temporarily form human damage", News Buzz, June 5. https://www.news18.com/news/buzz/how-coronavirus-lockdown-helped-nature-to-heal-even-if-temporarily-from-human-damages-2652815.html (accessed January 31, 2021). Arora, S., K.D. Bhaukhandi and P.K. Mishra. 2020. "Coronavirus lockdown helped the environment to bounce back," Science of the Total Environment, 742(140573) https://www.sciencedirect.com/science/article/pii/S004896972034095X#! (accessed January 31, 2021).
18. An exhibition of Mithila art focused on social justice at the ArtRage Gallery in Syracuse, NY, USA in 2019 included several paintings by young female artists that directly focused on climate change, industrialization, the loss of forests, and the effects of drought.
19. Kaur, R. and S. Ramaswamy. 2020. "The Goddess and The Virus", in V. Chaturvedi (ed.), *The Pandemic: Perspectives on Asia*. pp. 75–94. Ann Arbor, MI: Association of Asian Studies.
20. A Durga puja pandal in Kolkata presented this image in mid-October 2020 and is probably the initial inspiration for this painting. https://www.news18.com/news/buzz/after-migrant-mother-goddess-durga-reimagined-as-doctor-fighting-coronavirus-in-kolkata-pandal-2981213.html (accessed March 15, 2021).
21. Srinivas, T. 2020. "India's goddesses of contagion provide protection in the pandemic – just don't make them angry", The Conversation, June 15. https://theconversation.com/indias-goddesses-of-contagion-provide-protection-in-the-pandemic-just-dont-make-them-angry-139745 (accessed April 12, 2021).
22. https://english.alarabiya.net/coronavirus/2020/06/10/Indian-women-worship-coronavirus-leave-offerings-to-virus-goddess-say-reports (accessed April 12, 2021).
23. PDF sent by Facebook, along with painting, October 26, 2020. English translation by Nisha's brother.
24. See the forthcoming volume with its focus on the pandemic, with articles on gender, migrants, and class. Acharya, S. and S. Christopher (eds). 2022. *Caste, COVID-19, and Inequalities of Care: Lessons from South Asia*. Delhi: Springer.

BIBLIOGRAPHY

Acharya, S. and S. Christopher (eds). 2022. *Caste, COVID-19, and Inequalities of Care: Lessons from South Asia*. Delhi: Springer.

Amlôt, M. 2020. 'Indian women worship coronavirus, leave offerings to virus goddess, say reports', *AlArabiya.net* 10 June 2020: https://english.alarabiya.

net/coronavirus/2020/06/10/Indian-womenworship-coronavirus-leave-offerings-to-virus-goddess-say-reports (accessed April 12, 2021).

Archer, W.G. 1949. "Maithil Painting," *Marg* 3(3): 24–33.

Arora, S., K.D. Bhaukhandi and P.K. Mishra. 2020. 'Coronavirus lockdown helped the environment to bounce back,' *Science of the Total Environment*, 742(140573): https://www.sciencedirect.com/science/article/pii/S004896972034095X#! (accessed January 31, 2021).

Basak, S. 2020. 'How the Coronavirus Lockdown helped nature to heal even if temporarily from human damage', *News Buzz* 5 June: https://www.news18.com/news/buzz/how-coronavirus-lockdown-helped-nature-to-heal-even-if-temporarily-from-human-damages-2652815.html (accessed January 31, 2021).

Buzz Staff. 2020. 'Goddess Durga Reimagined as Doctor Slaying Coronavirus in Kolkata Pandal Goes Viral After Migrant Mother', *News 18* 20 October: https://www.news18.com/news/buzz/after-migrant-mother-goddess-durga-reimagined-as-doctorfighting-coronavirus-in-kolkata-pandal-2981213.html (accessed March 15, 2021).

Chakravarty, I. 2020. 'A story of swollen feet: The physical toll of walking home during lockdown.' *Scroll.in* 20 June 2020: https://scroll.in/article/963641/a-story-of-swollen-feet-the-physical-toll-of-walking-home-during-lockdown (accessed March 26, 2021).

Chaturvedi, A. 2020. '174 million travel and tourism jobs could be lost in 2020 due to Covid-19 and travel restrictions: WTTC', *Economic Times* 30 October 2020: https://economictimes.indiatimes.com/jobs/174-million-travel-and-tourism-jobs-could-be-lost-in-2020-due-to-covid-19-and-travel-restrictions-wttc/articleshow/78948740.cms?utm_source=contentofinterest&utm_medium=text&utm_campaign=cppst (Accessed June 16, 2023).

Frayer, L and Pathak, S. 2020. 'Indian Teen Bikes 700 Miles With Injured Dad, Gets Movie Deal—And Sparks Debate.' *NPR*, 20 July 2020: https://www.npr.org/sections/goatsandsoda/2020/06/02/866952444/indian-teen-bikes-700-miles-with-injured-dad-is-hailed-as-hero-and-sparks-debate (accessed March 2, 2021).

Ghosh, D. 2020. 'Boy Sleeps On Suitcase Wheeled By Mother: Video Tells Migrants' Plight', *India News* 14 May 2020: https://www.ndtv.com/india-news/coronavirus-india-lockdown-child-sleeps-on-suitcase-dragged-by-mother-migrants-tragedy-continues-2228557 (accessed June 16, 2023).

Jain, A. 2020. 'Madhya Pradesh: woman give birth on roadside, and marches on for 160km.' *Times of India*, May 10. https://timesofindia.indiatimes.com/city/indore/madhya-pradesh-woman-gives-birth-on-roadside-and-marches-on-for-160km/ articleshow/75654249.cms (accessed February 10, 2021).

Kaur, R. and S. Ramaswamy. 2020. 'The Goddess and The Virus', in V. Chaturvedi (ed.), *The Pandemic: Perspectives on Asia*. pp. 75–94. Ann Arbor, MI: Association of Asian Studies.

Outlook. 2020. 'Migrant Worker Delivers Baby on Road, Walks Another 150 KM to Get Help', *Outlook* 13 May 2020: https://www.outlookindia.com/website/story/india-news-migrant-worker-delivers-baby-on-road-walks-another-150-km-to-get-help/352658 (accessed June 21, 2023).

Ray, U.K. 2020. 'From Gurgaon to Bihar, 15-Year-Old Girl Cycles 1,200 km With Injured Father.' *The Wire,* 21 May 2020: https://thewire.in/rights/jyoti-kumari-bihar-gurgaon-cycle-covid-19-lockdown (accessed June 16, 2023).

Shukla, R. R. 2020. 'How River Yamuna Cleaned Itself In 60 Days Of Coronavirus Lockdown' *NDTV* 25 May: https://www.ndtv.com/india-news/coronavirus-lockdown-yamuna-cleanest-in-30-years-as-industrial-dumping-halts-2234790 (accessed March 2, 2021).

Srinivas, T. 2020. 'India's goddesses of contagion provide protection in the pandemic – just don't make them angry', *The Conversation*, June 15. https://theconversation.com/indias-goddesses-of-contagion-provide-protection-in-the-pandemic-just-dont-make-them-angry-139745 (accessed April 12, 2021).

Sur, P. and B. Westcott. 2020. 'Desperate to go Home, Indian migrant workers face tough choice amid world's largest Lockdown", *CNN.com* 28 March 2020: https:// www.cnn.com/2020/03/27/india/coronavirus-covid-19-india-2703-intl-hnk/ index.html (accessed February 21, 2021).

Wadley, S.S. 2014. 'Likhiyā: Paintings Women's Live in Rural Northern India', in S. Wadley (ed.), *South Asia in the World.* NY: M.S. Sharpe, pp. 241–60.

Afterword

Patricia Jeffery

Probably much to the consternation of the administrators in the School of Social and Political Science, University of Edinburgh, I made several attempts at retirement during the 2010s. To mark one such occasion, my colleagues organised a symposium in 2017. Long-term friends from far-flung places with common professional pre-occupations—colleagues, co-researchers, erstwhile doctoral students, postdoctoral mentees—assembled for a joyous and lively event, a day of sharing memories and discussing our academic passions.

Shortly afterwards, my wonderful colleagues in Sociology, Shruti Chaudhry, Hugo Gorringe and Radhika Govinda suggested that they would collect the papers presented at the symposium, commission further papers from others who had been unable to attend and create what has now become this Festschrift. I was very surprised and deeply honoured by their proposal—and I cannot fully express how grateful I am to them and the authors of the papers in the resulting volume for their enthusiasm and their dedication to this project.

In 1978, along with the late Rosemary Johnson, I taught the first undergraduate Gender course in the University of Edinburgh, at a time when Gender Studies were extremely novel and not universally accepted as serious academic pursuits (that's an understatement!). Since then, work on gender issues has increasingly trespassed in and enriched many arenas of academic endeavour, especially in Humanities and the Social Sciences. During the 1980s, the original Gender course morphed into the Gender and Development course. Meanwhile, some colleagues in Sociology and other parts of the university incorporated gender sessions in their courses. Others developed new gender courses focusing on a broad portfolio of themes—science and technology, law and social policy, health, education and employment, family and intimacy, among many others.

And quite right too. Gender studies should not be consigned to a 'women's studies' silo: teaching and research will only be impoverished if gender issues are ghettoised. Equally, teaching and research on any topic is bound to be partial if gender is not factored in. The social world does not come neatly packaged and it is unhelpful to be straitjacketed by conventional academic disciplinary boundaries. Gender issues are *everywhere*. But not only that: gender issues are also *different* everywhere.

The wide-ranging topics addressed in this volume echo these challenges that have been such inspiring starting points for my own academic work over the years. I am delighted that my 'retirement' has been the excuse for such a rich collection of fascinating and important contributions to scholarship.

I am deeply touched by the generosity of the contributors, of those who added such kind comments to the introduction, and to Shruti, Hugo and Radhika for pulling it all together. My heartfelt thanks to you all, and not only for the work that has gone into this Festschrift. Over the years, you have been among the many people from whom I have learned a great deal, and I have been a most fortunate beneficiary of your thoughts, advice, and support that have shaped what has been a most fulfilling and exciting career. Some, too, have been victims of my proverbial red pen (for which apologies, and thanks for responding with such dignified tolerance).

A Festschrift tends to direct our thoughts towards the past, but we should also think in the present and future tenses. As I write this Afterword, the real world increasingly resembles dystopian fictions. Unnatural ('man-made') calamities are pervasive. Women's reproductive rights, once thought safe in the US, have been retrenched, with the prospect of serious planet-wide ramifications. Across the globe, the many gains in (some) girls' access to education and (some) women's ability to attain comfortable economic independence since the 1970s are shored up by economic policies that result in growing inequalities within and between countries, in the inequitable impacts of environmental changes, in gender-based violence and obstetric and reproductive abuses across a broad spectrum, and raging culture wars in which dissenters are violently silenced and women all too often become the rhetorical playthings of regressive political ideologues. And so on.

Like the contributors to this volume, I am still 'work in progress', still armed with my red pen (although retirement means I shall probably use it more on my own writing than on other people's). I hope that we can nourish the new generations of researchers and protect the spaces that celebrate the free exchange of views about significant and often contentious issues, including the on-going and vital work of keeping gender issues to the fore. The political importance of continuing our academic research and writing is ever more urgent.

Edinburgh
June 2022

Notes on Contributors

Katharine Charsley is professor of Migration Studies in the School of Sociology, Politics and International Studies at the University of Bristol. Her research focuses on family, gender and migration, with a particular interest in transnational marriage. Her work in this field began with an ethnographic study of marriage between British Pakistanis and partners from Pakistan (*Transnational Pakistani Connections*, 2012), a starting point from which her interest in marriage and migration has expanded to include: interrogating policy discourses connecting ethnic minority marriage migration with problems of integration (*Marriage Migration and Integration*, 2020); masculinities in marriage migration ('The Invisible (Migrant) Man' with H. Wray, 2015); and the impacts on families separated by the UK's family immigration regime (Kept Apart, 2021).

Shruti Chaudhry is a Chancellor's Fellow in Sociology at the University of Edinburgh. Her doctoral research was completed at Edinburgh Sociology and was supervised by Patricia Jeffery. Her research focuses on migration, family and intimate relationships, ageing and the life-course, social change, gender and intersecting inequalities explored in the context of India and the South Asian diasporas in Scotland. She is the author of *Moving for Marriage: Inequalities, Intimacy and Women's Lives in Rural North India* (2021), a comparative ethnographic study of women who migrate for marriage, regionally and cross-regionally, to become brides in western Uttar Pradesh.

Archana Choksi in an independent researcher. She has a PhD from the Maharaji Sayajirao University in Vadodara, India, which is an ethnoarchaeological exploration of pastoralists' ceramics, and previous degrees in Fine Arts, Archaeology, and Museology. She moved to the UK in the late 1990s, where she has worked in the refugee sector, leading programmes for Oxfam, and establishing the Leeds One Community centre. She has combined her civil society work and activism with scholarly research, with continued interest in how 'development' impacts on mobile pastoralists in India. She has just completed a programme of work as senior research associate on the British Academy-funded HERDING project, which examines dignity, heritage and sustainable development among pastoralist women in Gujarat, Maharashtra and Himachal Pradesh.

Radhika Chopra is author of *Amritsar 1984: A City Remembers* and of *Militant and Migrant: The Politics and Social History of Punjab*. She has published extensively on militancy and its aftermath, on South Asian masculinities, and on visual cultures. Deeply interested in visual ethnography, she has two edited books of photographs from the field, *Ways of Worship* and *Migrant Lives*.

Caroline Dyer is professor of Education and International Development at the University of Leeds. She completed her PhD on educational policy implementation in India from the University of Edinburgh, since when she has largely focused on policies and practices of education inclusion for mobile pastoralists. She has worked on this topic across South Asia, Africa, and in Mongolia, where she was lead international consultant for UNESCO's 2020 Education Policy Review. As PI of three GCRF/ERSC/FCDO funded research projects, all in India, she has recently studied accountability in elementary education, NGO-generated secondary data, and heritage and dignity among mobile pastoralist women. Recent co-authored publications critique the sedentary ontology of education systems (*Compare*, DOI: 10.1080/03057925.2021.1907175), the social contract of India's right to education (*Development and Change*, DOI: 10.1111/dech.12715), and the bureaucratised relations of accountability in Indian education (*Third World Quarterly*, DOI: 10.1080/01436597.2022.2070469).

Hugo Gorringe is a senior lecturer in Sociology and former co-director of the Centre for South Asian Studies at The University of Edinburgh. His first academic post was as a replacement lecturer to Patricia Jeffery. His research interests focus on Dalit movements and politics in the south Indian state of Tamil Nadu. He is author of *Untouchable Citizens* (2005) and *Panthers in Parliament* (2017) which address the rise of the Viduthalai Chiruthaigal Katchi (VCK) and their entry into politics. He has co-edited a number of volumes including *From the Margins to the Mainstream* (2016, with Suryakant Waghmore and Roger Jeffery), *Civility in Crisis* (2020, with Suryakant Waghmore) and *Caste in Everyday Life* (2023, with Dhaneswar Bhoi). He has also written numerous articles on caste, violence and politics.

Radhika Govinda is a senior lecturer in Sociology at the School of Social and Political Science, University of Edinburgh and the Director of GENDER.ED – the University's interdisciplinary hub for gender and sexualities studies. She convenes Gender and Development – a postgraduate course that Patricia Jeffery designed and convened for many years. Her research focuses on the gender politics of development, intersecting inequalities and feminist knowledge production. She has co-edited *Doing Feminisms in the Academy in India and the UK* (Zubaan 2021, with Fiona Mackay, Krishna Menon and Rukmini Sen). She has also published a number of articles on gender, caste, masculinities, feminist activism and development in India.

Shalini Grover received her PhD in 2006 from the Department of Social Anthropology, University of Sussex. Thereafter, she was based in India for a decade and was Associate Professor in Anthropology at the Institute of Economic Growth (University of Delhi). She has published widely on marriage, love, kinship, legal pluralisms, labour relations and globalized care. Her 2011 monograph (*Marriage, Love, Caste and Kinship Support: Lived Experiences of the Urban Poor in India*) now features as a new international revised edition by Routledge (London and New York, 2018). In 2018, Grover returned to the United Kingdom and is now a Research Fellow at the International Inequalities Institute (III), London School of Economics (LSE). Her most recent publications in journal articles and edited volumes include 'Placement Agencies for Care-Domestic Labour' (*Modern Asian Studies*, 2022) and 'Family-Arranged Marriages in Globalizing India' (Rutgers University Press, 2022). She is currently preparing her second monograph, '*Caregivers of the 20th and 21st Centuries: Race, Coloniality and Global Elites in India*' for Cambridge University Press.

Barbara Harriss-White was in Patricia Jeffery's cohort at Newnham College, Cambridge. Starting off in geography, she turned through agricultural science to development economics before settling down in a political economy grounded in field research. Over a half-century since driving to India, she has researched rural capitalist development, dimensions of deprivation, small town economy and society and policy processes in these fields. Adviser to seven UN agencies, former director of Queen Elizabeth House, Oxford, co-founder of Oxford M Phil in Development Studies and founder director of Oxford's CSASP, she has supervised over 40 doctoral students, mentored as many post docs, co-produced as many books and won the Edgar Graham Prize for originality in development studies for *Rural Commercial Capital* (2008). Her recent books include *The Wild East* (2019) and *Rethinking Markets in Modern India* (2020). In retirement, she studies the economy as a waste-producing system.

Zoya Hasan is professor Emerita at Jawaharlal Nehru University and former Dean of the School of Social Sciences, JNU. She is currently Distinguished Professor, Council for Social Development, New Delhi. She is the author/editor of 18 books. Two of her recent books include, *Ideology and Organization in Indian Politics: Polarisation and the Growing Crisis of the Congress Party* (2009-2019) and *A Nation in Protest: Mobilizing for Equal Citizenship in India*, (Forthcoming).

Patricia Jeffery is Emerita professor of Sociology, University of Edinburgh, where her teaching included aspects of gender studies, especially gender and development, and race and ethnicity. Since 1970, she has conducted fieldwork in various parts of South Asia, focusing on gender politics, social demography, education and its links to women's status and demographic change, and childbearing (including pharmaceuticals and the [mis]use of oxytocin during childbirth). Her publications include *Migrants and Refugees: Muslim and Christian Pakistani Families in Bristol* (1976); *Frogs in a Well: Indian Women in Purdah* (1979); *Labour Pains and Labour Power: Women and Childbearing in India* (1989); *Don't Marry me to a Plowman: Women's Everyday Lives in Rural North India* (1996 [2019]); and *Confronting Saffron Demography: Religion, fertility and women's status in India* (2006). She is completing two book manuscripts based on her long-term ethnographic work in a Muslim village in rural western Uttar Pradesh, one on the demographic transition, child survival and fertility decline, the other on the intergenerational contract in the context of jobless growth, consumerism and communal politics. Details on her publications are available via **ORCID:** https://orcid.org/0000-0003-1257-854X

Ravinder Kaur is professor of Sociology and Social Anthropology at the Department of Humanities and Social Sciences, Indian Institute of Technology Delhi. She taught at the Delhi School of Economics and New York University before joining IIT Delhi in 1996. Her research interests are in the areas of the sociology of gender, family, marriage, kinship, middle class, technology, and women in science and technology. She has worked extensively on the issue of adverse sex ratios and their consequences in India and China and has published widely on the subject. Her work in this area spans gender-biased sex selection and its relationship with fertility, education, work, class mobility, crime, and marriage squeeze. Her ethnographic work on bride shortages and long-distance marriage migration in Haryana has been seminal to research in the area. She is co-author of *Planning Families, Planning Gender: The adverse child sex ratio in selected districts of Madhya Pradesh, Rajasthan, Himachal Pradesh, Haryana and Punjab* (2008), and co-editor of *Marrying in South Asia: Shifting Concepts, Changing Practices in a Globalising World* (2014) and editor of *Too Many Men, Too Few Women: Social Consequences of Gender Imbalance in India and China* (2016).

Rajni Palriwala recently retired from the University of Delhi, where she was a professor of Sociology. Her research falls within the broad area of gender relations, covering care and emotion, citizenship and the welfare state, kinship and marriage, dowry, women and work, migration, women's movements and feminist politics, cross-cultural and comparative studies, and research methodology, though her teaching went beyond. Other than numerous journal articles and book chapters, she has authored *Changing kinship, family, and gender relations in South Asia: Processes, trends and issues* (1994) and jointly authored *Care, culture and citizenship: Revisiting the politics of welfare in the Netherlands* (2005) and *Planning Families, Planning Gender: The adverse child sex ratio in selected districts of Madhya Pradesh, Rajasthan, Himachal Pradesh, Haryana and Punjab* (2008). She has jointly edited *Marrying in South Asia: Shifting Concepts, Changing Practices in a Globalised World* (2013), *Marriage, Migration, and Gender* (2008), *Shifting Circles of Support: Contextualising Kinship and Gender Relations in South Asia and Sub-Saharan Africa* (1996), *and Structures and Strategies: Women, Work and Family in Asia* (1990).

Helen Pankhurst CBE is a development and international women's rights activist working as an advisor to CARE International – primarily in Ethiopia and in the UK. She is also a Professor at MMU and the First Chancellor of the University of Suffolk. She holds an honorary doctorate from Edge Hill University and from the University of Manchester. The granddaughter of Sylvia, great-granddaughter of Emmeline Pankhurst, Helen carries on the legacy. This has included involvement in the Opening Ceremony of the 2012 London Olympics and in the 2015 film Suffragette and leading CARE International's events around International Women's Day. She convenes the Centenary Action (a coalition addressing barriers to women in politics) and GM4Women2028 (a charity looking at data and the lives of women and girls in Greater Manchester). Publications include the book: *Deeds Not Words, the Story of Women's Rights, Then and Now* (2018).

Kaveri Qureshi is senior lecturer in the Social Policy subject area at the School of Social and Political Science at the University of Edinburgh. She works in the UK and Pakistan, on the combined effects of racialization, class and gender in shaping health and family life. She has written two monographs: *Marital breakdown among British Asians: conjugality, legal pluralism and new kinship* and *Chronic illness in a Pakistani labour diaspora*.

Tanika Sarkar retired as Chair, Modern History, from the Centre for Historical Studies, Jawaharlal Nehru University, Delhi. She has also been a Visiting Professor at the universities of Yale, Chicago, Witswaterand, Gottingen, and at Grinnell College. Her monographs are related to political and cultural nationalism in colonial India and religious nationalism in contemporary India. She is currently working on sanitary workers and the problem of untouchability at the Calcutta Corporation as well as on colonial Personal Laws in nineteenth century India. She has recently completed a commissioned volume on Gender in Colonial and Post-Colonial Indian Subcontinent for the New Cambridge History of Modern India series. Her latest publication is *Hindu Nationalism in India*, (2021).

Jeevan R Sharma is professor in South Asia and International Development at the University of Edinburgh. He is the author of *Political Economy of Social Change and Development in Nepal* (2021) and *Crossing the Border to India: Youth, Migration and Masculinities in Nepal* (2018). He has carried out anthropological research on culture of migration, politics of aid-funded interventions in Nepal, maternal and child health interventions, and on low-income migrants in Indian cities. His work has focussed on labour migration in the context of social, economic and political transformations in Nepal, the Himalayas and the South Asian region, especially the culture of migration; border crossing; gendered, classed and racialised mobility of labour; ill treatment; access to justice and citizenship in South Asia. He is the co-editor of HIMALAYA and an associate editor of *South Asia: Journal of South Asian Studies*.

Sylvia Vatuk is professor Emerita of Anthropology at the University of Illinois-Chicago, with a BA in Sociology and Anthropology from Cornell University, an MA in Cultural Anthropology from the School of Oriental and African Studies, University of London, and a PhD in Anthropology from Harvard University. Her doctoral research in Meerut, Uttar Pradesh, led to the publication of *Kinship and Urbanization: White Collar Migrants in North India* (1972). She has subsequently carried out ethnographic research in Delhi, Hyderabad, and Chennai on both Hindu and Muslim marriage, family, and kinship organization, with a special emphasis on gender roles and intergenerational relationships, publishing her findings in academic journals and edited volumes. Most recently she has focused on legal-anthropological questions related to India's Muslim Personal Law, as administered in family courts, in the regular civil and criminal courts and by Islamic clerical functionaries. Her most recent publication, a collection of previously-published articles on Muslim women and the law, is *Marriage and its Discontents: Women, Islam and the Law in India* (2017).

Susan S Wadley is professor Emerita of Anthropology at Syracuse University where she taught for fifty years. She did extensive research on the village known as Karimpur in Uttar Pradesh since the late 1960s and remains in close contact with friends there, now observing the tremendous social changes from. In the early 2000s, she curated an exhibition of Mithila art owned by the Syracuse University Art Museum and has since worked extensively with Mithila artists while also adding recent paintings to the SU collection. Her contacts in Madhubani enabled the online Covid exhibition of Mithila art which forms the basis of her paper for this volume.